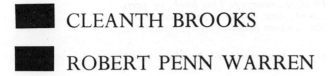

CLEANTH BROOKS

ROBERT PENN WARREN

The SCOPE

of FICTION

New York: APPLETON-CENTURY-CROFTS, Inc.

ACKNOWLEDGMENTS

Albert & Charles Boni: for "An Occurrence at Owl Creek Bridge" by Ambrose Bierce, from *In the Midst of Life.*

Criterion Books, Inc.: for "Crossing into Poland" by Isaac Babel, from *Isaac Babel: The Collected Stories,* copyright, 1955, by Criterion Books, Inc.

Doubleday & Company, Inc.: "I See You Never" by Ray Bradbury, from *The Golden Apples of the Sun,* copyright, 1947, by The New Yorker Magazine, Inc., reprinted by permission of Doubleday & Company, Inc.; for "The Furnished Room" by O. Henry, from *The Four Million,* copyright, 1904, by Doubleday & Company, Inc., reprinted by permission of the publisher; and for "The Man Who Would Be King" by Rudyard Kipling, from *Under the Deodars,* reprinted by permission of Mrs. George Bambridge and Doubleday & Company, Inc.

E. P. Dutton & Company, Inc.: for "War" by Luigi Pirandello, from *The Medals and Other Stories,* copyright, 1939, by E. P. Dutton & Company, Inc., reprinted by permission of the publishers.

Farrar, Straus and Cudahy, Inc.: for "The Lottery" by Shirley Jackson, from *The Lottery,* copyright, 1949, by Shirley Jackson, copyright, 1948, by The New Yorker Magazine, Inc.

Harcourt, Brace & Company, Inc.: for "A Good Man Is Hard to Find" by Flannery O'Connor, from *A Good Man Is Hard to Find and Other Stories* by Flannery O'Connor, copyright, 1953, 1954, 1955, by Flannery O'Connor, reprinted by permission of Harcourt, Brace & Company, Inc.; for "A Piece of News" by Eudora Welty, from *A Curtain of Green and Other Stories,* copyright, 1936, 1937, 1938, 1939, 1941, by Eudora Welty, reprinted by permission of Harcourt Brace & Company, Inc.; and for "Theft" by Katherine Anne Porter, from *Flowering Judas and Other Stories,* copyright, 1930, 1935, 1938, by Katherine Anne Porter, reprinted by permission of Harcourt, Brace & Company, Inc.

Harper & Brothers: for "Dermuche" by Marcel Aymé, from *Across Paris,* translated by Norman Denny, copyright, 1947, by Libraire Gallimard.

The Hogarth Press, Ltd.: for "Through the Quinquina Glass" by William Sansom, from *Fireman Flower,* Canadian rights.

Houghton Mifflin Company: for "Tennessee's Partner" by Bret Harte; and for "A Domestic Dilemma" by Carson McCullers, from *The Ballad of the Sad Cafe.*

Alfred A. Knopf, Inc.: for "The Bride Comes to Yellow Sky" by Stephen Crane, from *Stephen Crane: An Omnibus,* copyright, 1952, by Alfred A. Knopf, Inc.; for "The Fly" by Katherine Mansfield, from *The Short Stories of Katherine Mansfield,* copyright, 1922, 1937, by Alfred A. Knopf, Inc.; and for "The Drunkard" by Frank O'Connor, originally appeared in the *New Yorker,* from *The Stories of Frank O'Connor,* copyright, 1948, 1952, by Frank O'Connor.

John Lane: The Bodley Head, Ltd.: for "Dermuche" by Marcel Aymé, from *Across Paris,* Canadian rights.

Harold Matson Company: for "De Mortuis" by John Collier, originally appeared in the *New Yorker,* from *Fancies and Goodnights,* copyright, 1942, by John Collier; and for "The Drunkard" by Frank O'Connor, originally appeared in the *New Yorker,* from *The Stories of Frank O'Connor,* Canadian rights.

New Directions: for "Eventide" by James Purdy, from *Color of Darkness,* copyright, 1956, 1957, by James Purdy, reprinted by permission of New Directions.

The New Yorker Magazine, Inc.: for "The Secret Life of Walter Mitty" by James Thurber. Permission the author; copr. © 1939 The New Yorker Magazine, Inc.

Harold Ober Associates, Inc.: for "I Want to Know Why" by Sherwood Anderson, from *The Triumph of the Egg*, published by B. W. Huebsch, Inc., copyright © 1921, by Eleanor Anderson, reprinted by permission of Harold Ober Associates, Inc.

Random House, Inc.: for "A Rose for Emily" by William Faulkner, from *Collected Stories of William Faulkner*, copyright, 1930, and renewed, 1957, by William Faulkner, reprinted by permission of Random House, Inc.; and for "The Girls in Their Summer Dresses" by Irwin Shaw, from *Mixed Company* by Irwin Shaw, copyright, 1939, by Irwin Shaw, reprinted by permission of Random House, Inc.

Russell & Volkening, Inc.: for "Through the Quinquina Glass" by William Sansom, from *Fireman Flower* by William Sansom, copyright, 1945, by William Sansom.

Charles Scribner's Sons: for "The Killers" by Ernest Hemingway, copyright, 1927, Charles Scribner's Sons, renewal copyright, 1955, reprinted from *Men Without Women* by Ernest Hemingway with permission of Charles Scribner's Sons; for "Haircut" by Ring Lardner, copyright, 1925, Ellis A. Lardner, renewal copyright, 1953, reprinted from *The Love Nest and Other Stories* by Ring Lardner with permission of Charles Scribner's Sons; and for "The Far and the Near" by Thomas Wolfe, copyright, 1935, International Magazines, Inc., reprinted from *From Death to Morning* by Thomas Wolfe with permission of Charles Scribner's Sons.

Jesse Stuart: for his story "Love."

The Viking Press, Inc.: for "Araby " by James Joyce, from *Dubliners* by James Joyce, included in *The Portable James Joyce*, copyright, 1946, 1947, by The Viking Press, Inc., reprinted by permission of The Viking Press, Inc.; and for "Tickets, Please" by D. H. Lawrence from *England, My England* by D. H. Lawrence, included in *The Portable D. H. Lawrence*, copyright, 1922, by Thomas Seltzer, Inc., 1950, by Frieda Lawrence, reprinted by permission of The Viking Press, Inc.

A. P. Watt & Son: for "The Man Who Would Be King" by Rudyard Kipling, Canadian rights.

Preface

THIS BOOK is a shorter version of *Understanding Fiction. Understanding Fiction* is designed for a fairly elaborate course in the reading (and sometimes writing) of fiction, a course running, say, from a half to a full year. But since there are many courses in which the study of fiction occupies a relatively small part of the year, there is a demand for a shorter book embodying the same principles and methods. *The Scope of Fiction* is not, however, in any sense a watering down of *Understanding Fiction*, a mere collection of stories with casual commentary. It is, instead, the very core of the longer book, with a minimum of trimming and adapting. In the process of exposing this core, we have removed the more elaborately theoretical material and the most complex stories, and we have reduced the number of stories that are presented without editorial commentary. The student will, we trust, find here in shorter compass all the discussions, exercises, and illustrative materials that he needs for an induction into the art of fiction.

For a statement of the principles on which this text is based we are reprinting here, with some excisions, the Letter to the Teacher which appeared in the first edition of *Understanding Fiction*, in 1943.

C. B.
R. P. W.

Letter to the Teacher

MOST students read some kind of fiction of their own free will and for pleasure. This fact may lull the teacher of fiction into a false sense of security. He does not, he feels, have to "make" the student read fiction as he has to "make" the student read poetry or essays. He simply sets himself the easier problem of persuading the student that some fiction that is "good literature" or that has historical importance, is also interesting in itself. Frequently the student does discover that the "good" story or novel is interesting to him. Then the teacher says, in substance: "Look, you did like that story, and that story is literature. Therefore, you like literature, after all. You see, literature is not so bad." And having reached this conclusion, the teacher may feel that the objective of the course in fiction has been achieved.

But let us suppose that the student should read any number of stories which are called literature. No doubt, if he is somewhat more intelligent and sensitive than most, he will begin to ask questions of himself and to make comparisons, and his general taste will, as a result, be improved. But, unless he does attempt to read with deeper comprehension, it is doubtful whether any beneficial result can be had, no matter how many stories he reads or how many details of plot he can remember or how many characters he can name. The editors of this book believe that before extensive reading can be profitable, the student must have some practice in intensive reading. Otherwise, the interests which he originally brings to his reading will remain unchanged.

It is probably true, however, that a teacher must always build upon the interests which the student already possesses. But it is one thing to build upon those interests and quite another to take them as the standard of values by which the course is to be conducted. If the critical standards which the student possesses when he begins the course are adequate, then the course is superfluous and merely flatters him in his convictions. If the course merely encourages the student to systematize his views somewhat—to try to say why he likes or dislikes a story—some gain has certainly been made, for this process is essential to the development of taste. But if the views remain substantially unchanged, if the interests which he brings to fiction in the first place are not broadened and refined, the course has scarcely fulfilled its purpose: the student has merely grown more glib and complacent in his limitations.

Let us take a particular case. A student likes Kipling's "The Man Who Would Be King" because it is a story of romantic adventure, because he wants to know how it "comes out," but does not like Chekhov's "The Lament" because "nothing happens in it." One immediately realizes that the student is not giving a clear account of either story or even of his own reactions; that, in fact, he has not really "read" either story. In the first place, it is improbable that he likes "The Man Who Would Be King" simply because of the suspense concerning the external action. Matters of character, psychological development, and moral decision are inextricably involved with the action. It is true that the student may have a perfectly usual bias toward fiction of romantic setting and violent action, but it is only through a failure of introspection that he bases his case for the story merely on those elements. A little reflection should bring him to the conclusion that, even in the crudest story of violent action, he demands a certain modicum of characterization, a certain concern with the psychological basis of action, a certain interest in moral content and general meaning. And a little further reflection should lead him to the conclusion that his liking for the story may depend upon the organic relation existing among these elements—that his interest did not depend upon the element of violent plot, or the element of romantic setting, taken in isolation. If he has once faced this question, he may realize that his liking for a story does not depend finally upon his threshold interests, but rather depends, in one sense at least, upon the total structure, upon the logic of the whole, the relationships existing among elements of character and psychology, action, social situation, ideas and attitudes, style, and so on.

There are innumerable types of threshold interest which bring readers to fiction. Some of these types are clearly defined and well recognized in the field of magazine fiction. There are "sport" stories, "young love" stories, "marriage problem" stories, "moral" stories, "child" stories, "sea" stories, "Wild West" stories, "farm" stories, "business" stories, "crime" stories, and the like. Such threshold interests as are appealed to by these types may derive from a variety of factors. A man who knows the world of baseball may come to fiction that deals with that subject expecting the pleasure of recognition, of dwelling on what he knows and likes in real life. Such a reader demands a high degree of fidelity to the external facts of the world in which he is interested. But another reader may come, let us say, to baseball stories or to Wild West stories, expecting the pleasure of escape from a life which does not afford him sport or adventure. He is scarcely concerned with incidental realism, with recognizing a world which he already knows, but with extending his experience into a world which he does not know.

Both of these impulses, the impulse to dwell on the known world in fiction and to judge the fictional rendering by the facts of observation, and the impulse to enlarge experience through fiction, are perfectly normal and admirable; they are, in rudimentary form, the impulse toward contemplation and the impulse toward fulfillment, the demand for logic and the demand for imagination. They are pernicious only when they operate in isolation from each other and when they stop at the level of the threshold interest. For instance, if the baseball player or fan who reads only baseball stories should apply his criteria of realism, his tests of recognition and logic, to matters of characterization and psychology and theme as well as to the technical questions concerning the world of baseball, he would probably find unsatisfactory many of the stories which ordinarily satisfy his threshold interest. Or, if the reader who goes to adventure stories for escape from a humdrum existence could realize that his experience could be extended more fully by reading fiction which does not merely emphasize the elements of violent action and romantic setting but which also leads to some understanding of the inner lives of other people, or to some understanding of his own life, he might be less content with the escape based on merely external differences from the circumstances of his own experience.

The hypothetical student may object that he has lost, and not gained, by such a process, for his area of potential enjoyment has been limited by the process. But actually the process which leads him past the mere threshold interest to the fuller interests implicit in fiction causes an enlargement of the area of his potential enjoyment. As a human being, he has interests wider than baseball or Western adventure, and he may come to realize that, even in the shoddiest story dealing with baseball or the Wild West, his other more fundamental interests have been covertly engaged. And he may realize, further, that without the appeal to those other interests there would be no story at all. The Wild West and baseball, finally, interest him in terms of certain persons, with certain motivations and with certain characteristics, who have certain experiences; and these experiences themselves are of little interest to him except in so far as they involve certain meanings—success and failure, courage and cowardice, generosity and cruelty, and the like— which are dramatized in character and action. This returns us to the notion that the liking for a piece of fiction does not depend upon the satisfaction of the threshold interest, whatever it may be, football or moral message-hunting or sociological documentation, but upon the total structure, upon a set of organic relationships, upon the logic of the whole.

This book is based on the belief that the student can best be brought to an appreciation of the more broadly human values implicit in fiction by a course of study which aims at the close analytical and interpretative reading of concrete examples. It seems to us that the student may best come to understand a given piece of fiction by understanding the functions of the various elements which go to make up fiction and by understanding their relationships to each other in the whole construct. The editors believe that such an end may best be achieved by the use of an inductive method, by the use of concrete cases which can be investigated and interpreted and compared with each other. The organization of the book is based on that principle. . . .

Sections II, III, and IV are closely related to each other and really represent an extension and development of the principles touched on in Section I. Section II deals primarily with problems of plot. This is not to say that the stories involved are stories in which the plot interest obtrudes itself—that they are examples of what is called "the plot story." As a matter of fact, some of the stories in this section, such as "War," by Pirandello, and "A Piece of News," by Eudora Welty, scarcely involve overt action at all. Rather, the stories chosen for this section, along with their interpretations and exercises, are intended to illustrate a variety of types and functions of plot with a constant emphasis on the relationship of the plot to other factors. In Section III the same method is used in regard to certain problems of character in fiction; and in Section IV, in regard to certain problems of realizing theme in fiction. But in all of these sections other questions have been raised in the course of the discussions and in the exercises, questions of style and tone, for example, as related to the basic intentions of the stories. . . .

The selection of stories has been undertaken with the hope of providing as wide a range of examples in terms of fictional method as could be reasonably expected in a book of this size. There has been no attempt at great novelty in selection. Rather, the editors have, in large part, chosen stories which are popular and widely anthologized. Nor has there been any attempt at making this book a representative collection or a collection of masterpieces. Many authors of great importance, and many stories for which the editors feel the keenest admiration, are omitted. Furthermore, certain stories which are definitely inferior are included in order to give the student exercise in destructive analysis and criticism. Again, there has been no attempt to present key examples in the history of the short story. In fact, the history of the short story, except at the narrowest technical level, can scarcely be discussed at all in isolation from the history of fiction in general and of poetry. But the editors have undertaken to give materials for some historical investigation of the influences and methods found in the modern short story. . . .

It will no doubt be observed, and by some readers objected to, that for the most part the interpretations in this book are descriptive and analytical rather than evaluative. But the editors feel that, in general, the matter of the relative grading of stories, except for broad distinctions, should arise late rather than early in the critical process. The first problem is to understand the nature of fictional structure, to become acquainted with the idiom in terms of which the art operates, and to broaden the imaginative sympathies so that the student can transcend stock responses and threshold interests. But this process necessarily will lead to evaluation in a broad sense. A student does not have to go very far in the investigation of fictional structure before he understands that O. Henry's "The Furnished Room" depends for its effect not on a functional relationship among its elements but on arbitrary manipulation by the author, or before he understands that the irony here is accidental as compared with the irony in Pirandello's "War," or in Chekhov's "The Lament." Such a discrimination as this should come early and naturally, but an attempt to discriminate between the value of "The Lament" and that of "Tickets, Please," by Lawrence ought probably to come rather late. It is very important, to be sure, to be able to discriminate between the methods and effects of "The Lament" and those of "Tickets, Please," for such discrimination should lead to a fuller appreciation of both pieces; but an early effort to grade two such successful stories on their relative merits may encourage critical vindictiveness and literary priggishness. It has been aptly said that a literary dictator has no place in the republic of letters.

Another and more specific objection which may be raised concerns the apparent emphasis on formal considerations in the evaluation of fiction—what may be thought the editors' failure to give adequate heed to the importance, on ethical, religious, philosophical, or sociological grounds, of the "idea" in a piece of fiction. In attempting to reply to such an objection the editors would first say that idea or theme is one of the elements in the fictional structure, but that the structure is not to be set over against the idea in any mechanical fashion. Rather, it is their first article of faith that the structure of a piece of fiction, in so far as that piece of fiction is successful, must involve a vital and functional relationship between the idea and the other elements in that structure—plot, style, character, and the like. In the second place, they would agree that to be good, a piece of fiction must involve an idea of some real significance for mature and thoughtful human beings. This does not mean that to appreciate a piece of fiction such a mature and thoughtful reader must *agree* with the idea realized in it; but it does mean that the question raised by the piece of fiction must seem to him worthy of serious exploration. For instance, the mature and thoughtful reader whom we have posited might not accept the view of the world which underlies Hemingway's fiction, but he might very well realize the difficulty of transcending such a view of the world. That is, he might admit that the question implicit in Hemingway's fiction is a real question, even though he might feel that he himself had transcended Hemingway's solution. If, on the other hand, he is of such an unrelentingly dogmatic disposition that he restricts his approbation to works which involve ideas with which he is in precise accord, he will probably find himself subsisting on very poverty-stricken literary diet. Worse still, he will not even be able to receive nourishment from the diet which he accepts, for he will be reading merely in terms of his threshold interest and will not be submitting his beliefs to the test of imaginative experience. In literature, ideas leave their cloisters and descend into the dust and heat to prove their virtue anew.

But the editors would wish to make a further remark on this general point, a remark concerning the level at which an idea in fiction becomes important. The mere presence in a piece of fiction of an idea which is held to be important in itself on ethical, religious, philosophical, sociological, or other grounds, does not necessarily indicate anything about the importance of the piece of fiction. One might almost as well commend a piece of fiction for exemplifying good grammatical usage. The mere presence of the "good" idea or the "good" grammar tells us nothing about the final success of the item in question. The idea is important in a story in so far as it is incorporated into the total structure—in so far as the story lives out the idea and, in the process of living, modifies the idea. The idea as an abstraction is absolute; but the idea in a story forfeits that privilege of absoluteness and must accept the dangers of qualification and modification. Everyone is familiar with stories in which "good" ideas emerge as cruel parodies of themselves, brutally debased by insensitive style and crude characterization and arbitrary psychology, for instance, or else sentimentalized by defects in logic and mechanical plot management. In fact, most popular fiction aims at flattering the ethical sense of the public. That such fiction is often, in the last analysis, corrupt derives from the fact that the author does not recognize the necessity of attempting to realize the idea fully in the experience of his characters and in the structure of his story. The villain bites the dust; the good heart triumphs over all. The author does not recognize the difficulty, let us say, in making a moral decision, and simply follows the idea as blueprint, as dogma. Situations which qualify an idea of virtue and emphasize the difficulty of moral decision—such as the situation which confronts Cordelia in the first scene of *King Lear* or that which confronts Isabella in her condemned brother's cell in *Measure for Measure* —do not flourish in the fiction of our best family magazines. . . .

A piece of fiction is a unity, in so far as the piece of fiction is successful. Its elements are so related that we feel an expressive interpenetration among them, a set of vital relationships. But the unity which the fictional structure possesses is of a very special kind. It is not the result of a purely genial conspiracy among the constituent elements. There is conflict and tension present, and the structure involves almost as much of vindictive opposition as of genial conspiracy. One says "almost" because some sort of resolution, however provisional and marginal, must be implicit in the tensions of the fictional structure, if the unity is to be achieved—if the revelation is to be had. The fact of conflict as an essential aspect of fiction is clearly stated in every handbook. In its most obvious form it concerns a collision of interests in the external world. In a somewhat more subtle and sophisticated form conflict concerns a division of interests or obligations in the self. In an even more subtle and sophisticated form, it concerns the alignment of judgments and sympathies on the part of the author—the problem of his own self-division.

The dogmatist who is author paints a world of black and white, a world in which right and wrong, truth and falsehood, are clear with statutory distinctness, a world of villain and hero. The artist who is author paints a world in which there is, in the beginning, neither black nor white, neither right nor wrong which can be defined with absolute certainty. The certainty can only come in terms of the process, and must be *earned*, as it were, through the process. In other words, the artist is sporting enough to put the best case possible for the opposition. But this is not mere sportsmanship. The artist realizes that, if the opponent—"villain" or "idea"—is a straw man, the conflict will lack interest. In a simple example such as *Richard III*, we observe that Shakespeare makes the traditional and historical Tudor villain the vessel of certain virtues which the Tudor age seems to have admired inordinately. Without this ironical ambivalence, the play would be a tedious recital of butcheries to prove that you can't kill all of the people all of the time. It would have had no psychological center for tension, either in terms of the main character or in terms of the audience. Or, to glance at other simple cases, we may recall that in *Uncle Tom's Cabin* Simon Legree is a Yankee, and that in Hemingway's *For Whom the Bell Tolls* the scene of greatest brutality is that of the massacre of Fascists by Loyalists, or that the book closes with the distant figure of the young Fascist lieutenant (whom Hemingway has previously presented as a sympathetic character) caught in the gunsights of the hero. In all of these cases, the irony is intended, on the one hand, to intensify the implications of the conflict, and on the other, to raise the issue above the level of merely dogmatic and partisan vilification. But these two functions are closely interrelated and only by an act of abstraction can one, in many cases, separate them out.

Another function, also closely related, is to indicate an awareness of the multiplicity of options in conduct, idea, or attitude—an awareness of the full context. This suggests one of the objections which may be brought against the emphasis on irony; the objection that such an emphasis ends in the celebration of a smug and futile skepticism which is at variance with the actual effect which most successful literary compositions leave upon the reader. The editors would hope that, by this time, the grounds upon which they would answer this particular objection are clear. They would not endorse an irony which precluded resolution but they would endorse an irony which forced the resolution to take stock of as full a context as possible. The reader wants the resolution, but he does not want it too easy or too soon. He wants to see the knockout, but he does not want to see it until the fifteenth round. And, if he feels that the fight has been fixed, he will want to stop at the box office on the way out and demand his money back. . . .

The editors perhaps should crave the indulgence of the teacher for intruding this discussion of their general views into what should be a mere description of the aims and methods of this textbook. But they hope that the utility of this book for the individual teacher will not stand or fall by the teacher's assent to those views, just as they hope that it will not stand or fall by the teachers' assent to the editors' interpretation of particular stories. Certainly they do not wish to be dogmatic, for they realize too acutely the pitfalls in the way of even the most elementary critical analysis. They merely hope that this book raises certain profitable questions in a relatively systematic form for the student, and that by so doing it may render the task of the teacher a little easier. For the editors feel that no book, however much better than this, can do more than be of some slight assistance to the teacher in the classroom, upon whom the final responsibility must rest.

C. B.

R. P. W.

1943

Contents

SECTION I

Aspects of Fiction

SECTION II

How Plot Reveals

SECTION III

What Character Reveals

SECTION IV

What Theme Reveals

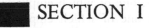 **SECTION I**

Aspects of Fiction

THERE are three questions that we ask, as naturally as breathing, about a story:

1. What happens?
2. Who does it?
3. What does it mean?

The questions are natural, for they represent the fundamental aspects of any story, aspects that in more technical language are labeled *plot*, *character*, and *theme*.

Notice that we have used the word *aspects*—and not such a word as *parts*. We must not think of plot, character, or theme as a part of a story that can be separated from the story. Each can be thought of separately, and discussed separately, but in actuality they are completely interfused. A plot cannot exist without characters who act and are acted upon; a character fulfills himself only in action; and all human action involves a judgment of values, that is, an idea, a theme. In other words, plot, character, and theme are abstracted from the organic unity which is the story, and when we discuss them we should always be aware that they are abstractions. And when we discuss them, we do so only in order to understand better the nature of that unity, the story, from which they are abstracted.

We make the abstraction in order to see how these aspects—these elements—and others which will come later under our consideration form an organic unity, a unity which is expressive and significant. It has the power to engage our interests and excite our feelings, not by reason of the particular elements that enter into it, but by reason of their interrelations.

1

The unity arising from such a fusion of elements we can grasp as an image of life.

To make what we have tried to say come alive, we must turn to some stories. Let us begin by examining three stories, one of which emphasizes plot, one of which emphasizes character, and one of which emphasizes theme. Our purpose, in each instance, will be to see how the aspect that seems so prominent, that first catches our interest, leads us back into the expressive unity which is the story.

Keeping in mind our general purpose here, the student will do well in reading these, and later, stories, to ask himself the following questions:

1. What are the characters like?
2. Are they "real"?
3. What do they want?
4. Why do they do what they do?
5. Do their actions logically follow from their natures?
6. What do their actions tell about their characters?
7. How are the individual pieces of action—the special incidents— related to each other?
8. How are the characters related to each other? What are the points of conflicts among them? Which are major and which minor?
9. What is the point—the theme?
10. How are the characters and incidents related to the theme?

RUDYARD KIPLING

The Man Who Would Be King

"Brother to a Prince and fellow to a beggar if he be found worthy."

THE law, as quoted, lays down a fair conduct of life, and one not easy to follow. I have been fellow to a beggar again and again under circumstances which prevented either of us finding out whether the other was worthy. I have still to be brother to a Prince, though I once came near to kinship with what might have been a veritable King and was promised the reversion of a Kingdom—army, law courts, revenue and policy all complete. But, today, I greatly fear that my King is dead, and if I want a crown I must go and hunt it for myself.

The beginning of everything was in a railway train upon the road to Mhow from Ajmir. There had been a Deficit in the Budget, which necessitated traveling, not Second-class, which is only half as dear as First-class, but by Intermediate, which is very awful indeed. There are no cushions in the Intermediate class, and the population are either Intermediate, which is Eurasian, or native, which for a long night journey is nasty, or Loafer, which is amusing though intoxicated. Intermediates do not patronize refreshment rooms. They carry their food in bundles and pots, and buy sweets from the native sweetmeat-sellers, and drink the roadside water. That is why in the hot weather Intermediates are taken out of the carriages dead, and in all weathers are most properly looked down upon.

My particular Intermediate happened to be empty till I reached Nasirabad, when a huge gentleman in shirt sleeves entered, and, following the custom of Intermediates, passed the time of day. He was a wanderer and a vagabond like myself, but with an educated taste for whisky. He told tales of things he had seen and done, of out-of-the-way corners of the Empire into which he had penetrated, and of adventures in which he risked his life for a few days' food. "If India was filled with men like you and me, not knowing more than the crows where they'd get their next day's rations, it isn't seventy millions of revenue the land would be paying —it's seven hundred millions," said he; and as I looked at his mouth and chin I was disposed to agree with him. We talked politics—the politics of Loaferdom that sees things from the underside where the lath and plaster is not smoothed off—and we talked postal arrangements because my friend wanted to send a telegram back from the next station to Ajmir, which is the turning-off place from the Bombay to the Mhow line as you travel westward. My friend had no money beyond eight annas which he wanted for dinner, and I had no money at all, owing to the hitch in the Budget before-mentioned. Further, I was going into a wilderness where, though I should resume touch with the Treasury, there were no telegraph offices. I was, therefore, unable to help him in any way.

"We might threaten a Stationmaster, and make him send a wire on tick," said my friend, "but that'd mean inquiries for you and for me, and I've got my hands full these days. Did you say you are traveling back along this line within any days?"

"Within ten," I said.

"Can't you make it eight?" said he. "Mine is rather urgent business."

"I can send your telegram within ten days if that will serve you," I said.

"I couldn't trust the wire to fetch him now I think of it. It's this way. He leaves Delhi on the twenty-third for Bombay. That means he'll be running through Ajmir about the night of the twenty-third."

"But I'm going into the Indian Desert," I explained.

"Well *and* good," said he. "You'll be changing at Marwar Junction to get into Jodhpore territory—you must do that—and he'll be coming through Marwar Junction in the early morning of the twenty-fourth by the Bombay Mail. Can you be at Marwar Junction on that time? 'Twon't be inconveniencing you because I know that there's precious few pickings to be got out of these Central India States—even though you pretend to be correspondent of the *Backwoodsman*."

"Have you ever tried that trick?" I asked.

"Again and again, but the Residents find you out, and then you get escorted to the Border before you've time to get your knife into them. But about my friend here. I *must* give him a word o' mouth to tell him what's come to me or else he won't know where to go. I would take it more than kind of you if you was to come out of Central India in time to catch him at Marwar Junction, and say to him, 'He has gone South for the week.' He'll know what that means. He's a big man with a red beard, and a great swell he is. You'll find him sleeping like a gentleman with all his luggage round him in a Second-class compartment. But don't you be afraid. Slip down the window, and say, 'He has gone South for the week,' and he'll tumble. It's only cutting your time of stay in those parts by two days. I ask you as a stranger—going to the West," he said, with emphasis.

"Where have *you* come from?" said I.

"From the East," said he, "and I am hoping that you will give him the message on the Square—for the sake of my Mother as well as your own."

Englishmen are not usually softened by appeals to the memory of their mothers, but for certain reasons, which will be fully apparent, I saw fit to agree.

"It's more than a little matter," said he, "and that's why I ask you to do it—and now I know that I can depend on you doing it. A Second-class carriage at Marwar Junction, and a red-haired man asleep in it. You'll be sure to remember. I get out at the next station, and I must hold on there till he comes or sends me what I want."

"I'll give the message if I catch him," I said, "and for the sake of your Mother as well as mine I'll give you a word of advice. Don't try to run the Central India States just now as the correspondent of the *Backwoodsman*. There's a real one knocking about here, and it might lead to trouble."

"Thank you," said he, simply, "and when will the swine be gone? I can't starve because he's ruining my work. I wanted to get hold of the Degumber Rajah down here about his father's widow, and give him a jump."

"What did he do to his father's widow, then?"

"Filled her up with red pepper and slippered her to death as she hung from a beam. I found that out myself, and I'm the only man that would dare going into the State to get hush money for it. They'll try to poison me, same as they did in Chortumna when I went on the loot there. But you'll give the man at Marwar Junction my message?"

He got out at a little roadside station, and I reflected. I had heard, more than once, of men personating correspondents of newspapers and bleeding small Native States with threats of exposure, but I had never met any of the caste before. They lead a hard life, and generally die with great suddenness. The Native States have a wholesome horror of English newspapers, which may throw light on their peculiar methods of government, and do their best to choke correspondents with champagne, or drive them out of their mind with four-in-hand barouches. They do not understand that nobody cares a straw for the internal administration of Native States so long as oppression and crime are kept within decent limits, and the ruler is not drugged, drunk, or diseased from one end of the year to the other. Native States were created by Providence in order to supply picturesque scenery, tigers, and tall writing. They are the dark places of the earth, full of unimaginable cruelty, touching the Railway and the Telegraph on one side, and, on the other, the days of Harun-al-Raschid. When I left the train I did business with divers Kings, and in eight days passed through many changes of life. Sometimes I wore dress clothes and consorted with Princes and Politicals, drinking from crystal and eating from silver. Sometimes I lay out upon the ground and devoured what I could get, from a plate made of a flapjack, and drank the running water, and slept under the same rug as my servant. It was all in the day's work.

Then I headed for the Great Indian Desert upon the proper date, as I had promised, and the night Mail set me down at Marwar Junction, where a funny little, happy-go-lucky, native-managed railway runs to Jodhpore. The Bombay Mail from Delhi makes a short halt at Marwar. She arrived as I got in, and I had just time to hurry to her platform and go down the carriages. There was only one Second-class on the train. I slipped the window, and looked down upon a flaming red beard, half covered by a railway rug. That was my man, fast asleep, and I dug him gently in the ribs. He woke with a grunt, and I saw his face in the light of the lamps. It was a great and shining face.

"Tickets again?" said he.

"No," said I. "I am to tell you that he is gone South for the week. He is gone South for the week!"

The train had begun to move out. The red man rubbed his eyes. "He has gone South for the week," he repeated. "Now that's just like his impidence. Did he say that I was to give you anything?—'Cause I won't."

"He didn't," I said, and dropped away, and watched the red lights die out in the dark. It was horribly cold, because the wind was blowing off the sands. I climbed into my own train—not an Intermediate Carriage this time—and went to sleep.

If the man with the beard had given me a rupee I should have kept it as a memento of a rather curious affair. But the consciousness of having done my duty was my only reward.

Later on I reflected that two gentlemen like my friends could not do any good if they foregathered and personated correspondents of newspapers, and might, if they "stuck up" one of the little rat-trap states of

Central India or Southern Rajputana, get themselves into serious difficulties. I therefore took some trouble to describe them as accurately as I could remember to people who would be interested in deporting them; and succeeded, so I was later informed, in having them headed back from Degumber borders.

Then I became respectable, and returned to an Office where there were no Kings and no incidents except the daily manufacture of a newspaper. A newspaper office seems to attract every conceivable sort of person, to the prejudice of discipline. Zenana-mission ladies arrive, and beg that the Editor will instantly abandon all his duties to describe a Christian prize-giving in a back-slum of a perfectly inaccessible village; Colonels who have been overpassed for commands sit down and sketch the outline of a series of ten, twelve, or twenty-four leading articles on Seniority *versus* Selection; missionaries wish to know why they have not been permitted to escape from their regular vehicles of abuse and swear at a brother missionary under special patronage of the editorial We; stranded theatrical companies troop up to explain that they cannot pay for their advertisements, but on their return from New Zealand or Tahiti will do so with interest; inventors of patent punkah-pulling machines, carriage couplings, and unbreakable swords and axletrees call with specifications in their pockets and hours at their disposal; tea companies enter and elaborate their prospectuses with the office pens; secretaries of ball committees clamor to have the glories of their last dance more fully expounded; strange ladies rustle in and say, "I want a hundred lady's cards printed *at once*, please," which is manifestly part of an Editor's duty; and every dissolute ruffian that ever tramped the Grand Trunk Road makes it his business to ask for employment as a proofreader. And, all the time, the telephone bell is ringing madly, and Kings are being killed on the Continent, and Empires are saying—"You're another," and Mister Gladstone is calling down brimstone upon the British Dominions, and the little black copy boys are whining, "*kaa-pi chay-ha-yeh*" (copy wanted) like tired bees, and most of the paper is as blank as Modred's shield.

But that is the amusing part of the year. There are other six months wherein none ever come to call, and the thermometer walks inch by inch up to the top of the glass, and the office is darkened to just above reading light, and the press machines are red-hot of touch, and nobody writes anything but accounts of amusements in the Hill stations or obituary notices. Then the telephone becomes a tinkling terror, because it tells you of the sudden deaths of men and women that you knew intimately, and the prickly heat covers you as with a garment, and you sit down and write: "A slight increase of sickness is reported from the Khuda Janta Khan District. The outbreak is purely sporadic in its nature, and, thanks to the energetic efforts of the District authorities, is now almost at an end. It is, however, with deep regret we record the death, etc."

Then the sickness really breaks out, and the less recording and reporting the better for the peace of the subscribers. But the Empires and the Kings continue to divert themselves as selfishly as before, and the Foreman thinks that a daily paper really ought to come out once in twenty-four hours, and all the people at the Hill stations in the middle of their amusements say, "Good gracious! Why can't the paper be sparkling? I'm sure there's plenty going on up here."

That is the dark half of the moon, and, as the advertisements say, "must be experienced to be appreciated."

It was in that season, and a remarkably evil season, that the paper began running the last issue of the week on Saturday night, which is to say, Sunday morning, after the custom of a London paper. This was a great convenience, for immediately after the paper was put to bed, the dawn would lower the thermometer from 96° to almost 84° for half an hour, and in that chill—you have no idea how cold is 84° on the grass until you begin to pray for it—a very tired man could set off to sleep ere the heat roused him.

One Saturday night it was my pleasant duty to put the paper to bed alone. A King or courtier or a courtesan or a community was going to die or get a new Constitution, or do something that was important on the other side of the world, and the paper was to be held open till the latest possible minute in order to catch the telegram. It was a pitchy black night, as stifling as a June night can be, and the *loo*, the red-hot wind from the westward, was booming among the tinder-dry trees and pretending that the rain was on its heels. Now and again a spot of almost boiling water would fall on the dust with the flop of a frog, but all our weary world knew that was only pretense. It was a shade cooler in the press room than the office, so I sat there, while the type clicked and clicked and the nightjars hooted at the windows, and the all but naked compositors wiped the sweat from their foreheads and called for water. The thing that was keeping us back, whatever it was, would not come off, though the *loo* dropped and the last type was set, and the whole round earth stood still in the choking heat, with its finger on its lip, to wait the event. I drowsed, and wondered whether the telegraph was a blessing, and whether this dying man, or struggling people, was aware of the inconvenience the delay was causing. There was no special reason beyond the heat and worry to make tension, but, as the clock hands crept up to three o'clock and the machines spun their flywheels two or three times to see that all was in order, before I said the word that would set them off, I could have shrieked aloud.

Then the roar and rattle of the wheels shivered the quiet into little bits. I rose to go away, but two men in white clothes stood in front of me. The first one said, "It's him!" The second said, "So it is!" And they both laughed almost as loudly as the machinery roared, and mopped their foreheads. "We see there was a light burning across the road and we were sleeping in that ditch there for coolness, and I said to my friend here, 'The office is open. Let's come along and speak to him as turned us back from the Degumber State.' " said the smaller of the two. He was the man I had met in the Mhow train, and his fellow was the red-bearded man of Marwar Junction. There was no mistaking the eyebrows of the one or the beard of the other.

I was not pleased, because I wished to go to sleep, not to squabble with loafers. "What do you want?" I asked.

"Half an hour's talk with you cool and comfortable, in the office," said the red-bearded man. "We'd *like* some drink—the Contrack doesn't begin yet, Peachey, so you needn't look—but what we really want is advice. We don't want money. We ask you as a favor, because you did us a bad turn about Degumber."

I led from the press room to the stifling office with the maps on the walls, and the red-haired man rubbed his hands. "That's something like," said he. "This was the proper shop to come to. Now, Sir, let me introduce to you Brother Peachey Carnehan, that's him, and Brother Daniel Dravot, that is *me*, and the less said about our professions the better, for we have been most things in our time. Soldier, sailor, compositor, photographer, proofreader, street preacher, and correspondents of the *Backwoodsman* when we thought the paper wanted one. Carnehan is sober, and so am I. Look at us first and see that's sure. It will save you cutting into my talk. We'll take one of your cigars apiece, and you shall see us light."

I watched the test. The men were absolutely sober, so I gave them each a tepid peg.

"Well *and* good," said Carnehan of the eyebrows, wiping the froth from his mustache. "Let me talk now, Dan. We have been all over India, mostly on foot. We have been boiler-fitters, engine-drivers, petty contractors, and all that, and we have decided that India isn't big enough for such as us."

They certainly were too big for the office. Dravot's beard seemed to fill half the room and Carnehan's shoulders the other half, as they sat on the big table. Carnehan continued: "The country isn't half worked out because they that governs it won't let you touch it. They spend all their blessed time in governing it, and you can't lift a spade, nor chip a rock, nor look for oil, nor anything like that without all the Government saying, 'Leave it alone and let us govern.' Therefore, such as it is, we will let it alone, and go away to some other place where a man isn't crowded and can come to his own. We are not little men, and there is nothing that we are afraid of except Drink, and we have signed a Contrack on that. *Therefore*, we are going away to be Kings."

"Kings in our own right," muttered Dravot.

"Yes, of course," I said. "You've been tramping in the sun, and it's a very warm night, and hadn't you better sleep over the notion? Come to-morrow."

"Neither drunk nor sunstruck," said Dravot. "We have slept over the notion half a year, and require to see Books and Atlases, and we have decided that there is only one place now in the world that two strong men can Sar-a-*whack*. They call it Kafiristan. By my reckoning it's the top right-hand corner of Afghanistan, not more than three hundred miles from Peshawur. They have two and thirty heathen idols there, and we'll be the thirty-third. It's a mountainous country, and the women of those parts are very beautiful."

"But that is provided against in the Contrack," said Carnehan. "Neither Women nor Liqu-or, Daniel."

"And that's all we know, except that no one has gone there, and they fight, and in any place where they fight, a man who knows how to drill men can always be a King. We shall go to those parts and say to any King we find, 'D'you want to vanquish your foes?' and we will show him how to drill men; for that we know better than anything else. Then we will sub-vert that King and seize his Throne and establish a Dy-nasty."

"You'll be cut to pieces before you're fifty miles across the Border," I said. "You have to travel through Afghanistan to get to that country. It's one mass of mountains and peaks and glaciers, and no Englishman has been through it. The people are utter brutes, and even if you reached them you couldn't do anything."

"That's more like," said Carnehan. "If you could think us a little more mad we would be more pleased. We have come to you to know about this country, to read a book about it, and be shown maps. We want you to tell us that we are fools and to show us your books." He turned to the bookcases.

"Are you at all in earnest?" I said.

"A little," said Dravot, sweetly. "As big a map as you have got, even if it's all blank where Kafiristan is, and any books you've got. We can read, though we aren't very educated."

I uncased the big thirty-two-miles-to-the-inch map of India, and two smaller Frontier maps, hauled down volume INF-KAN of the *Encyclopaedia Britannica*, and the men consulted them.

"See here!" said Dravot, his thumb on the map. "Up to Jagdallak, Peachey and me know the road. We was there with Roberts's Army. We'll have to turn off to the right at Jagdallak through Laghmann territory. Then we get among the hills—fourteen thousand feet—fifteen thousand—it will be cold work there, but it don't look very far on the map."

I handed him Wood on the *Sources of the Oxus*. Carnehan was deep in the *Encyclopaedia*.

"They're a mixed lot," said Dravot, reflectively; "and it won't help us to know the names of their tribes. The more tribes the more they'll fight, and the better for us. From Jagdallak to Ashang. H'mm!"

"But all the information about the country is as sketchy and inaccurate as can be," I protested. "No one knows anything about it really. Here's the file of the *United Services' Institute*. Read what Bellew says."

"Blow Bellew!" said Carnehan. "Dan, they're an all-fired lot of heathens, but this book here says they think they're related to us English."

I smoked while the men pored over *Raverty*, *Wood*, the maps, and the *Encyclopaedia*.

"There is no use your waiting," said Dravot, politely. "It's about four o'clock now. We'll go before six o'clock if you want to sleep, and we won't steal any of the papers. Don't you sit up. We're two harmless lunatics and if you come, tomorrow evening, down to the Serai we'll say good-by to you."

"You *are* two fools," I answered. "You'll be turned back at the Frontier or cut up the minute you set foot in Afghanistan. Do you want any money or a recommendation down-country? I can help you to the chance of work next week."

"Next week we shall be hard at work ourselves, thank you," said Dravot. "It isn't so easy being a King as it looks. When we've got our Kingdom in going order we'll let you know, and you can come up and help us to govern it."

"Would two lunatics make a Contrack like that?" said Carnehan, with subdued pride, showing me a greasy half sheet of note paper on which was written the following. I copied it, then and there, as a curiosity:

This Contract between me and you pursuing witnesseth in the name of God—Amen and so forth.

(ONE)   *That me and you will settle this matter together: i.e., to be Kings of Kafiristan.*

(TWO)   *That you and me will not, while this matter is being settled, look at any Liquor, nor any Woman, black, white or brown, so as to get mixed up with one or the other harmful.*

(THREE)   *That we conduct ourselves with dignity and discretion and if one of us gets into trouble the other will stay by him.*

Signed by you and me this day.
            PEACHEY TALIAFERRO CARNEHAN.
            DANIEL DRAVOT.
            Both Gentlemen at Large.

"There was no need for the last article," said Carnehan, blushing modestly; "but it looks regular. Now you know the sort of men that Loafers are—we *are* Loafers, Dan, until we get out of India—and *do* you think that we would sign a Contrack like that unless we was in earnest? We have kept away from the two things that make life worth having."

"You won't enjoy your lives much longer if you are going to try this idiotic adventure. Don't set the office on fire," I said, "and go away before nine o'clock."

I left them still poring over the maps and making notes on the back of the "Contrack." "Be sure to come down to the Serai tomorrow," were their parting words.

The Kumharsen Serai is the great four square sink of humanity where the strings of camels and horses from the North load and unload. All the nationalities of Central Asia may be found there, and most of the folk of India proper. Balkh and Bokhara there meet Bengal and Bombay, and try to draw eyeteeth. You can buy ponies, turquoises, Persian pussy cats, saddlebags, fat-tailed sheep, and musk in the Kumharsen Serai, and get many strange things for nothing. In the afternoon I went down there to see whether my friends intended to keep their word or were lying about drunk.

A priest attired in fragments of ribbons and rags stalked up to me, gravely twisting a child's paper whirligig. Behind was his servant bending under the load of a crate of mud toys. The two were loading up two camels, and the inhabitants of the Serai watched them with shrieks of laughter.

"The priest is mad," said a horse-dealer to me. "He is going up to Kabul to sell toys to the Amir. He will either be raised to honor or have his head cut off. He came in here this morning and has been behaving madly ever since."

"The witless are under the protection of God," stammered a flat-cheeked Usbeg in broken Hindi. "They foretell future events."

"Would they could have foretold that my caravan would have been cut up by the Shinwaris almost within shadow of the Pass!" grunted the Eusufzai agent of a Rajputana trading house whose goods had been feloniously diverted into the hands of other robbers just across the Border, and whose misfortunes were the laughingstock of the bazaar. "Ohé, priest, whence come you and whither do you go?"

"From Roum have I come," shouted the priest, waving his whirligig; "from Roum, blown by the breath of a hundred devils across the sea! O thieves, robbers, liars, the blessing of Pir Khan on pigs, dogs, and perjurers! Who will take the Protected of God to the North to sell charms that are never still to the Amir? The camels shall not gall, the sons shall not fall sick, and the wives shall remain faithful while they are away, of the men who give me place in their caravan. Who will assist me to slipper the King of the Roos with a golden slipper with a silver heel? The protection of Pir Khan be upon his labors!" He spread out the skirts of his garberdine and pirouetted between the lines of tethered horses.

"There starts a caravan from Peshawur to Kabul in twenty days, *Huzrut*," said the Eusufzai trader. "My camels go therewith. Do thou also go and bring us good luck."

"I will go even now!" shouted the priest. "I will depart upon my winged camels, and be at Peshawur in a day! Ho! Hazar Mir Khan," he yelled to his servant, "drive out the camels, but let me first mount my own."

He leaped on the back of his beast as it knelt, and, turning round to me, cried, "Come thou also, Sahib, a little along the road, and I will sell thee a charm—an amulet that shall make thee King of Kafiristan."

Then the light broke upon me, and I followed the two camels out of the Serai till we reached open road and the priest halted.

"What d'you think o' that?" said he in English. "Carnehan can't talk their patter, so I've made him my servant. He makes a handsome servant. 'Tisn't for nothing that I've been knocking about the country for fourteen years. Didn't I do that talk neat? We'll hitch on to a caravan at Peshawur till we get to Jagdallak, and then we'll see if we can get donkeys for our camels, and strike into Kafiristan. Whirligigs for the Amir, O Lor'! Put your hand under the camel bags and tell me what you feel."

I felt the butt of a Martini, and another and another.

"Twenty of 'em," said Dravot, placidly. "Twenty of 'em, and ammunition to correspond, under the whirligigs and the mud dolls."

"Heaven help you if you are caught with those things!" I said. "A Martini is worth her weight in silver among the Pathans."

"Fifteen hundred rupees of capital—every rupee we could beg, borrow, or steal—are invested on these two camels," said Dravot. "We won't get caught. We're going through the Khyber with a regular caravan. Who'd touch a poor mad priest?"

"Have you got everything you want?" I asked, overcome with astonishment.

"Not yet, but we shall soon. Give us a memento of your kindness, *Brother*. You did me a service yesterday, and that time in Marwar. Half my Kingdom shall you have, as the saying is." I slipped a small charm compass from my watch chain and handed it up to the priest.

"Good-by," said Dravot, giving me hand cautiously. "It's the last time we'll shake hands with an Englishman these many days. Shake hands with him, Carnehan," he cried, as the second camel passed me.

Carnehan leaned down and shook hands. Then the camels passed away along the dusty road, and I was left alone to wonder. My eye could detect no failure in the disguises. The scene in Serai attested that they were complete to the native mind. There was just the chance, therefore, that Carnehan and Dravot would be able to wander through Afghanistan without detection. But, beyond, they would find death, certain and awful death.

Ten days later a native friend of mine, giving me the news of the day from Peshawur, wound up his letter with:—"There has been much laughter here on account of a certain mad priest who is going in his estimation to sell petty gauds and insignificant trinkets which he ascribes as great charms to H. H. the Amir of Bokhara. He passed through Peshawur and associated himself to the Second Summer caravan that goes to Kabul. The merchants are pleased, because through superstition they imagine that such mad fellows bring good fortune."

The two, then, were beyond the Border. I would have prayed for them, but, that night, a real King died in Europe, and demanded an obituary notice.

*　*　*　*

The wheel of the world swings through the same phases again and again. Summer passed and winter thereafter, and came and passed again. The daily paper continued and I with it, and upon the third summer there fell a hot night, a night issue, and a strained waiting for something to be telegraphed from the other side of the world, exactly as had happened before. A few great men had died in the past two years, the machines worked with more clatter, and some of the trees in the Office garden were a few feet taller. But that was all the difference.

I passed over to the press room, and went through just such a scene as I have already described. The nervous tension was stronger than it had been two years before, and I felt the heat more acutely. At three o'clock I cried, "Print off," and turned to go, when there crept to my chair what was left of a man. He was bent into a circle, his head was sunk between his shoulders, and he moved his feet one over the other like a bear. I could hardly see whether he walked or crawled—this rag-wrapped, whining cripple who addressed me by name, crying that he was come back. "Can you give me a drink?" he whimpered. "For the Lord's sake, give me a drink!"

I went back to the office, the man followed with groans of pain, and I turned up the lamp.

"Don't you know me?" he gasped, dropping into a chair, and he turned his drawn face, surmounted by a shock of gray hair, to the light.

I looked at him intently. Once before had I seen eyebrows that met over the nose in an inch-broad black band, but for the life of me I could not tell where.

"I don't know you," I said, handing him the whisky. "What can I do for you?"

He took a gulp of the spirit raw, and shivered in spite of the suffocating heat.

"I've come back," he repeated; "and I was the King of Kafiristan—me and Dravot—crowned Kings we was! In this office we settled it—you setting there and giving us the books. I am Peachey—Peachey Taliaferro Carnehan, and you've been setting here ever since—O Lord!"

I was more than a little astonished, and expressed my feelings accordingly.

"It's true," said Carnehan, with a dry cackle, nursing his feet, which were wrapped in rags. "True as gospel. Kings we were, with crowns upon our heads—me and Dravot—poor Dan—oh, poor, poor Dan, that would never take advice, not though I begged of him!"

"Take the whisky," I said, "and take your own time. Tell me all you can recollect of everything from beginning to end. You got across the border on your camels, Dravot dressed as a mad priest and you his servant. Do you remember that?"

"I ain't mad—yet, but I shall be that way soon. Of course I remember. Keep looking at me, or maybe my words will go all to pieces. Keep looking at me in my eyes and don't say anything."

I leaned forward and looked into his face as steadily as I could. He dropped one hand upon the table and I grasped it by the wrist. It was twisted like a bird's claw, and upon the back was a ragged, red, diamond-shaped scar.

"No, don't look there. Look at *me*," said Carnehan.

"That comes afterward, but for the Lord's sake don't distrack me. We left with that caravan, me and Dravot playing all sorts of antics to amuse the people we were with. Dravot used to make us laugh in the evenings when all the people was cooking their dinners—cooking their dinners, and . . . what did they do then? They lit little fires with sparks that went into Dravot's beard, and we all laughed—fit to die. Little red fires they was, going into Dravot's big red beard—so funny." His eyes left mine and he smiled foolishly.

"You went as far as Jagdallak with that caravan," I said, at a venture, "after you had lit those fires. To Jagdallak, where you turned off to try to get into Kafiristan."

"No, we didn't neither. What are you talking about? We turned off before Jagdallak, because we heard the roads was good. But they wasn't good enough for our two camels—mine and Dravot's. When we left the caravan, Dravot took off all his clothes and mine too, and said we would be heathen, because the Kafirs didn't allow Mohammedans to talk to them. So we dressed betwixt and between, and such a sight as Daniel Dravot I never saw yet nor expect to see again. He burned half his beard, and slung a sheepskin over his shoulder, and shaved his head into patterns. He shaved mine, too, and made me wear outrageous things to look like a heathen. That was in a most mountaineous country, and our camels couldn't go along any more because of the mountains. They were tall and black, and coming home I saw them fight like wild goats—there are lots of goats in Kafiristan. And these mountains, they never keep still, no more than goats. Always fighting they are, and don't let you sleep at night."

"Take some more whisky," I said, very slowly. "What did you and Daniel Dravot do when the camels could go no further because of the rough roads that led into Kafiristan?"

"What did which do? There was a party called Peachey Taliaferro Carnehan that was with Dravot. Shall I tell you about him? He died out there in the cold. Slap from the bridge fell old Peachey, turning and twisting in the air like a penny whirligig that you can sell to the Amir— No; they was two for three ha'pence, those whirligigs, or I am much mistaken and woeful sore. And then these camels were no use, and Peachey said to Dravot—'For the Lord's sake, let's get out of this before our heads are chopped off,' and with that they killed the camels all among the mountains, not having anything in particular to eat, but first they took off the boxes with the guns and the ammunition, till two men came along driving four mules. Dravot up and dances in front of them, singing,—'Sell me four mules.' Says the first man,—'If you are rich enough to buy, you are rich enough to rob'; but before ever he could put his hand to his knife, Dravot breaks his neck over his knee, and the other party runs away. So Carnehan loaded the mules with the rifles that was taken off the camels, and together we starts forward into those bitter cold mountaineous parts, and never a road broader than the back of your hand."

He paused for a moment, while I asked him if he could remember the nature of the country through which he had journeyed.

"I am telling you as straight as I can, but my head isn't as good as it might be. They drove nails through it to make me hear better how Dravot died. The country was mountaineous and the mules were most contrary, and the inhabitants was dispersed and solitary. They went up and up, and down and down, and that other party, Carnehan, was imploring of Dravot not to sing and whistle so loud, for fear of bringing down the tremenjus avalanches. But Dravot says that if a King couldn't sing it wasn't worth being King, and whacked the mules over the rump, and never took no heed for ten cold days. We came to a big level valley all among the mountains, and the mules were near dead, so we killed them, not having anything in special for them or us to eat. We sat upon the boxes, and played odd and even with the cartridges that was jolted out.

"Then ten men with bows and arrows ran down that valley, chasing twenty men with bows and arrows, and the row was tremenjus. They was fair men—fairer than you or more—with yellow hair and remarkable well built. Says Dravot, unpacking the guns—'This is the beginning of the business. We'll fight for the ten men,' and with that he fires two rifles at the twenty men, and drops one of them at two hundred yards from the rock where we was sitting. The other men began to run, but Carnehan and Dravot sits on the boxes picking them off at all ranges, up and down the valley. Then we goes up to the ten men that had run across the snow too, and they fires a footy little arrow at us. Dravot he shoots above their heads and they all falls down flat. Then he walks over and kicks them, and then he lifts them up and shakes hands all around to make them friendly like. He calls them and gives them the boxes to carry, and waves his hand for all the world as though he was King already. They takes the boxes and him across the valley and up the hill into a pine wood on the top, where there was half a dozen big stone idols. Dravot he goes to the biggest—a fellow they call Imbra—and lays a rifle and a cartridge at his feet, rubbing his nose respectful with his own nose, patting him on the head, and saluting in front of it. He turns round to the men and nods his head, and says, 'That's all right. I'm in the know too, and all these old jim-jams are my friends.' Then he opens his mouth and points down it, and when the first man brings him food, he says 'No'; and when the second man brings him food, he says 'No'; but when one of the old priests and the boss of the village brings him food, he says 'Yes'; very haughty, and eats it slow. That was how we came to our first village, without any trouble, just as though we had tumbled from the skies. But we tumbled from one of those damned rope bridges, you see, and you couldn't expect a man to laugh much after that."

"Take some more whisky and go on," I said. "That was the first village you came into. How did you get to be King?"

"I wasn't King," said Carnehan. "Dravot he was the King, and a handsome man he looked with the gold crown on his head and all. Him and the other party stayed in that village, and every morning Dravot sat by the side of old Imbra, and the people came and worshiped. That was Dravot's order. Then a lot of men came into the valley, and Carnehan and Dravot picks them off with the rifles before they knew where they was, and runs down into the valley and up again the other side, and finds another village, same as the first one, and the people all falls down flat on their faces, and Dravot says, 'Now what is the trouble between you two villages?' and the people points to a woman, as fair as you or me, that was carried off, and Dravot takes her back to the first village and counts up the dead—eight there was. For each dead man Dravot pours a little milk on the ground and waves his arms like a whirligig and 'That's all right,' says he. Then he and Carnehan takes the big boss of each village by the arm and walks them down into the valley, and shows them how to scratch a line with a spear right down the valley, and gives each a sod of turf from both sides o' the line. Then all the people comes down and shouts like the devil and all, and Dravot says, 'Go and dig the land, and be fruitful and multiply,' which they did, though they didn't understand. Then we asks the names of things in their lingo—bread and water and fire and idols and such, and Dravot leads the priest of each village up to the idol, and says he must sit there and judge the people, and if anything goes wrong he is to be shot.

"Next week they was all turning up the land in the valley as quiet as bees and much prettier, and the priests heard all the complaints and told Dravot in dumb show what it was about. 'That's just the beginning,' says Dravot. 'They think we're Gods.' He and Carnehan picks out twenty good men and shows them how to click off a rifle, and form fours, and advance in line, and they was very pleased to do so, and clever to see the hang of it. Then he takes out his pipe and his 'baccy pouch and leaves one at one village and one at the other, and off we two goes to see what was to be done in the next valley. That was all rock, and there was a little village there, and Carnehan says, 'Send 'em to the old valley to plant,' and takes 'em there and gives 'em some land that wasn't took before. They were a poor lot, and we blooded 'em with a kid before letting 'em into the new Kingdom. That was to impress the people, and then they settled down quiet, and Carnehan went back to Dravot, who had got into another valley, all snow and ice and most mountaineous. There was no people there, and the Army got afraid, so Dravot shoots one of them, and goes on till he finds some people in a village, and the Army explains that unless the people wants to be killed they had better not shoot their little matchlocks; for they had matchlocks. We makes friends with the priest and I stays there alone with two of the Army, teaching the men how to drill, and a thundering big Chief comes across the snow with kettledrums and horns twanging, because he heard there was a new God kicking about. Carnehan sights for the brown of the men half a mile across the snow and wings one of them. Then he sends a message to the Chief that, unless he wished to be killed, he must come and shake hands with me and leave his arms behind. The Chief comes alone first, and Carnehan shakes hands with him and whirls his arms about, same as Dravot used, and very much surprised that Chief was, and strokes my eyebrows. Then Carnehan goes alone to the Chief, and asks him in dumb show if he had an enemy he hated. 'I have,' says the Chief. So Carnehan weeds out the pick of his men, and sets the two of the Army to show them drill, and at the end of two weeks the men can maneuver about as well as Volunteers. So he marches with the Chief to a great big plain on the top of a mountain, and the Chief's men rushes into a village and takes it; we three Martinis firing into the brown of the enemy. So we took that village too, and I gives the Chief a rag from my coat and says, 'Occupy till I come'; which was scriptural. By way of a reminder, when me and the Army was eighteen hundred yards away, I drops a bullet near him standing on the snow, and all the people falls flat on their faces. Then I sends a letter to Dravot, wherever he be by land or by sea."

At the risk of throwing the creature out of train I interrupted, "How could you write a letter up yonder?"

"The letter?—Oh!—The letter! Keep looking at me between the eyes, please. It was a string-talk letter, that we'd learned the way of it from a blind beggar in the Punjab."

I remember that there had once come to the office a blind man with a knotted twig and a piece of string which he wound round the twig according to some cipher of his own. He could, after the lapse of days or hours, repeat the sentence which he had reeled up. He had reduced the alphabet to eleven primitive sounds; and tried to teach me his method, but failed.

"I sent that letter to Dravot," said Carnehan; "and told him to come back because this Kingdom was growing too big for me to handle, and then I struck for the first valley, to see how the priests were working. They called the village we took along with the Chief, Bashkai, and the first village we took, Er-Heb. The priests at Er-Heb was doing all right, but they had a lot of pending cases about land to show me, and some men from another village had been firing arrows at night. I went out and looked for that village and fired four rounds at it from a thousand yards. That used all the cartridges I cared to spend, and I waited for Dravot, who had been away two or three months, and I kept my people quiet.

"One morning I heard the devil's own noise of drums and horns, and Dan Dravot marches down the hill with his Army and a tail of hundreds of men, and, which was the most amazing—a great gold crown on his head. 'My Gord, Carnehan,' says Daniel, 'this is a tremenjus business, and we've got the whole country as far as it's worth having. I am the son of Alexander by Queen Semiramis, and you're my younger brother and a God too! It's the biggest thing we've ever seen. I've been marching and fighting for six weeks with the Army, and every footy little village for fifty miles has come in rejoiceful; and more than that, I've got the key of the whole show, as you'll see, and I've got a crown for you! I told 'em to make two of 'em at a place called Shu, where the gold lies in the rock like suet in mutton. Gold I've seen, and turquoise I've kicked out of the cliffs, and there's garnets in the sands of the river, and here's a chunk of amber that a man brought me. Call up all the priests and, here, take your crown.'

"One of the men opens a black hair bag and I slips the crown on. It was too small and too heavy, but I wore it for the glory. Hammered gold it was—five pound weight, like a hoop of a barrel.

"'Peachey,' says Dravot, 'we don't want to fight no more. The Craft's the trick, so help me!' and he brings forward that same Chief that I left at Bashkai—Billy Fish we called him afterward, because he was so like Billy Fish that drove the big tank engine at Mach on the Bolan in the old days. 'Shake hands with him,' says Dravot, and I shook hands and nearly dropped, for Billy Fish gave me the Grip. I said nothing, but tried him with the Fellow Craft Grip. He answers, all right, and I tried the Master's Grip, but that was a slip. 'A Fellow Craft he is!' I says to Dan. 'Does he know the word?' 'He does,' says Dan, 'and all the priests know. It's a miracle! The Chiefs and the priests can work a Fellow Craft Lodge in a way that's very like ours, and they've cut the marks on the rocks, but they don't know the Third Degree, and they've come to find out. It's Gord's Truth. I've known these long years that the Afghans knew up to the Fellow Craft Degree, but this is a miracle. A God and a Grand Master of the Craft am I, and a Lodge in the Third Degree I will open, and we'll raise the head priests and the Chiefs of the villages.'

" 'It's against all the law,' I says, 'holding a Lodge without warrant from anyone; and we never held office in any Lodge.'

" 'It's a master stroke of policy,' says Dravot. 'It means running the country as easy as a four-wheeled bogy on a down grade. We can't stop to inquire now, or they'll turn against us. I've forty Chiefs at my heel, and passed and raised according to their merit they shall be. Billet these men on the villages and see that we run up a Lodge of some kind. The temple of Imbra will do for the Lodge room. The women must make aprons as you show them. I'll hold a levee of Chiefs tonight and Lodge tomorrow.'

"I was fair run off my legs, but I wasn't such a fool as not to see what a pull this Craft business gave us. I showed the priests' families how to make aprons of the degrees, but for Dravot's apron the blue border and marks was made of turquoise lumps on white hide, not cloth. We took a great square stone in the temple for the Master's chair, and little stones for the officers' chairs, and painted the black pavement with white squares, and did what we could to make things regular.

"At the levee which was held that night on the hillside with big bonfires, Dravot gives out that him and me were Gods and sons of Alexander, and Past Grand Masters in the Craft, and was come to make Kafiristan a country where every man should eat in peace and drink in quiet, and specially obey us. Then the Chiefs come round to shake hands, and they was so hairy and white and fair it was just shaking hands with old friends. We gave them names according as they was like men we had known in India—Billy Fish, Holly Wilworth, Pikky Kergan that was Bazaar-master when I was at Mhow, and so on and so on.

"*The* most amazing miracle was at Lodge next night. One of the old priests was watching us continuous, and I felt uneasy, for I knew we'd have to fudge the Ritual, and I didn't know what the men knew. The old priest was a stranger come in from beyond the village of Bashkai. The minute Dravot puts on the Master's apron that the girls had made for him, the priest fetches a whoop and a howl, and tried to overturn the stone that Dravot was sitting on. 'It's all up now,' I says. 'That comes of meddling with the Craft without warrant!' Dravot never winked an eye, not when ten priests took and tilted over the Grand Master's chair—which was to say the stone of Imbra. The priest begins rubbing the bottom end of it to clear away the black dirt, and presently he shows all the other priests the Master's Mark, same as was on Dravot's apron, cut into the stone. Not even the priests of the temple of Imbra knew it was there. The old chap falls flat on his face at Dravot's feet and kisses 'em. 'Luck again,' says Dravot, across the Lodge to me, 'they say it's the missing Mark that no one could understand the why of. We're more than safe now.' Then he bangs the butt of his gun for a gavel and says, 'By virtue of the authority vested in

me by my own right hand and the help of Peachey, I declare myself Grand
Master of all Freemasonry in Kafiristan in this the Mother Lodge o' the
country, and King of Kafiristan equally with Peachey!' At that he puts on
his crown and I puts on mine—I was doing Senior Warden—and we opens
the Lodge in most ample form. It was a amazing miracle! The priests
moved in Lodge through the first two degrees almost without telling, as if
the memory was coming back to them. After that, Peachey and Dravot
raised such as was worthy—high priests and Chiefs of far-off villages. Billy
Fish was the first, and I can tell you we scared the soul out of him. It was
not in any way according to Ritual, but it served our turn. We didn't
raise more than ten of the biggest men, because we didn't want to make
the Degree common. And they was clamoring to be raised.

" 'In another six months,' says Dravot, 'we'll hold another Communication and see how you are working.' Then he asks them about their villages, and learns that they was fighting one against the other and were fair
sick and tired of it. And when they wasn't doing that they was fighting
with the Mohammedans. 'You can fight those when they come into our
country,' says Dravot. 'Tell off every tenth man of your tribes for a
Frontier guard, and send two hundred at a time to this valley to be drilled.
Nobody is going to be shot or speared any more so long as he does well,
and I know that you won't cheat me because you're white people—sons of
Alexander—and not like common, black Mohammedans. You are *my* people
and by God,' says he, running off into English at the end—'I'll make a
damned fine Nation of you, or I'll die in the making!'

"I can't tell all we did for the next six months because Dravot did a lot
I couldn't see the hang of, and he learned their lingo in a way I never could.
My work was to help the people plow, and now and again go out with
some of the Army and see what the other villages were doing, and make
'em throw rope bridges across the ravines which cut up the country horrid.
Dravot was very kind to me, but when he walked up and down in the
pine wood pulling that bloody red beard of his with both fists I knew
he was thinking plans I could not advise him about, and I just waited for
orders.

"But Dravot never showed me disrespect before the people. They
were afraid of me and the Army, but they loved Dan. He was the best of
friends with the priests and the Chiefs; but anyone could come across the
hills with a complaint and Dravot would hear him out fair, and call four
priests together and say what was to be done. He used to call in Billy Fish
from Bashkai, and Pikky Kergan from Shu, and an old Chief we called
Kafuzelum—it was like enough to his real name—and hold councils with
'em when there was any fighting to be done in small villages. That was
his Council of War, and the four priests of Bashkai, Shu, Khawak, and
Madora was his Privy Council. Between the lot of 'em they sent me, with
forty men and twenty rifles, and sixty men carrying turquoises, into the

Ghorband country to buy those hand-made Martini rifles, that come out of the Amir's workshops at Kabul, from one of the Amir's Herati regiments that would have sold the very teeth out of their mouths for turquoises.

"I stayed in Ghorband a month, and gave the Governor there the pick of my baskets for hush money, and bribed the Colonel of the regiment some more, and, between the two and the tribespeople, we got more than a hundred hand-made Martinis, a hundred good Kohat Jezails that'll throw to six hundred yards, and forty manloads of very bad ammunition for the rifles. I came back with what I had, and distributed 'em among the men that the Chiefs sent to me to drill. Dravot was too busy to attend to those things, but the old Army that we first made helped me, and we turned out five hundred men that could drill, and two hundred that knew how to hold arms pretty straight. Even those corkscrewed, hand-made guns was a miracle to them. Dravot talked big about powder shops and factories, walking up and down in the pine wood when the winter was coming on.

" 'I won't make a Nation,' says he. 'I'll make an Empire! These men aren't niggers; they're English! Look at their eyes—look at their mouths. Look at the way they stand up. They sit on chairs in their own houses. They're the Lost Tribes, or something like it, and they've grown to be English. I'll take a census in the spring if the priests don't get frightened. There must be a fair two million of 'em in these hills. The villages are full o' little children. Two million people—two hundred and fifty thousand fighting men—and all English! They only want the rifles and a little drilling. Two hundred and fifty thousand men, ready to cut in on Russia's right flank when she tries for India! Peachey, man,' he says, chewing his beard in great hunks, 'we shall be Emperors—Emperors of the Earth! Rajah Brooke will be a suckling to us. I'll treat with the Vice-roy on equal terms. I'll ask him to send me twelve picked English—twelve that I know of—to help us govern a bit. There's Mackray, Sergeant-pensioner at Segowli—many's the good dinner he's given me, and his wife a pair of trousers. There's Donkin, the Warder of Tounghoo Jail; there's hundreds that I could lay my hand on if I was in India. The Vice-roy shall do it for me. I'll send a man through in the spring for those men, and I'll write for a dispensation from the Grand Lodge for what I've done as Grand Master. That—and all the Sniders that'll be thrown out when the native troops in India take up the Martini. They'll be worn smooth, but they'll do for fighting in these hills. Twelve English, a hundred thousand Sniders run through the Amir's country in driblets—I'd be content with twenty thousand in one year—and we'd be an Empire. When everything was shipshape, I'd hand over the crown—this crown I'm wearing now—to Queen Victoria on my knees, and she'd say: "Rise up, Sir Daniel Dravot." Oh, it's big! It's big, I tell you! But there's so much to be done in every place—Bashkai, Khawak, Shu, and everywhere else.'

" 'What is it?' I says. 'There are no more men coming in to be drilled this autumn. Look at those fat, black clouds. They're bringing the snow.'

" 'It isn't that,' says Daniel, putting his hand very hard on my shoulder; 'and I don't wish to say anything that's against you, for no other living man would have followed me and made me what I am as you have done. You're a first-class Commander-in-Chief, and the people know you; but—it's a big country, and somehow you can't help me, Peachey, in the way I want to be helped.'

" 'Go to your blasted priests, then!' I said, and I was sorry when I made that remark, but it did hurt me sore to find Daniel talking so superior when I'd drilled all the men, and done all he told me.

" 'Don't let's quarrel, Peachey,' says Daniel, without cursing. 'You're a King, too, and the half of this Kingdom is yours; but can't you see, Peachey, we want cleverer men than us now—three or four of 'em, that we can scatter about for our Deputies. It's a hugeous great State, and I can't always tell the right thing to do, and I haven't time for all I want to do, and here's the winter coming on and all.' He put half his beard into his mouth, and it was as red as the gold of his crown.

" 'I'm sorry, Daniel,' says I. 'I've done all I could. I've drilled the men and shown the people how to stack their oats better; and I've brought in those tinware rifles from Ghorband—but I know what you're driving at. I take it Kings always feel oppressed that way.'

" 'There's another thing too,' says Dravot, walking up and down. 'The winter's coming and these people won't be giving much trouble and if they do we can't move about. I want a wife.'

" 'For Gord's sake leave the women alone!' I says. 'We've both got all the work we can, though I *am* a fool. Remember the Contrack, and keep clear o' women.'

" 'The Contrack only lasted till such time as we was Kings; and Kings we have been these months past,' says Dravot, weighing his crown in his hand. 'You go get a wife too, Peachey—a nice, strappin', plump girl that'll keep you warm in the winter. They're prettier than English girls, and we can take the pick of 'em. Boil 'em once or twice in hot water, and they'll come as fair as chicken and ham.'

" 'Don't tempt me!' I says. 'I will not have any dealings with a woman not till we are a dam' side more settled than we are now. I've been doing the work o' two men, and you've been doing the work o' three. Let's lie off a bit, and see if we can get some better tobacco from Afghan country and run in some good liquor; but no women.'

" 'Who's talking o' *women?*' says Dravot. 'I said *wife*—a Queen to breed a King's son for the King. A Queen out of the strongest tribe, that'll make them your blood brothers, and that'll lie by your side and tell you all the people thinks about you and their own affairs. That's what I want.'

" 'Do you remember that Bengali woman I kept at Mogul Serai when

I was a plate layer?' says I. 'A fat lot o' good she was to me. She taught me the lingo and one or two other things; but what happened? She ran away with the Stationmaster's servant and half my month's pay. Then she turned up at Dadur Junction in tow of a half-caste, and had the impidence to say I was her husband—all among the drivers in the running shed!'

" 'We've done with that,' says Dravot. 'These women are whiter than you or me, and a Queen I will have for the winter months.'

" 'For the last time o' asking, Dan, do *not*,' I says. 'It'll only bring us harm. The Bible says that Kings ain't to waste their strength on women, 'specially when they've got a new raw Kingdom to work over.'

" 'For the last time of answering, I will,' said Dravot, and he went away through the pine trees looking like a big red devil. The low sun hit his crown and beard on one side and the two blazed like hot coals.

"But getting a wife was not as easy as Dan thought. He put it before the Council, and there was no answer till Billy Fish said that he'd better ask the girls. Dravot damned them all round. 'What's wrong with me?' he shouts, standing by the idol Imbra. 'Am I a dog or am I not enough of a man for your wenches? Haven't I put the shadow of my hand over this country? Who stopped the last Afghan raid?' It was me really, but Dravot was too angry to remember. 'Who brought your guns? Who repaired the bridges? Who's the Grand Master of the sign cut in the stone?' and he thumped his hand on the block that he used to sit on in Lodge, and at Council, which opened like Lodge always. Billy Fish said nothing, and no more did the others. 'Keep your hair on, Dan,' said I; 'and ask the girls. That's how it's done at Home, and these people are quite English.'

" 'The marriage of the King is a matter of State,' says Dan, in a white-hot rage, for he could feel, I hope, that he was going against his better mind. He walked out of the Council room, and the others sat still, looking at the ground.

" 'Billy Fish,' says I to the Chief of Bashkai, 'what's the difficulty here? A straight answer to a true friend.' 'You know,' says Billy Fish. 'How should a man tell you who know everything? How can daughters of men marry Gods or Devils? It's not proper.'

"I remembered something like that in the Bible; but if, after seeing us as long as they had, they still believed we were Gods, it wasn't for me to undeceive them.

" 'A God can do anything,' says I. 'If the King is fond of a girl he'll not let her die.' 'She'll have to,' said Billy Fish. 'There are all sorts of Gods and Devils in these mountains, and now and again a girl marries one of them and isn't seen any more. Besides, you two know the Mark cut in the stone. Only the Gods know that. We thought you were men till you showed the sign of the Master.'

"I wished then that we had explained about the loss of the genuine secrets of a Master Mason at the first go-off; but I said nothing. All that

night there was a blowing of horns in a little dark temple halfway down
the hill, and I heard a girl crying fit to die. One of the priests told us that
she was being prepared to marry the King.

" 'I'll have no nonsense of that kind,' says Dan. 'I don't want to interfere with your customs, but I'll take my own wife.' 'The girl's a little bit
afraid,' says the priest. 'She thinks she's going to die, and they are a-
heartening of her up down in the temple.'

" 'Hearten her very tender, then,' says Dravot, 'or I'll hearten you
with the butt of a gun so that you'll never want to be heartened again.'
He licked his lips, did Dan, and stayed up walking about more than half
the night, thinking of the wife that he was going to get in the morning.
I wasn't any means comfortable, for I knew that dealings with a woman
in foreign parts, though you was a crowned King twenty times over, could
not but be risky. I got up very early in the morning while Dravot was
asleep, and I saw the priests talking together in whispers, and the Chiefs
talking together too, and they looked at me out of the corners of their
eyes.

" 'What is up, Fish?' I says to the Bashkai man, who was wrapped up
in his furs and looking splendid to behold.

" 'I can't rightly say,' says he; 'but if you can induce the King to
drop all this nonsense about marriage, you'll be doing him and me and
yourself a great service.'

" 'That I do believe,' says I. 'But sure, you know, Billy, as well as
me, having fought against and for us, that the King and me are nothing
more than two of the finest men that God Almighty ever made. Nothing
more, I do assure you.'

" 'That may be,' says Billy Fish, 'and yet I should be sorry if it was.'
He sinks his head upon his great fur cloak for a minute and thinks. 'King,'
says he, 'be you man or God or Devil, I'll stick by you today. I have
twenty of my men with me, and they will follow me. We'll go to Bashkai
until the storm blows over.'

"A little snow had fallen in the night, and everything was white except
the greasy fat clouds that blew down and down from the north. Dravot
came out with his crown on his head, swinging his arms and stamping his
feet, and looking more pleased than Punch.

" 'For the last time, drop it, Dan,' says I, in a whisper. 'Billy Fish here
says that there will be a row.'

" 'A row among my people!' says Dravot. 'Not much. Peachey, you're
a fool not to get a wife too. Where's the girl?' says he, with a voice as
loud as the braying of a jackass. 'Call up all the Chiefs and priests, and
let the Emperor see if his wife suits him.'

"There was no need to call anyone. They were all there leaning on
their guns and spears round the clearing in the center of the pine wood.
A deputation of priests went down to the little temple to bring up the

girl, and the horns blew up fit to wake the dead. Billy Fish saunters round and gets as close to Daniel as he could, and behind him stood his twenty men with matchlocks. Not a man of them under six feet. I was next to Dravot, and behind me was twenty men of the regular Army. Up comes the girl, and a strapping wench she was, covered with silver and turquoises, but white as death, and looking back every minute at the priests.

" 'She'll do,' said Dan, looking her over. 'What's to be afraid of, lass? Come and kiss me.' He puts his arm round her. She shuts her eyes, gives a bit of a squeak, and down goes her face in the side of Dan's flaming red beard.

" 'The slut's bitten me!' says he, clapping his hand to his neck, and, sure enough, his hand was red with blood. Billy Fish and two of his matchlock men catches hold of Dan by the shoulders and drags him into the Bashkai lot, while the priests howl in their lingo, 'Neither God nor Devil, but a man!' I was all taken aback, for a priest cut at me in front, and the Army behind began firing into the Bashkai men.

" 'God A-mighty!' says Dan. 'What is the meaning o' this?'

" 'Come back! Come away!' says Billy Fish, 'Ruin and Mutiny is the matter. We'll break for Bashkai if we can.'

"I tried to give some sort of orders to my men—the men o' the regular Army—but it was no use, so I fired into the brown of 'em with an English Martini and drilled three beggars in a line. The valley was full of shouting, howling creatures, and every soul was shrieking, 'Not a God not a Devil, but only a man!' The Bashkai troops stuck to Billy Fish all they were worth, but their matchlocks wasn't half as good as the Kabul breechloaders, and four of them dropped. Dan was bellowing like a bull, for he was very wrathy; and Billy Fish had a hard job to prevent him running out at the crowd.

" 'We can't stand,' says Billy Fish. 'Make a run for it down the valley! The whole place is against us.' The matchlock men ran, and we went down the valley in spite of Dravot's protestations. He was swearing horribly and crying out that he was a King. The priests rolled great stones on us, and the regular Army fired hard, and there wasn't more than six men, not counting Dan, Billy Fish, and Me, that came down to the bottom of the valley alive.

"Then they stopped firing and the horns in the temple blew again. 'Come away—for Gord's sake come away!' says Billy Fish. 'They'll send runners out to all the villages before ever we get to Bashkai. I can protect you there, but I can't do anything now.'

"My own notion is that Dan began to go mad in his head from that hour. He stared up and down like a stuck pig. Then he was all for walking back alone and killing the priests with his bare hands; which he could have done. 'An Emperor am I,' says Daniel, 'and next year I shall be a Knight of the Queen.'

" 'All right, Dan,' says I; 'but come along now while there's time.'

" 'It's your fault,' says he, 'for not looking after your Army better. There was mutiny in the midst and you didn't know—you damned engine-driving, plate-laying, missionary's-pass-hunting hound!' He sat upon a rock and called me every foul name he could lay tongue to. I was too heartsick to care, though it was all his foolishness that brought the smash.

" 'I'm sorry, Dan,' says I, 'but there's no accounting for natives. This business is our Fifty-Seven. Maybe we'll make something out of it yet, when we've got to Bashkai.'

" 'Let's get to Bashkai, then,' says Dan, 'and, by God, when I come back here again I'll sweep the valley so there isn't a bug in a blanket left!'

"We walked all that day, and all that night Dan was stumping up and down on the snow, chewing his beard and muttering to himself.

" 'There's no hope o' getting clear,' said Billy Fish. 'The priests will have sent runners to the villages to say that you are only men. Why didn't you stick on as Gods till things was more settled? I'm a dead man,' says Billy Fish, and he throws himself down on the snow and begins to pray to his Gods.

"Next morning we was in a cruel bad country—all up and down, no level ground at all, and no food either. The six Bashkai men looked at Billy Fish hungrywise as if they wanted to ask something, but they said never a word. At noon we came to the top of a flat mountain all covered with snow, and when we climbed up into it, behold, there was an Army in position waiting in the middle!

" 'The runners have been very quick,' says Billy Fish, with a little bit of a laugh. 'They are waiting for us.'

"Three or four men began to fire from the enemy's side, and a chance shot took Daniel in the calf of the leg. That brought him to his senses. He looks across the snow at the Army, and sees the rifles that we had brought into the country.

" 'We're done for,' says he. 'They are Englishmen, these people—and it's my blasted nonsense that has brought you to this. Get back, Billy Fish, and take your men away; you've done what you could, and now cut for it. Carnehan,' says he, 'shake hands with me and go along with Billy. Maybe they won't kill you. I'll go and meet 'em alone. It's me that did it. Me, the King!'

" 'Go!' says I. 'Go to Hell, Dan. I'm with you here. Billy Fish, you clear out, and we two will meet those folk.'

" 'I'm a Chief,' says Billy Fish, quite quiet. 'I stay with you. My men can go.'

"The Bashkai fellows didn't wait for a second word, but ran off, and Dan and Me and Billy Fish walked across to where the drums were drumming and the horns were horning. It was cold—awful cold. I've got that cold in the back of my head now. There's a lump of it there."

The punkah coolies had gone to sleep. Two kerosene lamps were blazing in the office, and the perspiration poured down my face and splashed on the blotter as I leaned forward. Carnehan was shivering, and I feared that his mind might go. I wiped my face, took a fresh grip of the piteously mangled hands, and said, "What happened after that?"

The momentary shift of my eyes had broken the clear current.

"What was you pleased to say?" whined Carnehan. "They took them without any sound. Not a little whisper all along the snow, not though the King knocked down the first man that set hand on him—not though old Peachey fired his last cartridge into the brown of 'em. Not a single solitary sound did those swines make. They just closed up tight, and I tell you their furs stunk. There was a man called Billy Fish, a good friend of us all, and they cut his throat, Sir, then and there, like a jig; and the King kicks up the bloody snow and says, 'We've had a dashed fine run for our money. What's coming next?' But Peachey, Peachey Taliaferro, I tell you, Sir, in confidence as betwixt two friends, he lost his head, Sir. No, he didn't neither. The King lost his head, so he did, all along o' one of those cunning rope bridges. Kindly let me have the paper cutter, Sir. It tilted this way. They marched him a mile across that snow to a rope bridge over a ravine with a river at the bottom. You may have seen such. They prodded him behind like an ox. 'Damn your eyes!' says the King. 'D'you suppose I can't die like a gentleman?' He turns to Peachey—Peachey that was crying like a child. 'I've brought you to this, Peachey,' says he. 'Brought you out of your happy life to be killed in Kafiristan, where you was late Commander-in-Chief of the Emperor's forces. Say you forgive me, Peachey,' 'I do,' says Peachey. 'Fully and freely do I forgive you, Dan.' 'Shake hands, Peachey,' says he. 'I'm going now.' Out he goes, looking neither right nor left, and when he was plumb in the middle of those dizzy dancing ropes, 'Cut, you beggars,' he shouts; and they cut, and old Dan fell, turning round and round and round twenty thousand miles, for he took half an hour to fall till he struck the water, and I could see his body caught on a rock with the gold crown close beside.

"But do you know what they did to Peachey between two pine trees? They crucified him, Sir, as Peachey's hand will show. They used wooden pegs for his hands and his feet; and he didn't die. He hung there and screamed, and they took him down next day, and said it was a miracle that he wasn't dead. They took him down—poor old Peachey that hadn't done them any harm—that hadn't done them any . . ."

He rocked to and fro and wept bitterly, wiping his eyes with the back of his scarred hands and moaning like a child for some ten minutes.

"They was cruel enough to feed him up in the temple, because they said he was more of a God than old Daniel that was a man. Then they turned him out on the snow, and told him to go home, and Peachey came home in about a year, begging along the roads quite safe; for Daniel Dravot he walked before and said, 'Come along, Peachey. It's a big thing we're doing.' The mountains they danced at night, and the mountains they tried to fall on Peachey's head, but Dan he held up his hand, and Peachey came along bent double. He never let go of Dan's hand, and he never let go of Dan's head. They gave it to him as a present in the temple, to remind him not to come again, and though the crown was pure gold, and Peachey was starving, never would Peachey sell the same. You knew Dravot, Sir! You knew Right Worshipful Brother Dravot! Look at him now!"

He fumbled in the mass of rags round his bent waist; brought out a black horsehair bag embroidered with silver thread; and shook therefrom on to my table—the dried, withered head of Daniel Dravot! The morning sun that had long been paling the lamps struck the red beard and blind sunken eyes; struck, too, a heavy circlet of gold studded with raw turquoises, that Carnehan placed tenderly on the battered temples.

"You behold now," said Carnehan, "the Emperor in his habit as he lived—the King of Kafiristan with his crown upon his head. Poor old Daniel that was a monarch once!"

I shuddered, for, in spite of defacements manifold, I recognized the head of the man of Marwar Junction. Carnehan rose to go. I attempted to stop him. He was not fit to walk abroad. "Let me take away the whisky, and give me a little money," he gasped. "I was a King once. I'll go to the Deputy Commissioner and ask to set in the Poorhouse till I get my health. No, thank you, I can't wait till you get a carriage for me. I've urgent private affairs—in the South—at Marwar."

He shambled out of the office and departed in the direction of the Deputy Commissioner's house. That day at noon I had occasion to go down the blinding hot Mall, and I saw a crooked man crawling along the white dust of the roadside, his hat in his hand, quavering dolorously after the fashion of street-singers at Home. There was not a soul in sight, and he was out of all possible earshot of the houses. And he sang through his nose, turning his head from right to left:

> The Son of Man goes forth to war,
>   A golden crown to gain;
> His blood-red banner streams afar—
>   Who follows in his train?

I waited to hear no more, but put the poor wretch into my carriage and drove him off to the nearest missionary for eventual transfer to the Asylum. He repeated the hymn twice while he was with me, whom he did not in the least recognize, and I left him singing it to the missionary.

Two days later I inquired after his welfare of the Superintendent of the Asylum.

"He was admitted suffering from sunstroke. He died early yesterday morning," said the Superintendent. "Is it true that he was half an hour bareheaded in the sun at midday?"

"Yes," said I, "but do you happen to know if he had anything upon him by any chance when he died?"

"Not to my knowledge," said the Superintendent.

And there the matter rests.

INTERPRETATION

At first glance, this seems to be merely a good story of adventure in a far-off and exotic place. There are difficult journeys, mysterious strangers, battles, pagan temples, madness, a crucifixion. The reader's curiosity about the turn of events is whetted by many cunning devices for provoking suspense. For instance, the first stranger's mysterious message leads to the red-bearded man in the second-class carriage. The trader and his servant in the bazaar turn out to be the adventurers ready for their journey. Or, to go further, in the *episode* (see Glossary) concerning the mark on the stone, everything hangs for a moment in the balance until the mark is disclosed. Kipling, in other words, not only plays on the reader's curiosity about the final outcome, but plays up our suspense as to the outcome of the individual steps in the story's development.

Furthermore, we can see how, in this story in which *plot* (see Glossary) seems to be so dominant in interest, one incident is caused by another. For instance, the marriage causes the discovery which brings on the ruin of the kings. But though we can link up the various episodes into a chain of cause and effect, we can see that this chain really depends upon the characters themselves.

Again, considered superficially, the matter of *motivation* (see Glossary) seems to present little difficulty. Many men desire riches and power, as do Peachey and Dravot; and it may seem that we need go no further into the matter in our discussion of motivation and character. (Indeed, this is as far as most adventure stories do go in presenting motivation.) But we can see that in this story, despite its apparent emphasis on action, the motivation is more complicated. For example, as the kings acquire their power, the simple desire for riches and power begins to change. There is a growing sense of responsibility for, and pride in, the people that they rule. Dravot begins to talk about bringing in skilled administrators, recognizing with an unexpected kind of humility that the business of kingship is more complicated than he had thought. He even begins to dream of turning over his kingdom to Queen Victoria—of taking his place in history as one of the Empire Builders. Actually, it is this development of character that proves to be one of the factors leading to his downfall, for the desire for marriage is not merely his simple human desire for companionship—though this is present—but it is also a desire to found a royal line, to leave someone to carry on the kingdom after his death. The wedding, therefore, must be public, and it must be carried out with due ceremony and ritual.

The course of the adventure itself has gone hand in hand with a development of character. That is, the men whom we meet at the beginning of the story are loafers—even if rather unusual loafers—yet men who are outcasts and who see "things from the underside where the lath and plaster is not smoothed off." But Dravot does not die like the loafer: "They prodded him behind like an ox. 'Damn your eyes!' says the King. 'D'you suppose I can't die like a gentleman?' "

He dies like a king, "like a gentleman," not like the trapped animal, the ox. And even Peachey, whose position is subordinate to Dravot's throughout the story, participates in this new dignity. Peachey comes back through the wild mountains, through terrors and hardships, but he never relinquishes the bag in which are the head of the King, and the crown, the symbol of kingship. So, as a *paradox* (see Glossary), the two loafers become most truly kings in the moment when their false kingship is taken from them. That is, when external kingship is lost, internal kingship is achieved.

This idea may prompt us to look back again at the meaning of the situation which brings about the ruin of the adventurers. The natives have thought of them as gods—not as human kings. The power of Peachey and Dravot is, thus, that of the king-as-god, not that of the king-as-man. But Dravot, the king-as-god, wants to be a man—he has human instincts which the mere exercise of godlike power cannot satisfy. He wants to have power, to be a god (for, to have power over the natives, he must be a god, as we discover), and he longs to be a man. This is the dilemma in which he is caught, and the dilemma which ruins him. The story at this point shows itself to be in a sense, then, a study of kingship; and there is a continuation of this study of kingship as the story goes on to recount Dravot's death, where, as we have seen, Dravot achieves another kind of kingship, and the nature of kingship is redefined.

Perhaps the general point may be summarized as follows: The loafers are impelled by a dream of kingship, but not a kingship hedged about by constitutional limitations, not a kingship which depends upon a mere social arrangement, not a kingship which is a mere figurehead or symbol for the real power of the state, but a "real" kingship, a kingship of absolute power. Such power depends upon their remaining aloof from humanity as gods; yet they are men, and man, not even for power, will forfeit his humanity. It is ironical that Dravot finally exercises his godlike power only in order to become a man—to satisfy his basic human desires. This step brings ruin, but there is a further irony in the fact that Dravot becomes most truly kingly at the moment of his ruin. Especially is this true for the reader who sees simply a kind of tawdry showmanship and deception in the parade of godlike power over the ignorant tribesmen, but who admires the way in which Dravot meets his death. Thus the story involves a contrast between kinds of kingship, between kinds of power, external and internal, power over others and power over oneself.

To recur to the list of questions suggested earlier on page 2: it ought to be apparent that the account of "The Man Who Would Be King" just given represents what may be regarded as at least a beginning to an answer to those questions. But the account also makes it very plain that the questions are all interrelated, and that a full answer to one of them tends to involve the answers to the others. It should also be plain that such questions as are suggested at the beginning of this story actually go on to raise many further questions. The account of the story given above does not pretend to provide a full interpretation of the story. For instance, the following are some of the questions which would be involved in a full interpretation of the story:

1. Why is it appropriate that Peachey should be heard singing the particular hymn which he sings? Is it in his character to sing this particular hymn? How is the hymn related to the "meaning" of the story? Define the ironies involved in this incident.

2. Is Billy Fish loyal to Dravot as "god" or as "man"? What light does the fact of his loyalty shed on the rest of the story?

3. Is the contract signed by Dravot and Peachey humorous, pathetic, or heroic?

4. How does the fact that this story is told by a first-person narrator help us to define the characters?

5. What is the significance of the crucifixion of Peachey?

These are only a few of the possible questions which might be raised about the story. The student should choose several of these topics as exercises and write a full discussion of them.

JAMES THURBER

The Secret Life of Walter Mitty

"WE'RE going through!" The Commander's voice was like thin ice breaking. He wore his full-dress uniform, with the heavily braided white cap pulled down rakishly over one cold gray eye. "We can't make it, sir. It's spoiling for a hurricane, if you ask me." "I'm not asking you, Lieutenant Berg," said the Commander. "Throw on the power lights! Rev her up to 8,500! We're going through!" The pounding of the cylinders increased; ta-pocketa-pocketa-pocketa-pocketa-pocketa. The Commander stared at the ice forming on the pilot window. He walked over and twisted a row of complicated dials. "Switch on No. 8 auxiliary!" he shouted. "Switch on No. 8 auxiliary!" repeated Lieutenant Berg. "Full strength in No. 3 turret!" shouted the Commander. "Full strength in No. 3 turret!" The crew, bending to their various tasks in the huge, hurtling eight-engined Navy hydroplane, looked at each other and grinned. "The Old Man'll get us through," they said to one another. "The Old Man ain't afraid of Hell!" . . .

"Not so fast! You're driving too fast!" said Mrs. Mitty. "What are you driving so fast for?"

"Hmm?" said Walter Mitty. He looked at his wife, in the seat beside him, with shocked astonishment. She seemed grossly unfamiliar, like a strange woman who had yelled at him in a crowd. "You were up to fifty-five," she said. "You know I don't like to go more than forty. You were up to fifty-five." Walter Mitty drove on toward Waterbury in silence, the roaring of the SN202 through the worst storm in twenty years of Navy flying fading in the remote, intimate airways of his mind. "You're tensed up again," said Mrs. Mitty. "It's one of your days. I wish you'd let Dr. Renshaw look you over."

Walter Mitty stopped the car in front of the building where his wife went to have her hair done. "Remember to get those overshoes while I'm having my hair done," she said. "I don't need overshoes," said Mitty. She put her mirror back into her bag. "We've been all through that," she said, getting out of the car. "You're not a young man any longer." He raced the engine a little. "Why don't you wear your gloves? Have you lost your gloves?" Walter Mitty reached in a pocket and brought out the gloves. He put them on, but after she had turned and gone into the building and he had driven on to a red light, he took them off again. "Pick it up, brother!" snapped a cop as the light changed, and Mitty hastily pulled on his gloves and lurched ahead. He drove around the streets aimlessly for a time, and then he drove past the hospital on his way to the parking lot.

. . . "It's the millionaire banker, Wellington McMillan," said the pretty nurse. "Yes?" said Walter Mitty, removing his gloves slowly. "Who has the case?" "Dr. Renshaw and Dr. Benbow, but there are two specialists here, Dr. Remington from New York and Dr. Pritchard-Mitford from London. He flew over." A door opened down a long, cool corridor and Dr. Renshaw came out. He looked distraught and haggard. "Hello, Mitty," he said. "We're having the devil's own time with McMillan, the millionaire banker and close personal friend of Roosevelt. Obstreosis of the ductal tract. Tertiary. Wish you'd take a look at him." "Glad to." said Mitty.

In the operating room there were whispered introductions: "Dr. Remington, Dr. Mitty. Dr. Pritchard-Mitford, Dr. Mitty." "I've read your book on streptothricosis," said Pritchard-Mitford, shaking hands. "A brilliant performance, sir." "Thank you," said Walter Mitty. "Didn't know you were in the States, Mitty," grumbled Remington. "Coals to Newcastle, bringing Mitford and me up here for a tertiary." "You are very kind," said Mitty. A huge, complicated machine, connected to the operating table, with many tubes and wires, began at this moment to go pocketa-pocketa-pocketa. "The new anaesthetizer is giving away!" shouted an interne. "There is no one in the East who knows how to fix it!" "Quiet, man!" said Mitty, in a low, cool voice. He sprang to the machine, which was now going pocketa-pocketa-queep-pocketa-queep. He began fingering delicately a row of glistening dials. "Give me a fountain pen!" he snapped. Someone handed him a fountain pen. He pulled a faulty piston out of the machine and inserted the pen in its place. "That will hold for ten minutes," he said. "Get on with the operation." A nurse hurried over and whispered to Renshaw, and Mitty saw the man turn pale. "Coreopsis has set in," said Renshaw nervously. "If you would take over, Mitty?" Mitty looked at him and at the craven figure of Benbow, who drank, and at the grave, uncertain faces of the two great specialists. "If you wish," he said. They slipped a white gown on him; he adjusted a mask and drew on thin gloves; nurses handed him shining . . .

"Back it up, Mac! Look out for that Buick!" Walter Mitty jammed on the brakes. "Wrong lane, Mac," said the parking-lot attendant, looking at Mitty closely. "Gee. Yeh," muttered Mitty. He began cautiously to back out of the lane marked "Exit Only." "Leave her sit there," said the attendant. "I'll put her away." Mitty got out of the car. "Hey, better leave the key." "Oh," said Mitty, handing the man the ignition key. The attendant vaulted into the car, backed it up with insolent skill, and put it where it belonged.

They're so damn cocky, thought Walter Mitty, walking along Main Street; they think they know everything. Once he had tried to take his chains off, outside New Milford, and he had got them wound around the axles. A man had had to come out in a wrecking car and unwind them, a young, grinning garage man. Since then Mrs. Mitty always made him drive to a garage to have the chains taken off. The next time, he thought, I'll wear my right arm in a sling; they won't grin at me then. I'll have my right arm in a sling and they'll see I couldn't possibly take the chains off myself. He kicked at the slush on the sidewalk. "Overshoes," he said to himself, and he began looking for a shoe store.

When he came out into the street again, with the overshoes in a box under his arm, Walter Mitty began to wonder what the other thing was his wife had told him to get. She had told him, twice before they set out from their house for Waterbury. In a way he hated these weekly trips to town—he was always getting something wrong. Kleenex, he thought, Squibb's, razor blades? No. Toothpaste, toothbrush, bicarbonate, carborundum, initiative and referendum? He gave it up. But she would remember it. "Where's the what's-its-name?" she would ask. "Don't tell me you forgot the what's-its-name." A newsboy went by shouting something about the Waterbury trial.

. . . "Perhaps this will refresh your memory." The District Attorney suddenly thrust a heavy automatic at the quiet figure on the witness stand. "Have you ever seen this before?" Walter Mitty took the gun and examined it expertly. "This is my Webley-Vickers 50.80," he said calmly. An excited buzz ran around the courtroom. The judge rapped for order. "You are a crack shot with any sort of firearms, I believe?" said the District Attorney, insinuatingly. "Objection!" shouted Mitty's attorney. "We have shown the the defendant could not have fired the shot. We have shown that he wore his right arm in a sling on the night of the fourteenth of July." Walter Mitty raised his hand briefly and the bickering attorneys were stilled. "With any known make of gun," he said evenly, "I could have killed Gregory Fitzhurst at three hundred feet *with my left hand*." Pandemonium broke loose in the courtroom. A woman's scream rose above the bedlam and suddenly a lovely, dark-haired girl was in Walter Mitty's arms. The District Attorney struck at her savagely. Without rising from his chair, Mitty let the man have it on the point of the chin. "You miserable cur!" . . .

"Puppy biscuit," said Walter Mitty. He stopped walking and the buildings of Waterbury rose up out of the misty courtroom and surrounded him again. A woman who was passing laughed. "He said 'Puppy biscuit,' " she said to her companion. "That man said 'Puppy biscuit' to himself." Walter Mitty hurried on. He went into an A. & P., not the first one he came to but a smaller one farther up the street. "I want some biscuit for small, young dogs," he said to the clerk. "Any special brand, sir?" The greatest pistol shot in the world thought a moment. "It says 'Puppies Bark for It' on the box," said Walter Mitty.

His wife would be through at the hairdresser's in fifteen minutes, Mitty saw in looking at his watch, unless they had trouble drying it; sometimes they had trouble drying it. She didn't like to get to the hotel first; she would want him to be there waiting for her as usual. He found a big leather chair in the lobby, facing a window, and he put the overshoes and the puppy biscuit on the floor beside it. He picked up an old copy of *Liberty* and sank down into the chair. "Can Germany Conquer the World through the Air?" Walter Mitty looked at the pictures of bombing planes and of ruined streets.

. . . "The cannonading has got the wind up in young Raleigh, sir," said the sergeant. Captain Mitty looked up at him through tousled hair. "Get him to bed," he said wearily, "with the others. I'll fly alone." "But you can't, sir," said the sergeant anxiously. "It takes two men to handle that bomber and the Archies are pounding hell out of the air. Von Richtman's circus is between here and Saulier." "Somebody's got to get that ammunition dump," said Mitty. "I'm going over. Spot of brandy?" He poured a drink for the sergeant and one for himself. War thundered and whined around the dugout and battered at the door. There was a rending of wood and splinters flew through the room. "A bit of a near thing," said Captain Mitty carelessly. "The box barrage is closing in," said the sergeant. "We only live once, sergeant," said Mitty, with his faint, fleeting smile. "Or do we?" He poured another brandy and tossed it off. "I never see a man could hold his brandy like you, sir," said the sergeant. "Begging your pardon, sir." Captain Mitty stood up and strapped on his huge Webley-Vickers automatic. "It's forty kilometers through hell, sir," said the sergeant. Mitty finished one last brandy. "After all," he said softly, "what isn't?" The pounding of the cannon increased; there was the rat-tat-tatting of machine guns, and from somewhere came the menacing pocketa-pocketa-pocketa of the new flame-throwers. Walter Mitty walked to the door of the dugout humming "*Après de Ma Blonde.*" He turned and waved to the sergeant. "Cheerio!" he said. . . .

Something struck his shoulder. "I've been looking all over this hotel for you," said Mrs. Mitty. "Why do you have to hide in this old chair? How did you expect me to find you?" "Things close in," said Walter Mitty vaguely. "What?" Mrs. Mitty said. "Did you get the what's-its-name? The puppy biscuit? What's in that box?" "Overshoes," said Mitty. "Couldn't you have put them on in the store?" "I was thinking," said Walter Mitty. "Does it ever occur to you that I am sometimes thinking?" She looked at him. "I'm going to take your temperature when I get you home," she said.

They went out through the revolving doors that made a faintly derisive whistling sound when you pushed them. It was two blocks to the parking lot. At the drugstore on the corner she said, "Wait here for me. I forgot something. I won't be a minute." She was more than a minute.

Walter Mitty lighted a cigarette. It began to rain, rain with sleet in it. He stood up against the wall of the drugstore, smoking. . . . He put his shoulders back and his heels together. "To hell with the handkerchief," said Walter Mitty scornfully. He took one last drag on his cigarette and snapped it away. Then, with that faint, fleeting smile playing about his lips, he faced the firing squad; erect and motionless, proud and disdainful, Walter Mitty the Undefeated, inscrutable to the last.

INTERPRETATION

This story may seem to be merely a character sketch, and not fiction at all. True, certain things do happen here, but are the happenings meaningful? Mr. Mitty, a suburbanite, drives his wife into the center for some shopping. After having been reproved for driving too fast, he lets her out at the hairdresser's, and leaves his car at the parking lot. He buys a pair of overshoes and a box of dog biscuit, and goes to the lobby of the hotel where his wife is to meet him. On their way back to the parking lot, his wife remembers something that she needs to buy in the drugstore and the story ends as Mr. Mitty waits for her outside. If we call this the "action" of the story, then indeed precious little happens. And if we go on to say that Mr. Mitty's daydreaming, which actually makes up most of the story, is not really connected with the action at all, being a direct expression of character, then the case for denying that the story is fiction becomes rather grave. It looks as if the very sketchy "plot" is simply a convenient rack on which to hang the various manifestations of Mr. Mitty's interior life. Looking at the story in this way, we may be tempted to deny that Thurber's story constitutes that revelation of character *through* action which is essential to fiction.

There is a sense, of course, in which the foregoing account of the story is true: the whole narrative *is* constructed to reveal the character of the man, and aside from that revelation, very little does happen. This story, it must be confessed, is very close to a mere character sketch. Yet, it will not be difficult to show that it is a genuine piece of fiction after all.

In the first place, the author never once makes a direct comment upon Walter Mitty's character. We have no difficulty, it is true, in deducing what kind of figure Mitty cuts in the eyes of the parking-lot attendant or of the woman who passes him as he mutters "puppy biscuit." But the author never tells us in his own person what we are to think. He is really quite objective in his report of what happens. We learn what people think of Walter Mitty through the actions and comments of those people—not through any summary made by the author.

In the second place, when it comes to a matter of the way in which Mitty sees himself, that too is mediated through "action." We see Mitty at his business of daydreaming. We see how Mrs. Mitty's mention of the family physician, Dr. Renshaw, sends Mitty into a fantasy in which he becomes the medical hero in the operating room of a great hospital, or how his withering retort to the District Attorney, "You miserable cur"—itself a part of one of his daydreams—suddenly reminds him that it is puppy biscuit that he is to remember to purchase.

Most important of all, however, the "action," trivial though it is, gives point and meaning to Mitty's daydreams. It indicates the motivation for these fantasies by revealing Mitty's need to escape from the world in which he lives. His is not only a trivial and boring world; it is a world in which his own role is that of the husband henpecked by an overbearing and unimaginative wife who evidently long ago effectually suppressed Mr. Mitty's yearnings for the heroic and venturesome. The "action" in this little story effectively dramatizes this relationship, and though the events in question are in themselves commonplace—Mitty's driving at 55 miles an hour or Mitty's protest at wearing overshoes—they illuminate the very core of Mitty's life.

What attitude are we to take toward Walter Mitty? The situation portrayed is in essence the Maggie-and-Jiggs comic-strip sort of situation. Yet the effect aimed at here is not so blatant as that of the comic strip. Walter Mitty, though his daydreams embody the stalest of clichés of adventure fiction and the movies, is not made farcically grotesque. He is allowed a certain kind of pathos, even though his creator is obviously amused at his ineffectuality. Are we to take him rather seriously, then, and see in his plight the imprisonment of a high-hearted soul condemned to frustration? Scarcely that, either. The nature of the daydreams and the way in which they are grotesquely piled up one upon another effectually prevent our taking the plight of Walter Mitty really seriously. But the reader will need no special help in deciding how to "take" this story. Here again the "action" of the story serves to suggest the proper blend of sympathy and amusement with which we are to view Mr. Mitty. Far from telling us what to feel, the author gives us a dramatic presentation of a few hours of Mr. Mitty's life and leaves it up to us to make our own inferences. The "point" of the story is thus also rendered by the drama of presentation.

We began the previous paragraph by asking what attitude we should take toward Walter Mitty. We might have put this question by asking: What is the *tone* (see Glossary) of the story. For the tone is the reflection in the makeup of the story of the author's attitudes—toward his material and toward his reader. The tone of a story may be characterized as grave or gay, reserved or ebullient, straightforward or mocking, merry or melancholy, solemn, playful, prim, sentimental—and one might continue through a hundred other adjectives. Actually, however, the tone of most stories will usually be too special and too complicated to be adequately described by any one adjective. The tone of Thurber's story, for example, is one of amused playfulness, but we have seen that it has nothing of scorn in it and that it even allows for a trace of pathos. But to give an exact description of the tone will involve us in the same difficulties as those met with in the attempt to characterize the author's attitude.

Tone as a term used to characterize style derives from the tone of the voice. The tone in which a thing is uttered modifies what is said and may even reverse the meaning. "He's a fine fellow" delivered in a sarcastic tone, means that the speaker does not think that the person in question is a fine fellow at all. In our spoken language, we are constantly giving exact qualifications to what our words literally say by the tone in which we say them. The literary artist usually cannot read us his work aloud; yet if he is an artist, he can control very powerfully and exactly the way in which we are to "take" what he puts on the page. In the stories that follow, the problem of the "tone" is frequently a matter of primary importance. We shall often have to ask what is the tone of a passage or of a whole story. (If we are thinking primarily not of the story but of the author we may prefer to transpose our question from the tone of the story to the attitude of the author.)

1. In its distortion, the portrait of Walter Mitty may be regarded as a kind of caricature. In this instance is the distortion, like that employed by a good cartoonist, justified?

2. May the last sentence of the story be said to be an appropriate conclusion? Literally, of course, this sentence refers to the pose he assumes in the particular fantasy in which he is absorbed, but can it be said to apply at another level? Is there a sense in which Walter Mitty is indeed "the Undefeated, inscrutable to the last"?

3. Consider the function of the following items in making for the humorous effect: Mr. Mitty's fondness for the syllables "pocketa-pocketa" as expressive of certain sounds; the *alliteration* (see Glossary) involved in such phrases as "sir, said the sergeant"; the use, in the parts of the story which recount Mitty's various fantasies, of *clichés* (see Glossary) drawn from thriller stories.

SHIRLEY JACKSON

The Lottery

THE morning of June 27th was clear
and sunny, with the fresh warmth of a full-summer day; the flowers
were blossoming profusely and the grass was richly green. The people
of the village began to gather in the square, between the post office
and the bank, around ten o'clock; in some towns there were so many
people that the lottery took two days and had to be started on June
26th, but in this village, where there were only about three hundred
people, the whole lottery took less than two hours, so it could begin at
ten o'clock in the morning and still be through in time to allow the
villagers to get home for noon dinner.

The children assembled first, of course. School was recently over
for the summer, and the feeling of liberty sat uneasily on most of them;
they tended to gather together quietly for a while before they broke
into boisterous play, and their talk was still of the classroom and the
teacher, of books and reprimands. Bobby Martin had already stuffed his
pockets full of stones, and the other boys soon followed his example, selecting the smoothest and roundest stones; Bobby and Harry Jones and
Dickie Delacroix—the villagers pronounced this name "Dellacroy"—eventually made a great pile of stones in one corner of the square and guarded
it against the raids of the other boys. The girls stood aside, talking among
themselves, looking over their shoulders at the boys, and the very small
children rolled in the dust or clung to the hands of their older brothers or
sisters.

Soon the men began to gather, surveying their own children, speaking of planting and rain, tractors and taxes. They stood together, away
from the pile of stones in the corner, and their jokes were quiet and they
smiled rather than laughed. The women, wearing faded house dresses
and sweaters, came shortly after their menfolk. They greeted one another
and exchanged bits of gossip as they went to join their husbands. Soon the
women, standing by their husbands, began to call to their children, and
the children came reluctantly, having to be called four or five times.
Bobby Martin ducked under his mother's grasping hand and ran, laughing, back to the pile of stones. His father spoke up sharply, and Bobby
came quickly and took his place between his father and his oldest brother.

The lottery was conducted—as were the square dances, the teen-age club, the Halloween program—by Mr. Summers, who had time and energy to devote to civic activities. He was a round-faced, jovial man and he ran the coal business, and people were sorry for him, because he had no children and his wife was a scold. When he arrived in the square, carrying the black wooden box, there was a murmur of conversation among the villagers, and he waved and called, "Little late today, folks." The post-master, Mr. Graves, followed him, carrying a three-legged stool, and the stool was put in the center of the square and Mr. Summers set the black box down on it. The villagers kept their distance, leaving a space between themselves and the stool, and when Mr. Summers said, "Some of you fellows want to give me a hand?" there was a hesitation before two men, Mr. Martin and his oldest son, Baxter, came forward to hold the box steady on the stool while Mr. Summers stirred up the papers inside it.

The original paraphernalia for the lottery had been lost long ago, and the black box now resting on the stool had been put into use even before Old Man Warner, the oldest man in town, was born. Mr. Sum-mers spoke frequently to the villagers about making a new box, but no one liked to upset even as much tradition as was represented by the black box. There was a story that the present box had been made with some pieces of the box that had preceded it, the one that had been con-structed when the first people settled down to make a village here. Every year, after the lottery, Mr. Summers began talking again about a new box, but every year the subject was allowed to fade off without any-thing's being done. The black box grew shabbier each year; by now it was no longer completely black but splintered badly along one side to show the original wood color, and in some places faded or stained.

Mr. Martin and his oldest son, Baxter, held the black box securely on the stool until Mr. Summers had stirred the papers thoroughly with his hand. Because so much of the ritual had been forgotten or discarded, Mr. Summers had been successful in having slips of paper substituted for the chips of wood that had been used for generations. Chips of wood, Mr. Summers had argued, had been all very well when the village was tiny, but now that the population was more than three hundred and likely to keep on growing, it was necessary to use something that would fit more easily into the black box. The night before the lottery, Mr. Summers and Mr. Graves made up the slips of paper and put them in the box, and it was then taken to the safe of Mr. Summers' coal company and locked up until Mr. Summers was ready to take it to the square next morning. The rest of the year, the box was put away, sometimes one place, sometimes another: it had spent one year in Mr. Graves's barn and another year underfoot in the post office, and sometimes it was set on a shelf in the Martin grocery and left there.

There was a great deal of fussing to be done before Mr. Summers declared the lottery open. There were the lists to make up—of heads of families, heads of households in each family, members of each household in each family. There was the proper swearing-in of Mr. Summers by the postmaster, as the official of the lottery; at one time, some people remembered, there had been a recital of some sort, performed by the official of the lottery, a perfunctory, tuneless chant that had been rattled off duly each year; some people believed that the official of the lottery used to stand just so when he said or sang it, others believed that he was supposed to walk among the people, but years and years ago this part of the ritual had been allowed to lapse. There had been, also, a ritual salute, which the official of the lottery had had to use in addressing each person who came up to draw from the box, but this also changed with time, until now it was felt necessary only for the official to speak to each person approaching. Mr. Summers was very good at all this; in his clean white shirt and blue jeans, with one hand resting carelessly on the black box, he seemed very proper and important as he talked interminably to Mr. Graves and the Martins.

Just as Mr. Summers finally left off talking and turned to the assembled villagers, Mrs. Hutchinson came hurriedly along the path to the square, her sweater thrown over her shoulders, and slid into place in the back of the crowd. "Clean forgot what day it was," she said to Mrs. Delacroix, who stood next to her, and they both laughed softly. "Thought my old man was out back stacking wood," Mrs. Hutchinson went on, "and then I looked out the window and the kids was gone, and then I remembered it was the twenty-seventh and came a-running." She dried her hands on her apron, and Mrs. Delacroix said, "You're in time though. They're still talking away up there."

Mrs. Hutchinson craned her neck to see through the crowd and found her husband and children standing near the front. She tapped Mrs. Delacroix on the arm as a farewell and began to make her way through the crowd. The people separated good-humoredly to let her through; two or three people said, in voices just loud enough to be heard across the crowd, "Here comes your Missus, Hutchinson," and "Bill, she made it after all." Mrs. Hutchinson reached her husband, and Mr. Summers, who had been waiting, said cheerfully, "Thought we were going to have to get on without you, Tessie." Mrs. Hutchinson said, grinning, "Wouldn't have me leave m'dishes in the sink, now, would you, Joe?," and soft laughter ran through the crowd as the people stirred back into position after Mrs. Hutchinson's arrival.

"Well, now," Mr. Summers said soberly, "guess we better get started, get this over with, so's we can go back to work. Anybody ain't here?"

"Dunbar," several people said. "Dunbar, Dunbar."

Mr. Summers consulted his list. "Clyde Dunbar," he said. "That's right. He's broke his leg, hasn't he. Who's drawing for him?"

"Me, I guess," a woman said, and Mr. Summers turned to look at her. "Wife draws for her husband," Mr. Summers said. "Don't you have a grown boy to do it for you, Janey?" Although Mr. Summers and everyone else in the village knew the answer perfectly well, it was the business of the official of the lottery to ask such questions formally. Mr. Summers waited with an expression of polite interest while Mrs. Dunbar answered.

"Horace's not but sixteen yet," Mrs. Dunbar said regretfully. "Guess I gotta fill in for the old man this year."

"Right," Mr. Summers said. He made a note on the list he was holding. Then he asked, "Watson boy drawing this year?"

A tall boy in the crowd raised his hand. "Here," he said. "I'm drawing for m'mother and me." He blinked his eyes nervously and ducked his head as several voices in the crowd said things like "Good fellow, Jack," and "Glad to see your mother's got a man to do it."

"Well," Mr. Summers said, "guess that's everyone. Old Man Warner make it?"

"Here," a voice said, and Mr. Summers nodded.

A sudden hush fell on the crowd as Mr. Summers cleared his throat and looked at the list. "All ready?" he called. "Now, I'll read the names—heads of families first—and the men come up and take a paper out of the box. Keep the paper folded in your hand without looking at it until everyone has had a turn. Everything clear?"

The people had done it so many times that they only half listened to the directions; most of them were quiet, wetting their lips, not looking around. Then Mr. Summers raised one hand high and said, "Adams." A man disengaged himself from the crowd and came forward. "Hi, Steve," Mr. Summers said, and Mr. Adams said, "Hi, Joe." They grinned at one another humorlessly and nervously. Then Mr. Adams reached into the black box and took out a folded paper. He held it firmly by one corner as he turned and went hastily back to his place in the crowd, where he stood a little apart from his family, not looking down at his hand.

"Allen," Mr. Summers said. "Anderson . . . Bentham."

"Seems like there's no time at all between lotteries any more," Mrs. Delacroix said to Mrs. Graves in the back row. "Seems like we got through with the last one only last week."

"Time sure goes fast," Mrs. Graves said.

"Clark. . . . Delacroix."

"There goes my old man," Mrs. Delacroix said. She held her breath while her husband went forward.

"Dunbar," Mr. Summers said, and Mrs. Dunbar went steadily to the box while one of the women said, "Go on, Janey," and another said, "There she goes."

"We're next," Mrs. Graves said. She watched while Mr. Graves came around from the side of the box, greeted Mr. Summers gravely, and selected a slip of paper from the box. By now, all through the crowd there were men holding the small folded papers in their large hands, turning them over and over nervously. Mrs. Dunbar and her two sons stood together, Mrs. Dunbar holding the slip of paper.

"Harburt. . . . Hutchinson."

"Get up there, Bill," Mrs. Hutchinson said, and the people near her laughed.

"Jones."

"They do say," Mr. Adams said to Old Man Warner, who stood next to him, "that over in the north village they're talking of giving up the lottery."

Old Man Warner snorted. "Pack of crazy fools," he said. "Listening to the young folks, nothing's good enough for *them*. Next thing you know, they'll be wanting to go back to living in caves, nobody work any more, live *that* way for a while. Used to be a saying about 'Lottery in June, corn be heavy soon.' First thing you know, we'd all be eating stewed chickweed and acorns. There's *always* been a lottery," he added petulantly. "Bad enough to see young Joe Summers up there joking with everybody."

"Some places have already quit lotteries," Mrs. Adams said.

"Nothing but trouble in *that*," Old Man Warner said stoutly. "Pack of young fools."

"Martin." And Bobby Martin watched his father go forward. "Overdyke. . . . Percy."

"I wish they'd hurry," Mrs. Dunbar said to her older son. "I wish they'd hurry."

"They're almost through," her son said.

"You get ready to run tell Dad," Mrs. Dunbar said.

Mr. Summers called his own name and then stepped forward precisely and selected a slip from the box. Then he called, "Warner."

"Seventy-seventh year I been in the lottery," Old Man Warner said as he went through the crowd. "Seventy-seventh time."

"Watson." The tall boy came awkwardly through the crowd. Someone said, "Don't be nervous, Jack," and Mr. Summers said, "Take your time, son."

"Zanini."

After that, there was a long pause, a breathless pause, until Mr. Summers, holding his slip of paper in the air, said, "All right, fellows." For a minute, no one moved, and then all the slips of paper were opened. Suddenly, all the women began to speak at once, saying, "Who is it?," "Who's got it?," "Is it the Dunbars?," "Is it the Watsons?" Then the voices began to say, "It's Hutchinson. It's Bill," "Bill Hutchinson's got it."

"Go tell your father," Mrs. Dunbar said to her older son.

People began to look around to see the Hutchinsons. Bill Hutchinson was standing quiet, staring down at the paper in his hand. Suddenly, Tessie Hutchinson shouted to Mr. Summers, "You didn't give him time enough to take any paper he wanted. I saw you. It wasn't fair!"

"Be a good sport, Tessie," Mrs. Delacroix called, and Mrs. Graves said, "All of us took the same chance."

"Shut up, Tessie," Bill Hutchinson said.

"Well, everyone," Mr. Summers said, "that was done pretty fast, and now we've got to be hurrying a little more to get done in time." He consulted his next list. "Bill," he said, "you draw for the Hutchinson family. You got any other households in the Hutchinsons?"

"There's Don and Eva," Mrs. Hutchinson yelled. "Make *them* take their chance!"

"Daughters draw with their husbands' families, Tessie," Mr. Summers said gently. "You know that as well as anyone else."

"It wasn't *fair*," Tessie said.

"I guess not, Joe," Bill Hutchinson said regretfully. "My daughter draws with her husband's family, that's only fair. And I've got no other family except the kids."

"Then, as far as drawing for families is concerned, it's you," Mr. Summers said in explanation, "and as far as drawing for households is concerned, that's you, too. Right?"

"Right," Bill Hutchinson said.

"How many kids, Bill?" Mr. Summers asked formally.

"Three," Bill Hutchinson said. "There's Bill, Jr., and Nancy, and little Dave. And Tessie and me."

"All right, then," Mr. Summers said. "Harry, you got their tickets back?"

Mr. Graves nodded and held up the slips of paper. "Put them in the box, then," Mr. Summers directed. "Take Bill's and put it in."

"I think we ought to start over," Mrs. Hutchinson said, as quietly as she could. "I tell you it wasn't *fair*. You didn't give him time enough to choose. Everybody saw that."

Mr. Graves had selected the five slips and put them in the box, and he dropped all the papers but those onto the ground, where the breeze caught them and lifted them off.

"Listen, everybody," Mrs. Hutchinson was saying to the people around her.

"Ready, Bill?" Mr. Summers asked, and Bill Hutchinson, with one quick glance around at his wife and children, nodded.

"Remember," Mr. Summers said, "take the slips and keep them folded until each person has taken one. Harry, you help little Dave." Mr. Graves took the hand of the little boy, who came willingly with him up to the box. "Take a paper out of the box, Davy," Mr. Summers said. Davy put his hand into the box and laughed. "Take just *one* paper," Mr. Summers said. "Harry, you hold it for him." Mr. Graves took the child's hand and removed the folded paper from the tight fist and held it while little Dave stood next to him and looked up at him wonderingly.

"Nancy next," Mr. Summers said. Nancy was twelve, and her school friends breathed heavily as she went forward, switching her skirt, and took a slip daintily from the box. "Bill, Jr.," Mr. Summers said, and Billy, his face red and his feet overlarge, nearly knocked the box over as he got a paper out. "Tessie," Mr. Summers said. She hesitated for a minute, looking around defiantly, and then set her lips and went up to the box. She snatched a paper out and held it behind her.

"Bill," Mr. Summers said, and Bill Hutchinson reached into the box and felt around, bringing his hand out at last with the slip of paper in it.

The crowd was quiet. A girl whispered, "I hope it's not Nancy," and the sound of the whisper reached the edges of the crowd.

"It's not the way it used to be," Old Man Warner said clearly. "People ain't the way they used to be."

"All right," Mr. Summers said. "Open the papers. Harry, you open little Dave's."

Mr. Graves opened the slip of paper and there was a general sigh through the crowd as he held it up and everyone could see that it was blank. Nancy and Bill, Jr., opened theirs at the same time, and both beamed and laughed, turning around to the crowd and holding their slips of paper above their heads.

"Tessie," Mr. Summers said. There was a pause, and then Mr. Summers looked at Bill Hutchinson, and Bill unfolded his paper and showed it. It was blank.

"It's Tessie," Mr. Summers said, and his voice was hushed. "Show us her paper, Bill."

Bill Hutchinson went over to his wife and forced the slip of paper out of her hand. It had a black spot on it, the black spot Mr. Summers had made the night before with the heavy pencil in the coal-company office. Bill Hutchinson held it up, and there was a stir in the crowd.

"All right, folks," Mr. Summers said. "Let's finish quickly."

Although the villagers had forgotten the ritual and lost the original black box, they still remembered to use stones. The pile of stones the boys had made earlier was ready; there were stones on the ground with the blowing scraps of paper that had come out of the box. Mrs. Delacroix selected a stone so large she had to pick it up with both hands and turned to Mrs. Dunbar. "Come on," she said. "Hurry up."

Mrs. Dunbar had small stones in both hands, and she said, gasping for breath, "I can't run at all. You'll have to go ahead and I'll catch up with you."

The children had stones already, and someone gave little Davy Hutchinson a few pebbles.

Tessie Hutchinson was in the center of a cleared space by now, and she held her hands out desperately as the villagers moved in on her. "It isn't fair," she said. A stone hit her on the side of the head.

Old Man Warner was saying, "Come on, come on, everyone." Steve Adams was in the front of the crowd of villagers, with Mrs. Graves beside him.

"It isn't fair, it isn't right," Mrs. Hutchinson screamed, and then they were upon her.

INTERPRETATION

This story certainly differs very sharply from both of the stories that precede it. The plot is so simple that to some readers it may seem to lack sufficient complication to be interesting. The story seems to do no more than recount the drawing of lots to determine which citizen of the village shall be stoned to death. There is no conflict—at least of the kind that occurs between tangible forces—no decision to be arrived at, no choice between two goods or two evils. There is no development of plot through human struggle and effort: the issue of life and death turns upon pure chance. The suspense secured is the simplest kind possible: which unlucky person will chance determine to be the victim?

Even this suspense is largely undercut by the fact that character interest in the story is also at a minimum. We are not brought close up to any of the characters. We learn little about their inner natures. There is nothing to distinguish them from ten thousand other people and indeed it becomes clear that they represent no more than the typical inhabitants of a New England village. The author seems deliberately to have played down any distinguishing traits. The victim herself, it is made very clear, is simply the typical small-town housewife.

Yet the story makes a very powerful impact, and the handling of plot and character must finally be judged, in terms of the story's development, to be very skillful. Obviously this story, unlike "The Man Who Would Be King," and "The Secret Life of Walter Mitty," has been sharply tilted toward theme. The reaction of most readers, as a matter of fact, tends to center on this problem: what does the story—granted its power—mean? It is not really a story about the victim, Mrs. Hutchinson. It is not literally about life in an American village, since the events portrayed are fantastic events. What then is the story "about"?

Before trying to answer the question specifically, one ought to say that this story is a kind of *fable* (see Glossary). The general flatness of characterization—the fact that the characters are all simply variants of the ordinary human being, and the fantastic nature of the plot make this rather clear. The most famous early fables, Aesop's fables, for example, give us fantastic situations in which animals are actuated by human motivations, speak like human beings, and reveal themselves as rather transparent instances of certain human types. But Aesop's fables usually express a fairly explicit comment on life which can be expressed as a moral. For example, a popular translation of the fable of the fox and the grapes concludes with the moral tag: "It is easy to despise what you cannot get."

The family resemblance of "The Lottery" to the fable is concealed in part by the fact that "The Lottery" does not end with a neat moral tag and indeed avoids focusing upon a particular meaning. This latter point, however, we shall consider a little later.

The general pattern of this story may also be said to resemble that of the *parable* (see Glossary). In a parable the idea or truth is presented by a simple narrative in which the events, persons, and the like, of the narrative are understood as being directly equivalent to terms involved in the statement of the truth. For example, let us look at the parable of the sower, in the Gospel according to Saint Mark:

Hearken; Behold, there went out a sower to sow:

And it came to pass, as he sowed, some fell by the way side, and the fowls of the air came and devoured it up.

And some fell on stony ground, where it had not much earth; and immediately it sprang up, because it had no depth of earth:

But when the sun was up, it was scorched; and because it had no root, it withered away.

And some fell among thorns, and the thorns grew up, and choked it, and it yielded no fruit.

And other fell on good ground, and did yield fruit that sprang up and increased; and brought forth, some thirty, and some sixty, and some an hundred.

Later, Jesus explains and interprets the parable to his disciples:

The sower soweth the word.

And these are they by the way side, where the word is sown; but when they have heard, Satan cometh immediately, and taketh away the word that was sown in their hearts.

And these are they likewise which are sown on stony ground; who, when they have heard the word, immediately receive it with gladness;

And have no root in themselves, and so endure but for a time: afterward, when affliction or persecution ariseth for the word's sake, immediately they are offended.

And these are they which are sown among thorns; such as hear the word.

And the cares of this world, and the deceitfulness of riches, and the lusts of other things entering in, choke the word, and it becometh unfruitful.

And these are they which are sown on good ground; such as hear the word, and receive it, and bring forth fruit, some thirtyfold, some sixty, and some an hundred.

In a parable, it is plain, characterization is reduced to a minimum: the *sower* is any sower. And the action is reduced to a minimum too. We need only so much of narrative as will make the point that the speaker wishes to make. But if "The Lottery" in its relative thinness of characterization and its relative simplicity of narration resembles the parable, it is obviously not a naked parable. The author has taken pains to supply a great deal of concrete detail to make us "believe" in her village, in its goings on this morning of June 27th. It is also obvious that she has preferred to give no key to her parable but to leave its meaning to our inference. One may summarize by saying that "The Lottery" is a normal piece of fiction, even if tilted over toward the fable and the parable form. Yet the comparison with these two forms may be useful in indicating the nature of the story.*

What of its meaning? We had best not try to restrict the meaning to some simple dogmatic statement. The author herself has been rather careful to allow a good deal of flexibility in our interpretation of the meaning. Yet surely a general meaning does emerge. This story comments upon the all-too-human tendency to seize upon a scapegoat and to visit upon the scapegoat the cruelties that most of us seem to have dammed up within us. An example out of our own time might be the case in which some sensational happening occurs in a family—a child is kidnapped, or a youthful member of the family is implicated in a weird crime. The newspapers sometimes hound the family past all decency, and we good citizens, who support those newspapers, batten upon their misery with a cruelty that

---

* Since we have used the terms *fable* and *parable* in connection with this story, it may be well at this point to relate it also to the more general term *symbol*, which we will often have occasion to use in this book. We have used the term *symbol* earlier (p. 30) with reference to "The Man Who Would Be King" in referring to the crown as a symbol of kingship.

Here we need to distinguish between two kinds of symbols. The crown, like the cross and the flag, is a *conventional* symbol. That is, men *have agreed* that the figure of the cross should stand for Christianity, that a flag of a certain design should stand for the United States of America, and that the circlet of gold should stand for the power and authority of kingship. Such conventional symbols occur in literature just as they occur in our daily speech, but the symbolism with which we are characteristically concerned as we read poems and stories is not conventional. It is special and it is related to a particular context. Consider "The Lottery" itself, where an incident is so handled as to express an interpretation of human life. In literature, objects and events often become symbolic, possessing a wider significance and thus becoming expressive of the author's meaning. Since fiction is concrete and dramatic in its presentation, the author must necessarily make use of symbols at some level; for he does not "state" his meanings abstractly but renders them through the presentation of concrete particulars.

would shock us if we ever could realize what we were doing. Or to take another case, a man's patriotism is impugned quite falsely; or, whether the charge against him is false or true, let us say that his wife is completely guiltless. Yet she is "stoned" by her self-righteous neighbors who are acting, of course, out of pure virtue and fervent patriotism. These two instances are merely suggestive. Neither would answer fully to the terms of the story, but they may indicate that the issues with which the story is concerned are thoroughly live issues in our time.

But the author has been wise not to confine the meaning to any precise happening of the sort we have suggested. For evidently she is concerned with the more general psychological basis for such cruelty as a community tends to manifest. "The Lottery" makes such points as these: the cruel stoning is carried out by "decent" citizens who in many other respects show themselves kind and thoughtful. The cruel act is kept from seeming the cruel thing it is by the fact that it has been sanctioned by custom and long tradition. When Mrs. Adams remarks that "Some places have already quit lotteries," Old Man Warner says, "Nothing but trouble in *that*. Pack of young fools." A further point is this: human beings find it difficult to become exercised over ills not their own. Once a family group sees that the victim is not to be selected from among themselves, they proceed to observe matters with a certain callous disinterest. Moreover, even the individual members of the Hutchinson family are themselves relatively unconcerned once each discovers that he is not the victim chosen. Thus, "Nancy and Bill, Jr., opened theirs at the same time, and both beamed and laughed, turning round to the crowd and holding their slips of paper above their heads." The French moralist Rochefoucald ruefully observed that we obtain a certain pleasure from news of misfortune to friends. There is truth in this, and our story savagely makes a related point. Only the victim protests "It isn't fair," and she makes her protest only after she has chosen a slip of paper marked with the black spot. We remember that earlier Mrs. Hutchinson had said to Mrs. Delacroix in neighborly good humor, "Clean forgot what day it was," and both had "laughed softly" together.

"The Lottery," then, deals indeed with live issues and issues relevant to our time. If we hesitate to specify a particular "point" that the story makes, it is not because the story is vague and fuzzy, but rather because its web of observations about human nature is too subtle and too complex to be stated in one or two brief maxims.

What requires a little further attention is a problem of a quite different sort: how does this story differ from a tract or a treatise on human nature? Are we actually justified in calling it a piece of fiction?

An answer to these questions might run like this: This is obviously not a tract or merely an essay. The village is made to exist for us; the characters of Old Man Warner and Mr. Summers and Mrs. Hutchinson do come alive. They are not fully developed, to be sure, and there is a sense in which even the personality of the victim is finally subservient to the "point" to be made and is not developed in its own right and for its own sake. But, as we have said, this is not a "naked parable"—and the fact that we get an impression of a real village and real people gives the sense of grim terror.

The fictional form thus justifies itself by making vivid and forceful what would otherwise have to be given prosaically and undramatically. But it does something else that is very important: it provides a special shaping of the reader's attitude toward the climactic event and toward that from which the climactic event stems. The reader's attitude has been moulded very carefully from the very beginning. Everything in the story has been devised to let us know how we are to "take" the final events in the story. (In this general connection, see the discussion of *tone* on pp. 37–38.)

The very fact that an innocent woman is going to be stoned to death by her friends and neighbors and that this is to happen in an American small town during our own present day of enlightenment requires a special preparation. The apparently fantastic nature of the happening means that everything else in the story must be made plausible, down-to-earth, sensible, commonplace, everyday. We must be made to feel that what is happening on this June morning is perfectly credible. Making it seem credible will do two things: it will increase the sense of shock when we suddenly discover what is really going on, but it will ultimately help us to believe that what the story asserts does come to pass. In general, then, the horror of the ending is counter-balanced by the dry, even cheery, atmosphere of the scene. This contrast between the matter-of-factness and the cheery atmosphere, on one side, and the grim terror, on the other, gives us a dramatic shock. But it also indicates that the author's point in general has to do with the awful doubleness of the human spirit—a doubleness that expresses itself in the blended good neighborliness and cruelty of the community's action. The fictional form, therefore, does not simply "dress up" a specific comment on human nature. The fictional form actually gives point and definition to the social commentary.

1. Attempt to characterize the tone of this story.

2. Why does the author hold up any information about the purpose of the lottery until late in the story? What is gained by her doing so?

3. What is gained by having Mrs. Delacroix select the first stone?

How Plot Reveals

■ LET us now try to make a more systematic statement about the nature of the plot. We may begin with the most off-hand notion: Plot may be said to be what happens in a story. It is the string of events *thought of* as different from the persons involved in the events and different from the meaning of the events. We make such a distinction even though we know that, in fact, we cannot very well separate an act from the person who commits it, or from its meaning as an act. The distinction is one we make in our heads and do not find ready-made for us in fiction. In order better to understand the nature of a story itself, we analyze the unity which is the story and which is what we actually experience before the process of analysis begins.

Plot is what happens in a story—that is a good rough-and-ready way to put the matter. But let us go a step farther. Plot, we may say, is the structure of an action as presented in a piece of fiction. It is not, we shall note, the structure of an action as we happen to find it out in the world, but the structure within a story. It is, in other words, what the teller of the story has done to the action in order to present it to us. Let us hang on to this distinction between a "raw" action—action as it occurs out in the world—and an action in a story, that is, action manipulated by the teller of the story.

Here we are using the word *action* (see Glossary) in a special way. We do not mean a single event—John struck Jim with a stone, Mary put the book on the shelf. We mean a series of events, a movement through time, exhibiting unity and significance. It is a series of connected events moving

51

through three logical stages—the beginning, the middle, and the end.

The beginning of an action always presents us with a situation in which there is some element of instability, some conflict; in the middle of an action there is a period of readjustment of forces in the process of seeking a new kind of stability; in the end of an action, some point of stability is reached, the forces that have been brought into play have been resolved. At the dawn of the day of Waterloo, the fate of Europe hung in the balance; at sunset Napoleon was a broken man. On June 7, 1776, Richard Henry Lee, of Virginia, presented to the Continental Congress a resolution declaring that "these United States are, and of right ought to be, free and independent States"; on July 4 the Declaration of Independence was signed. When Tom Smith met Evelyn Pembroke, he immediately recognized her vain and frivolous nature, but that recognition could not overcome the attraction she exerted over him; and he was the only person in Morristown not surprised when T. P. Smith, the wealthy, middle-aged banker, the very pillar of respectability, was arrested for embezzlement. In each of these actions, two of them historical and one made up, we recognize a movement toward a point of rest, of resolution.

In these actions we recognize, too, unity and significance. That is, these actions move toward an end, and the end settles something. We shall postpone for a page or two our fuller discussion of unity and significance in relation to action (and to plot), and for the moment content ourselves with saying that what constitutes an action always depends upon the perspective in which we view the events involved. The Battle of Waterloo may be regarded as an action, but it may also be regarded as merely an event in the broader action of Napoleon's career, or even as one event in a very different broader action, say the rise of the British Empire or the growth of the theory of free trade. Or to refer to our imaginary action above, the account of the banker and the vain, frivolous Evelyn Pembroke with whom he falls in love, though we may think of this as a complete action, we may, in another perspective, regard it as merely an episode in the life of one of the two persons concerned, or even in the life of, say, Smith's son.

The unity and significance of an action must, however, be felt really to inhere in the action. They cannot be regarded as being merely arbitrary fabrications imposed by us upon the action—even if their nature changes according to the perspective in which we place an action, and according to our interest in the facts and our interpretation of them. The patterns giving unity and significance must be grounded in the facts themselves.

We have just used the word *facts*—speaking of the facts that constitute an action. But we must hasten to say that we do not necessarily mean historical facts, actual happenings. As we have already implied by our reference to Tom Smith and Evelyn Pembroke, the "facts" may be imaginary ones, which in their turn can be placed in some special perspective of interest and interpretation so as to constitute an action. And this brings us to the relation between an action and the manipulation necessary in order to turn an action into a plot.

Let us begin this discussion by thinking of some action—it doesn't matter whether it is real or imaginary—in its full and massive array of facts, all disposed in their chronological order. The teller of a story, whether in idle conversation or in the serious business of writing a thousand-page novel, could not possibly use all the facts involved in the situation. He has to *select* the facts that seem to him useful for his particular purpose.

There are two kinds of usefulness, we may say. A fact is useful if it is vivid, that is, if it stirs the imagination to accept the story. One vivid fact may, suddenly, make a whole passage of narrative seem real to us. And a fact is also useful if it indicates, directly or indirectly, the line of development a story is pursuing, that is, if it indicates how one thing leads to another, or what is the meaning of the movement of events. Vividness and significance—these are the tests of usefulness in selection. But the two tend to merge. The vivid detail that catches the imagination helps to create the special quality, the "feel" of a story, and this "feel", this *atmosphere* (see Glossary) is an element of the meaning.

So if we examine fiction we are continually faced with the questions: Why was this particular thing selected? What has led the writer to use these facts and reject others? How would the choice of other available facts have made this a very different story?

The answers to such questions are always complicated, but the questions are worth pondering. They may lead us toward the full meaning of a story.

After a writer has selected his facts, there comes the question of order. Thus far we have thought of the action as existing in all of its intricate detail out in the world, with all of its components disposed in their strict chronological order. Yet many stories—indeed, in a strict sense, all stories —violate in one way or another the strict chronological sequence of an action as thought of in the actual world. To take an example, no writer can give simultaneously in his narrative two things that occur simultaneously in the action. His order of narration is bound to be artificial. To take another example, the beginning of a story may, or may not, happen to pick up the beginning of the action which it presents. The plot may plunge us into the very middle of things, and then, stage by stage, take us back to the beginning of the action. Or there may be a complicated interweaving of times. A little chart of a hypothetical story may indicate this notion:

Sequence of Action: a b c d e f g h i j k l m n o p q r s t u v w x y z

SEQUENCE OF PLOT: F A B H I J E R S T V Y Z

We see, in our chart, that the plot does not use all of the facts of the action, and that the chronological order has been scrambled. The plot, then, is the structure of the action *as presented* in a piece of fiction. It represents the treatment the story-teller makes of the events of his action.

In discussing the nature of an action we have necessarily touched on unity and significance. Let us now return to these topics with more special reference to plot.

When we say "*a* novel," "*a* story," or "*a* plot," we instinctively imply the idea of a unity. We imply that the parts, the various individual events, hang together. There is the matter of cause and effect. In any story we expect to find one thing bringing on another. If we can detect no reasonable connection between them, if there is no "logic" whatever, we lose interest. Every story must indicate some basis for the relation among its parts, for the story itself is a *particular writer's way of saying how you can make sense of human experience.*

Cause and effect constitute one of the ways of saying this. In works of fiction, however, we cannot think of cause as a mechanical thing—as though one event were one domino knocking over the next in the series. The events are human events; that is, they involve human responses to changing situations, including the possibility of action taken to change existing situations. Many nonhuman things may enter into the logic of a story—the weather that ruins a crop, the iceberg that sinks a ship, the explosion that wrecks a mine, the nail lost from the shoe of the horse of the king's messenger—but in the end the central logic we are concerned with is the logic of human motivation. How do human needs work themselves out? Plot, then, is character in action.

Logic, including the logic of motivation, binds the events of a plot together into a unity. This unity is, of course, a dynamic unity. It is a unity involving change: no change, no story. At the beginning of a story we find a situation with some element of instability in it. At the end of the story, we find that things have become stable once more. Something has been settled: Dravot has discovered the true meaning of kingship and godhood through manhood; Walter Mitty, we have come to know, will never wake from his dream. This movement from instability toward stability involves, as we have said, certain natural stages—the beginning, the middle, and the end.

When we come to consider how these natural stages are treated in terms of plot, we find that we need some special terms. The beginning of a plot action is called the *exposition* (see Glossary)—the "setting forth" of the assumptions from which the story will develop. The middle is called the *complication* (see Glossary), for it presents the increasing difficulty encountered in the movement toward stability. If, for example, a character moves easily toward his triumph, or his ruin, there is really no story. It is no story to tell how a barrel rolls downhill. The story interest inheres in the resistances encountered and overcome, or not overcome—in the logic by which resistance evokes responses which, in their turn, encounter or create new resistances to be dealt with. The complication moves toward a moment, an event, when something has to happen, when something has to crack. This moment is the point of highest tension, the moment when the story turns toward its solution. This is called the *climax* (see Glossary). The story, then, is the story of *conflict* developing logically through the stages of the complication.

The end—the *denouement* (see Glossary)—gives us the outcome of the conflict, the solution to the problem, the basis of a new stability. We realize, of course, that the basis of stability now reached may be only provisional and temporary, that something may come along to upset the hard-won stability. If, for example, we have the story of a stormy courtship and "boy gets girl" in the end, we know that, except in the fairy-tale formula of "they lived happily ever after," no promise is made of an end to all conflict, all struggle, all problems. The denouement simply gives us the settling of a particular action, which is the story that the author has elected to tell.

The denouement, as we have just said, gives us the settling of the particular action. But the meaning of the settlement always reaches out beyond the particular action. And this idea takes us back to the question of significance in plot. In so far, of course, as the development of a plot exhibits logic, it is already exhibiting significance—it is telling us, or showing us, something about human nature and human conduct. The conclusion which stems from this logic aims to give us not only an evaluation of the particular experience which is the story, but a *generalized* evaluation. Always the end of a successful story leaves us with an attitude to take toward things in general. The story embodies a comment on human values—on what is good or bad in human nature and human conduct, on what attitude one may take, finally, toward life and the business of living. That is, any particular story will always appear, in our imagination and feelings, as an image, however shadowy, of the meaning of experience.

The way in which the meaning is presented may vary from instance to instance. There may be a perfectly explicit general statement, more or less complete—as in the epigraph of "The Man Who Would Be King." Or a story may, again like "The Man Who Would Be King," use symbolism which can be read back into statement, as we have done in our comment on the end of the story. Even when the denouement may seem merely to wind up events and avoid interpretation, we shall find that the story, if it is a successful one, will turn us back toward some basic quality in the story itself; and we shall find that that quality may have subtly modified our feelings and attitudes. It may have enlarged our sympathies—as with "The Lament," by Chekhov—so that we may now more readily regard other people with charity and humility. Or it may have given us a liberating sense of the comedy of experience—as with "The Drunkard," by Frank O'Connor, or "The Secret Life of Walter Mitty," by James Thurber. Or the story may conclude on a note of savage satire or chilling irony. Always, however, we expect in fiction an idea about, some stance toward, experience, and if we do not get it we are dissatisfied. We feel cheated. We don't know what the shooting has been about. We feel, in other words, that the story is not coherent—the plot has not fulfilled itself, even though stage by stage the logic of motivation, and the like, may have been seeming to work itself out. We do not like to be preached at, but we do demand a sense of meaningfulness.

So our discussion of plot brings us back to theme, just as it has already led us, in discussing motivation, to the question of character. And that is only natural, for a good story is, after all, a unity. It is consistent within itself. The world of imagination that it presents must hang together—must make sense in its own terms—must be *coherent*.

We have tried to indicate something of the function of the parts of a plot, and something of the relation among them. Let us ask the next question: Are we to be concerned with any particular *proportion* among the parts? The answer is no. In some pieces of fiction—whether novels or stories—a great deal of exposition is required; there is a great weight of the past behind the moment in which the story comes to crisis and if we are to understand the story we must understand what lies behind it. Or sometimes to understand a story we must know something of a special world that may be unfamiliar to us.

Or to consider the denouement, sometimes a story needs a long and elaborate treatment in this part. In one sense "The Man Who Would Be King" ends when Dravot walks boldly out on the bridge and yells, "Cut, you beggars!" But a good deal of space, and a good deal of narrative, is required before we have the full implications of that moment. Think, however, how little is required to end "The Lottery." Of course, one story is longer than the other, and more complicated, but even so, there is a fundamental difference that has little to do with the question of length as such. "The Man Who Would Be King" is a story giving the development of a character and when the development is over it requires some time and some elaboration for its full weight to be felt. "The Lottery," however, is concerned with a shocking contrast, the contrast between thinking yourself in one position, thinking yourself at one with society, accepting its values and habits, and then suddenly finding yourself in another position, the victim of the values and habits of that society. The shock is the point. If we were to spin out the denouement, we should lose the sense of shock, and add nothing significant. The story does have weighty implications, but they do not need to be elaborated; their force depends on the shock.

What all this amounts to is simple: Proportion is not mechanically determined. It depends on the materials of the particular story and the kind of story the writer is trying to make of those materials. As we read, we must try to sense the needs of the situation, and try to understand the intention of the writer.

One more question presents itself in regard to the divisions of a plot. Are we to expect to find a sharp line between exposition and complication, or between complication and denouement? There may, of course, be sharp division, and sometimes the sharpness contributes greatly to the effect—as in "The Lottery." But, as we have indicated on our little chart distinguishing between action and plot, there is sometimes considerable interpenetration between one part and another, and especially between exposition and complication. There may be certain advantages, for example, in presenting an element of complication very early, at the very start perhaps, to catch the reader's attention, even before he can get the full import of the event before him. And sometimes a piece of exposition may be withheld until fairly late until the reader feels the need for it and it will come with dramatic force. Our principle here, again, is one of tact, of flexibility. There is no hard and fast rule. As readers, we must try to see how sharp separations or intricate interpenetrations among the parts of a plot are related to the final effect.

In this section we shall not confine ourselves to reading and discussing stories in which the element of plot is strongly marked—stories, for example, like "The Man Who Would Be King." We shall, in fact, read some stories in which the plot is seemingly slight. This is a reasonable procedure, for we are concerned here to see how the element of plot, whether strongly marked or recessive, works in relation to other aspects of fiction.

Furthermore, we shall not confine ourselves to stories in which the plot fulfills the requirements of a good plot, that is, exhibits significant order. We shall look at some instances in which the events are not in significant order, in which they do not adequately embody human values— instances, in short, in which the plot is incoherent. Of all the stories we read in this book we shall be asking ourselves: Is the plot coherent? Does it makes sense? If it does not make sense, in what particular way does it fail? We must, in other words, constantly consider the relation of plot to character and theme.

But not only to character and theme. Stories and novels are composed in words, and so we shall have to think a little about the relation of plot to the resources of language which the writer uses well or badly. Problems of coherence, as we shall see, arise here too.

IRWIN SHAW

The Girls in Their Summer Dresses

FIFTH Avenue was shining in the sun when they left the Brevoort. The sun was warm, even though it was February, and everything looked like Sunday morning—the buses and the well-dressed people walking slowly in couples and the quiet buildings with the windows closed.

Michael held Frances' arm tightly as they walked toward Washington Square in the sunlight. They walked lightly, almost smiling, because they had slept late and had a good breakfast and it was Sunday. Michael unbuttoned his coat and let it flap around him in the mild wind.

"Look out," Frances said as they crossed Eighth Street. "You'll break your neck." Michael laughed and Frances laughed with him.

"She's not so pretty," Frances said. "Anyway, not pretty enough to take a chance of breaking your neck."

Michael laughed again. "How did you know I was looking at her?"

Frances cocked her head to one side and smiled at her husband under the brim of her hat. "Mike, darling," she said.

"O.K.," he said. "Excuse me."

Frances patted his arm lightly and pulled him along a little faster toward Washington Square. "Let's not see anybody all day," she said. "Let's just hang around with each other. You and me. We're always up to our neck in people, drinking their Scotch or drinking our Scotch; we only see each other in bed. I want to go out with my husband all day long. I want him to talk only to me and listen only to me."

"What's to stop us?" Michael asked.

"The Stevensons. They want us to drop by around one o'clock and they'll drive us into the country."

"The cunning Stevensons," Mike said. "Transparent. They can whistle. They can go driving in the country by themselves."

"Is it a date?"

"It's a date."

Frances leaned over and kissed him on the tip of the ear.

"Darling," Michael said, "this is Fifth Avenue."

"Let me arrange a program," Frances said. "A planned Sunday in New York for a young couple with money to throw away."

"Go easy."

"First let's go to the Metropolitan Museum of Art," Frances suggested, because Michael had said during the week he wanted to go. "I haven't been there in three years and there're at least ten pictures I want to see again. Then we can take the bus down to Radio City and watch them skate. And later we'll go down to Cavanagh's and get a steak as big as a blacksmith's apron, with a bottle of wine, and after that there's a French picture at the Filmarte that everybody says—say, are you listening to me?"

"Sure," he said. He took his eyes off the hatless girl with the dark hair, cut dancer-style like a helmet, who was walking past him.

"That's the program for the day," Frances said flatly. "Or maybe you'd just rather walk up and down Fifth Avenue."

"No," Michael said. "Not at all."

"You always look at other women," Frances said. "Everywhere. Every damned place we go."

"No, darling," Michael said, "I look at everything. God gave me eyes and I look at women and men in subway excavations and moving pictures and the little flowers of the field. I casually inspect the universe."

"You ought to see the look in your eye," Frances said, "as you casually inspect the universe on Fifth Avenue."

"I'm a happily married man." Michael pressed her elbow tenderly. "Example for the whole twentieth century—Mr. and Mrs. Mike Loomis. Hey, let's have a drink," he said, stopping.

"We just had breakfast."

"Now listen, darling," Mike said, choosing his words with care, "it's a nice day and we both felt good and there's no reason why we have to break it up. Let's have a nice Sunday."

"All right. I don't know why I started this. Let's drop it. Let's have a good time."

They joined hands consciously and walked without talking among the baby carriages and the old Italian men in their Sunday clothes and the young women with Scotties in Washington Square Park.

"At least once a year everyone should go to the Metropolitan Museum of Art," Frances said after a while, her tone a good imitation of the tone she had used at breakfast and at the beginning of their walk. "And it's nice on Sunday. There're a lot of people looking at the pictures and you get the feeling maybe Art isn't on the decline in New York City, after all—"

"I want to tell you something," Michael said very seriously. "I have not touched another woman. Not once. In all the five years."

"All right," Frances said.

"You believe that, don't you?"

"All right."

They walked between the crowded benches, under the scrubby city-park trees.

"I try not to notice it," Frances said, "but I feel rotten inside, in my stomach, when we pass a woman and you look at her and I see that look in your eye and that's the way you looked at me the first time. In Alice Maxwell's house. Standing there in the living room, next to the radio, with a green hat on and all those people."

"I remember the hat," Michael said.

"The same look," Frances said. "And it makes me feel bad. It makes me feel terrible."

"Sh-h-h, please, darling, sh-h-h."

"I think I would like a drink now," Frances said.

They walked over to a bar on Eighth Street, not saying anything. Michael automatically helping her over curbstones and guiding her past automobiles. They sat near a window in the bar and the sun streamed in and there was a small, cheerful fire in the fireplace. A little Japanese waiter came over and put down some pretzels and smiled happily at them.

"What do you order after breakfast?" Michael asked.

"Brandy, I suppose," Frances said.

"Courvoisier," Michael told the waiter, "Two Courvoisiers."

The waiter came with the glasses and they sat drinking the brandy in the sunlight. Michael finished half his and drank a little water.

"I look at women," he said. "Correct. I don't say it's wrong or right. I look at them. If I pass them on the street and I don't look at them, I'm fooling you, I'm fooling myself."

"You look at them as though you want them," Frances said, playing with her brandy glass. "Every one of them."

"In a way," Michael said, speaking softly and not to his wife, "in a way that's true. I don't do anything about it, but it's true."

"I know it. That's why I feel bad."

"Another brandy," Michael called. "Waiter, two more brandies."

He sighed and closed his eyes and rubbed them gently with his finger-tips. "I love the way women look. One of the things I like best about New York is the battalions of women. When I first came to New York from Ohio that was the first thing I noticed, the million wonderful women, all over the city. I walked around with my heart in my throat."

"A kid," Frances said. "That's a kid's feeling."

"Guess again," Michael said. "Guess again. I'm older now. I'm a man getting near middle age, putting on a little fat, and I still love to walk along

Fifth Avenue at three o'clock on the east side of the street between Fiftieth and the Fifty-seventh Streets. They're all out then, shopping, in their furs and their crazy hats, everything all concentrated from all over the world into seven blocks—the best furs, the best clothes, the handsomest women, out to spend money and feeling good about it."

The Japanese waiter put the two drinks down, smiling with great happiness.

"Everything is all right?" he asked.

"Everything is wonderful," Michael said.

"If it's just a couple of fur coats," Frances said, "and forty-five dollar hats—"

"It's not the fur coats. Or the hats. That's just the scenery for that particular kind of women. Understand," he said, "you don't have to listen to this."

"I want to listen."

"I like the girls in the offices. Neat, with their eyeglasses, smart, chipper, knowing what everything is about. I like the girls on Forty-fourth Street at lunchtime, the actresses, all dressed up on nothing a week. I like the salesgirls in the stores, paying attention to you first because you're a man, leaving lady customers waiting. I got all this stuff accumulated in me because I've been thinking about it for ten years and now you've asked for it and here it is."

"Go ahead," Frances said.

"When I think of New York City, I think of all the girls on parade in the city. I don't know whether it's something special with me or whether every man in the city walks around with the same feeling inside him, but I feel as though I'm at a picnic in this city. I like to sit near the women in the theatres, the famous beauties who've taken six hours to get ready and look it. And the young girls at the football games, with the red cheeks, and when the warm weather comes, the girls in their summer dresses." He finished his drink. "That's the story."

Frances finished her drink and swallowed two or three times extra. "You say you love me?"

"I love you."

"I'm pretty, too," Frances said. "As pretty as any of them."

"You're beautiful," Michael said.

"I'm good for you," Frances said, pleading. "I've made a good wife, a good housekeeper, a good friend. I'd do any damn thing for you."

"I know," Michael said. He put his hand out and grasped hers.

"You'd like to be free to—" Frances said.

"Sh-h-h."

"Tell the truth." She took her hand away from under his.

Michael flicked the edge of his glass with his finger. "O.K.," he said gently. "Sometimes I feel I would like to be free."

"Well," Frances said, "any time you say."

"Don't be foolish." Michael swung his chair around to her side of the table and patted her thigh.

She began to cry silently into her handkerchief, bent over just enough so that nobody else in the bar would notice. "Someday," she said, crying, "you're going to make a move."

Michael didn't say anything. He sat watching the bartender slowly peel a lemon.

"Aren't you?" Frances asked harshly. "Come on, tell me. Talk. Aren't you?"

"Maybe," Michael said. He moved his chair back again. "How the hell do I know?"

"You know," Frances persisted. "Don't you know?"

"Yes," Michael said after a while, "I know."

Frances stopped crying then. Two or three snuffles into the handkerchief and she put it away and her face didn't tell anything to anybody. "At least do me one favor," she said.

"Sure."

"Stop talking about how pretty this woman is or that one. Nice eyes, nice breasts, a pretty figure, good voice." She mimicked his voice. "Keep it to yourself. I'm not interested."

Michael waved to the waiter. "I'll keep it to myself," he said.

Frances flicked the corners of her eyes. "Another brandy," she told the waiter.

"Two," Michael said.

"Yes, Ma'am, yes, sir," said the waiter, backing away.

Frances regarded Michael coolly across the table. "Do you want me to call the Stevensons?" she asked. "It'll be nice in the country."

"Sure," Michael said. "Call them."

She got up from the table and walked across the room toward the telephone. Michael watched her walk, thinking what a pretty girl, what nice legs.

INTERPRETATION

The plot structure of this story is quite simple. The exposition gives us a young couple out for a Sunday morning walk, planning on a happy private day together. By the time Michael asks, "What's to stop us?" we know a good deal about them—enough anyway for the limited purposes of the story. We have even had the first element of the complication, when Michael turns around to look at the first girl. It comes in lightly, as a joke, but the germ of instability in the happy situation has been isolated.

It comes in, we have said, as a joke, and this is as it should be. The story is very short, and one of the problems of the author is to give it a sense of rising interest, increasing tension, growing suspense. If much were to be made of Michael's first look, the story would sacrifice something of its development, the suspense. The episode comes in quite casually, but something signals: *This is it, watch now!*

Frances continues her planning of the day, gaily and affectionately, but before long Michael has noticed another girl. Now Frances strikes out at him, and the complication begins in dead earnest. With this repetition, the look at the second girl to pass—we may comment on another principle of plot, the principle of *pattern* (see Glossary). A pattern implies repetition, and pattern in plot is significant repetition. We know that the fact of Michael's looking at the passing girls is now what the story will hinge on, and we know that this will give the key to our understanding of the relationship.

Let us interrupt ourselves for a moment to ask what was the pattern in "The Man Who Would Be King." There is, of course, the series of efforts to gain a kingdom, a series of events pointing toward the same end. But there is a deeper and more significant pattern. As Dravot moves toward power, toward kingship and godhood, he discovers, step by step, the inner meaning of power. He has started out as a simple looter to grab a kingdom and live on the fat of the land. Bit by bit, his acts assume a pattern; he is moving toward a sense of responsibility in power, toward a depersonalizing of power, toward pride in his people, toward a desire to bring order and peace, toward the ambition, not merely to loot and indulge his appetites, but to enter history, to achieve something worthwhile and memorable. This movement is not over when Dravot does achieve full manhood. It continues with Peachey's return, after Dravot's death, and the symbolic presentation, by Peachey's delirium in the mountains, of Dravot as now somehow godlike, able to hold up the mountains. And it is this movement, the pattern of recognitions in ascending order, a pattern that continues after the progress toward practical success is finished, that constitutes the pattern of the plot.

To return to "The Girls in Their Summer Dresses," we can see how the recurrence of the topic of Michael's glances at the passing girls will lead, in the end, to the sad recognition—and the bitter acceptance—of the fact that the couple really mean nothing to each other. Each is, as it were, merely a convenience to the other. This is, of course, especially true of Michael's attitude toward Frances. Despite his actual faithfulness, Frances is just another girl, the one he "happens" to have married. They have now stumbled on the recognition of their plight, and Frances does not, somehow, do more than bitterly accept it. She hasn't the idealism, after all, to struggle for more. She will go and call the Stevensons, for she and her husband have nothing more to say to each other. The last line, as Frances moves toward the telephone, sums up the whole thing: Frances is just another pretty girl worth Michael's attention, and she might be anybody.

This story is a very good example of the compact, well-made short story. The method is about as simple as possible, and a simple method is all that the material requires. Not much of the past needs to be told. We need only a minimum of individualization. The conflict between the two characters progresses in an obvious pattern of repetitions. The main movement is carried by dialogue, as though we were actually unseen eavesdroppers, hearing the pair speak for themselves. The conclusion is quick and sharp. The point is clear and carries with its little ironic turn a serious idea—the failure of love through the failure to recognize the beloved as a person, as more than a convenience.

Many stories, however, use subject matter and express ideas and attitudes that cannot be treated this simply and directly. We must, then, expect other effects, more complicated and indirect methods. But we may use this story as a sort of measuring stick against which to test and define others.

1. What are the stages in the exposition of "The Man Who Would Be King"? In the denouement?

2. What principle of pattern is used in "The Secret Life of Walter Mitty"?

3. Try to imagine a story by James Thurber about Frances and Michael on their Sunday morning walk. What differences in treatment, feeling, and meaning can you imagine between his version and the present one?

O. HENRY

The Furnished Room

RESTLESS, shifting, fugacious as time itself is a certain vast bulk of the population of the red brick district of the lower West Side. Homeless, they have a hundred homes. They flit from furnished room to furnished room, transients forever—transients in abode, transients in heart and mind. They sing "Home, Sweet Home" in ragtime; they carry their *lares et penates* in a bandbox; their vine is entwined about a picture hat; a rubber plant is their fig tree.

Hence the houses of this district, having had a thousand dwellers, should have a thousand tales to tell, mostly dull ones, no doubt; but it would be strange if there could not be found a ghost or two in the wake of all these vagrant guests.

One evening after dark a young man prowled among these crumbling red mansions, ringing their bells. At the twelfth he rested his lean hand baggage upon the step and wiped the dust from his hatband and forehead. The bell sounded faint and far away in some remote, hollow depths.

To the door of this, the twelfth house whose bell he had rung, came a housekeeper who made him think of an unwholesome, surfeited worm that had eaten its nut to a hollow shell and now sought to fill the vacancy with edible lodgers.

He asked if there was a room to let.

"Come in," said the housekeeper. Her voice came from her throat; her throat seemed lined with fur. "I have the third floor, back, vacant since a week back. Should you wish to look at it?"

The young man followed her up the stairs. A faint light from no particular source mitigated the shadows of the halls. They trod noiselessly upon a stair carpet that its own loom would have foresworn. It seemed to have become vegetable; to have degenerated in that rank, sunless air to lush lichen or spreading moss that grew in patches to the staircase and was viscid under the foot like organic matter. At each turn of the stairs were vacant niches in the wall. Perhaps plants had once been set within them. If so, they had died in that foul and tainted air. It may be that statues of the saints had stood there, but it was not difficult to conceive that imps and devils had dragged them forth in the darkness and down to the unholy depths of some furnished pit below.

"This is the room," said the housekeeper, from her furry throat. "It's a nice room. It ain't often vacant. I had some most elegant people in it last summer—no trouble at all, and paid in advance to the minute. The water's at the end of the hall. Sprowls and Mooney kept it three months. They done a vaudeville sketch. Miss B'retta Sprowls—you may have heard of her—oh, that was just the stage names—right there over the dresser is where the marriage certificate hung, framed. The gas is here, and you see there is plenty of closet room. It's a room everybody likes. It never stays idle long."

"Do you have many theatrical people rooming here?" asked the young man.

"They comes and goes. A good proportion of my lodgers is connected with the theaters. Yes, sir, this is the theatrical district. Actor people never stays long anywhere. I get my share. Yes, they comes and they goes."

He engaged the room, paying for a week in advance. He was tired, he said, and would take possession at once. He counted out the money. The room had been made ready, she said, even to towels and water. As the housekeeper moved away he put, for the thousandth time, the question that he carried at the end of his tongue.

"A young girl—Miss Vashner—Miss Eloise Vashner—do you remember such a one among your lodgers? She would be singing on the stage, most likely. A fair girl, of medium height and slender, with reddish, gold hair and a dark mole near her left eyebrow."

"No, I don't remember the name. Them stage people has names they change as often as their rooms. They comes and they goes. No, I can't call that one to mind."

No. Always no. Five months of ceaseless interrogation and the inevitable negative. So much time spent by day in questioning managers, agents, schools, and choruses; by night among the audiences of theaters from all-star casts down to music halls so low that he dreaded to find what he most hoped for. He who had loved her best had tried to find her. He was sure that since her disappearance from home this great, water-girt city held her somewhere, but it was like a monstrous quicksand, shifting its particles constantly, with no foundation, its upper granules of today buried tomorrow in ooze and slime.

The furnished room received its latest guest with a first glow of pseudo-hospitality, a hectic, haggard, perfunctory welcome like the specious smile of a demirep. The sophistical comfort came in reflected gleams from the decayed furniture, the ragged brocade upholstery of a couch and two chairs, a foot-wide cheap pier glass between the two windows, from one or two gilt picture frames and a brass bedstead in a corner.

The guest reclined, inert, upon a chair, while the room, confused in speech as though it were an apartment in Babel, tried to discourse to him of its divers tenantry.

A polychromatic rug like some brilliant-flowered rectangular, tropical islet lay surrounded by a billowy sea of soiled matting. Upon the gay-papered wall were those pictures that pursue the homeless one from house to house—The Huguenot Lovers, The First Quarrel, The Wedding Breakfast, Psyche at the Fountain. The mantel's chastely severe outline was ingloriously veiled behind some pert drapery drawn rakishly askew like the sashes of the Amazonian ballet. Upon it was some desolate flotsam cast aside by the room's marooned when a lucky sail had borne them to a fresh port—a trifling vase or two, pictures of actresses, a medicine bottle, some stray cards out of a deck.

One by one, as the characters of a cryptograph become explicit, the little signs left by the furnished room's procession of guests developed a significance. The threadbare space in the rug in front of the dresser told that lovely women had marched in the throng. The tiny finger prints on the wall spoke of little prisoners trying to feel their way to sun and air. A splattered stain, raying like the shadow of a bursting bomb, witnessed where a hurled glass or bottle had splintered with its contents against the wall. Across the pier glass had been scrawled with a diamond in staggering letters the name "Marie." It seemed that the succession of dwellers in the furnished room had turned in fury—perhaps tempted beyond forbearance by its garish coldness—and wreaked upon it their passions. The furniture was chipped and bruised; the couch, distorted by bursting springs, seemed a horrible monster that had been slain during the stress of some grotesque convulsion. Some more potent upheaval had cloven a great slice from the marble mantel. Each plank in the floor owned its particular cant and shriek as from a separate and individual agony. It seemed incredible that all this malice and injury had been wrought upon the room by those who had called it for a time their home; and yet it may have been the cheated home instinct surviving blindly, the resentful rage at false household gods that had kindled their wrath. A hut that is our own we can sweep and adorn and cherish.

The young tenant in the chair allowed these thoughts to file, softshod, through his mind, while there drifted into the room furnished sounds and furnished scents. He heard in one room a tittering and incontinent, slack laughter; in others the monologue of a scold, the rattling of dice, a lullaby, and one crying dully; above him a banjo tinkled with spirit. Doors banged somewhere; the elevated trains roared intermittently; a cat yowled miserably upon a back fence. And he breathed the breath of the house— a dank savor rather than a smell—a cold, musty effluvium as from underground vaults mingled with the reeking exhalations of linoleum and mildewed and rotten woodwork.

Then, suddenly, as he rested there, the room was filled with the strong, sweet odor of mignonette. It came as upon a single buffet of wind with such sureness and fragrance and emphasis that it almost seemed a living visitant. And the man cried aloud: "What, dear?" as if he had been called, and sprang up and faced about. The rich odor clung to him and wrapped him around. He reached out his arms for it, all his senses for the time confused and commingled. How could one be peremptorily called by an odor? Surely it must have been a sound. But, was it not the sound that had touched, that had caressed him?

"She has been in this room," he cried, and he sprang to wrest from it a token, for he knew he would recognize the smallest thing that had belonged to her or that she had touched. This enveloping scent of mignonette, the odor that she had loved and made her own—whence came it?

The room had been but carelessly set in order. Scattered upon the flimsy dresser scarf were half a dozen hairpins—those discreet, indistinguishable friends of womankind, feminine of gender, infinite of mood and uncommunicative of tense. These he ignored, conscious of their triumphant lack of identity. Ransacking the drawers of the dresser, he came upon a discarded, tiny, ragged handkerchief. He pressed it to his face. It was racy and insolent with heliotrope; he hurled it to the floor. In another drawer he found odd buttons, a theater program, a pawnbroker's card, two lost marshmallows, a book on the divination of dreams. In the last was a woman's black satin hair bow, which halted him, poised between ice and fire. But the black satin hair bow also is femininity's demure, impersonal, common ornament and tells no tales.

And then he traversed the room like a hound on the scent, skimming the walls, considering the corners of the bulging matting on his hands and knees, rummaging mantel and tables, the curtains and hangings, the drunken cabinet in the corner, for a visible sign, unable to perceive that she was there beside, around, against, within, above him, clinging to him, wooing him, calling him so poignantly through the finer senses that even his grosser ones became cognizant of the call. Once again he answered loudly: "Yes, dear!" and turned, wildeyed, to gaze on vacancy, for he could not yet discern form and color and love and outstretched arms in the odor of mignonette. Oh, God! whence that odor, and since when have odors had a voice to call? Thus he groped.

He burrowed in crevices and corners, and found corks and cigarettes. These he passed in passive contempt. But once he found in a fold of the matting a half-smoked cigar, and this he ground beneath his heel with a green and trenchant oath. He sifted the room from end to end. He found dreary and ignoble small records of many a peripatetic tenant; but of her whom he sought, and who may have lodged there, and whose spirit seemed to hover there, he found no trace.

And then he thought of the housekeeper.

He ran from the haunted room downstairs and to a door that showed a crack of light. She came out to his knock. He smothered his excitement as best he could.

"Will you tell me, madam," he besought her, "who occupied the room I have before I came?"

"Yes, sir. I can tell you again. 'Twas Sprowls and Mooney, as I said. Miss B'retta Sprowls it was in the theaters, but Missis Mooney she was. My house is well known for respectability. The marriage certificate hung, framed, on a nail over—"

"What kind of a lady was Miss Sprowls—in looks, I mean?"

"Why, black-haired, sir, short, and stout, with a comical face. They left a week ago Tuesday."

"And before they occupied it?"

"Why, there was a single gentleman connected with the draying business. He left owing me a week. Before him was Missis Crowder and her two children that stayed four months; and back of them was old Mr. Doyle, whose sons paid for him. He kept the room six months. That goes back a year, sir, and further I do not remember."

He thanked her and crept back to his room. The room was dead. The essence that had vivified it was gone. The perfume of mignonette had departed. In its place was the old, stale odor of moldy house furniture, of atmosphere in storage.

The ebbing of his hope drained his faith. He sat staring at the yellow, singing gaslight. Soon he walked to the bed and began to tear the sheets into strips. With the blade of his knife he drove them tightly into every crevice around windows and door. When all was snug and taut, he turned out the light, turned the gas full on again, and laid himself gratefully upon the bed.

* * * *

It was Mrs. McCool's night to go with the can for beer. So she fetched it and sat with Mrs. Purdy in one of those subterranean retreats where housekeepers foregather and the worm dieth seldom.

"I rented out my third floor, back, this evening," said Mrs. Purdy, across a fine circle of foam. "A young man took it. He went up to bed two hours ago."

"Now, did ye, Mrs. Purdy, ma'am?" said Mrs. McCool, with intense admiration. "You do be a wonder for rentin' rooms of that kind. And did ye tell him, then?" she concluded in a husky whisper laden with mystery.

"Rooms," said Mrs. Purdy, in her furriest tones, "are furnished for to rent. I did not tell him, Mrs. McCool."

" 'Tis right ye are, ma'am; 'tis by rentin' rooms we kape alive. Ye have the rale sense for business, ma'am. There be many people will rayjict the rentin' of a room if they be tould a suicide has been after dyin' in the bed of it."

"As you say, we has our living to be making," remarked Mrs. Purdy.

"Yis, ma'am; 'tis true. 'Tis just one wake ago this day I helped ye lay out the third floor, back. A pretty slip of a colleen she was to be killin' herself wid the gas—a swate little face she had, Mrs. Purdy, ma'am."

"She'd a-been called handsome, as you say," said Mrs. Purdy, assenting but critical, "but for that mole she had a-growin' by her left eyebrow. Do fill up your glass again, Mrs. McCool."

INTERPRETATION

This story is obviously divided into two parts. The first part, which ends with the death of the lodger, concerns his failure in the search for his sweetheart and the motivation of his suicide; the second part concerns the revelation, by the landlady to her crony, that his sweetheart had, a week earlier, committed suicide in the same room. What accounts for the fact that O. Henry felt it necessary to treat the story in this fashion? What holds the two parts of the story together?

The most interesting question has to do with the young man's motivation. In one sense, O. Henry has deliberately made the problem of his motivation more difficult by withholding the information that the sweetheart is dead. The young man does not know that she is dead; indeed, in the room, he gets, with the scent of mignonette, a renewed hope. Why then, under these circumstances, does he commit suicide? Presumably, the explanation is this: he has been searching fruitlessly for five months; he is, we are told, tired—and, we assume, not only momentarily tired physically, but spiritually weary. Indeed, we are told: "He was sure that since her disappearance from home this great water-girt city held her somewhere, but it was like a monstrous quicksand, shifting its particles constantly, with no foundation, its upper granules of today buried tomorrow in ooze and slime." But we are not supposed to believe, even so, that he would have necessarily turned on the gas this particular evening, except as a despairing reaction from the hope which has been raised by the scent of mignonette. This is the author's account of the motivation of the suicide.

But is the motivation, as presented, really convincing? That will depend on the character of the man. What sort of man is he? Actually, O. Henry has told us very little about him except that he is young, has searched for his sweetheart for five months, and is tired. Especially does the question of the man's character, and state of mind, come up in the incident in which he notices the odor of mignonette. Did he really smell it? Did he merely imagine that he smelled it? "And he breathed the breath of the house . . . a cold, musty effluvium . . . mingled with the reeking exhalations of linoleum and mildewed and rotten woodwork. . . . Then, suddenly, as he rested there, the room was filled with the strong, sweet odor of mignonette. It came as upon a single buffet of wind. . . . The rich odor clung to him and wrapped him around."

The suddenness with which he notices the odor, the power of the odor, the fact that he can find no source for the odor, and finally the complete disappearance of the odor, all tend to imply that he merely imagines it. But over against this view, we have the testimony of the landlady that the sweetheart had actually occupied the room. This question is important, for it is crucial for the young man's lapse into acute despair. If the odor is real, the author must convince his reader that it exists; if it is imaginary, the author must convince his reader that the psychological condition of the young man will account for its apparent existence. These are the tests which the reader must apply to the situation. We have already pointed out that there is some evidence on both sides of the question. The reader must, of course, decide for himself which explanation must be taken, and more importantly, whether the explanation is convincing, and renders the action credible. The author, however, seems to weight the evidence toward the presence of the real odor. If this is the case, how are we to account for the fact that the search reveals no source of it, especially since the odor is so overpoweringly strong? Or, perhaps the author has in mind some idea that the odor provokes a mystical communion between the two lovers. But this does not relieve the fiction writer from the necessity for furnishing some sort of specific clue to his meaning. (Morever, if we are to take the whole experience as an hallucination, the author is certainly not relieved from providing some clear motivation for the event.)

To sum up: it is obvious enough, from the detailed description of the room, that O. Henry is trying to suggest a ground for the man's experience in the nature of the room itself. That is, the room in its disorder, its squalor, its musty smell, its rubbish and debris of nameless lives, reflects the great city, or the world, in which his sweetheart has been lost, and in which all humanity seems to become degraded and brutalized. It is easy enough to see why O. Henry should want to suggest the contrast between what the sordid surroundings mean to the hero and what the odor of mignonette means to him. As the girl is lost somewhere in the great city, so the odor is lost somewhere in the room. After the young man is told that the girl has not been there, and after he has been unable to find the source of the odor, the room itself is supposed to become a sort of overwhelming symbol for the futility of his effort. This intention on the part of the author may be sound enough, but the fact that we see what the intention is does not mean that the intention has been carried out. The whole effect of the story depends on the incident of the odor, and we have seen that the handling of this detail is confused.

Assuming that this objection is valid, the basic remedy suggests itself at once. The author needed to go back and fill in the character of the young man much more fully. The reader might then have been able to follow the processes of his mind as he goes through his crucial experience, and the specific nature of his response to the odor would have been clarified. But O. Henry chooses an easier solution. Resting upon his rather thin and sketchy characterization of the young man, the author chooses to give a turn to the plot by a last-minute surprise. In the second part of the story the landlady tells her crony that she has lied to the young man about the girl.

What is the effect of this revelation? It is intended, obviously, to underline the "irony of fate," to illustrate the hard-heartedness of the city in which the young man finds himself, to justify the young man's overwhelming sense that the girl has been in the room, and, all in all, to pull the story together. For the sympathetic reader this conclusion is supposed to suggest that the bonds of love stretch across the confusion and squalor of the great city, and that, in a sense, the young man has finally succeeded in his search, for the lovers are at last united in death. The young man finds, as it were, the proper room in the great city in which to die.

But is the story really pulled together? The end of the story depends on the lie. But are the lives of the lovers altered by the lie? Does the lie cause the death of the young man? It is conceivable that, had the landlady told the truth, the shock of the information might have saved the young man from suicide, but this is the merest speculation. The character, as given in the story, commits suicide in despair when the landlady tells him that the girl has not been there; the landlady's telling him that the girl is irretrievably lost, is dead, would presumably have had the same effect.

Actually, is there any point in the lie except to trick the reader—to provide the illusion of a meaningful ending? Whatever irony lies in the ending is based on a far-fetched coincidence, and does not depend on the fact that the woman said one thing rather than another. (Readers who are inclined to accept the conclusion of the story as meaningful might try reconstructing the story with the young man's calling at the door, finding with horror that his sweetheart has committed suicide there a week before, renting the room, and turning on the gas. We would then still have the ironical coincidence and a sort of union of the lovers, but the story would seem very tame and flat.) O. Henry, by withholding certain information and thus surprising us with it at the end, has simply tried to give the reader the illusion that the information was meaningful. The irony, in the story as we have it, simply resides in a trick played on the reader rather than in a trick which fate has played on the young man.

Readers who feel that the end of this story is a shabby trick will be able to point out other symptoms of cheapness: the general thinness of characterization, the cluttered and sometimes mawkish description, the wheedling tone taken by the author, and the obvious play for emotional sympathy in such writing as the following: "Oh, God! whence that odor, and since when have odors had a voice to call?" In other words, we can readily surmise that the trickery involved in the surprise ending may be an attempt to compensate for defects within the body of the story itself. The straining to stir the emotions of the reader, the mawkish and wheedling tone— all are attempts to make up for a lack of logic, a lack of coherence, in the story itself. *Sentimentality* (see Glossary) often springs from such a lack of coherence—emotionalism without reference to a reasonable occasion for it.

A trick of plot does not make a story. A surprise ending may appear in a very good story, but only if the surprise has been prepared for so that, upon second thought, the reader realizes that it is, after all, a logical and meaningful development from what has gone before, and not merely a device employed by the author to give him an easy way out of his difficulties. The same principle applies to *coincidence* (see Glossary) in general. Coincidences do occur in real life, sometimes quite startling ones, and in one sense every story is based on a coincidence—namely, that the particular events happen to occur together, that such and such characters happen to meet, for example. But since fiction is concerned with a logic of character and action, coincidence, in so far as it is purely illogical, has little place in fiction. Truth can afford to be stranger than fiction, because truth is "true"—is acceptable on its own merits—but the happenings of fiction, as we have seen, must justify themselves in terms of logical connection with other elements in fiction and in terms of meaningfulness. Certainly coincidence is never acceptable when it is used to solve the problem of a story—to bail the author out of his difficulties.

JOHN COLLIER

De Mortuis

DR. Rankin was a large and raw-boned man on whom the newest suit at once appeared outdated, like a suit in a photograph of twenty years ago. This was due to the squareness and flatness of his torso, which might have been put together by a manufacturer of packing cases. His face also had a wooden and a roughly constructed look; his hair was wiglike and resentful of the comb. He had those huge and clumsy hands which can be an asset to a doctor in a small upstate town where people still retain a rural relish for paradox, thinking that the more apelike the paw, the more precise it can be in the delicate business of a tonsillectomy.

This conclusion was perfectly justified in the case of Dr. Rankin. For example, on this particular fine morning, though his task was nothing more ticklish than the cementing over of a large patch on his cellar floor, he managed those large and clumsy hands with all the unflurried certainty of one who would never leave a sponge within or create an unsightly scar without.

The doctor surveyed his handiwork from all angles. He added a touch here and a touch there till he had achieved a smoothness altogether professional. He swept up a few last crumbs of soil and dropped them into the furnace. He paused before putting away the pick and shovel he had been using, and found occasion for yet another artistic sweep of his trowel, which made the new surface precisely flush with the surrounding floor. At this moment of supreme concentration the porch door upstairs slammed with the report of a minor piece of artillery, which, appropriately enough, caused Dr. Rankin to jump as if he had been shot.

The Doctor lifted a frowning face and an attentive ear. He heard two pairs of heavy feet clump across the resonant floor of the porch. He heard the house door opened and the visitors enter the hall, with which his cellar communicated by a short flight of steps. He heard whistling and then the voices of Buck and Bud crying, "Doc! Hi, Doc! They're biting!"

Whether the Doctor was not inclined for fishing that day, or whether, like others of his large and heavy type, he experienced an especially sharp, unsociable reaction on being suddenly startled, or whether he was merely anxious to finish undisturbed the job in hand and proceed to more important duties, he did not respond immediately to the inviting outcry of his friends. Instead, he listened while it ran its natural course, dying down at last into a puzzled and fretful dialogue.

"I guess he's out."

"I'll write a note—say we're at the creek to come on down."

"We could tell Irene."

"But she's not here, either. You'd think *she'd* be around."

"Ought to be, by the look of the place."

"You said it, Bud. Just look at this table. You could write your name—"

"Sh-h-h! Look!"

Evidently the last speaker had noticed that the cellar door was ajar and that a light was shining below. Next moment the door was pushed wide open and Bud and Buck looked down.

"Why, Doc! There you are!"

"Didn't you hear us yelling?"

The Doctor, not too pleased at what he had overheard, nevertheless smiled his rather wooden smile as his two friends made their way down the steps. "I thought I heard someone," he said.

"We were bawling our heads off," Buck said. "Thought nobody was home. Where's Irene?"

"Visiting," said the Doctor. "She's gone visiting."

"Hey, what goes on?" said Bud. "What are you doing? Burying one of your patients, or what?"

"Oh, there's been water seeping up through the floor," said the Doctor. "I figured it might be some spring opened up or something."

"You don't say!" said Bud, assuming instantly the high ethical standpoint of the realtor. "Gee, Doc, I sold you this property. Don't say I fixed you up with a dump where there's an underground spring."

"There was water," said the Doctor.

"Yes, but, Doc, you can look on that geological map the Kiwanis Club got up. There's not a better section of subsoil in the town."

"Looks like he sold you a pup," said Buck, grinning.

"No," said Bud. "Look. When the Doc came here he was green. You'll admit he was green. The things he didn't know!"

"He bought Ted Webber's jalopy," said Buck.

"He'd have bought the Jessop place if I'd let him," said Bud. "But I wouldn't give him a bum steer."

"Not the poor, simple city slicker from Poughkeepsie," said Buck.

"Some people would have taken him," said Bud. "Maybe some people did. Not me. I recommended this property. He and Irene moved straight in as soon as they were married. I wouldn't have put the Doc on to a dump where there'd be a spring under the foundations."

"Oh, forget it," said the Doctor, embarrassed by this conscientiousness. "I guess it was just the heavy rains."

"By gosh!" Buck said, glancing at the besmeared point of the pick-axe. "You certainly went deep enough. Right down into the clay, huh?"

"That's four feet down, the clay," Bud said.

"Eighteen inches," said the Doctor.

"Four feet," said Bud. "I can show you on the map."

"Come on. No arguments," said Buck. "How's about it, Doc? An hour or two at the creek, eh? They're biting."

"Can't do it, boys," said the Doctor. "I've got to see a patient or two."

"Aw, live and let live, Doc," Bud said. "Give 'em a chance to get better. Are you going to depopulate the whole darn town?"

The Doctor looked down, smiled, and muttered, as he always did when this particular jest was trotted out. "Sorry, boys," he said. "I can't make it."

"Well," said Bud, disappointed, "I suppose we'd better get along. How's Irene?"

"Irene?" asked the Doctor. "Never better. She's gone visiting. Albany. Got the eleven o'clock train."

"Eleven o'clock?" said Buck. "For Albany?"

"Did I say Albany?" said the Doctor. "Watertown, I meant."

"Friends in Watertown?" Buck asked.

"Mrs. Slater," said the Doctor. "Mr. and Mrs. Slater. Lived next door to 'em when she was a kid, Irene said, over on Sycamore Street."

"Slater?" said Bud. "Next door to Irene. Not in *this* town."

"Oh, yes," said the Doctor. "She was telling me all about them last night. She got a letter. Seems this Mrs. Slater looked after her when her mother was in the hospital one time."

"No," said Bud.

"That's what she told me," said the Doctor. "Of course, it was a good many years ago."

"Look, Doc," said Buck. "Bud and I were raised in this town. We've known Irene's folks all our lives. We were in and out of their house all the time. There was never anybody next door called Slater."

"Perhaps," said the Doctor, "she married again, this woman. Perhaps it was a different name."

Bud shook his head.

"What time did Irene go to the station?" Buck asked.

"Oh, about a quarter of an hour ago," said the Doctor.

"You didn't drive her?" said Buck.

"She walked," said the Doctor.

"We came down Main Street," Buck said. "We didn't meet her."

"Maybe she walked across the pasture," said the Doctor.

"That's a tough walk with a suitcase," said Buck.

"She just had a couple of things in a little bag," said the Doctor.

Bud was still shaking his head.

Buck looked at Bud, and then at the pick, at the new, damp cement on the floor. "Jesus Christ!" he said.

"Oh, God, Doc!" Bud said. "A guy like you!"

"What in the name of heaven are you two bloody fools thinking?" asked the Doctor. "What are you trying to say?"

"A spring!" said Bud. "I ought to have known right away it wasn't any spring."

The Doctor looked at his cement-work, at the pick, at the large worried faces of his two friends. His own face turned livid. "Am I crazy?" he said. "Or are you? You suggest that I've—that Irene—my wife—oh, go on! Get out! Yes, go and get the sheriff. Tell him to come here and start digging. You—get out!"

Bud and Buck looked at each other, shifted their feet, and stood still again.

"Go on," said the Doctor.

"I don't know," said Bud.

"It's not as if he didn't have the provocation," Buck said.

"God knows," Bud said.

"God knows," Buck said. "You know. I know. The whole town knows. But try telling it to a jury."

The Doctor put his hand to his head. "What's that?" he said. "What is it? Now what are you saying? What do you mean?"

"If this ain't being on the spot!" said Buck. "Doc, you can see how it is. It takes some thinking. We've been friends right from the start. Damn good friends."

"But we've got to think," said Bud. "It's serious. Provocation or not, there's a law in the land. There's such a thing as being an accomplice."

"You were talking about provocation," said the Doctor.

"You're right," said Buck. "And you're our friend. And if ever it could be called justified—"

"We've got to fix this somehow," said Bud.

"Justified?" said the Doctor.

"You were bound to get wised up sooner or later," said Buck.

"We could have told you," said Bud. "Only—what the hell?"

"We could," said Buck. "And we nearly did. Five years ago. Before ever you married her. You hadn't been here six months, but we sort of cottoned to you. Thought of giving you a hint. Spoke about it. Remember, Bud?"

Bud nodded. "Funny," he said. "I came right out in the open about that Jessop property. I wouldn't let you buy that, Doc. But getting married, that's something else again. We could have told you."

"We're that much responsible," Buck said.

"I'm fifty," said the Doctor. "I suppose it's pretty old for Irene."

"If you was Johnny Weissmuller at the age of twenty-one, it wouldn't make any difference," said Buck.

"I know a lot of people think she's not exactly a perfect wife," said the Doctor. "Maybe she's not. She's young. She's full of life."

"Oh, skip it!" said Buck sharply, looking at the raw cement. "Skip it, Doc, for God's sake."

The Doctor brushed his hand across his face. "Not everybody wants the same thing," he said. "I'm a sort of dry fellow. I don't open up very easily. Irene—you'd call her gay."

"You said it," said Buck.

"She's no housekeeper," said the Doctor. "I know it. But that's not the only thing a man wants. She's enjoyed herself."

"Yeah," said Buck. "She did."

"That's what I love," said the Doctor. "Because I'm not that way myself. She's not very deep, mentally. All right. Say she's stupid. I don't care. Lazy. No system. Well, I've got plenty of system. She's enjoyed herself. It's beautiful. It's innocent. Like a child."

"Yes. If that was all," Buck said.

"But," said the Doctor, turning his eyes full on him, "You seem to know there was more."

"Everybody knows it," said Buck.

"A decent, straightforward guy comes to a place like this and marries the town floozy," Bud said bitterly. "And nobody'll tell him. Everybody just watches."

"And laughs," said Buck. "You and me, Bud, as well as the rest."

"We told her to watch her step," said Bud. "We warned her."

"Everybody warned her," said Buck. "But people get fed up. When it got to truck-drivers—"

"It was never us, Doc," said Bud, earnestly. "Not after you came along, anyway."

"The town'll be on your side," said Buck.

"That won't mean much when the case comes to trial in the county seat," said Bud.

"Oh!" cried the Doctor, suddenly. "What shall I do? What shall I do?"

"It's up to you, Bud," said Buck. "I can't turn him in."

"Take it easy, Doc," said Bud. "Calm down. Look, Buck. When we came in here the street was empty, wasn't it?"

"I guess so," said Buck. "Anyway, nobody saw us come down cellar."

"And we haven't been down," Bud said, addressing himself forcefully to the Doctor. "Get that, Doc? We shouted upstairs, hung around a minute or two, and cleared out. But we never came down into this cellar."

"I wish you hadn't," the Doctor said heavily.

"All you have to do is say Irene went out for a walk and never came back," said Buck. "Bud and I can swear we saw her headed out of town with a fellow in a—well, say in a Buick sedan. Everybody'll believe that, all right. We'll fix it. But later. Now we'd better scram."

"And remember, now. Stick to it. We never came down here and we haven't seen you today," said Bud. "So long!"

Buck and Bud ascended the steps, moving with a rather absurd degree of caution. "You'd better get that . . . that thing covered up," Buck said over his shoulder.

Left alone, the Doctor sat down on an empty box, holding his head with both hands. He was still sitting like this when the porch door slammed again. This time he did not start. He listened. The house door opened and closed. A voice cried, "Yoo-hoo! Yoo-hoo! I'm back."

The Doctor rose slowly to his feet. "I'm down here, Irene!" he called.

The cellar door opened. A young woman stood at the head of the steps. "Can you beat it?" she said. "I missed the damn train."

"Oh!" said the Doctor. "Did you come back across the field?"

"Yes, like a fool," she said. "I could have hitched a ride and caught the train up the line. Only I didn't think. If you'd run me over to the junction, I could still make it."

"Maybe," said the Doctor. "Did you meet anyone coming back?"

"Not a soul," she said. "Aren't you finished with that old job yet?"

"I'm afraid I'll have to take it all up again," said the Doctor. "Come down here, my dear, and I'll show you."

INTERPRETATION

This story, like "The Furnished Room," involves coincidence and has a trick ending. But are those two things more acceptable here than in "The Furnished Room"? Perhaps we can best answer the question by considering the difference between the pretensions of the two stories.

"The Furnished Room" aspires to be a serious story. O. Henry wants us to feel the pathos and irony of life, the brutality and anonymity of the great city in contrast with the loves and hopes of the lost individuals. The story aims to stir our emotions and evoke our sympathies.

"De Mortuis," on the other hand, is a kind of extended joke. It deals with serious materials, the betrayal of a simple, decent man by an immoral wife, and his murder of her, but the emphasis is not on the human passions and suffering. The treatment is the treatment to be found in a joke, and the point, in a way, lies in the contrast between the potentially serious, even tragic, human situation, on the one hand, and the reversal and punch of the joke, on the other. It's a great joke on Irene. Just wait till she gets downstairs! Won't she be surprised! Well, she had it coming. She stepped into it that time. We have the comic effect—the liberation from the demands of sympathy and seriousness.

As a matter of fact, the joke isn't merely on Irene. There is a joke on everybody, on Buck and Bud, who unwittingly get the thing worked up, and on the doctor himself. Life has some rather grim little jokes, the story implies, but the best thing to do is to recognize them as jokes and laugh at them. Even the fact of coincidence—Bud and Buck just happen to drop in at the right time, Irene just happens to miss the train and come back, unseen, across the pasture—are consistent with the comic effect. We accept the coincidences as the machinery of the joke life is playing—for the illogic of life, not the logic, is what gives us the comedy. Poor Irene, and the others, are caught in the improbable coincidences and the unexpected turn, and we laugh at the fact. No appeal has been made to our sympathies. The tone is one of calm detachment, coolly reportorial. We are not involved in the human situation. The fact of the seriousness and the suffering merely gives a grim little edge to the comedy.

To sum up, it is the particular comic tone which makes us accept the coincidences and the trick ending. By tone, as we have already suggested (p. 37–38), we mean the impression that the author gives of his attitude toward his subject and his reader. Collier here takes life as a sardonic joke, full of traps and tricks. Careful, Irene, dear, watch that banana peel. It's right there before your eyes.

1. It may help us in developing some of the principles involved here, if we make a comparison with "The Lottery." That story, too, depends on coincidence and on a trick ending, again a grim joke. But the tone is certainly different. Try to describe the basic difference. Which story is, in its basic intention, more serious? Which do you like better? Why?

2. Try to distinguish between exposition and complication in "De Mortuis." Can you point out any elements of exposition that are withheld until complication has begun?

3. Suppose Collier had interpolated toward the end of the story a passage in which the doctor remembers his loneliness before his marriage, dwells on certain moments of tenderness of which Irene had been capable, shudders at the horror of the impulse that seizes him, then steels himself to the act. How would this change the effect of the story? What would be the effect on the tone? Would the story still be coherent?

4. What value for the story does the first paragraph have?

GUY DE MAUPASSANT

The Necklace

SHE was one of those pretty and charming girls who are sometimes, as if by a mistake of destiny, born in a family of clerks. She had no dowry, no expectations, no means of being known, understood, loved, wedded by any rich and distinguished man; and she let herself be married to a little clerk at the Ministry of Public Instruction.

She dressed plainly because she could not dress well, but she was as unhappy as though she had really fallen from her proper station, since with women there is neither caste nor rank: and beauty, grace, and charm act instead of family and birth. Natural fineness, instinct for what is elegant, suppleness of wit, are the sole hierarchy, and make from women of the people the equals of the very greatest ladies.

She suffered ceaselessly, feeling herself born for all the delicacies and all the luxuries. She suffered from the poverty of her dwelling, from the wretched look of the walls, from the worn-out chairs, from the ugliness of the curtains. All those things, of which another woman of her rank would never even have been conscious, tortured her and made her angry. The sight of the little Breton peasant who did her humble housework aroused in her regrets which were despairing, and distracted dreams. She thought of the silent antechambers hung with Oriental tapestry, lit by tall bronze candelabra, and of the two great footmen in knee breeches who sleep in the big armchairs, made drowsy by the heavy warmth of the hot-air stove. She thought of the long *salons* fitted up with ancient silk, of the delicate furniture carrying priceless curiosities, and of the coquettish perfumed boudoirs made for talks at five o'clock with intimate friends, with men famous and sought after, whom all women envy and whose attention they all desire.

When she sat down to dinner, before the round table covered with a tablecloth three days old, opposite her husband, who uncovered the soup tureen and declared with an enchanted air, "Ah, the good *pot-au-feu!* I don't know anything better than that," she thought of dainty dinners, of shining silverware, of tapestry which peopled the walls with ancient personages and with strange birds flying in the midst of a fairy forest; and she thought of delicious dishes served on marvelous plates, and of the whispered gallantries which you listen to with a sphinxlike smile, while you are eating the pink flesh of a trout or the wings of a quail.

She had no dresses, no jewels, nothing. And she loved nothing but that; she felt made for that. She would so have liked to please, to be envied, to be charming, to be sought after.

She had a friend, a former schoolmate at the convent, who was rich, and whom she did not like to go and see any more, because she suffered so much when she came back.

But one evening, her husband returned home with a triumphant air, and holding a large envelope in his hand.

"There," said he. "Here is something for you."

She tore the paper sharply, and drew out a printed card which bore these words:

"The Minister of Public Instruction and Mme. Georges Ramponneau request the honor of M. and Mme. Loisel's company at the palace of the Ministry on Monday evening, January eighteenth."

Instead of being delighted, as her husband hoped, she threw the invitation on the table with disdain, murmuring:

"What do you want me to do with that?"

"But, my dear, I thought you would be glad. You never go out, and this is such a fine opportunity. I had awful trouble to get it. Everyone wants to go; it is very select, and they are not giving many invitations to clerks. The whole official world will be there."

She looked at him with an irritated glance, and said, impatiently:

"And what do you want me to put on my back?"

He had not thought of that; he stammered:

"Why, the dress you go to the theater in. It looks very well, to me."

He stopped, distracted, seeing his wife was crying. Two great tears descended slowly from the corners of her eyes toward the corners of her mouth. He stuttered:

"What's the matter? What's the matter?"

But, by violent effort, she had conquered her grief, and she replied, with a calm voice, while she wiped her wet cheeks:

"Nothing. Only I have no dress and therefore I can't go to this ball. Give your card to some colleague whose wife is better equipped than I."

He was in despair. He resumed:

"Come, let us see, Mathilde. How much would it cost, a suitable dress, which you could use on other occasions, something very simple?"

She reflected several seconds, making her calculations and wondering also what sum she could ask without drawing on herself an immediate refusal and a frightened exclamation from the economical clerk.

Finally, she replied, hesitatingly:

"I don't know exactly, but I think I could manage it with four hundred francs."

He had grown a little pale, because he was laying aside just that amount to buy a gun and treat himself to a little shooting next summer on the plain of Nanterre, with several friends who went to shoot larks down there, of a Sunday.

But he said:

"All right. I will give you four hundred francs. And try to have a pretty dress."

The day of the ball drew near, and Mme. Loisel seemed sad, uneasy, anxious. Her dress was ready, however. Her husband said to her one evening:

"What is the matter? Come, you've been so queer these last three days."

And she answered:

"It annoys me not to have a single jewel, not a single stone, nothing to put on. I shall look like distress. I should almost rather not go at all."

He resumed:

"You might wear natural flowers. It's very stylish at this time of the year. For ten francs you can get two or three magnificent roses."

She was not convinced.

"No; there's nothing more humiliating than to look poor among other women who are rich."

But her husband cried:

"How stupid you are! Go look up your friend Mme. Forestier, and ask her to lend you some jewels. You're quite thick enough with her to do that."

She uttered a cry of joy:

"It's true. I never thought of it."

The next day she went to her friend and told of her distress.

Mme. Forestier went to a wardrobe with a glass door, took out a large jewel-box, brought it back, opened it, and said to Mme. Loisel:

"Choose, my dear."

She saw first of all some bracelets, then a pearl necklace, then a Venetian cross, gold and precious stones of admirable workmanship. She tried on the ornaments before the glass, hesitated, could not make up her mind to part with them, to give them back. She kept asking:

"Haven't you any more?"

"Why, yes. Look. I don't know what you like."

All of a sudden she discovered, in a black satin box, a superb necklace of diamonds, and her heart began to beat with an immoderate desire. Her hands trembled as she took it. She fastened it around her throat, outside her high-necked dress, and remained lost in ecstasy at the sight of herself.

Then she asked, hesitating, filled with anguish:

"Can you lend me that, only that?"

"Why, yes, certainly."

She sprang upon the neck of her friend, kissed her passionately, then fled with her treasure.

The day of the ball arrived. Mme. Loisel made a great success. She was prettier than them all, elegant, gracious, smiling, and crazy with joy. All the men looked at her, asked her name, endeavored to be introduced. All the attachés of the Cabinet wanted to waltz with her. She was remarked by the minister himself.

She danced with intoxication, with passion, made drunk by pleasure, forgetting all, in the triumph of her beauty, in the glory of her success, in a sort of cloud of happiness composed of all this homage, of all this admiration, of all these awakened desires, and of that sense of complete victory which is so sweet to a woman's heart.

She went away about four o'clock in the morning. Her husband had been sleeping since midnight, in a little deserted anteroom, with three other gentlemen whose wives were having a very good time. He threw over her shoulders the wraps which he had brought, modest wraps of common life, whose poverty contrasted with the elegance of the ball dress. She felt this, and wanted to escape so as not to be remarked by the other women, who were enveloping themselves in costly furs.

Loisel held her back.

"Wait a bit. You will catch cold outside. I will go and call a cab."

But she did not listen to him, and rapidly descended the stairs. When they were in the street they did not find a carriage; and they began to look for one, shouting after the cabmen whom they saw passing by at a distance.

They went down toward the Seine, in despair, shivering with cold. At last they found on the quay one of those ancient noctambulant coupés which, exactly as if they were ashamed to show their misery during the day, are never seen round Paris until after nightfall.

It took them to their door in the Rue des Martyrs, and once more, sadly, they climbed up homeward. All was ended, for her. And as to him, he reflected that he must be at the Ministry at ten o'clock.

She removed the wraps which covered her shoulders, before the glass, so as once more to see herself in all her glory. But suddenly she uttered a cry. She no longer had the necklace around her neck!

Her husband, already half undressed, demanded:

"What is the matter with you?"

She turned madly towards him:

"I have—I have—I've lost Mme. Forestier's necklace."

He stood up, distracted.

"What!—how?—impossible!"

And they looked in the folds of her dress, in the folds of her cloak, in her pockets, everywhere. They did not find it.

He asked:

"You're sure you had it on when you left the ball?"

"Yes, I felt it in the vestibule of the palace."

"But if you had lost it in the street we should have heard it fall. It must be in the cab."

"Yes. Probably. Did you take his number?"

"No. And you, didn't you notice it?"

"No."

They looked, thunderstruck, at one another. At last Loisel put on his clothes.

"I shall go back on foot," said he, "over the whole route which we have taken to see if I can find it."

And he went out. She sat waiting on a chair in her ball dress, without strength to go to bed, overwhelmed, without fire, without a thought.

Her husband came back about seven o'clock. He had found nothing.

He went to Police Headquarters, to the newspaper offices, to offer a reward; he went to the cab companies—everywhere, in fact, whither he was urged by the least suspicion of hope.

She waited all day, in the same condition of mad fear before this terrible calamity.

Loisel returned at night with a hollow, pale face; he had discovered nothing.

"You must write to your friend," said he, "that you have broken the clasp of her necklace and that you are having it mended. That will give us time to turn round."

She wrote at his dictation.

At the end of a week they had lost all hope.

And Loisel, who had aged five years, declared:

"We must consider how to replace that ornament."

The next day they took the box which had contained it, and they went to the jeweler whose name was found within. He consulted his books.

"It was not I, madame, who sold that necklace; I must simply have furnished the case."

Then they went from jeweler to jeweler, searching for a necklace like the other, consulting their memories, sick both of them with chagrin and anguish.

They found, in a shop at the Palais Royal, a string of diamonds which seemed to them exactly like the one they looked for. It was worth forty thousand francs. They could have it for thirty-six.

So they begged the jeweler not to sell it for three days yet. And they made a bargain that he should buy it back for thirty-four thousand francs, in case they found the other one before the end of February.

Loisel possessed eighteen thousand francs which his father had left him. He would borrow the rest.

He did borrow, asking a thousand francs of one, five hundred of another, five louis here, three louis there. He gave notes, took up ruinous obligations, dealt with usurers and all the race of lenders. He compromised all the rest of his life, risked his signature without even knowing if he could meet it; and, frightened by the pains yet to come, by the black misery which was about to fall upon him, by the prospect of all the physical privation and of all the moral tortures which he was to suffer, he went to get the new necklace, putting down upon the merchant's counter thirty-six thousand francs.

When Mme. Loisel took back the necklace, Mme. Forestier said to her, with a chilly manner:

"You should have returned it sooner; I might have needed it."

She did not open the case, as her friend had so much feared. If she had detected the substitution, what would she have thought, what would she have said? Would she not have taken Mme. Loisel for a thief?

Mme. Loisel now knew the horrible existence of the needy. She took her part, moreover, all of a sudden, with heroism. That dreadful debt must be paid. She would pay it. They dismissed their servant; they changed their lodgings; they rented a garret under the roof.

She came to know what heavy housework meant and the odious cares of the kitchen. She washed the dishes, using her rosy nails on the greasy pots and pans. She washed the dirty linen, the shirts, and the dishcloths, which she dried upon a line; she carried the slops down to the street every morning, and carried up the water, stopping for breath at every landing. And, dressed like a woman of the people, she went to the fruiterer, the grocer, the butcher, her basket on her arm, bargaining, insulted, defending her miserable money sou by sou.

Each month they had to meet some notes, renew others, obtain more time.

Her husband worked in the evening making a fair copy of some tradesman's accounts, and late at night he often copied manuscript for five sous a page.

And this life lasted for ten years.

At the end of ten years, they had paid everything, everything, with the rates of usury, and the accumulations of the compound interest.

Mme. Loisel looked old now. She had become the woman of improverished households—strong and hard and rough. With frowsy hair, skirts askew, and red hands, she talked loud while washing the floor with great swishes of water. But sometimes, when her husband was at the office, she sat down near the window, and she thought of that gay evening of long ago, of that ball where she had been so beautiful and so fêted.

What would have happened if she had not lost that necklace? Who knows? Who knows? How life is strange and changeful! How little a thing is needed for us to be lost or to be saved!

But, one Sunday, having gone to take a walk in the Champs Elysées to refresh herself from the labor of the week, she suddenly perceived a woman who was leading a child. It was Mme. Forestier, still young, still beautiful, still charming.

Mme. Loisel felt moved. Was she going to speak to her? Yes, certainly. And now that she had paid, she was going to tell her all about it. Why not?

She went up.

"Good-day, Jeanne."

The other, astonished to be familiarly addressed by this plain good-wife, did not recognize her at all, and stammered:

"But—madam!—I do not know— You must be mistaken."

"No. I am Mathilde Loisel."

Her friend uttered a cry.

"Oh, my poor Mathilde! How you are changed!"

"Yes, I have had days hard enough, since I have seen you, days wretched enough—and that because of you!"

"Of me! How so?"

"Do you remember that diamond necklace which you lent me to wear at the ministerial ball?"

"Yes. Well?"

"Well, I lost it."

"What do you mean? You brought it back."

"I brought you back another just like it. And for this we have been ten years paying. You can understand that it was not easy for us, us who had nothing. At last it is ended, and I am very glad."

Mme. Forestier had stopped.

"You say that you bought a necklace of diamonds to replace mine?"

"Yes. You never noticed it, then! They were very like."

And she smiled with a joy which was proud and naïve at once.

Mme. Forestier, strongly moved, took her two hands.

"Oh, my poor Mathilde! Why, my necklace was paste. It was worth at most five hundred francs!"

INTERPRETATION

This story ends with a surprising turn. The heroine, after years of privation and struggle caused by the loss of the borrowed necklace, learns that the jewels had, after all, been valueless. At first glance this revelation may seem to be a trick, just as the conclusion of "The Furnished Room" is a trick. To determine whether or not the conclusion of "The Necklace" is a trick, one should investigate the following questions:

1. Has Maupassant made use of the fact that the jewels are paste as a starting point from which to develop his story, or has he used it as merely a piece of trickery to provide a surprise ending? In other words, is there a really important difference between the fundamental fact that the jewels are paste, and the fact that the heroine eventually discovers them to be paste? Would there be an irony in the story even if the woman had never discovered the true nature of the jewels?

2. Waiving the question of the nature of the jewels: some people, having lost them, would have made a clean breast of the situation at once. Is the heroine's refusal to do so adequately motivated? Is the pride from which this refusal springs a true and admirable pride or merely a false pride? Or is it an ironical mixture of the two? The heroine's actions subsequent to the loss of the jewels are presumably conditioned by her character. Are these two elements logically related in the story?

3. Finally, does the fundamental meaning of the story depend on the fact of the loss of the jewels, whether paste or real? In other words, is not this the sort of woman who, in one way or another, would have wasted her life on some sort of vanity? (In this connection read the first paragraph of the story.) Does Maupassant not use the accident of the loss of the jewels as a means to speed up and intensify a process which is already inherent in the woman's character? If this can be maintained, then does not the falsity of the jewels become a kind of symbol for the root situation of the story? That is, does not the "falsity" of the jewels stand as a symbol for the falsity of the values by which the woman once lived?

4. Have we any evidence that the author intended to indicate a regeneration of the heroine? If so, what are we to make of the fact that the heroine discovers in the end that she has now paid for "real" jewels?

5. We may say that the irony of "De Mortuis" is based on a general view of life, the surprising and comic way in which things happen, and that the irony of "The Lottery" is based on a general view of human nature, the doubleness of human nature. The irony of "The Necklace" is based on something more specific. How would you describe it?

6. We have said that Madame Forestier's revelation that the original necklace was paste carries to us, the readers, the point of the story. What does it carry to Madame Loisel?

This story gives us a good chance to consider the problem of the treatment of time in fiction. The story takes Madame Loisel from youth to middle age. Her girlhood is passed over in one sentence in the first paragraph, and the early years of marriage are treated in the second to the fifth paragraphs. Then the time of the ball is treated at considerable length in five direct scenes, the conversation about the dress, the conversation about the jewels, the visit to Madame Forestier, the ball itself, the search for the lost necklace. Then the time of deprivation and payment, ten years, occupies a page or so. Then comes the denouement, the encounter with Madame Forestier in the park.

There is, we see, a sort of balance between the long periods of time treated by summary, and the short periods, treated more or less dramatically by direct rendering. In treating the long periods, in which the eye sweeps, as it were, over a panorama, the writer needs to hit on the important fact, or the essential feeling of the period. He needs to distill out the thing fundamental to the story—the character of the young Madame Loisel, or the way she lived through the ten years of deprivation. In the dramatic—or scenic—treatment the need, however, is to show the process of the movement through the time involved, how there is, step by step, a development; how, for example, Madame Loisel decides to speak to her old friend in the park, how she accosts her, how she discovers the unexpected joy in the thought that the necklace she had bought had successfully deceived Madame Forestier, how Madame Forestier makes the revelation which, for us, will carry the burden of meaning. The scene, in other words, gives the "close-ups" of time, and the summary the "long shots." These are, we may say, questions of distance (see Glossary).

Often in a summary a writer must give more than mere summary. After all, he is writing fiction, and fiction wants to give the feeling of life, not merely the bare facts. Let us notice how even in the relatively bare summary in which Maupassant presents the years of hardship, he manages by a few specific touches to make us sense the quality of the life of the Loisels. Madame Loisel scraped "her rosy nails on the greasy pots and pans." When she carried up her household water every morning, she had to stop "for breath at every landing." She had become, Maupassant tells us, strong, hard, and rough. Then he writes: "With frowsy hair, skirts askew, and red hands, she talked loud while washing the floor with great swishes of water." It all comes alive with the phrase "great swishes of water." We *see* that.

Some pieces of fiction, even some novels, can proceed almost entirely by scenes, by direct presentation. For instance, "De Mortuis" gives us a single little segment of time, as does "The Girls in Their Summer Dresses," with only a minimum of summarized exposition from the past. In fact, both of these stories, in treating the present time, depend almost entirely on conversation and direct action—more so, for instance, than even "The Lottery," which, also, occupies a single short section of continuing time.

Many stories and almost all novels, however, must swing back and forth between more or less direct treatments and narrative summary with more or less of description and analysis thrown in. It is well to begin to notice how these two basic kinds of treatment (with the various shadings and combinations) are related. We must ask ourselves how much the feeling of a particular story, the logic of its telling, the effect it has on us, are related to the writer's handling of this question of time. Again, there is no rule. We must try to inspect our own reactions as carefully and candidly as possible, and try to imagine what would be the effect, in instance after instance, if a different method were used.

WILLIAM SANSOM

Through the Quinquina Glass

ALTHOUGH we shared the same table, Jean sat in the shade whereas I was able to enjoy the sunlight. Between us the crenelated shadow of the café awning drew a sharp division across the table. Cigarette tips burned like white gold in the light and in the shade siphons made from blue glass glinted evilly.

Over on the quay a sailor in a striped sweater trundled a barrel of oil through the hot sunlight. Three curiously tall boys played a game of bowls with some small wooden balls. In the very middle of the road a lean honey-colored dog with degenerate pale blue eyes stretched itself lazily for the flies. An old woman sat knitting beneath a dusty plane tree. This was the only life on an empty stage. From the campanile back in the town came the slow tolling of a funeral bell. It was three o'clock, the hour for siesta, and no time for men to be abroad. And yet . . . here was a man in a severe black coat just arrived and taking his place in the long row of empty café tables. The man was a stranger to us. We watched him lazily. He looked like an office worker from the town, an advocate perhaps.

Jean was saying, "Damn that waiter! Why must he bring me quinquina instead of pastis? Why must he be insolent in the bargain?"

"Because he's a man," I said. "Because he has a private life beneath his dicky. Because his wife may be delivering and he just can't stand being a waiter this afternoon. How can you know the facts?"

Jean mumbled, "Nevertheless he's a waiter—and on duty."

"But I can't agree. You are influenced in advance by the dicky. You deny the man. If you had seen the man first, you would deny the waiter. We see a man cleaning a car—and we say to ourselves 'There is a man cleaning a car.' But perhaps that man is really wondering whether he should propose marriage to his girl. That, of course, is of more moment than cleaning a car. So what we are seeing is in truth a man wondering about a proposal—not a man cleaning a car. We should be more humble in our judgments: we should say, at the most, 'There is a man.' "

I raised my glass and drank the quinquina. Then, holding the glass to the light, I looked through it. In that café, they serve quinquina in green glasses. Framed in the green glass I found the stranger who had recently arrived.

"Take our new arrival," I said. "There he sits, a man. By some accident of taste, he chooses to wear a black coat. Let us reconstruct his story. He is not only a man in a black coat. His name, let us say, is . . . Aristide Fougeres. He is forty years old, he is an advocate in this small Corsican town, he discovered six months ago that his wife had deceived him. Let us see what might be the story of Aristide."

Through the quinquina glass the scene was sunless. The life had left it. It had taken the quality of a picture in oils when the pigments have faded with age. Or it seemed that a mysterious storm had drifted from nowhere, that sudden clouds shrouded our world with gloom. I lowered the glass. I was just beginning to speak when I realized that something was wrong. Something unearthly had happened. I had lowered the glass—yet the scene retained its lurid quality. There was no sun—yet the green gloom persisted. The air was leaden. I could not believe it. I knew there was no real storm. The fact was simply that the quinquina glass had left its imprint on the world. I refused to admit this. I imagined it to be a momentary hallucination. So that I went on talking—consciously avoiding my fearful impression.

"Well, this M. Fougeres discovered that his wife had spent the night with a commercial traveler from Auxerres. Let us return through six months to that occasion. The circumstances of the discovery are unimportant. Perhaps it was a letter, a word from an unkind neighbor, or a sock found at the bottom of his bed. However it went, the evidence was confirmed. What is more important is the action taken by M. Fougeres on his discovery. For he neither sought the man out, nor accused his wife. M. Fougeres remained silent upon the matter. He contained his misery within himself, never breathing a word to a living soul.

"The shock of the discovery affected M. Fougeres in two ways. First his vanity was wounded. Secondly, he found himself in possession of a secret which he soon discovered he was using as a weapon. Mme. Fougeres was a woman whose forceful character dominated husband and household. Now M. Fougeres found that he held a trump card with which he could annihilate his wife's ascendancy at any moment of his choosing. On the production of such an accusation her composure would crumble, a sense of guilt would sweep the certainty from her eyes, her voice would tremble with a refreshing note of appeal. Thus he felt a sudden secret sensation of power. Yet this was not the only effect the discovery had on M. Fougeres."

(This story was coming to my lips with a peculiar fluency. Ordinarily I would have hesitated. I would have paused before the choice of alternatives to the story. Now, it was as if I repeated a story already known to me. I would not say that I felt actually *impelled* to speak. But I was curiously *sure* of my words. The dull light of the quinquina glass alone illumined the scene. The air was breathless.)

"They lived in a narrow house just off the market square. M. Fougeres occupied the ground floor with his offices, while the two upper floors served as dwelling quarters. M. Fougeres had managed to maintain the privacy of his own personal office. This was his holy of holies, upon the door of which even Mme. must knock and wait his leisured 'Entrez.' In this room stood the big desk. It was a heavy mahogany piece with a sturdy roll-top that could drop a reassuring curtain over his private affairs. One day, two weeks after the discovery, Mr. Fougeres cleared out one half of this desk. All the old papers he crammed away into a strong-box—and there lay eight empty pigeon-holes and three clean drawers! This clearance was to be part of a new system. Its purpose was to house evidence of the guilt of Mme. and the collection of evidence relating to any future misdemeanor. For M. Fougeres had decided to employ a detective.

"M. Fougeres wanted more information for a variety of reasons. I have said that his vanity had suffered. In addition to this, the memory of his courting days had been sullied. He had not treasured his wife's body for some years now. She was still a handsome woman, but the perfection he himself had once known was fading. Yet he still treasured the memory of her young loveliness. And for this he felt a fierce jealousy. This memory lived somewhere within the frame of his wife in her present form. That another man should know intimately even the ghost of his young love brought a thrill of horror to the stomach. At night in bed, in the privacy of darkness, with his wife asleep and unseeing beside him, he would torment himself with deliberate images of the commercial traveler's caresses. The torture was voluntary, and it was he who exerted every imaginative effort to devise new and ingenious refinements. His first, and understandable, sense of injury changed to a deliberate masochistic delight. And that was why M. Fougeres had commissioned a detective. He told himself that he must be sure that her infidelity had been no more than a passing 'one night affair. He deprecated that this was 'wishful thinking'; yet excused himself on these same grounds. Actually, it was 'wishful thinking'—of another sort. Perversely, he really wished to discover a new infidelity. He did not yet admit this to himself. But soon he realized that he was disappointed when the detective brought him no news of an incriminating nature.

"As the weeks went by, he developed new and exciting methods of detection. First, he took great trouble to obtain a duplicate key to his wife's bureau. There he found and read her private letters. From these he gleaned nothing—except for one short note from the commercial traveler himself, alongside a photograph of that gentleman. With these trophies M. Fougeres would amuse himself for hours on end. He would choose an hour when there could be no fear of disturbance. Nevertheless he would lock the door behind him with precise care. As he walked from the door to the desk, he would experience a delightful sense of anticipation. He was like a child who stores up a secret moment for the inspection of some very special treasure—a bird's nest, a hidden cupboard in a doll's house, the hour when the candle is snuffed and the nursery fire flickers strangely on the ceiling, the hour reserved for delicious speculation on fine times to come.

"M. Fougeres would unroll his desk and spend some time selecting his first subject. Then he would sit for perhaps two hours, sometimes reading a detective's report, sometimes studying the photograph, sometimes the letter. He would invent new interconnections, new possibilities. At times his temples would throb with the hot blood of indignation, at times he would sink into an apathy of self-pity. There were occasions when he granted himself the luxury of striding the length of his office—right on the point of a stern decision to go and 'have it out' with the commercial traveler. Again, he would engineer periods of 'clear thinking,' when his was the generous, logical mind that could honestly admit a sympathy with the commercial traveler; after all, they were surely men of similar taste? And then he would dream of the day when he would reveal his knowledge to his wife. But most of all he would sit and wonder at the absolute ir- revocability of what had been done. Nothing could undo this terrible wrong. And the tears would well in his eyes as he exaggerated the im- portance of the injury done to him. Each one of these different sensations was a lasting pleasure. And to refine his torment still further, M. Fougeres would constantly accuse himself for his whole attitude over the matter. Normally he was a balanced man. Up to this point he realized that he, too, was committing an underhand action. Two wrongs do not make a right. In deceiving the deceiver, he was acting in a mean and ungenerous manner. M. Fougeres accused himself.

"Added to these pleasures was a more elementary thrill. It was the thrill of adventure. He took risks, he gambled at 'not being found out.' When, for instance, he would quickly run through his wife's bag while she was in the very next room, while he could actually hear the rustle of her skirts! How quickly his fingers worked on such occasions! How alert was his brain!

"But as the weeks passed into months, such little perverted pleasures developed into a dangerous mania. This happened because no new evidence of infidelity presented itself. M. Fougeres sensed that the importance of the matter was fading. Perhaps the moment for taking some dramatic advantage of his secret had slipped by. Time dulls the finer edges of resentment. Gradually he could only think of the episode in minuscule—much as though he were regarding some grand object through the wrong end of a telescope. As its importance eluded him, so he redoubled his efforts to discover something new.

"On returning from any period of absence—even an afternoon's business in some neighboring town—he would examine immediately and in detail every ash-tray in the house. Perhaps one day he would find a cigar stub, the end of an unfamiliar brand of cigarette! He took great care to smell the cushions and the curtains for the aroma of a strange pomade or the stale breath of tobacco. He interrupted for a period his usual custom of shaving in the wash basin: he endured the discomfort of shaving over the bath, some yards from his mirror, because he wished to leave the wash basin plughole free from the trace of his own shaved whiskers. Thus, returning from some overnight absence, he would make his way immediately to the bathroom, lock the door, and scrape out the film of soap and dirt that clung to the dark sides of the hole. He would spread this film over a shaving paper and inspect it thoroughly. One day he might discover a bristle shaved off by his own razor! His own razor callously lent by his wife to her visitor of the night!

"The mania developed and M. Fougeres endured greater discomforts, went to greater lengths to achieve his object. He would arrange fake visits to fictitious friends in the country. During these periods he would watch for hours outside the house, sitting in the darkness of a workman's cafe or pressed self-consciously into the shade of a small alley. Then he would have to sleep at an hotel in the town. The money he spent! And the valuable hours of business wasted! For sometimes, having previously arranged to be absent for the night, he would interrupt negotiations in a distant town to catch the last bus home so that he might appear unexpectedly. On these occasions, his excitement rose to great heights. For on his entrance he would imagine that the man might still be secreted somewhere in the house. He delighted to scrutinize his wife's face for a revealing embarrassment. He loved to search every room and every closet, watching her in between operations and at the same time making subtle excuses that he was looking for this thing or that thing. Sometimes he would make some casual reference to a fictitious acquaintance bearing the same name as the commercial traveler. Once, even, he hinted that he had run into the fellow on a fictitious visit to Auxerres. On this occasion his wife's eyes had brightened and she had looked away. So she still remembered! In addition he would engineer long conversations with his wife on the subject of infidelity.

"Some two months ago M. Fougeres tried another tack. In a moment of delirious misery he visited a brothel. He parted the bead curtains of a brothel and accompanied a girl up the stairs. Every night for a week he continued to visit this place. His pleasure was vicarious. He bathed in the squalor of this medical experience. He delighted in the clinical efficiency of the beds and the bathrooms. He prolonged the money bargain, enjoying its indignity. He always chose the ugliest and oldest woman in the house.

"But these visits were soon to cease. In the first place, they had been a gesture and became tedious on reiteration. In the second place, Fougeres became terrified that his wife would by chance find him out—and in her turn remain silent. Thus she would again be in the ascendant. So M. Fougeres cast around for some other plan. And he found one. It was the finest plan of all. He hit upon it only last week. It was so ingenious that he shuddered to imagine that perhaps it might never have entered his mind. Perhaps he would have died without thinking of it! It was so simple a plan as to be elusive: it was so far-reaching a plan that it might never have occurred to him. It was this. It was that he should go to Auxerres, meet the commercial traveler, and make of him a bosom friend. In this way he would always have the man near him—a far more satisfactory instrument of torture than a photograph. And in a certain sense, the situation would make up a deficiency in his wife's guilt. For his wife's liaison of one night might have been but a passionate lapse, duly regretted, which a generous husband might even forgive. But now, in a roundabout way, she would have deceived him with his best friend. Oh, the injustice of it! And, to make matters worse, she might even be tempted to offer herself to this man again.

"Well . . . M. Fougeres has just returned from Auxerres. After four days of inquiries at the hotels—and later at the Town Hall—he has discovered that the commercial traveler has died from a tubercular kidney five months before. So that all this time he has been jealous of a dead man! Death can turn the tables completely on life. Dead men tell no tales, dead men feel no pride in the past possession of women. In a sense, his wife is a widow—and in some artificial manner suddenly rendered blameless. M. Fougeres has just left the station. He is sitting down to a glass of coffee. Dressed in his fusty black coat, he sits there bereft in a moment of his exclusive interest in life—his secret. Now just what is M. Fougeres to do?"

I paused. I did not quite know how to finish the story.

Just then the sunlight snapped on. The green of the quinquina glass vanished as queerly as it had arrived. Suddenly the air was fresh.

At that identical moment, the man in the black coat rose from his chair. He stood for a few seconds staring at the ground just in front of his table. Then he raised his hand quickly to his ear. A shot rang out. I saw the black revolver fall from his hand before he himself toppled stupidly over the table, off the table, and down onto the ground.

INTERPRETATION

Is this a trick ending? Write an interpretative essay focussed on this question. Be sure you refer to the fact of a narrator and the use of the quinquina glass.

AMBROSE BIERCE

An Occurrence at Owl Creek Bridge

A MAN stood upon a railroad bridge in northern Alabama, looking down into the swift water twenty feet below. The man's hands were behind his back, the wrists bound with a cord. A rope closely encircled his neck. It was attached to a stout cross-timber above his head and the slack fell to the level of his knees. Some loose boards laid upon the sleepers supporting the metals of the railway supplied a footing for him and his executioners—two private soldiers of the Federal army, directed by a sergeant who in civil life may have been a deputy sheriff. At a short remove upon the same temporary platform was an officer in the uniform of his rank, armed. He was a captain. A sentinel at each end of the bridge stood with his rifle in the position known as "support," that is to say, vertical in front of the left shoulder, the hammer resting on the forearm thrown straight across the chest—a formal and unnatural position, enforcing an erect carriage of the body. It did not appear to be the duty of these two men to know what was occurring at the center of the bridge; they merely blockaded the two ends of the foot planking that traversed it.

Beyond one of the sentinels nobody was in sight; the railroad ran straight away into a forest for a hundred yards, then, curving, was lost to view. Doubtless there was an outpost farther along. The other bank of the stream was open ground—a gentle acclivity topped with a stockade of vertical tree trunks, loopholed for rifles, with a single embrasure through which protruded the muzzle of a brass cannon commanding the bridge.

Midway of the slope between the bridge and fort were the spectators—a single company of infantry in line, at "parade rest," the butts of the rifles on the ground, the barrels inclining slightly backward against the right shoulder, the hands crossed upon the stock. A lieutenant stood at the right of the line, the point of his sword upon the ground, his left hand resting upon his right. Excepting the group of four at the center of the bridge, not a man moved. The company faced the bridge, staring stonily, motionless. The sentinels, facing the banks of the stream, might have been statues to adorn the bridge. The captain stood with folded arms, silent, observing the work of his subordinates, but making no sign. Death is a dignitary who when he comes announced is to be received with formal manifestations of respect, even by those most familiar with him. In the code of military etiquette silence and fixity are forms of deference.

The man who was engaged in being hanged was apparently about thirty-five years of age. He was a civilian, if one might judge from his habit, which was that of a planter. His features were good—a straight nose, firm mouth, broad forehead, from which his long, dark hair was combed straight back, falling behind his ears to the collar of his well-fitting frock coat. He wore a mustache and pointed beard, but no whiskers; his eyes were large and dark gray, and had a kindly expression which one would hardly have expected in one whose neck was in the hemp. Evidently this was no vulgar assassin. The liberal military code makes provision for hanging many kinds of persons, and gentlemen are not excluded.

The preparations being complete, the two private soldiers stepped aside and each drew away the plank upon which he had been standing. The sergeant turned to the captain, saluted and placed himself immediately behind that officer, who in turn moved apart one pace. These movements left the condemned man and the sergeant standing on the two ends of the same plank, which spanned three of the crossties of the bridge. The end upon which the civilian stood almost, but not quite, reached a fourth. This plank had been held in place by the weight of the captain; it was now held by that of the sergeant. At a signal from the former the latter would step aside, the plank would tilt and the condemned man go down between two ties. The arrangement commended itself to his judgment as simple and effective. His face had not been covered nor his eyes bandaged. He looked a moment at his "unsteadfast footing," then let his gaze wander to the swirling water of the stream racing madly beneath his feet. A piece of dancing driftwood caught his attention and his eyes followed it down the current. How slowly it appeared to move! What a sluggish stream!

He closed his eyes in order to fix his last thoughts upon his wife and children. The water, touched to gold by the early sun, the brooding mists under the banks at some distance down the stream, the fort, the soldiers, the piece of drift—all had distracted him. And now he became conscious of a new disturbance. Striking through the thought of his dear ones was a sound which he could neither ignore nor understand, a sharp, distinct, metallic percussion like the stroke of a blacksmith's hammer upon the anvil; it had the same ringing quality. He wondered what it was, and whether immeasurably distant or near by—it seemed both. Its recurrence was regular, but as slow as the tolling of a death knell. He awaited each stroke with impatience and—he knew not why—apprehension. The intervals of silence grew progressively longer; the delays became maddening. With their greater infrequency the sounds increased in strength and sharpness. They hurt his ear like the thrust of a knife; he feared he would shriek. What he heard was the ticking of his watch.

He unclosed his eyes and saw again the water below him. "If I could free my hands," he thought, "I might throw off the noose and spring into the stream. By diving I could evade the bullets and, swimming vigorously, reach the bank, take to the woods and get away home. My home, thank God, is as yet outside their lines; my wife and little ones are still beyond the invader's farthest advance."

As these thoughts, which have here to be set down in words, were flashed into the doomed man's brain rather than evolved from it the captain nodded to the sergeant. The sergeant stepped aside.

Peyton Farquhar was a well-to-do planter, of an old and highly respected Alabama family. Being a slave owner and like other slave owners a politician, he was naturally an original secessionist and ardently devoted to the Southern cause. Circumstances of an imperious nature, which it is unnecessary to relate here, had prevented him from taking service with the gallant army that had fought the disastrous campaigns ending with the fall of Corinth, and he chafed under the inglorious restraint, longing for the release of his energies, the larger life of the soldier, the opportunity for distinction. That opportunity, he felt, would come, as it comes to all in war time. Meanwhile he did what he could. No service was too humble for him to perform in aid of the South, no adventure too perilous for him to undertake if consistent with the character of a civilian who was at heart a soldier, and who in good faith and without too much qualification assented to at least a part of the frankly villainous dictum that all is fair in love and war.

One evening while Farquhar and his wife were sitting on a rustic bench near the entrance to his grounds, a gray-clad soldier rode up to the gate and asked for a drink of water. Mrs. Farquhar was only too happy to serve him with her own white hands. While she was fetching the water her husband approached the dusty horseman and inquired eagerly for news from the front.

"The Yanks are repairing the railroads," said the man, "and are getting ready for another advance. They have reached the Owl Creek bridge, put it in order and built a stockade on the north bank. The commandant has issued an order, which is posted everywhere, declaring that any civilian caught interfering with the railroad, its bridges, tunnels or trains will be summarily hanged. I saw the order."

"How far is it to the Owl Creek bridge?" Farquhar asked.

"About thirty miles."

"Is there no force on this side of the creek?"

"Only a picket post half a mile out, on the railroad, and a single sentinel at this end of the bridge."

"Suppose a man—a civilian and student of hanging—should elude the picket post and perhaps get the better of the sentinel," said Farquhar, smiling, "what could he accomplish?"

The soldier reflected. "I was there a month ago," he replied. "I observed that the flood of last winter had lodged a great quantity of driftwood against the wooden pier at this end of the bridge. It is now dry and would burn like tow."

The lady had now brought the water, which the soldier drank. He thanked her ceremoniously, bowed to her husband and rode away. An hour later, after nightfall, he re-passed the plantation, going northward in the direction from which he had come. He was a Federal scout.

As Peyton Farquhar fell straight downward through the bridge he lost consciousness and was as one already dead. From this state he was awakened—ages later, it seemed to him—by the pain of a sharp pressure up his throat, followed by a sense of suffocation. Keen, poignant agonies seemed to shoot from his neck downward through every fiber of his body and limbs. These pains appeared to flash along well-defined lines of ramification and to beat with an inconceivably rapid periodicity. They seemed like streams of pulsating fire heating him to an intolerable temperature. As to his head, he was conscious of nothing but a feeling of fullness—of congestion. These sensations were unaccompanied by thought. The intellectual part of his nature was already effaced; he had power only to feel, and feeling was torment. He was conscious of motion. Encompassed in a luminous cloud, of which he was now merely the fiery heart, without material substance, he swung through unthinkable arcs of oscillation, like a vast pendulum. Then all at once, with terrible suddenness, the light about him shot upward with the noise of a loud splash; a frightful roaring was in his ears, and all was cold and dark. The power of thought was restored; he knew that the rope had broken and he had fallen into the stream. There was no additional strangulation; the noose about his neck was already suffocating him and kept the water from his lungs. To die of hanging at the bottom of a river!—the idea seemed to him ludicrous. He opened his eyes in the darkness and saw above him a gleam of light, but how distant, how inaccessible! He was still sinking, for the light became fainter and fainter until it was a mere glimmer. Then it began to grow and brighten, and he knew that he was rising toward the surface—knew it with reluctance, for he was now very comfortable. "To be hanged and drowned," he thought, "that is not so bad; but I do not wish to be shot. No; I will not be shot; that is not fair."

He was not conscious of an effort, but a sharp pain in his wrist apprised him that he was trying to free his hands. He gave the struggle his attention, as an idler might observe the feat of a juggler, without interest in the outcome. What splendid effort! What magnificent, what superhuman strength! Ah, that was a fine endeavor! Bravo! The cord fell away; his arms parted and floated upward, the hands dimly seen on each side in the growing light. He watched them with a new interest as first one and then the other pounced upon the noose at his neck. They tore it away and thrust it fiercely aside, its undulations resembling those of a water snake. "Put it back, put it back!" He thought he shouted these words to his hands, for the undoing of the noose had been succeeded by the direst pang that he had yet experienced. His neck ached horribly; his brain was on fire; his heart, which had been fluttering faintly, gave a great leap, trying to force itself out at his mouth. His whole body was racked and wrenched with an insupportable anguish! But his disobedient hands gave no heed to the command. They beat the water vigorously with quick, downward strokes, forcing him to the surface. He felt his head emerge; his eyes were blinded by the sunlight; his chest expanded convulsively, and with a supreme and crowning agony his lungs engulfed a great draught of air, which instantly he expelled in a shriek!

He was now in full possession of his physical senses. They were, indeed, preternaturally keen and alert. Something in the awful disturbance of his organic system had so exalted and refined them that they made record of things never before perceived. He felt the ripples upon his face and heard their separate sounds as they struck. He looked at the forest on the bank of the stream, saw the individual trees, the leaves and the veining of each leaf—saw the very insects upon them: the locusts, the brilliant-bodied flies, the gray spiders stretching their webs from twig to twig. He noted the prismatic colors in all the dew-drops upon a million blades of grass. The humming of the gnats that danced above the eddies of the stream, the beating of the dragonflies' wings, the strokes of the water spiders' legs, like oars which had lifted their boat—all these made audible music. A fish slid along beneath his eyes and he heard the rush of its body parting the water.

He had come to the surface facing down the stream; in a moment the visible world seemed to wheel slowly round, himself the pivotal point, and he saw the bridge, the fort, the soldiers upon the bridge, the captain, the sergeant, the two privates, his executioners. They were in silhouette against the blue sky. They shouted and gesticulated, pointing at him. The captain had drawn his pistol, but did not fire; the others were unarmed. Their movements were grotesque and horrible, their forms gigantic.

Suddenly he heard a sharp report and something struck the water smartly within a few inches of his head, spattering his face with spray. He heard a second report, and saw one of the sentinels with his rifle at his shoulder, a light cloud of blue smoke rising from the muzzle. The man in the water saw the eye of the man on the bridge gazing into his own through the sights of the rifle. He observed that it was a gray eye and remembered having read that gray eyes were keenest, and that all famous marksmen had them. Nevertheless, this one had missed.

A counter-swirl had caught Farquhar and turned him half round; he was again looking into the forest on the bank opposite the fort. The sound of a clear, high voice in a monotonous singsong now rang out behind him and came across the water with a distinctness that pierced and subdued all other sounds, even the beating of the ripples in his ears. Although no soldier, he had frequented camps enough to know the dread significance of that deliberate, drawling, aspirated chant, the lieutenant on shore was taking a part in the morning's work. How coldly and pitilessly—with what an even, calm intonation, presaging, and enforcing tranquillity in the men—with what accurately measured intervals fell those cruel words:

"Attention, company! . . . Shoulder arms! . . . Ready! . . . Aim! . . . Fire!"

Farquhar dived—dived as deeply as he could. The water roared in his ears like the voice of Niagara, yet he heard the dulled thunder of the volley and, rising again toward the surface, met shining bits of metal, singularly flattened, oscillating slowly downward. Some of them touched him on the face and hands, then fell away, continuing their descent. One lodged between his collar and neck; it was uncomfortably warm and he snatched it out.

As he rose to the surface, gasping for breath, he saw that he had been a long time under water; he was perceptibly farther down stream—nearer to safety. The soldiers had almost finished reloading; the metal ramrods flashed all at once in the sunshine as they were drawn from the barrels, turned in the air, and thrust into their sockets. The two sentinels fired again, independently and ineffectually.

The hunted man saw all this over his shoulder; he was now swimming vigorously with the current. His brain was as energetic as his arms and legs; he thought with the rapidity of lightning.

"The officer," he reasoned, "will not make that martinet's error a second time. It is as easy to dodge a volley as a single shot. He has probably already given the command to fire at will. God help me, I cannot dodge them all!"

An appalling splash within two yards of him was followed by a loud, rushing sound, *diminuendo*, which seemed to travel back through the air to the fort and died in an explosion which stirred the very river to its deeps! A rising sheet of water curved over him, fell down upon him, blinded him, strangled him! The cannon had taken a hand in the game. As he shook his head free from the commotion of the smitten water he heard the deflected shot humming through the air ahead, and in an instant it was cracking and smashing the branches in the forest beyond.

"They will not do that again," he thought; "the next time they will use a charge of grape. I must keep my eye upon the gun; the smoke will apprise me—the report arrives too late; it lags behind the missile. That is a good gun."

Suddenly he felt himself whirled round and round—spinning like a top. The water, the banks, the forests, the now distant bridge, fort and men —all were commingled and blurred. Objects were represented by their colors only; circular horizontal streaks of color—that was all he saw. He had been caught in a vortex and was being whirled on with a velocity of advance and gyration that made him giddy and sick. In a few moments he was flung upon the gravel at the foot of the left bank of the stream— the southern bank—and behind a projecting point which concealed him from his enemies. The sudden arrest of his motion, the abrasion of one of his hands on the gravel, restored him, and he wept with delight. He dug his fingers into the sand, threw it over himself in handfuls and audibly blessed it. It looked like diamonds, rubies, emeralds; he could think of nothing beautiful which it did not resemble. The trees upon the bank were giant garden plants; he noted a definite order in their arrangement, in-haled the fragrance of their blooms. A strange, roseate light shone through the spaces among their trunks and the wind made in their branches the music of Aeolian harps. He had no wish to perfect his escape—was content to remain in that enchanting spot until retaken.

A whiz and rattle of grapeshot among the branches high above his head roused him from his dream. The baffled cannoneer had fired him a random farewell. He sprang to his feet, rushed up the sloping bank, and plunged into the forest.

All that day he traveled, laying his course by the rounding sun. The forest seemed interminable; nowhere did he discover a break in it, not even a woodman's road. He had not known that he lived in so wild a region. There was something uncanny in the revelation.

By nightfall he was fatigued, footsore, famishing. The thought of his wife and children urged him on. At last he found a road which led him in what he knew to be the right direction. It was as wide and straight as a city street, yet it seemed untraveled. No fields bordered it, no dwelling any-where. Not so much as the barking of a dog suggested human habitation. The black bodies of the trees forced a straight wall on both sides, termi-nating on the horizon in a point, like a diagram in a lesson in perspective. Overhead, as he looked up through this rift in the wood, shone great golden stars looking unfamiliar and grouped in strange constellations. He was sure they were arranged in some order which had a secret and malign sig-

nificance. The wood on either side was full of singular noises, among which
—once, twice, and again—he distinctly heard whispers in an unknown
tongue.

His neck was in pain and lifting his hand to it he found it horribly
swollen. He knew that it had a circle of black where the rope had bruised
it. His eyes felt congested; he could no longer close them. His tongue was
swollen with thirst; he relieved its fever by thrusting it forward from between his teeth into the cold air. How softly the turf had carpeted the untraveled avenue—he could no longer feel the roadway beneath his feet!

Doubtless, despite his suffering, he had fallen asleep while walking,
for now he sees another scene—perhaps he has merely recovered from a
delirium. He stands at the gate of his own home. All is as he left it, and
all bright and beautiful in the morning sunshine. He must have traveled
the entire night. As he pushes open the gate and passes up the wide white
walk, he sees a flutter of female garments; his wife, looking fresh and cool
and sweet, steps down from the veranda to meet him. At the bottom of
the steps she stands waiting, with a smile of ineffable joy, an attitude of
matchless grace and dignity. Ah, how beautiful she is! He springs forward
with extended arms. As he is about to clasp her he feels a stunning blow
upon the back of the neck; a blinding white light blazes all about him with
a sound like the shock of a cannon—then all is darkness and silence!

Peyton Farquhar was dead; his body, with a broken neck, swung
gently from side to side beneath the timbers of the Owl Creek bridge.

INTERPRETATION

This story, like "The Necklace" and "The Furnished Room," involves a surprise ending, an ironical turn. The basic question, then, which
the story raises is this: Is the surprise ending justified; is it validated by the
body of the story; is it, in other words, a mere trick, or is it expressive and
functional?

Perhaps the best way to clear the ground for a consideration of this
basic question is to raise another question which no doubt will occur to
many readers of the story. Is it possible for a man in the last moment of
his life to have a vision of the sort which Farquhar has as he falls from the
bridge? Many people may be inclined to judge the story in terms of their
acceptance or rejection of the psychological realism of this incident. But
is it possible to have absolutely convincing evidence on this point? Isn't
the fact of the vision something which, in itself, can be accepted without
too much strain on the reader's credulity? But there is a much more important consideration to be taken into account. Even if we could arrive at
a completely satisfying decision about the psychological realism of the
incident, would this fact actually determine the nature of our judgment
concerning the story? For reasons to be suggested below, it would not

determine our judgment, and therefore preoccupation with this question is likely to prove a red herring—is likely to distract us from the real problem.

Suppose that we assume for the moment that the incident is psychologically valid; there remain these questions to be answered:

1. Why does the author withhold from the reader the knowledge that the dying man's vision is merely a vision?

2. Is any revelation of character accomplished thereby?

3. Does the withholding of this information throw any light on the development of a theme for the story?

4. There is an irony generated by the end of the story, but is it a meaningful irony?

What we are leading up to by means of these questions is this:

Fiction is concerned with people, and one of the interests we take in it arises from the presentation of human character and human experience as merely human. Both the common and the uncommon human character or experience interest us, the common because we share in it, and the uncommon because it wakes us to marvel at new possibilities. But it is a great—and not uncommon—error to equate the presentation of character as such, or experience as such, with the specific meaning of fiction. Fiction, as we have tried to indicate in our first section, involves a theme, an idea, an interpretation, an attitude toward life developed and embodied in the piece of fiction. Directly or indirectly, through the experience of the characters in the piece of fiction, an evaluation is made—an evaluation which is assumed to have some claim to a general validity.

The plot that depends on some peculiarity of human psychology—as does "An Occurrence at Owl Creek Bridge"—may give as a shock of surprise, but it does not carry a fictional meaning. The peculiar quirk of psychology—the "case study"—must also involve some significant human evaluation, some broadening or deepening of our human attitudes, if it is to be acceptable as fiction. Fiction involves all kinds of human characters and human experiences, common and uncommon, but it is concerned to do more than make a clinical report, medical or psychological. We must keep this firmly in mind.

EUDORA WELTY

A Piece of News

SHE had been out in the rain. She stood in front of the cabin fireplace, her legs wide apart, bending over, shaking her wet yellow head crossly, like a cat reproaching itself for not knowing better. She was talking to herself—only a small fluttering sound, hard to lay hold of in the sparsity of the room.

"The pouring-down rain, the pouring-down rain"—was that what she was saying over and over, like a song? She stood turning in little quarter turns to dry herself, her head bent forward and the yellow hair hanging out streaming and tangled. She was holding her skirt primly out to draw the warmth in.

Then, quite rosy, she walked over to the table and picked up a little bundle. It was a sack of coffee, marked "sample" in red letters, which she unwrapped from a wet newspaper. But she handled it tenderly.

"Why, how come he wrapped it in a newspaper!" she said, catching her breath, looking from one hand to the other. She must have been lonesome and slow all her life, the way things would take her by surprise.

She set the coffee on the table, just in the center. Then she dragged the newspaper by one corner in a dreamy walk across the floor, spread it all out, and lay down full length on top of it in front of the fire. Her little song about the rain, her cries of surprise, had been only a preliminary, only playful pouting with which she amused herself when she was alone. She was pleased with herself now. As she sprawled close to the fire, her hair began to slide out of its damp tangles and hung all displayed down her back like a piece of bargain silk. She closed her eyes. Her mouth fell into a deepness, into a look of unconscious cunning. Yet in her very stillness and pleasure she seemed to be hiding there, all alone. And at moments when the fire stirred and tumbled in the grate, she would tremble, and her hand would start out as if in impatience or despair.

Presently she stirred and reached under her back for the newspaper. Then she squatted there, touching the printed page as if it were fragile. She did not merely look at it—she watched it, as if it were unpredictable, like a young girl watching a baby. The paper was still wet in places where her body had lain. Crouching tensely and patting the creases away with small cracked red fingers, she frowned now and then at the blotched drawing of something and big letters that spelled a word underneath. Her lips trembled, as if looking and spelling so slowly had stirred her heart.

All at once she laughed.

She looked up.

"Ruby Fisher!" she whispered.

An expression of utter timidity came over her flat blue eyes and her soft mouth. Then a look of fright. She stared about. . . . What eye in the world did she feel looking in on her? She pulled her dress down tightly and began to spell through a dozen words in the newspaper.

The little item said:

"Mrs. Ruby Fisher had the misfortune to be shot in the leg by her husband this week."

As she passed from one word to the next she only whispered; she left the long word, "misfortune," until the last, and came back to it, then she said it all over out loud, like conversation.

"That's me," she said softly, with deference, very formally.

The fire slipped and suddenly roared in the house already deafening with the rain which beat upon the roof and hung full of lightning and thunder outside.

"You Clyde!" screamed Ruby Fisher at last, jumping to her feet. "Where are you, Clyde Fisher?"

She ran straight to the door and pulled it open. A shudder of cold brushed over her in the heat, and she seemed striped with anger and bewilderment. There was a flash of lightning, and she stood waiting, as if she half thought that would bring him in, a gun leveled in his hands.

She said nothing more and, backing against the door, pushed it closed with her hip. Her anger passed like a remote flare of elation. Neatly avoiding the table where the bag of coffee stood, she began to walk nervously about the room, as if a teasing indecision, an untouched mystery, led her by the hand. There was one window, and she paused now and then, waiting, looking out at the rain. When she was still, there was a passivity about her, or a deception of passivity, that was not really passive at all. There was something in her that never stopped.

At last she flung herself onto the floor, back across the newspaper, and looked at length into the fire. It might have been a mirror in the cabin, into which she could look deeper and deeper as she pulled her fingers through her hair, trying to see herself and Clyde coming up behind her.

"Clyde?"

But of course her husband, Clyde, was still in the woods. He kept a thick brushwood roof over his whisky still, and he was mortally afraid of lightning like this, and would never go out in it for anything.

And then, almost in amazement, she began to comprehend her predicament: it was unlike Clyde to take up a gun and shoot her.

She bowed her head toward the heat, onto her rosy arms, and began to talk and talk to herself. She grew voluble. Even if he heard about the coffee man, with a Pontiac car, she did not think he would shoot her. When Clyde would make her blue, she would go out onto the road, some car would slow down, and if it had a Tennessee license, the lucky kind, the chances were that she would spend the afternoon in the shed of the empty gin. (Here she rolled her head about on her arms and stretched her legs tiredly behind her, like a cat.) And if Clyde got word, he would slap her. But the account in the paper was wrong. Clyde had never shot her, even once. There had been a mistake made.

A spark flew out and nearly caught the paper on fire. Almost in fright she beat it out with her fingers. Then she murmured and lay back more firmly upon the pages.

There she stretched, growing warmer and warmer, sleepier and sleepier. She began to wonder out loud how it would be if Clyde shot her in the leg. . . . If he were truly angry, might he shoot her through the heart?

At once she was imagining herself dying. She would have a nightgown to lie in, and a bullet in her heart. Anyone could tell, to see her lying there with that deep expression about her mouth, how strange and terrible that would be. Underneath a brand-new nightgown her heart would be hurting with every beat, many times more than her toughened skin when Clyde slapped at her. Ruby began to cry softly, the way she would be crying from the extremity of pain; tears would run down in a little stream over the quilt. Clyde would be standing there above her, as he once looked, with his wild black hair hanging to his shoulders. He used to be very handsome and strong!

He would say, "Ruby, I done this to you."

She would say—only a whisper—"That is the truth, Clyde—you done this to me."

Then she would die; her life would stop right there.

She lay silently for a moment, composing her face into a look which would be beautiful, desirable, and dead.

Clyde would have to buy her a dress to bury her in. He would have to dig a deep hole behind the house, under the cedar, a grave. He would have to nail her up a pine coffin and lay her inside. Then he would have to carry her to the grave, lay her down and cover her up. All the time he would be wild, shouting, and all distracted, to think he could never touch her one more time.

She moved slightly, and her eyes turned toward the window. The white rain splashed down. She could hardly breathe, for thinking that this was the way it was to fall on her grave, where Clyde would come and stand, looking down in the tears of some repentance.

A whole tree of lightning stood in the sky. She kept looking out the window, suffused with the warmth from the fire and with the pity and beauty and power of her death. The thunder rolled.

Then Clyde was standing there, with dark streams flowing over the floor where he had walked. He poked at Ruby with the butt of his gun, as if she were asleep.

"What's keepin' supper?" he growled.

She jumped up and darted away from him. Then, quicker than lightning, she put away the paper. The room was dark, except for the firelight. From the long shadow of his steamy presence she spoke to him glibly and lighted the lamp.

He stood there with a stunned, yet rather good-humored look of delay and patience in his face, and kept on standing there. He stamped his mud-red boots, and his enormous hands seemed weighted with the rain that fell from him and dripped down the barrel of the gun. Presently he sat down with dignity in the chair at the table, making a little tumult of his rightful wetness and hunger. Small streams began to flow from him everywhere.

Ruby was going through the preparations for the meal gently. She stood almost on tiptoe in her bare, warm feet. Once as she knelt at the safe, getting out the biscuits, she saw Clyde looking at her and she smiled and bent her head tenderly. There was some way she began to move her arms that was mysteriously sweet and yet abrupt and tentative, a delicate and vulnerable manner, as though her breasts gave her pain. She made many unnecessary trips back and forth across the floor, circling Clyde where he sat in his steamy silence, a knife and fork in his fists.

"Well, where you been, anyway?" he grumbled at last, as she set the first dish on the table.

"Nowheres special."

"Don't you talk back to me. You been hitchhikin' again, ain't you?" He almost chuckled.

She gave him a quick look straight into his eyes. She had not even heard him. She was filled with happiness. Her hand trembled when she poured the coffee. Some of it splashed on his wrist.

At that he let his hand drop heavily down upon the table and made the plates jump.

"Some day I'm goin' to smack the livin' devil outa you," he said.

Ruby dodged mechanically. She let him eat. Then, when he had crossed his knife and fork over his plate, she brought him the newspaper. Again she looked at him in delight. It excited her even to touch the paper with her hand, to hear its quiet secret noise when she carried it, the rustle of surprise.

"A newspaper!" Clyde snatched it roughly and with a grabbing disparagement. "Where'd you git that? Hussy."

"Look at this-here," said Ruby in her small singsong voice. She opened the paper while he held it and pointed gravely to the paragraph.

Reluctantly, Clyde began to read it. She watched his damp bald head slowly bend and turn.

Then he made a sound in his throat and said, "It's a lie."

"That's what's in the newspaper about me," said Ruby, standing up straight. She took up his plate and gave him that look of joy.

He put his big crooked finger on the paragraph and poked at it.

"Well, I'd just like to see the place I shot you!" he cried explosively. He looked up, his face blank and bold.

But she drew herself in, still holding the empty plate, faced him straightened and hard, and they looked at each other. The moment filled full with their helplessness. Slowly they both flushed, as though with a double shame and a double pleasure. It was as though Clyde might really have killed Ruby, and as though Ruby might really have been dead at his hand. Rare and wavering, some possibility stood timidly like a stranger between them and made them hang their heads.

Then Clyde walked over in his water-soaked boots and laid the paper on the dying fire. It floated there a moment and then burst into flame. They stood still and watched it burn. The whole room was bright.

"Look," said Clyde suddenly. "It's a Tennessee paper. See 'Tennessee'? That wasn't none of you it wrote about." He laughed, to show that he had been right all the time.

"It was Ruby Fisher!" cried Ruby. "My name is Ruby Fisher!" she declared passionately to Clyde.

"Oho, it was another Ruby Fisher—in Tennessee," cried her husband. "Fool me, huh? Where'd you get that paper?" He spanked her good-humoredly across her backside.

Ruby folded her still trembling hands into her skirt. She stood stooping by the window until everything, outside and in, was quieted before she went to her supper.

It was dark and vague outside. The storm had rolled away to faintness like a wagon crossing a bridge.

INTERPRETATION

At first glance this story may seem to be no story at all—merely a trivial incident, which is meaningless except as it may provoke our amusement: an all but illiterate girl happens, quite by accident, to come upon a newspaper story in which a girl with the same name as hers is shot by her husband. She goes off into a reverie in which she imagines that she has been shot by her own husband—imagines that she is really the girl of the newspaper story. This reverie is interrupted by the return of her husband, who reads the account, is for his own part momentarily shocked by the coincidence of names, but with an overriding common sense, throws the newspaper into the fire, and dismisses the incident.

Even the reader who tries to deal with the story sympathetically, who knows, for instance, the authority which the written word carries for many simple people, and who is willing to believe that the coincidence of names might really provoke in the simple girl the action ascribed to her in this story—even such a reader might feel that the story was finally pointless. That is, even if we feel that the motivation of the characters in the story is sound, we still may not be convinced that the story has a "meaning" apart from its humorous commentary on the psychology of simple and primitive folk.

The story does have a meaning, but the author has been careful to dramatize it for us in terms of the action. Perhaps the most fruitful approach to a discussion of the meaning will take into account the dramatic, though gradual, presentation of this meaning.

In the first place, the girl and her husband, Ruby and Clyde, are isolated from the world which we know. Clyde Fisher keeps a still. He is an outlaw, and is properly suspicious of strangers. He and his wife live in a world which reverses most of the conventions of the ordinary world: it is a world in which, for example, guns are common and newspapers uncommon—mention in newspapers, least common of all.

Ruby, as the story opens, has just made a visit to that outside world, to get the sack of coffee. She comes back with the chance-acquired newspaper. Now that she is back inside her own house, the storm builds up the sense of her isolation. The storm has soaked her, and thus accounts for her idling over the newspaper before the fire; with its lightning and thunder, the storm supplies a background for the excited imaginings that possess her. But Miss Welty's use of the natural background is modest, probable, and subdued: the background remains background, yet contributes to the story.

The background helps to create the atmosphere of the story, by which we mean the general feeling that seems inherent in the materials themselves or in the way they are treated. For instance, in Poe's celebrated story, "The Fall of the House of Usher," we speak of the atmosphere of horror, as we may speak of the sunny, cheerful atmosphere of another story. Our general words for describing the atmosphere of a story are relatively few, and often metaphorical, as though we had to appeal to metaphor to make up for the poverty of the language available to us for this purpose. We say horrible, terrible, gay, sunny, cheerful, depressing, morbid, dank, dreamy, mysterious, cold, and so on, but we recognize how inadequate such terms are to describe and discriminate among the great variety and the subtle variations of atmosphere which we find in fiction. The good story is apt to carry with it a certain "feel" which eludes our general descriptions but which we recognize as being essential and meaningful in the story. It is the atmosphere, we may say metaphorically, in which the story can breathe and live.

Though background, feeling, and atmosphere are important in varying degrees in all fiction (no story can exist in a vacuum) this element is more important in some stories than others. In "A Piece of News," we realize that the world in which Ruby Fisher lives is, as we have said, immediately important for the story—much more immediately important, for instance, than the world in which Michael and Frances encounter their dilemma in "The Girls in Their Summer Dresses." Factually, as we have said, it is a world where the newspaper has some magical significance. It is an isolated world, isolated by Clyde's outlawry, by ignorance, by poverty, by distance from the ordinary world. It is also a world in which Ruby moves in a dream divorced from ordinary reality, from ordinary moral standards, locked in her loneliness, humming her little songs to herself, in the monotony of her life breaking out, now and then, to the highway and the sordid adventures of the gin house, or into her dreamy musings, both the adventures of the gin house and those of the musings being somehow innocent, or merely childish—as even Clyde, who might slap her good and hard, but would never shoot her, instinctively recognizes. It is a world of dreaminess, of the mysterious confusions of dreams. How does the writer create this atmosphere for us?

The writer does, as a matter of fact, give us the words *dreamy, mystery, mysteriously*. A cruder writer might have insisted on such words, and have exhorted us, by the their use, to notice and appreciate the effect being created. But here the words are casually absorbed into the body of the story. Ruby drags the newspaper "by one corner in a dreamy walk across the floor," and the dreaminess appears as natural to the specific act, the childish handling of the newspaper, the drifting aimlessness of the walk, and not as a direct comment on the atmosphere. It does, of course, do its work in helping to create the atmosphere, but primarily because it is an accurate description of the act, and not by definition of the atmosphere as such.

To take another example, later in the story, after Clyde has come home and Ruby is getting supper ready, we find the sentence: "There was some way she began to move her arms that was mysteriously sweet and yet abrupt and tentative, a delicate and vulnerable manner, as though her breasts gave her pain." A mysterious thing is indeed happening here: we may say that the daydream Ruby has had of herself as caught in a violent, dramatic, and pitifully sweet experience now overlaps back on real life and she feels the ordinary events and her old relation with Clyde touched by sweetness and romance. Because of the daydream, actuality has become mysteriously rich, full, and sweet. But here again we see that the writer has used the general word as tied to a specific moment; in the end it may also work toward a comment and an interpretation, but it does not come directly to us at that level.

We have seen that the words generally descriptive of the atmosphere are absorbed into the story itself. We could, in fact, dispense entirely with them, so strongly and subtly has the writer created her atmosphere. The girl's talking to herself with the little rhythmic sing-song, her shaking her yellow wet hair crossly "like a cat reproaching itself for not knowing better" than to get wet, her "playful pouting with which she amused herself when . . . alone," the "deepness" of her mouth, the impersonal crashes and flashes of the storm and the rain "hung full of lightning and thunder," the cat-like stretching as she thinks of the gin house, her sweet, sensual self-pitying sleepiness as she thinks of being shot and dying and of Clyde weeping over her grave in the rain—all these things *are* the world, are the atmosphere, of the story. We don't need to describe it, for it exists and does its work upon us by the vividness with which the writer has realized them. And so we begin to understand that that story itself, the events, the very plot, could not exist except in this world, in this atmosphere, for, as we shall see, the story is about an adventure in dream and the return to reality. That is the plot.

To return to the sequence of events in the story itself, we find that Ruby, who "must have been lonesome and slow all her life," is first surprised when she sees her name, surprised and even delighted as a child is delighted. But her next reaction is fright: "What eye in the world did she feel looking in on her?" The isolation has been penetrated. She "pulled her dress down tightly"—as if her modesty were being violated.

The reader soon guesses the common-sense explanation of the matter —the explanation which after a few moments occurs to the husband Clyde when he comes in: the newspaper is referring to another Mrs. Ruby Fisher. But this is not the explanation which occurs in her bewilderment to the girl. The author, however, is not anxious to convince us of the strained and improbable psychology involved in the girl's belief that the newspaper account is true. The girl knows really that it is not true. She even reasons out to herself the impossibility of its being true; Clyde wouldn't do that. Indeed, there had been occasions which might have provoked a husband to shoot his wife, but Clyde had never shot her. Even if she told him about the coffee salesman, Clyde would only strike her—he wouldn't shoot her. But the line which the author has Ruby take in arguing against the impossibility of the action suggests another motive which works against her making a realistic and common-sense dismissal of the newspaper story. It is exciting to imagine herself shot by Clyde—to imagine a Clyde who would shoot her. And after he had shot her, what would she be like, and what would he say, and do? The coincidence of names has stirred her imagination. It allows her—indeed, has seemed to force upon her—a new focus of attention in terms of which both she and Clyde take on new perspectives to each other. By being seen in a new role—reading about "herself" in the newspaper—she takes on the new role; she becomes somehow a stranger to her husband. Even her own body becomes something strange and new to her: "There was some way she began to move her arms that was mysteriously sweet and yet abrupt and tentative. . . ." Throughout the reverie she thinks of herself in a nightgown ("She would have a nightgown to lie in . . .") like a bride.

This sense of illumination in which old and familiar things, by acquiring an altered focus, become mysterious and strange, is a recurrent theme in fiction as it is a basic fact in human existence. A shocking and surprising incident, an emotional crisis, may very well force on us such an alteration of focus. For a person who lives in a surburban world, say, where newspapers and electrical toastmakers are familiar, and guns and whisky stills unfamiliar, such an alteration would hardly be effected by the coincidence of names in a scrap of newspaper. But the fact of the experience is universal. In this story, it comes about in terms consonant with the characters depicted in the story and with their situation, and the accident which brings it about for them is a—to us, ironically—trivial incident.

Ruby's reverie is broken by Clyde's prodding her with the gun. His act is the impingement of common sense, the return to reality. But, ironically, the fact that Clyde stands there with the gun in his hand ties the reverie to the reality. For a moment, to the girl, it almost seems that the imagined situation will become real.

We have seen how concretely—and delicately—the theme is developed. Equally noteworthy is the way the author has played down the ending of the story. The effect of the revelation on both Clyde and Ruby is given quietly, almost by suggestion.

1. Analyze the character of Clyde in relation to the ending of the story.

2. How is coincidence used in this story: is it used to set up the problem of the story or to solve the problem of the story?

3. In this story there is a good deal of interpenetration of exposition and complication. Indicate some of this. Has this fluid blurring of the line between exposition and complication any relation to the general atmosphere of the story and the character of Ruby?

4. Compare the different ways used to create atmosphere here with those used in "The Furnished Room." Is there, furthermore, any difference in the purposes for which the atmosphere is used?

5. In the middle of "A Piece of News" (the paragraph beginning, "She said nothing more, and backing against the door . . . ."), we find the third use of a general word descriptive of the atmosphere of the story, in the sentence: "Neatly avoiding the table where the bag of coffee stood, she began to walk nervously about the room, as if a teasing indecision, an untouched mystery, led her by the hand." Is this instance as thoroughly

"absorbed" (see pp. 110–111) as the other two discussed. Do you consider this instance justifiable?

6. Suppose John Collier had written a story about Ruby and the newspaper. On the basis of his story "De Mortuis," how do you imagine he might have ended it? What differences, then, would you expect in the atmosphere of the story?

7. "The Secret Life of Walter Mitty" is about the relation of dream and reality. What differences do you detect between that story and this. Both have comic, or humorous, elements, but is there a difference between them?

RAY BRADBURY

I See You Never

THE soft knock came at the kitchen door, and when Mrs. O'Brian opened it, there on the back porch were her best tenant, Mr. Ramirez, and two police officers, one on each side of him. Mr. Ramirez just stood there, walled in and small.

"Why, Mr. Ramirez!" said Mrs. O'Brian.

Mr. Ramirez was overcome. He did not seem to have words to explain.

He had arrived at Mrs. O'Brian's rooming house more than two years earlier and had lived there ever since. He had come by bus from Mexico City to San Diego and had then gone up to Los Angeles. There he had found the clean little room, with glossy blue linoleum, and pictures and calendars on the flowered walls, and Mrs. O'Brian as the strict but kindly landlady. During the war he had worked at the airplane factory and made parts for the planes that flew off somewhere, and even now, after the war, he still held his job. From the first he had made big money. He saved some of it, and he got drunk only once a week—a privilege that, to Mrs. O'Brian's way of thinking, every good workingman deserved, unquestioned and unreprimanded.

Inside Mrs. O'Brian's kitchen, pies were baking in the oven. Soon the pies would come out with complexions like Mr. Ramirez'—brown and shiny and crisp, with slits in them for the air almost like the slits of Mr. Ramirez' dark eyes. The kitchen smelled good. The policemen leaned forward, lured by the odor. Mr. Ramirez gazed at his feet, as if they had carried him into all this trouble.

"What happened, Mr. Ramirez?" asked Mrs. O'Brian.

Behind Mrs. O'Brian, as he lifted his eyes, Mr. Ramirez saw the long table laid with clean white linen and set with a platter, cool, shining glasses, a water pitcher with ice cubes floating inside it, a bowl of fresh potato salad and one of bananas and oranges, cubed and sugared. At this table sat Mrs. O'Brian's children—her three grown sons, eating and conversing, and her two younger daughters, who were staring at the policemen as they ate.

"I have been here thirty months," said Mr. Ramirez quietly, looking at Mrs. O'Brian's plump hands.

"That's six months too long," said one policeman. "He only had a temporary visa. We've just got around to looking for him."

Soon after Mr. Ramirez had arrived he bought a radio for his little room; evenings, he turned it up very loud and enjoyed it. And he bought a wrist watch and enjoyed that too. And on many nights he had walked silent streets and seen the bright clothes in the windows and bought some of them, and he had seen the jewels and bought some of them for his few lady friends. And he had gone to pictures shows five nights a week for a while. Then, also, he had ridden the streetcars—all night some nights— smelling the electricity, his dark eyes moving over the advertisements, feeling the wheels rumble under him, watching the little sleeping houses and big hotels slip by. Besides that, he had gone to large restaurants, where he had eaten many-course dinners, and to the opera and the theater. And he had bought a car, which later, when he forgot to pay for it, the dealer had driven off angrily from in front of the rooming house.

"So here I am," said Mr. Ramirez now, "to tell you I must give up my room, Mrs. O'Brian. I come to get my baggage and clothes and go with these men."

"Back to Mexico?"

"Yes. To Lagos. That is a little town north of Mexico City."

"I'm sorry, Mr. Ramirez."

"I'm packed," said Mr. Ramirez hoarsely, blinking his dark eyes rapidly and moving his hands helplessly before him. The policemen did not touch him. There was no necessity for that.

"Here is the key, Mrs. O'Brian," Mr. Ramirez said. "I have my bag already."

Mrs. O'Brian, for the first time, noticed a suitcase standing behind him on the porch.

Mr. Ramirez looked in again at the huge kitchen, at the bright silver cutlery and the young people eating and the shining waxed floor. He turned and looked for a long moment at the apartment house next door, rising up three stories, high and beautiful. He looked at the balconies and fire escapes and back-porch stairs, at the lines of laundry snapping in the wind.

"You've been a good tenant," said Mrs. O'Brian.

"Thank you, thank you, Mrs. O'Brian," he said softly. He closed his eyes.

Mrs. O'Brian stood holding the door half open. One of her sons, behind her, said that her dinner was getting cold, but she shook her head at him and turned back to Mr. Ramirez. She remembered a visit she had once made to some Mexican border towns—the hot days, the endless crickets leaping and falling or lying dead and brittle like the small cigars in the shopwindows, and the canals taking river water out to the farms, the dirt roads, the scorched landscape. She remembered the silent towns, the warm beer, the hot, thick foods each day. She remembered the slow, dragging horses and the parched jack rabbits on the road. She remembered the iron mountains and the dusty valleys and the ocean beaches that spread hundreds of miles with no sound but the waves—no cars, no buildings, nothing.

"I'm sure sorry, Mr. Ramirez," she said.

"I don't want to go back, Mrs. O'Brian," he said weakly. "I like it here, I want to stay here. I've worked, I've got money. I look all right, don't I? And I don't want to go back!"

"I'm sorry, Mr. Ramirez," she said. "I wish there was something I could do."

"Mrs. O'Brian!" he cried suddenly, tears rolling out from under his eyelids. He reached out his hands and took her hand fervently, shaking it, wringing it, holding to it. "Mrs. O'Brian, I see you never, I see you never!"

The policemen smiled at this, but Mr. Ramirez did not notice it, and they stopped smiling very soon.

"Good-by, Mrs. O'Brian. You have been good to me. Oh, good-by, Mrs. O'Brian. I see you never!"

The policemen waited for Mr. Ramirez to turn, pick up his suitcase, and walk away. Then they followed him, tipping their caps to Mrs. O'Brian. She watched them go down the porch steps. Then she shut the door quietly and went slowly back to her chair at the table. She pulled the chair out and sat down. She picked up the shining knife and fork and started once more upon her steak.

"Hurry up, Mom," said one of the sons. "It'll be cold."

Mrs. O'Brian took one bite and chewed on it for a long, slow time; then she stared at the closed door. She laid down her knife and fork.

"What's wrong, Ma?" asked her son.

"I just realized," said Mrs. O'Brian—she put her hand to her face—"I'll never see Mr. Ramirez again."

INTERPRETATION

1. This story, like "A Piece of News," has very little action, only a minimal plot. In fact, some readers might argue that it is not a story at all, a mere episode. One way to think of this problem would be to ask what is the point, the theme? Can you state it?

In thinking about this you should remember that "what happens" in a story may be only the growth of an awareness—a realization. It does not have to be an event out in the physical world. It is also well to remember that the awareness may be what comes both to a person in the story and to the reader, or merely to the reader, who, to speak metaphorically, sees over and beyond the characters in the story. For example, we see more of the meaning of Dravot's experience than does Peachey, who tells about it. (But do we see more than the newspaperman who tells about Peachey?) In the present story, "I See You Never," Mrs. O'Brian "realizes" something —and through her realization we come to the meaning of the story.

2. Let us suppose that Mrs. O'Brian were alone in her kitchen when the police bring Mr. Ramirez, and that as soon as he says, "I see you never," she bursts into tears and stands there watching him go away with the policemen. What difference would that make for the story? Would it make the story less of a story? Would there be less sense of conflict? If so, what is the nature of the conflict in the present version?

3. What kind of pattern, if any, do you detect in the complication here?

RING LARDNER

Haircut

I GOT another barber that comes over from Carterville and helps me out Saturdays, but the rest of the time I can get along all right alone. You can see for yourself that this ain't no New York City and besides that, the most of the boys works all day and don't have no leisure to drop in here and get themselves prettied up.

You're a newcomer, ain't you? I thought I hadn't seen you round before. I hope you like it good enough to stay. As I say, we ain't no New York City or Chicago, but we have pretty good times. Not as good, though, since Jim Kendall got killed. When he was alive, him and Hod Meyers used to keep this town in an uproar. I bet they was more laughin' done here than any town its size in America.

Jim was comical, and Hod was pretty near a match for him. Since Jim's gone, Hod tries to hold his end up just the same as ever, but it's tough goin' when you ain't got nobody to kind of work with.

They used to be plenty fun in here Saturdays. This place is jam-packed Saturdays, from four o'clock on. Jim and Hod would show up right after their supper round six o'clock. Jim would set himself down in that big chair, nearest the blue spitoon. Whoever had been settin' in that chair, why, they'd get up when Jim come in and give it to him.

You'd of thought it was a reserved seat like they have sometimes in a theaytre. Hod would generally always stand or walk up and down or some Saturdays, of course, he'd be settin' in this chair part of the time, gettin' a haircut.

Well, Jim would set there a w'ile without openin' his mouth only to spit, and then finally he'd say to me, "Whitey,"—my right name, that is, my right first name, is Dick, but everybody round here calls me Whitey— Jim would say, "Whitey, your nose looks like a rosebud tonight. You must of been drinkin' some of your aw de cologne."

So I'd say, "No, Jim, but you look like you'd been drinkin' somethin' of that kind or somethin' worse."

Jim would have to laugh at that, but then he'd speak up and say, "No, I ain't had nothin' to drink, but that ain't sayin' I wouldn't like somethin'. I wouldn't even mind if it was wood alcohol."

Then Hod Meyers would say, "Neither would your wife." That would set everybody to laughin' because Jim and his wife wasn't on very good terms. She'd of divorced him only they wasn't no chance to get alimony and she didn't have no way to take care of herself and the kids. She couldn't never understand Jim. He *was* kind of rough, but a good fella at heart.

Him and Hod had all kinds of sport with Milt Sheppard. I don't suppose you've seen Milt. Well, he's got an Adam's apple that looks more like a mushmelon. So I'd been shavin' Milt and when I'd start to shave down here on his neck, Hod would holler, "Hey, Whitey, wait a minute! Before you cut into it, let's make up a pool and see who can guess closest to the number of seeds."

And Jim would say, "If Milt hadn't of been so hoggish, he'd of ordered a half a cantaloupe instead of a whole one and it might not of stuck in his throat."

All the boys would roar at this and Milt himself would force a smile, though the joke was on him. Jim certainly was a card!

There's his shavin' mug, setting on the shelf, right next to Charley Vail's. "Charles M. Vail." That's the druggist. He comes in regular for his shave three times a week. And Jim's is the cup next to Charley's. "James H. Kendall." Jim won't need no shavin' mug no more, but I'll leave it there just the same for old time's sake. Jim certainly was a character!

Years ago, Jim used to travel for a canned goods concern over in Carterville. They sold canned goods. Jim had the whole northern half of the State and was on the road five days out of every week. He'd drop in here Saturdays and tell his experiences for that week. It was rich.

I guess he paid more attention to playin' jokes than makin' sales. Finally the concern let him out and he come right home here and told everybody he'd been fired instead of sayin' he'd resigned like most fellas would of.

It was a Saturday and the shop was full and Jim got up out of that chair and says, "Gentlemen, I got an important announcement to make. I been fired from my job."

Well, they asked him if he was in earnest and he said he was and nobody could think of nothin' to say till Jim finally broke the ice himself. He says, "I been sellin' canned goods and now I'm canned goods myself."

You see, the concern he'd been workin' for was a factory that made canned goods. Over in Carterville. And now Jim said he was canned himself. He was certainly a card!

Jim had a great trick that he used to play w'ile he was travelin'. For instance, he'd be ridin' on a train and they'd come to some little town like, well, like, well, like, we'll say, like Benton. Jim would look out the train window and read the signs on the stores.

For instance, they'd be a sign, "Henry Smith, Dry Goods." Well, Jim would write down the name and the name of the town and when he got to wherever he was goin' he'd mail back a postal card to Henry Smith at Benton and not sign no name to it, but he'd write on the card, well, somethin' like "Ask your wife about that book agent that spent the afternoon last week," or "Ask your Missus who kept her from gettin' lonesome the last time you was in Carterville." And he'd sign the card, "A Friend."

Of course, he never knew what really come of none of these jokes, but he could picture what *probably* happened and that was enough.

Jim didn't work very steady after he lost his position with the Carterville people. What he did earn, doin' odd jobs round town, why, he spent pretty near all of it on gin, and his family might of starved if the stores hadn't of carried them along. Jim's wife tried her hand at dressmakin', but they ain't nobody goin' to get rich makin' dresses in this town.

As I say, she'd of divorced Jim, only she seen that she couldn't support herself and the kids and she was always hopin' that some day Jim would cut out his habits and give her more than two or three dollars a week.

They was a time when she would go to whoever he was workin' for and ask them to give her his wages, but after she done this once or twice, he beat her to it by borrowin' most of his pay in advance. He told it all round town, how he had outfoxed his Missus. He certainly was a caution!

But he wasn't satisfied with just outwittin' her. He was sore the way she had acted, tryin' to grab off his pay. And he made up his mind he'd get even. Well, he waited till Evans's Circus was advertised to come to town. Then he told his wife and two kiddies that he was goin' to take them to the circus. The day of the circus, he told them he would get the tickets and meet them outside the entrance to the tent.

Well, he didn't have no intentions of bein' there or buyin' tickets or nothin'. He got full of gin and laid round Wright's poolroom all day. His wife and the kids waited and waited and of course he didn't show up. His wife didn't have a dime with her, or nowhere else, I guess. So she finally had to tell the kids it was all off and they cried like they wasn't never goin' to stop.

Well, it seems, w'ile they was cryin', Doc Stair come along and he asked what was the matter, but Mrs. Kendall was stubborn and wouldn't tell him, but the kids told him and he insisted on takin' them and their mother in the show. Jim found this out afterwards and it was one reason why he had it in for Doc Stair.

Doc Stair come here about a year and a half ago. He's a mighty handsome young fella and his clothes always look like he has them made to order. He goes to Detroit two or three times a year and w'ile he's there must have a tailor take his measure and then make him a suit to order. They cost pretty near twice as much, but they fit a whole lot better than if you just bought them in a store.

For a w'ile everybody was wonderin' why a young doctor like Doc Stair should come to a town like this where we already got old Doc Gamble and Doc Foote that's both been here for years and all the practice in town was always divided between the two of them.

Then they was a story got round that Doc Stair's gal had throwed him over, a gal up in the Northern Peninsula somewhere, and the reason he come here was to hide himself away and forget it. He said himself that he thought they wasn't nothin' like general practice in a place like ours to fit a man to be a good all round doctor. And that's why he'd came.

Anyways, it wasn't long before he was makin' enough to live on, though they tell me that he never dunned nobody for what they owed him, and the folks here certainly has got the owin' habit, even in my business. If I had all that was comin' to me for just shaves alone, I could go to Carterville and put up at the Mercer for a week and see a different picture every night. For instance, they's old George Purdy—but I guess I shouldn't ought to be gossipin'.

Well, last year, our coroner died, died of the flu. Ken Beatty, that was his name. He was the coroner. So they had to choose another man to be coroner in his place and they picked Doc Stair. He laughed at first and said he didn't want it, but they made him take it. It ain't no job that anybody would fight for and what a man makes out of it in a year would just about buy seeds for their garden. Doc's the kind, though, that can't say no to nothin' if you keep at him long enough.

But I was goin' to tell you about a poor boy we got here in town—Paul Dickson. He fell out of a tree when he was about ten years old. Lit on his head and it done somethin' to him and he ain't never been right. No harm in him, but just silly. Jim Kendall used to call him cuckoo; that's a name Jim had for anybody that was off their head, only he called people's head their bean. That was another of his gags, callin' head bean and callin' crazy people cuckoo. Only poor Paul ain't crazy, but just silly.

You can imagine that Jim used to have all kinds of fun with Paul. He'd send him to the White Front Garage for a left-handed monkey wrench. Of course they ain't no such thing as a left-handed monkey wrench.

And once we had a kind of a fair here and they was a baseball game between the fats and the leans and before the game started Jim called Paul over and sent him away down to Schrader's hardware store to get a key for the pitcher's box.

They wasn't nothin' in the way of gags that Jim couldn't think up, when he put his mind to it.

Poor Paul was always kind of suspicious of people, maybe on account of how Jim had kept foolin' him. Paul wouldn't have much to do with anybody only his own mother and Doc Stair and a girl here in town named Julie Gregg. That is, she ain't a girl no more, but pretty near thirty or over.

When Doc first came to town, Paul seemed to feel like here was a real friend and he hung round Doc's office most of the w'ile; the only time he wasn't there was when he'd go home to eat or sleep or when he seen Julie Gregg doin' her shoppin'.

When he looked out Doc's window and seen her, he'd run downstairs and join her and tag along with her to the different stores. The poor boy was crazy about Julie and she always treated him mighty nice and made him feel like he was welcome, though of course it wasn't nothin' but pity on her side.

Doc done all he could to improve Paul's mind and he told me once that he really thought the boy was getting better, that they was times when he was as bright and sensible as anybody else.

But I was goin' to tell you about Julie Gregg. Old man Gregg was in the lumber business, but got to drinkin' and lost the most of his money and when he died, he didn't leave nothin' but the house and just enough insurance for the girl to skimp along on.

Her mother was a kind of a half invalid and didn't hardly ever leave the house. Julie wanted to sell the place and move somewheres else after the old man died, but the mother said she was born here and would die here. It was tough on Julie as the young people round this town—well, she's too good for them.

She'd been away to school and Chicago and New York and different places and they ain't no subject she can't talk on, where you take the rest of the young folks here and you mention anything to them outside of Gloria Swanson or Tommy Meighan and they think you're delirious. Did you see Gloria in *Wages of Virtue?* You missed somethin'!

Well, Doc Stair hadn't been here more than a week when he come in one day to get shaved and I recognized who he was, as he had been pointed out to me, so I told him about my old lady. She's been ailin' for a couple years and either Doc Gamble or Doc Foote, neither one, seemed to be helpin' her. So he said he would come out and see her, but if she was able to get out herself, it would be better to bring her to his office where he could make a completer examination.

So I took her to his office and w'ile I was waitin' for her in the reception room, in come Julie Gregg. When somebody comes in Doc Stair's office, they's a bell that rings in his inside office so as he can tell they's somebody to see him.

So he left my old lady inside and come out to the front office and that's the first time him and Julie met and I guess it was what they call love at first sight. But it wasn't fifty-fifty. This young fella was the slickest lookin' fella she'd ever seen in this town and she went wild over him. To him she was just a lady that wanted to see the doctor.

She'd came on about the same business I had. Her mother had been doctorin' for years with Doc Gamble and Doc Foote and without no results. So she'd heard they was a new doc in town and decided to give him a try. He promised to call and see her mother that same day.

I said a minute ago that it was love at first sight on her part. I'm not only judgin' by how she acted afterwards but how she looked at him that first day in his office. I ain't no mind reader, but it was wrote all over her face that she was gone.

Now Jim Kendall, besides bein' a jokesmith and a pretty good drinker, well, Jim was quite a lady-killer. I guess he run pretty wild durin' the time he was on the road for them Carterville people, and besides that, he'd had a couple little affairs of the heart right here in town. As I say, his wife would have divorced him, only she couldn't.

But Jim was like the majority of men, and women, too, I guess. He wanted what he couldn't get. He wanted Julie Gregg and worked his head off tryin' to land her. Only he'd of said bean instead of head.

Well, Jim's habits and his jokes didn't appeal to Julie and of course he was a married man, so he didn't have no more chance than, well, than a rabbit. That's an expression of Jim's himself. When somebody didn't have no chance to get elected or somethin', Jim would always say they didn't have no more chance than a rabbit.

He didn't make no bones about how he felt. Right in here, more than once, in front of the whole crowd, he said he was stuck on Julie and anybody that could get her for him was welcome to his house and his wife and kids included. But she wouldn't have nothin' to do with him; wouldn't even speak to him on the street. He finally seen he wasn't gettin' nowheres with his usual line so he decided to try the rough stuff. He went right up to her house one evenin' and when she opened the door he forced his way in and grabbed her. But she broke loose and before he could stop her, she run in the next room and locked the door and phoned to Joe Barnes. Joe's the marshal. Jim could hear who she was phonin' to and he beat it before Joe got there.

Joe was an old friend of Julie's pa. Joe went to Jim the next day and told him what would happen if he ever done it again.

I don't know how the news of this little affair leaked out. Chances is that Joe Barnes told his wife and she told somebody else's wife and they told their husband. Anyways, it did leak out and Hod Meyers had the nerve to kid Jim about it, right here in this shop. Jim didn't deny nothin' and kind of laughed it off and said for us all to wait; that lots of people had tried to make a monkey out of him, but he always got even.

Meanw'ile everybody in town was wise to Julie's bein' wild mad over the Doc. I don't suppose she had any idear how her face changed when him and her was together; of course she couldn't of, or she'd of kept away from him. And she didn't know that we was all noticin' how many times she made excuses to go up to his office or pass it on the other side of the street and look up in his window to see if he was there. I felt sorry for her and so did most other people.

Hod Meyers kept rubbin' it into Jim about how the Doc had cut him out. Jim didn't pay no attention to the kiddin' and you could see he was plannin' one of his jokes.

One trick Jim had was the knack of changin' his voice. He could make you think he was a girl talkin' and he could mimic any man's voice. To show you how good he was along this line, I'll tell you the joke he played on me once.

You know, in most towns of any size, when a man is dead and needs a shave, why, the barber that shaves him soaks him five dollars for the job; that is, he don't soak *him*, but whoever ordered the shave. I just charge three dollars because personally I don't mind much shavin' a dead person. They lay a whole lot stiller than live customers. The only thing is that you don't feel like talkin' to them and you get kind of lonesome.

Well, about the coldest day we ever had here, two years ago last winter, the phone rung at the house w'ile I was home to dinner and I answered the phone and it was a woman's voice and she said she was Mrs. John Scott and her husband was dead and would I come out and shave him.

Old John had always been a good customer of mine. But they live seven miles out in the country, on the Streeter road. Still I didn't see how I could say no.

So I said I would be there, but would have to come in a jitney and it might cost three or four dollars besides the price of the shave. So she, or the voice, it said that was all right, so I got Frank Abbott to drive me out to the place and when I got there, who should open the door but old John himself! He wasn't no more dead than, well, than a rabbit.

It didn't take no private detective to figure out who had played me this little joke. Nobody could of thought it up but Jim Kendall. He certainly was a card!

I tell you this incident just to show you how he could disguise his voice and make you believe it was somebody else talkin'. I'd of swore it was Mrs. Scott had called me. Anyways, some woman.

Well, Jim waited till he had Doc Stair's voice down pat; then he went after revenge.

He called Julie up on a night when he knew Doc was over in Carterville. She never questioned but what it was Doc's voice. Jim said he must see her that night; he couldn't wait no longer to tell her somethin'. She was all excited and told him to come to the house. But he said he was expectin' an important long distance call and wouldn't she please forget her manners for once and come to his office. He said they couldn't nothin' hurt her and nobody would see her and he just *must* talk to her a little w'ile. Well, poor Julie fell for it.

Doc always keeps a night light in his office, so it looked to Julie like they was somebody there.

Meanw'ile Jim Kendall had went to Wright's poolroom, where they was a whole gang amusin' themselves. The most of them had drank plenty of gin, and they was a rough bunch when sober. They was always strong for Jim's jokes and when he told them to come with him and see some fun they give up their card games and pool games and followed along.

Doc's office is on the second floor. Right outside his door they's a flight of stairs leadin' to the floor above. Jim and his gang hid in the dark behind these stairs.

Well, Julie come up to Doc's door and rung the bell and they was nothin' doin'. She rung it again and she rung it seven or eight times. Then she tried the door and found it locked. Then Jim made some kind of a noise and she heard it and waited a minute, and then she says, "Is that you, Ralph?" Ralph is Doc's first name.

They was no answer and it must of came to her all of a sudden that she'd been bunked. She pretty near fell downstairs and the whole gang after her. They chased her all the way home, hollerin', "Is that you, Ralph?" and "Oh, Ralphie, dear, is that you?" Jim says he couldn't holler it himself, as he was laughin' too hard.

Poor Julie! She didn't show up here on Main Street for a long, long time afterward.

And of course Jim and his gang told everybody in town, everybody but Doc Stair. They was scared to tell him, and he might of never knowed only for Paul Dickson. The poor cuckoo, as Jim called him, he was here in the shop one night when Jim was still gloatin' yet over what he'd done to Julie. And Paul took in as much of it as he could understand and he run to Doc with the story.

It's a cinch Doc went up in the air and swore he'd make Jim suffer. But it was a kind of a delicate thing, because if it got out that he had beat Jim up, Julie was bound to hear of it and then she'd know that Doc knew and of course knowin' that he knew would make it worse for her than ever. He was goin' to do somethin', but it took a lot of figurin'.

Well, it was a couple days later when Jim was here in the shop again, and so was the cuckoo. Jim was goin' duck-shootin' the next day and had came in lookin' for Hod Meyers to go with him. I happened to know that Hod had went over to Carterville and wouldn't be home till the end of the week. So Jim said he hated to go alone and he guessed he would call it off. Then poor Paul spoke up and said if Jim would take him he would go along. Jim thought a w'ile and then he said, well, he guessed a half-wit was better than nothin'.

I suppose he was plottin' to get Paul out in the boat and play some joke on him, like pushin' him in the water. Anyways, he said Paul could go. He asked him had he ever shot a duck and Paul said no, he'd never even had a gun in his hands. So Jim said he could set in the boat and watch him and if he behaved himself, he might lend him his gun for a couple of shots. They made a date to meet in the mornin' and that's the last I seen of Jim alive.

Next mornin', I hadn't been open more than ten minutes when Doc Stair come in. He looked kind of nervous. He asked me had I seen Paul Dickson. I said no, but I knew where he was, out duck-shootin' with Jim Kendall. So Doc says that's what he had heard, and he couldn't understand it because Paul had told him he wouldn't never have no more to do with Jim as long as he lived.

He said Paul had told him about the joke Jim had played on Julie. He said Paul had asked him what he thought of the joke and the Doc told him that anybody that would do a thing like that ought not to be let live.

I said it had been a kind of a raw thing, but Jim just couldn't resist no kind of a joke, no matter how raw. I said I thought he was all right at heart, but just bubblin' over with mischief. Doc turned and walked out.

At noon he got a phone call from old John Scott. The lake where Jim and Paul had went shootin' is on John's place. Paul had came runnin' up to the house a few minutes before and said they'd been an accident. Jim had shot a few ducks and then give the gun to Paul and told him to try his luck. Paul hadn't never handled a gun and he was nervous. He was shakin' so hard that he couldn't control the gun. He let fire and Jim sunk back in the boat, dead.

Doc Stair, bein' the coroner, jumped in Frank Abbott's flivver and rushed out to Scott's farm. Paul and old John was down on the shore of the lake. Paul had rowed the boat to shore, but they'd left the body in it, waiting for Doc to come.

Doc examined the body and said they might as well fetch it back to town. They was no use leavin' it there or callin' a jury, as it was a plain case of accidental shootin'.

Personally I wouldn't never leave a person shoot a gun in the same boat I was in unless I was sure they knew somethin' about guns. Jim was a sucker to leave a new beginner have his gun, let alone a half-wit. It probably served Jim right, what he got. But still we miss him round here. He certainly was a card! Comb it wet or dry?

INTERPRETATION

The main action here is the story of the "card," the practical joker. He has no shred of human perception or feeling, and his jokes are, naturally, brutal and stupid, only a way of inflating his own ego. In the end, one of his jokes backfires, and we have the moral satisfaction of seeing the biter bit, the joker caught in the destructive consequences of a joke whose destructive nature for other people he could never have understood or cared about. Assuming that the card is adequately characterized, that the setting of the small town is adequately rendered for us, and that the plot is logically worked out, we might still feel that this main action, taken by itself, is somewhat over-simple and predictable, even too moralistic and too obviously an illustration of brutal arrogance being paid off. Anyway, it would seem that Ring Lardner must have felt some dissatisfaction with a naked presentation of the main action, such as we might have if it were told on the author's own responsibility; for he provides a narrator, the barber, who gives us his version of the business.

The use of the narrator does make the story seem less bare and simple, but, of course, complication for the mere sake of complication would scarcely justify itself. What positive values is Ring Lardner aiming at in the use of the barber? To answer this we may well begin by asking another question: What is the barber like? More specifically, what is his attitude toward the story he tells?

The barber, we quickly discover, admires the card, and thinks that life is pretty dull around town now that the card is gone. The barber has accepted the card at his own evaluation, has vicariously participated in the brutal jokes, and is, therefore, a kind of accomplice. So we have a deepening of the originally simple action—a sense that brutality and evil thrive by a kind of connivance on the part of those who do not directly participate in it, a sense of the spreading ripples of complicity always around the evil act.

There is, also, another kind of deepening, not in content this time but in the way of presentation. Let us suppose that the narrator of the story had merely told us about people like the barber, people who had some tacit complicity with the card's jokes, and that he himself, the narrator, found such people reprehensible. Given this treatment, we would find ourselves in immediate agreement with his attitude. There would be no shock of the collision between the narrator's attitude and our own. But as things actually stand, there is a shock of collision between the narrator's attitude and our own, a growing need to reassess things and repudiate his attitude. In other words, Lardner has used an inverted and ironical method. The narrator does not represent the author's view, nor our own. The barber is put there to belie, as it were, the meaning of the story, and by so doing to heighten our own feelings—even to irritate us to a fuller awareness of what is at stake in the story.

If the story were told directly, or told by a narrator whose attitudes were congenial with our own, we should be inclined to say: "Of course, the card is a brute, a louse, and got just what he deserved." But we might say it too quickly, too easily, and we might be inclined to dismiss the whole business. As it is, we are compelled, in a greater or lesser degree, to take issue with the barber, and in taking issue we are drawn more deeply into the story.

The use of this kind of narrator is, then, a fairly simple device for provoking what we may call "reader participation"—for making the reader do some of the interpreting himself, for drawing him into the inside of the story by making him invert an apparent meaning (here the barber's valuations) or develop meaning beyond the point where the story actually comes to rest. Irony, *understatement* (see Glossary), withholding—these are ways to provoke the reader to reassess things, to reassess his own feelings, and thus enter more deeply into the process of the piece of fiction.

Here it might be well to consider the general problem of the *point of view* or the *focus of narration* (see Glossary). We have just seen how important it is that "Haircut" is presented through the mentality of the barber, and have seen how the use of this point of view affects the whole story and our reception of the story. The point of view—the choice of the teller of the story—is a question of the greatest importance for any piece of fiction. The action has to come to us through words, but through whose words? On the answer to that question, all else may often hinge. So we have such subsidiary questions as these:

1. What does the narrator know of the total action lying beyond the story? What can he tell?

2. Does he tell all he knows? If not, why not? What accounts for his withholding any information or narrative? If there is withholding, is it reasonable and justifiable, or merely trickery and mystification?

3. Why does he tell what he does tell? What is his motivation as narrator?

4. What is the narrator's attitude toward what he tells?

5. Assuming that the narrator is not the author himself, as he is not in "Haircut," is the narrator's attitude toward what he tells the same as the attitude of the author?

6. Is the narrator's attitude supposed to be the same as that of the reader? If not, why not? If the narrator's attitude is supposed to be a sort

of guide to the reader's reaction, does the narrator go all the way in interpretation, or does he stop short, withhold, or understate the meaning of
the story?

Though there are many other important questions that may develop
around the point of view of a piece of fiction, we can see from these that
the point of view bears most important relations to the structure and
meaning of fiction. Before we go into such relations, however, we should
sort out what points of view are possible in fiction.

There is, obviously, the first person—the story told, as in "Haircut,"
by an "I," speaking in his own person and in his own language, telling only
what he himself can be reasonably supposed to know and what he is interested in telling. We are immediately aware that the relation of such a
narrator varies from case to case. The "I" may be the main character, or
one of the main characters, telling of his own experience, as in Sherwood
Anderson's "I Want To Know Why," a story which we shall come to
later; or, to take the other extreme, the "I" may be a mere observer who
sees the action of the story but has no stake in it beyond curiosity, as for
example the newspaper man who is supposed to narrate "The Man Who
Would Be King." In between these two extremes, there may be all sorts
of shadings of relationships, from the narrator who is not central but
who is deeply involved, like Peachey in "The Man Who Would Be King,"
through the narrator like the barber, who is not involved in any direct
sense but has some moral connection with the action, or a narrator who is
an observer but who is affected in some significant way, for better or
worse, by what he observes.

The other general point of view from which a story may be told is
the third person, the unidentified author speaking impersonally. But there
are many variations and shadings possible also in this point of view. The
narrator may tell only what can be seen or heard from the outside—as
though he were a camera and sound machine making the objective record.
"The Girls in Their Summer Dresses," except for the last line, when we
enter the head of Michael, is such a story. We see the young couple and
hear their conversation as though we were eavesdropping or watching a
play on the stage. The method is, we may say, dramatic, objective; we
never get a glimpse inside anyone's head except by his actions or words,
no thoughts, no feelings, directly given. That is, until the last line, when
we are admitted into Michael's head: "Michael watched her walk, thinking what a pretty girl, what nice legs." John Collier's "De Mortuis" is
another almost perfect example of the dramatic method, the immediate
reportorial method, without summary or psychological interpretation or
any entering into the heads of characters.

In the third person, however, we find at the other extreme from the
objective method, a method which does let us into the thoughts and feel-

ings of one or more characters, sometimes most intimately into them so that the story is little more than the tracing of their reactions. "Walter Mitty" is such a story; his dream world is the world of the story, and by being admitted into it we make a judgment on it. "A Piece of News," though not as pure an example of this subjective treatment, gives us the same kind of intimate knowledge of the inner goings-on of Ruby Fisher. But we may, of course, enter into a character's head, not to follow more or less sympathetically the flow of thought and feeling, but to dissect, analyze, and summarize, as in the subjective moments of "The Necklace."

We may summarize what we have said of kinds of point of view by the following chart:

	Internal analysis of events	*External observation of events*
Narrator as a character in story	1. Main character tells own story	2. Minor character tells main character's story
Narrator not a character in story	4. Analytic or omniscient author tells story, entering thoughts and feelings	3. Author tells story as external observer

To return to our remarks about the relation of point of view to structure and meaning, we may take a backward glance at "The Man Who Would Be King." That story has not only one narrator, but two. There is the newspaper man who gives us the general narration in his own person, a sort of shadow of Kipling, but within his narration there is the action narrated by Peachey, again in the first person. What is the logic of Kipling's choice of method?

First, we may observe that by taking a first-person narrator, a certain naturalness may be gained. This is not to say that the reader is so innocent that he more readily "believes" a story told in the first person, but it is to say that certain things can be introduced into a story more informally and casually, even though we recognize that the first-person itself is a *convention* (see Glossary), a fiction. In this particular story we need to know something about the strange world of India, and if that information were given in the third person the burden of mere exposition would be more apparent. As it is, the newspaperman can more or less casually and incidentally give us a fairly complete notion of his world; he can feed the expository material in without making us feel that it is labelled, for it is part of his life.

Second, the presence of a first-person narrator introduces naturally into a story a device for *selectivity* (see p. 53 and Glossary). Since the

narrator can tell only what he has observed, heard, or reasonably surmised, a considerable body of material from the hypothetical underlying
action is not available to him. If for a particular story the narrator is well
chosen, then the deletions he must make will seem natural, and the selec-
tions significant. We feel that what he has to tell is what he can tell and
must tell.

For example, in "The Man Who Would Be King" we are dealing with
an action which, taken in itself, is potentially a novel—the conquest of
Kafiristan. Kipling is, however, interested in only one thing—the idea of
kingship, godhood, and manhood—and he wants to render only so much
of the general action as is needed to make vivid and credible the development of Dravot. By the time Dravot's story is filtered through Peachey
and the newspaperman only vivid and telling strokes are left. A piece of
action that might require pages if given any ordinary development comes
down to a sentence or two—for example, the taking of the four mules in
the mountains. The scale of treatment can be controlled in terms of the
narrator's presence—he tells it in his way, he makes the emphasis. Selection,
foreshortening, summary—these things are natural to all fiction, but with
the first-person narrator we have, as it were, a built-in device for con-
trolling them. In other words, the plot of a story—that is, the structure of
action as it is actually presented to us—depends on the point of view.

Not only does structure depend on point of view. Let us take
Peachey again. He is useful in the way we have said, as a narrator of events,
the giver of the structure, but he is also a mirror to Dravot's development,
a device of interpretation as well as of control. We can ask not merely
what he knows of the action, but what he knows of the meaning of the
action. We sense immediately that Dravot is the powerful one of the pair,
the one with ambition and imagination, the one who starts the great
scheme of looting a kingdom. Peachey is content to follow at an admiring
distance. This same relationship prevails as Dravot begins his spiritual
journey from mere looter up to the point that he achieves in the end.
Each new phase of his development is played off against Peachey, the unimaginative follower who if left alone, would be perfectly content to be
merely the self-indulgent loafer and looter. It is through Peachey's not
entirely comprehending response and blundering account that we sense
the depth of experience represented by Dravot. We may say that Peachey,
with his blunt lack of sensitivity and his simplicity of mind, is a device of
irony and understatement. The fact that the spiritual significance of the
theme comes through the man who, except for his association with
Dravot, would remain loafer and looter, gives an ironical contrast—though
the irony here, as is not the case with the barber, makes us think not
worse, but better, of the narrator. The meaning of the story, as filtered to
us through Peachey, is understated: the full significance is not offered.
Peachey is, as it were, a guide for our response, though a rather limping

one; and in the end it is he who, in his delirium in the mountains, presents the image of the godlike Dravot who can hold up the peaks. Peachey's simplicity of mind makes possible the image which we can reasonably accept—we accept the thematic truth of it and at the same time, because it comes from the delirium of Peachey's simple mind, accept the plausibility of it.

This is perhaps enough to indicate something of the importance of point of view for both structure and meaning. Let us glance at some other stories we have already read:

1. Try to think of "The Girls in Their Summer Dresses" as narrated by Frances. What difference do you think this shift in point of view would make to the story? What is our attitude toward the events of the story as it now stands? If she told it would we be more inclined to think her nagging and self-pitying? What would be lost at the very end? All this is not to say that for every story there is an absolutely right way to narrate the action, but it is to say that a shift in point of view creates new considerations and new problems.

2. We have discussed the tone of "De Mortuis." How is the point of view related to the tone of the story?

3. What is the point of view of "The Necklace"? How is this related to questions of scale in the story?

4. How is the point of view related to questions of atmosphere in "A Piece of News"?

ISAAC BABEL

Crossing into Poland

THE Commander of the VI Division reported: Novgorod-Volynsk was taken at dawn today. The Staff had left Krapivno, and our baggage train was spread out in a noisy rearguard over the highroad from Brest to Warsaw built by Nicholas I upon the bones of peasants.

Fields flowered around us, crimson with poppies; a noontide breeze played in the yellowing rye; on the horizon virginal buckwheat rose like the wall of a distant monastery. The Volyn's peaceful stream moved away from us in sinuous curves and was lost in the pearly haze of the birch groves; crawling between flowery slopes, it wound weary arms through a wilderness of hops. The orange sun rolled down the sky like a lopped-off head, and mild light glowed from the cloud gorges. The standards of the sunset flew above our heads. Into the cool of evening dripped the smell of yesterday's blood, of slaughtered horses. The blackened Zbruch roared, twisting itself into foamy knots at the falls. The bridges were down, and we waded across the river. On the waves rested a majestic moon. The horses were in to the cruppers, and the noisy torrent gurgled among hundreds of horses' legs. Somebody sank, loudly defaming the Mother of God. The river was dotted with the square black patches of the wagons, and was full of confused sounds, of whistling and singing, that rose above the gleaming hollows, the serpentine trails of the moon.

Far on in the night we reached Novograd. In the house where I was billeted I found a pregnant woman and two red-haired, scraggy-necked Jews. A third, huddled to the wall with his head covered up, was already asleep. In the room I was given I discovered turned-out wardrobes, scraps of women's fur coats on the floor, human filth, fragments of the occult crockery the Jews use only once a year, at Eastertime.

"Clear this up," I said to the woman. "What a filthy way to live!" The two Jews rose from their places and, hopping on their felt soles, cleared the mess from the floor. They skipped about noiselessly, monkey-fashion, like Japs in a circus act, their necks swelling and twisting. They put down for me a feather bed that had been disemboweled, and I lay down by the wall next to the third Jew, the one who was asleep. Faint-hearted poverty closed in over my couch.

Silence overcame all. Only the moon, clasping in her blue hands her round, bright, carefree face, wandered like a vagrant outside the window.

I kneaded my numbed legs and, lying on the ripped-open mattress, fell asleep. And in my sleep the Commander of the VI Division appeared to me; he was pursuing the Brigade Commander on a heavy stallion, fired at him twice between the eyes. The bullets pierced the Brigade Commander's head, and both his eyes dropped to the ground. "Why did you turn back the brigade?" shouted Savitsky, the Divisional Commander, to the wounded man—and here I woke up, for the pregnant woman was groping over my face with her fingers.

"Good sir," she said, "you're calling out in your sleep and you're tossing to and fro. I'll make you a bed in another corner, for you're pushing my father about."

She raised her thin legs and rounded belly from the floor and removed the blanket from the sleeper. Lying on his back was an old man, a dead old man. His throat had been torn out and his face cleft in two; in his beard blue blood was clotted like a lump of lead.

"Good sir," said the Jewess, shaking up the feather bed, "the Poles cut his throat, and he begging them: 'Kill me in the yard so that my daughter shan't see me die.' But they did as suited them. He passed away in this room, thinking of me.—And now I should wish to know," cried the woman with sudden and terrible violence, "I should wish to know where in the whole world you could find another father like my father?"

INTERPRETATION

This, like "I See You Never," may be regarded by some readers as a mere episode, not a story at all, lacking conflict and complication and any acceptable resolution. What do you think? In considering this question you may find some help in imagining, by way of contrast, the same action told in the third person, very impersonally. Does the fact of a first-person narrator, who, presumably, arrives at the unspecified awareness, give more fictional shape and significance than would be possible otherwise? What is the awareness arrived at?

LUIGI PIRANDELLO

War

THE passengers who had left Rome by the night express had had to stop until dawn at the small station of Fabriano in order to continue their journey by the small old-fashioned local joining the main line with Sulmona.

At dawn, in a stuffy and smoky second-class carriage in which five people had already spent the night, a bulky woman in deep mourning was hoisted in—almost like a shapeless bundle. Behind her, puffing and moaning, followed her husband—a tiny man, thin and weakly, his face death-white, his eyes small and bright and looking shy and uneasy.

Having at last taken a seat he politely thanked the passengers who had helped his wife and who had made room for her; then he turned round to the woman trying to pull down the collar of her coat, and politely inquired:

"Are you all right, dear?"

The wife, instead of answering, pulled up her collar again to her eyes, so as to hide her face.

"Nasty world," muttered the husband with a sad smile.

And he felt it his duty to explain to his traveling companions that the poor woman was to be pitied, for the war was taking away from her her only son, a boy of twenty to whom both had devoted their entire life, even breaking up their home at Sulmona to follow him to Rome, where he had to go as a student, then allowing him to volunteer for war with an assurance, however, that at least for six months he would not be sent to the front and now, all of a sudden, receiving a wire saying that he was due to leave in three days' time and asking them to go and see him off.

The woman under the big coat was twisting and wriggling, at times growling like a wild animal, feeling certain that all those explanations would not have aroused even a shadow of sympathy from those people who—most likely—were in the same plight as herself. One of them, who had been listening with particular attention, said:

"You should thank God that your son is only leaving now for the front. Mine has been sent there the first day of the war. He has already come back twice wounded and been sent back again to the front."

"What about me? I have two sons and three nephews at the front," said another passenger.

"Maybe, but in our case it is our *only* son," ventured the husband.

"What difference can it make? You may spoil your only son with excessive attentions, but you cannot love him more than you would all your other children if you had any. Paternal love is not like bread that can be broken into pieces and split amongst the children in equal shares. A father gives *all* his love to each one of his children without discrimination, whether it be one or ten, and if I am suffering now for my two sons, I am not suffering half for each of them but double . . ."

"True . . . true . . ." sighed the embarrassed husband, "but suppose (of course we all hope it will never be your case) a father has two sons at the front and he loses one of them, there is still one left to console him . . . while . . ."

"Yes," answered the other, getting cross, "a son left to console him but also a son left for whom he must survive, while in the case of the father of an only son if the son dies the father can die too and put an end to his distress. Which of the two positions is the worse? Don't you see how my case would be worse than yours?"

"Nonsense," interrupted another traveler, a fat, red-faced man with bloodshot eyes of the palest gray.

He was panting. From his bulging eyes seemed to spurt inner violence of an uncontrolled vitality which his weakened body could hardly contain.

"Nonsense," he repeated, trying to cover his mouth with his hand so as to hide the two missing front teeth. "Nonsense. Do we give life to our children for our own benefit?"

The other travelers stared at him in distress. The one who had had his son at the front since the first day of the war sighed: "You are right. Our children do not belong to us, they belong to the Country. . . ."

"Bosh," retorted the fat traveler. "Do we think of the Country when we give life to our children? Our sons are born because . . . well, because they must be born and when they come to life they take our own life with them. This is the truth. We belong to them but they never belong to us. And when they reach twenty they are exactly what we were at their age. We too had a father and mother, but there were so many other things as well . . . girls, cigarettes, illusions, new ties . . . and the Country, of course, whose call we would have answered—when we were twenty—even if father and mother had said no. Now at our age, the love of our Country is still great, of course, but stronger than it is the love for our children. Is there any one of us here who wouldn't gladly take his son's place at the front if he could?"

There was a silence all round, everybody nodding as to approve.

"Why then," continued the fat man, "shouldn't we consider the feelings of our children when they are twenty? Isn't it natural that at their age they should consider the love for their Country (I am speaking of decent boys, of course) even greater than the love for us? Isn't it natural that it should be so, as after all they must look upon us as upon old boys who cannot move any more and must stay at home? If Country exists, if Country is a natural necessity, like bread, of which each of us must eat in order not to die of hunger, somebody must go to defend it. And our sons go, when they are twenty, and they don't want tears, because if they die, they die inflamed and happy (I am speaking, of course, of decent boys). Now, if one dies young and happy, without having the ugly sides of life, the boredom of it, the pettiness, the bitterness of disillusion . . . what more can we ask for him? Everyone should stop crying; everyone should laugh, as I do . . . or at least thank God—as I do—because my son, before dying, sent me a message saying that he was dying satisfied at having ended his life in the best way he could have wished. That is why, as you see, I do not even wear mourning. . . ."

He shook his light fawn coat as to show it; his livid lip over his missing teeth was trembling, his eyes were watery and motionless, and soon after he ended with a shrill laugh which might well have been a sob.

"Quite so . . . quite so . . ." agreed the others.

The woman who, bundled in a corner under her coat, had been sitting and listening had—for the last three months—tried to find in the words of her husband and her friends something to console her in her deep sorrow, something that might show her how a mother should resign herself to send her son not even to death but to a probably dangerous life. Yet not a word had she found amongst the many which had been said . . . and her grief had been greater in seeing that nobody—as she thought—could share her feelings.

But now the words of the traveler amazed and almost stunned her. She suddenly realized that it wasn't the others who were wrong and could not understand her but herself who could not rise up to the same height of those fathers and mothers willing to resign themselves, without crying, not only to the departure of their sons but even to their death.

She lifted her head, she bent over from her corner trying to listen with great attention to the details which the fat man was giving to his companions about the way his son had fallen as a hero, for his King and his Country, happy and without regrets. It seemed to her that she had stumbled into a world she had never dreamt of, a world so far unknown to her and she was so pleased to hear everyone joining in congratulating that brave father who could so stoically speak of his child's death.

Then suddenly, just as if she had heard nothing of what had been said and almost as if waking up from a dream, she turned to the old man, asking him:

"Then . . . is your son really dead?"

Everybody stared at her. The old man, too, turned to look at her, fixing his great, bulging, horribly watery light gray eyes, deep in her face. For some little time he tried to answer, but words failed him. He looked and looked at her, almost as if only then—at that silly, incongruous question—he had suddenly realized at last that his son was really dead—gone for ever—for ever. His face contracted, became horribly distorted, then he snatched in haste a handkerchief from his pocket and, to the amazement of everyone, broke into harrowing, heart-rending, uncontrollable sobs.

INTERPRETATION

This story may seem peculiarly lacking in action, if by the term we mean physical action. After the fat woman has been "hoisted" into the compartment and her shy, apologetic husband has climbed in after her, there is no physical movement indicated except the wriggling and twisting of the fat woman under her coat, the attempt of the old man to cover his mouth with his hand when he talks in order to conceal the fact that two of his teeth are missing, his shaking of his fawn-colored overcoat to show that he does not wear mourning, the fat woman's bending forward to listen to the old man, the turning of all eyes upon the woman when she finally asks the old man about his son, and the contortion of the old man's face as he tries to answer. These physical actions are important in the story, but their importance lies in the fact that they are clues to the feelings and attitudes of the persons involved in the story. They do not, in other words, actually constitute the plot.

The plot itself is constituted of the conflicts among the various attitudes held by the characters toward the subject: the giving of children to the country. The form, then, is almost the form of a debate—different points of view are stated and argued, one after another. But this is not a debate for the mere sake of debate. The persons involved are persons for whom the issue is very real; they have sons in the war, and one man, the old man in the fawn-colored overcoat, has already lost his son. That is, the debate is dramatically meaningful for the participants.

The two extreme positions in the debate are held by the fat woman and the old man. The fat woman says nothing, but we know what her position is: "The woman under the big coat was twisting and wriggling, at times growling like a wild animal, feeling certain that all those explanations would not have aroused even a shadow of sympathy from those people who—most likely—were in the same plight as herself." Her grief has a kind of immediacy, like physical pain; it is beyond reasoning or discussion; she can only twist as in pain or utter meaningless animal-like sounds. The other extreme position, that of the old man whose son has been actually killed, is the most fully stated. He argues that one does not, in the first place, have children for one's own benefit; that, in the second place, a son, being young and idealistic, is more drawn by love of country than by love of parents; that if a son dies for his country he dies happy— if he is "decent"; that one who dies young and happy has been spared the ugly side of life, boredom, pettiness, disillusion; that, therefore, a parent whose son has died heroically should be happy and laugh, as he says he does, or should at least thank God. That is, the old man has completely argued away, philosophized away, all of the fundamental sense of loss and grief. Such are the two extremes of attitude.

Now, what may be called the plot pattern of the story depends upon the opposition between these two extreme views. But it is not a static opposition—a mere statement of difference. Both views are modified.

First, the fat woman, who had been unable to take consolation from her husband or her friends, because, as she felt, nobody could share her feelings, begins to take consolation from the words of the stranger. He has actually lost a son, and therefore he must know, must be able to share, her own feelings. He must be wise, because his loss is greater than hers, for her son is yet alive. Furthermore, the very violence of the old man's position, its difference from all the views given her by husband and friends, its absolute denial of grief by its heroic terms, make her feel that she has "stumbled into a world she had never dreamt of." It seems incredible to her that a man whose son is really dead can speak thus of his loss. So "almost as if waking up from a dream" she asks him: "Then . . . is your son really dead?"

Presumably, if the man should say, simply, "Yes, he is dead," she would be prepared to accept, for the moment at least, his position. If the man could assure her once more that the son is "really" dead, then she could try to imitate his heroic attitude. She, too, would be able to face the fact of death.

But her question, which provides the climax, the focal point of the story, reveals something to the old man, just as his previous words have revealed something to her. So, as in the first place, we find her position modified by him, we find now, in the second place, his position modified by her. When she utters the words "really dead" everybody "stares" at her—as though she had said something out of place, something impolite and embarrassing, as though she had divulged some horrible and shocking secret. The old man stares at her too, and cannot answer. For the first time, he realizes that his son is "really dead—gone for ever—for ever." He is caught now in the abject, animal-like, unreasoning misery, in which she had previously been held, and bursts into sobs.

The story, then, depends on a conflict between the basic, personal, un-formulable emotion on the one hand, and systems, codes, reason, ideal compensations, and interpretations on the other. There is here an ironical contrast, an irreconcilable contrast—or a contrast, which if reconcilable is reconcilable only by the greatest effort. The equilibrium of the man who has made the reconciliation is upset, we see, by the slightest touch, by the woman's "silly, incongruous question," but a question which is fundamental. Are we to assume, therefore, that the author is simply saying that codes, systems, reason, obligations, ideals do not matter, that the only thing which matters is the fact of personal emotion? It would not seem to be the case. If that were the case, why would he illustrate the powerful appeal which the old man's words make to the woman who is sunk in grief? No, it seems that the author is putting, in dramatic terms, a basic conflict in human experience—is saying that the two terms of the opposition are always in existence and that neither can be ignored. (Compare the author's attitude toward his theme with that of Bradbury toward the theme of "I See You Never," see pp. 113–115.)

Let us turn again to the pattern of the story. We have said that we find a movement away from the two extreme positions, a process of mutual modification focused, finally, on the question which the woman asks the old man. In other words, we have, in a sense, two "stories" within a story—the story of the woman's change of attitude and the story of the old man's change of attitude. Each of the two persons seems, when introduced, to be firmly fixed in a special attitude. How are we to account for the changes? Are the changes prepared for and made acceptable in the story?

The author devotes some analysis to the woman's change. It is the novelty, the heroic quality, of the consolation offered by the old man, that attract her. Further, the fact that he has really lost a son makes her feel that he will "understand" her. But we have no such explicit analysis of the change on the part of the old man. His change of attitude comes as a surprise. But does he not overstate his case in the earlier part of the story? Is there not an inkling of the fact that he is trying to argue against himself rather than against other people? Is there not a hint of hysteria? In this connection one might investigate the following sentence, which comes just after he has said that he does not even wear mourning: "He shook his light fawn coat as to show it; his livid lip over his missing teeth was trembling, his eyes were watery and motionless, and soon after he ended with a shrill laugh which might well have been a sob."

The foregoing analysis of the story is not complete. Certain other questions are important for a full interpretation and for an understanding of the author's method.

1. What is the importance of the physical actions in the story? We have said that they offer clues to the feelings and attitudes of the characters. How is this true? Take, for instance, the fact that the old man at first tries to cover his mouth but later forgets to do so.

2. What is the significance of the words which are italicized in the following sentence: "The old man, too, turned to look at her, fixing his great, bulging, *horribly* watery light gray eyes, *deep* in her face."

3. The following version of the story would be inferior to the present version: The old man's son is merely at the front. He argues with the other people in the compartment, and persuades them, as in the present version of the story. At a station, he receives a telegram saying that his son has been killed and bursts into "heart-rending, uncontrollable sobs," while they stare at him in amazement. Why would this version be inferior to the story as given?

STEPHEN CRANE

The Bride Comes to Yellow Sky

I

THE great Pullman was whirling onward with such dignity of motion that a glance from the window seemed simply to prove that the plains of Texas were pouring eastward. Vast flats of green grass, dull-hued spaces of mesquit and cactus, little groups of frame houses, woods of light and tender trees, all were sweeping into the east, sweeping over the horizon, a precipice.

A newly married pair had boarded this coach at San Antonio. The man's face was reddened from many days in the wind and sun, and a direct result of his new black clothes was that his brick-coloured hands were constantly performing in a most conscious fashion. From time to time he looked down respectfully at his attire. He sat with a hand on each knee, like a man waiting in a barber's shop. The glances he devoted to other passengers were furtive and shy.

The bride was not pretty, nor was she very young. She wore a dress of blue cashmere, with small reservations of velvet here and there, and with steel buttons abounding. She continually twisted her head to regard her puff sleeves, very stiff, straight, and high. They embarrassed her. It was quite apparent that she had cooked, and that she expected to cook, dutifully. The blushes caused by the careless scrutiny of some passengers as she had entered the car were strange to see upon this plain, under-class countenance, which was drawn in placid, almost emotionless lines.

They were evidently very happy. "Ever been in a parlor-car before?" he asked, smiling with delight.

"No," she answered; "I never was. It's fine, ain't it?"

"Great! And then after a while we'll go forward to the diner, and get a big lay-out. Finest meal in the world. Charge a dollar."

"Oh, do they?" cried the bride. "Charge a dollar? Why, that's too much—for us—ain't it, Jack?"

"Not this trip, anyhow," he answered bravely. "We're going to go the whole thing."

Later he explained to her about the trains. "You see, it's a thousand miles from one end of Texas to the other; and this train runs right across it, and never stops but four times." He had the pride of an owner. He pointed out to her the dazzling fittings of the coach; and in truth her eyes opened wider as she contemplated the sea-green figured velvet, the shining brass, silver, and glass, the wood that gleamed as darkly brilliant as the surface of a pool of oil. At one end a bronze figure sturdily held a support for a separated chamber, and at convenient places on the ceiling were frescos in olive and silver.

To the minds of the pair, their surroundings reflected the glory of their marriage that morning in San Antonio; this was the environment of their new estate; and the man's face in particular beamed with an elation that made him appear ridiculous to the Negro porter. This individual at times surveyed them from afar with an amused and superior grin. On other occasions he bullied them with skill in ways that did not make it exactly plain to them that they were being bullied. He subtly used all the manners of the most unconquerable kind of snobbery. He oppressed them; but on this oppression they had small knowledge, and they speedily forgot that infrequently a number of travellers covered them with stares of derisive enjoyment. Historically there was supposed to be something infinitely humorous in their situation.

"We are due in Yellow Sky at 3:42," he said, looking tenderly into her eyes.

"Oh, are we?" she said, as if she had not been aware of it. To evince surprise at her husband's statement was part of her wifely amiability. She took from a pocket a little silver watch; and as she held it before her, and stared at it with a frown of attention, the new husband's face shone.

"I bought it in San Anton' from a friend of mine," he told her gleefully.

"It's seventeen minutes past twelve," she said, looking up at him with a kind of shy and clumsy coquetry. A passenger. noting this play, grew excessively sardonic, and winked at himself in one of the numerous mirrors.

At last they went to the dining-car. Two rows of Negro waiters, in glowing white suits, surveyed their entrance with the interest, and also the equanimity, of men who had been forewarned. The pair fell to the lot of a waiter who happened to feel pleasure in steering them through their meal. He viewed them with the manner of a fatherly pilot, his countenance radiant with benevolence. The patronage, entwined with the ordinary deference, was not plain to them. And yet, as they returned to their coach, they showed in their faces a sense of escape.

To the left, miles down a long purple slope, was a little ribbon of mist where moved the keening Rio Grande. The train was approaching it at an angle, and the apex was Yellow Sky. Presently it was apparent that, as the distance from Yellow Sky grew shorter, the husband became commensurately restless. His brick-red hands were more insistent in their prominence. Occasionally he was even rather absent-minded and far-away when the bride leaned forward and addressed him.

As a matter of truth, Jack Potter was beginning to find the shadow of a deed weigh upon him like a leaden slab. He, the town marshal of Yellow Sky, a man known, liked, and feared in his corner, a prominent person, had gone to San Antonio to meet a girl he believed he loved, and there, after the usual prayers, had actually induced her to marry him, without consulting Yellow Sky for any part of the transaction. He was now bringing his bride before an innocent and unsuspecting community.

Of course people in Yellow Sky married as it pleased them, in accordance with a general custom; but such was Potter's thought of his duty to his friends, or of their idea of his duty, or of an unspoken form which does not control men in these matters, that he felt he was heinous. He had committed an extraordinary crime. Face to face with this girl in San Antonio, and spurred by his sharp impulse, he had gone headlong over all the social hedges. At San Antonio he was like a man hidden in the dark. A knife to sever any friendly duty, any form, was easy to his hand in that remote city. But the hour of Yellow Sky—the hour of daylight—was approaching.

He knew full well that his marriage was an important thing to his town. It could only be exceeded by the burning of the new hotel. His friends could not forgive him. Frequently he had reflected on the advisability of telling them by telegraph, but a new cowardice had been upon him. He feared to do it. And now the train was hurrying him toward a scene of amazement, glee, and reproach. He glanced out of the window at the line of haze swinging slowly in toward the train.

Yellow Sky had a kind of brass band, which played painfully, to the delight of the populace. He laughed without heart as he thought of it. If the citizens could dream of his prospective arrival with his bride, they would parade the band at the station and escort them, amid cheers and laughing congratulations to his adobe home.

He resolved that he would use all the devices of speed and plainscraft in making the journey from the station to his house. Once within that safe citadel, he could issue some sort of vocal bulletin, and then not go among the citizens until they had time to wear off a little of their enthusiasm.

The bride looked anxiously at him. "What's worrying you, Jack?"

He laughed again. "I'm not worrying, girl; I'm only thinking of Yellow Sky."

She flushed in comprehension.

A sense of mutual guilt invaded their minds and developed a finer tenderness. They looked at each other with eyes softly aglow. But Potter often laughed the same nervous laugh; the flush upon the bride's face seemed quite permanent.

The traitor to the feelings of Yellow Sky narrowly watched the speeding landscape. "We're nearly there," he said.

Presently the porter came and announced the proximity of Potter's home. He held a brush in his hand, and, with all his airy superiority gone, he brushed Potter's new clothes as the latter slowly turned this way and that way. Potter fumbled out a coin and gave it to the porter, as he had seen others do. It was a heavy and muscle-bound business, as that of a man shoeing his first horse.

The porter took their bag, and as the train began to slow they moved forward to the hooded platform of the car. Presently the two engines and their long string of coaches rushed into the station of Yellow Sky.

"They have to take water here," said Potter, from a constricted throat and in mournful cadence, as one announcing death. Before the train stopped his eyes had swept the length of the platform, and he was glad and astonished to see there was none upon it but the station-agent, who, with a slightly hurried and anxious air, was walking toward the water-tanks. When the train had halted, the porter alighted first, and placed in position a little temporary step.

"Come on, girl," said Potter, hoarsely. As he helped her down they each laughed on a false note. He took the bag from the Negro, and bade his wife cling to his arm. As they slunk rapidly away, his hang-dog glance perceived that they were unloading the two trunks, and also that the station-agent, far ahead near the baggage-car, had turned and was running toward him, making gestures. He laughed, and groaned as he laughed, when he noted the first effect of his marital bliss upon Yellow Sky. He gripped his wife's arm firmly to his side, and they fled. Behind them the porter stood, chuckling fatuously.

II

The California express on the Southern Railway was due at Yellow Sky in twenty-one minutes. There were six men at the bar of the Weary Gentleman saloon. One was a drummer who talked a great deal and rapidly; three were Texans who did not care to talk at that time; and two were Mexican sheepherders, who did not talk as a general practice in the Weary Gentleman saloon. The barkeeper's dog lay on the board walk that crossed in front of the door. His head was on his paws, and he glanced drowsily here and there with the constant vigilance of a dog that is kicked on occasion. Across the sandy street were some vivid green grass-plots, so wonderful in appearance, amid the sands that burned near them in a blazing sun, that they caused a doubt in the mind. They exactly resembled the grass mats used to represent lawns on the stage. At the cooler end of the railway station, a man without a coat sat in a tilted chair and smoked his pipe. The fresh-cut bank of the Rio Grande circled near the town, and there could be seen beyond it a great plum-coloured plain of mesquit.

Save for the busy drummer and his companions in the saloon, Yellow Sky was dozing. The new-comer leaned gracefully upon the bar, and recited many tales with the confidence of a bard who has come upon a new field.

"—and at the moment that the old man fell downstairs with the bureau in his arms, the old woman was coming up with two scuttles of coal, and of course—"

The drummer's tale was interrupted by a young man who suddenly appeared in the open door. He cried: "Scratchy Wilson's drunk, and has turned loose with both hands." The two Mexicans at once set down their glasses and faded out of the rear entrance of the saloon.

The drummer, innocent and jocular, answered: "All right, old man. S'pose he has? Come in and have a drink, anyhow."

But the information had made such an obvious cleft in every skull in the room that the drummer was obliged to see its importance. All had become instantly solemn. "Say," said he, mystified, "what is this?" His three companions made the introductory gesture of eloquent speech; but the young man at the door forestalled them.

"It means, my friend," he answered, as he came into the saloon, "that for the next two hours this town won't be a health resort."

The barkeeper went to the door, and locked and barred it; reaching out of the window, he pulled in heavy wooden shutters, and barred them. Immediately a solemn, chapel-like gloom was upon the place. The drummer was looking from one to another.

"But say," he cried, "what is this, anyhow? You don't mean there is going to be a gun-fight?"

"Don't know whether there'll be a fight or not," answered one man, grimly; "but there'll be some shootin'—some good shootin'."

The young man who had warned them waved his hand. "Oh, there'll be a fight fast enough, if any one wants it. Anybody can get a fight out there in the street. There's a fight just waiting."

The drummer seemed to be swayed between the interest of a foreigner and a perception of personal danger.

"What did you say his name was?" he asked.

"Scratchy Wilson," they answered in chorus.

"And will he kill anybody? What are you going to do? Does this happen often? Does he rampage around like this once a week or so? Can he break in that door?"

"No; he can't break down that door," replied the barkeeper. "He's tried it three times. But when he comes you'd better lay down on the floor, stranger. He's dead sure to shoot at it, and a bullet may come through."

Thereafter the drummer kept a strict eye upon the door. The time had not yet been called for him to hug the floor, but, as a minor precaution, he sidled near to the wall. "Will he kill anybody?" he said again.

The man laughed low and scornfully at the question.

"He's out to shoot, and he's out for trouble. Don't see any good in experimentin' with him."

"But what do you do in a case like this? What do you do?"

A man responded: "Why, he and Jack Potter—"

"But," in chorus the other men interrupted, "Jack Potter's in San Anton'."

"Well, who is he? What's he got to do with it?"

"Oh, he's the town marshal. He goes out and fights Scratchy when he gets on one of these tears."

"Wow!" said the drummer, mopping his brow. "Nice job he's got."

The voices had toned away to mere whisperings. The drummer wished to ask further questions, which were born of an increasing anxiety and bewilderment; but when he attempted them, the men merely looked at him in irritation and motioned him to remain silent. A tense waiting hush was upon them. In the deep shadows of the room their eyes shone as they listened for sounds from the street. One man made three gestures at the barkeeper; and the latter, moving like a ghost, handed him a glass and a bottle. The man poured a full glass of whisky, and set down the bottle noiselessly. He gulped the whisky in a swallow, and turned again toward the door in immovable silence. The drummer saw that the barkeeper, without a sound, had taken a Winchester from beneath the bar. Later he saw this individual beckoning to him, so he tiptoed across the room.

"You better come with me back of the bar."

"No, thanks," said the drummer, perspiring; "I'd rather be where I can make a break for the back door."

Whereupon the man of bottles made a kindly but peremptory gesture. The drummer obeyed it, and, finding himself seated on a box with his head below the level of the bar, balm was laid upon his soul at sight of various zinc and copper fittings that bore a resemblance to armour-plate. The barkeeper took a seat comfortably upon an adjacent box.

"You see," he whispered, "this here Scratchy Wilson is a wonder with a gun—a perfect wonder; and when he goes on the war-trail, we hunt our holes—naturally. He's about the last one of the old gang that used to hang out along the river here. He's a terror when he's drunk. When he's sober he's all right—kind of simple—wouldn't hurt a fly—nicest fellow in town. But when he's drunk—whoo!"

There were periods of stillness. "I wish Jack Potter was back from San Anton'," said the barkeeper. "He shot Wilson up once—in the leg—and he would sail in and pull out the kinks in this thing."

Presently they heard from a distance the sound of a shot, followed by three wild yowls. It instantly removed a bond from the men in the darkened saloon. There was a shuffling of feet. They looked at each other. "Here he comes," they said.

III

A man in a maroon-colored flannel shirt, which had been purchased for purposes of decoration, and made principally by some Jewish women on the East Side of New York, rounded a corner and walked into the middle of the main street of Yellow Sky. In either hand the man held a long, heavy, blue-black revolver. Often he yelled, and these cries rang through a semblance of a deserted village, shrilly flying over the roofs in a volume that seemed to have no relation to the ordinary vocal strength of a man. It was as if the surrounding stillness formed the arch of a tomb over him. These cries of ferocious challenge rang against walls of silence. And his boots had red tops with gilded imprints, of the kind beloved in winter by little sledding boys on the hillsides of New England.

The man's face flamed in a rage begot of whisky. His eyes, rolling, and yet keen for ambush, hunted the still doorways and windows. He walked with the creeping movement of the midnight cat. As it occurred to him, he roared menacing information. The long revolvers in his hands were as easy as straws; they were moved with an electric swiftness. The little fingers of each hand played sometimes in a musician's way. Plain from the low collar of the shirt, the cords of his neck straightened and sank, straightened and sank, as passion moved him. The only sounds were his terrible invitations. The calm adobes preserved their demeanour at the passing of this small thing in the middle of the street.

There was no offer of fight—no offer of fight. The man called to the sky. There were no attractions. He bellowed and fumed and swayed his revolvers here and everywhere.

The dog of the barkeeper of the Weary Gentleman saloon had not appreciated the advance of events. He yet lay dozing in front of his master's door. At sight of the dog, the man paused and raised his revolver humorously. At sight of the man, the dog sprang up and walked diagonally away, with a sullen head, and growling. The man yelled, and the dog broke into a gallop. As it was about to enter an alley, there was a loud noise, a whistling, and something spat the ground directly before it. The dog screamed, and, wheeling in terror, galloped headlong in a new direction. Again there was a noise, a whistling, and sand was kicked viciously before it. Fear-stricken, the dog turned and flurried like an animal in a pen. The man stood laughing, his weapons at his hips.

Ultimately the man was attracted by the closed door of the Weary Gentleman saloon. He went to it and, hammering with a revolver, demanded drink.

The door remaining imperturbable, he picked a bit of paper from the walk, and nailed it to the framework with a knife. He then turned his back contemptuously upon this popular resort and, walking to the opposite side of the street and spinning there on his heel quickly and lithely, fired at the bit of paper. He missed it by a half-inch. He swore at himself, and went away. Later he comfortably fusilladed the windows of his most intimate friend. The man was playing with this town; it was a toy for him.

But still there was no offer of fight. The name of Jack Potter, his ancient antagonist, entered his mind, and he concluded that it would be a glad thing if he should go to Potter's house, and by bombardment induce him to come out and fight. He moved in the direction of his desire, chanting Apache scalp-music.

When he arrived at it, Potter's house presented the same still front as had the other adobes. Taking up a strategic position, the man howled a challenge. But this house regarded him as might a great stone god. It gave no sign. After a decent wait, the man howled further challenges, mingling with them wonderful epithets.

Presently there came the spectacle of a man churning himself into deepest rage over the immobility of a house. He fumed at it as the winter wind attacks a prairie cabin in the North. To the distance there should have gone the sound of a tumult like the fighting of two hundred Mexicans. As necessity bade him, he paused for breath or to reload his revolvers.

IV

Potter and his bride walked sheepishly and with speed. Sometimes they laughed together shamefacedly and low.

"Next corner, dear," he said finally.

They put forth the efforts of a pair walking bowed against a strong wind. Potter was about to raise a finger to point the first appearance of the new home when, as they circled the corner, they came face to face with a man in a maroon-colored shirt, who was feverishly pushing cartridges into a large revolver. Upon the instant the man dropped his revolver to the ground and, like lightning, whipped another from its holster. The second weapon was aimed at the bridegroom's chest.

There was a silence. Potter's mouth seemed to be merely a grave for his tongue. He exhibited an instinct to at once loosen his arm from the woman's grip, and he dropped the bag to the sand. As for the bride, her face had gone as yellow as old cloth. She was a slave to hideous rites, gazing at the apparitional snake.

The two men faced each other at a distance of three paces. He of the revolver smiled with a new and quiet ferocity.

"Tried to sneak up on me," he said. "Tried to sneak up on me!" His eyes grew more baleful. As Potter made a slight movement, the man thrust his revolver venomously forward. "No; don't you do it, Jack Potter. Don't you move a finger toward a gun just yet. Don't you move an eyelash. The time has come for me to settle with you, and I'm goin' to do it my own way, and loaf along with no interferin'. So if you don't want a gun bent on you, just mind what I tell you."

Potter looked at his enemy. "I ain't got a gun on me, Scratchy," he said. "Honest, I ain't." He was stiffening and steadying, but yet somewhere at the back of his mind a vision of the Pullman floated: the sea-green figured velvet, the shining brass, silver, and glass, the wood that gleamed as darkly brilliant as the surface of a pool of oil—all the glory of the marriage, the environment of the new estate. "You know I fight when it comes to fighting, Scratchy Wilson; but I ain't got a gun on me. You'll have to do all the shootin' yourself."

His enemy's face went livid. He stepped forward, and lashed his weapon to and fro before Potter's chest. "Don't you tell me you ain't got no gun on you, you whelp. Don't tell me no lie like that. There ain't a man in Texas ever seen you without no gun. Don't take me for no kid." His eyes blazed with light, and his throat worked like a pump.

"I ain't takin' you for no kid," answered Potter. His heels had not moved an inch backward. "I'm takin' you for a damn fool. I tell you I ain't got a gun, and I ain't. If you're goin' to shoot me up, you better begin now; you'll never get a chance like this again."

So much enforced reasoning had told on Wilson's rage; he was calmer. "If you ain't got a gun, why ain't you got a gun?" he sneered. "Been to Sunday-school?"

"I ain't got a gun because I've just come from San Anton' with my wife. I'm married," said Potter. "And if I'd thought there was going to be any galoots like you prowling around when I brought my wife home, I'd had a gun, and don't you forget it."

"Married!" said Scratchy, not at all comprehending.

"Yes, married. I'm married," said Potter, distinctly.

"Married?" said Scratchy. Seemingly for the first time, he saw the drooping, drowning woman at the other man's side. "No!" he said. He was like a creature allowed a glimpse of another world. He moved a pace backward, and his arm, with the revolver, dropped to his side. "Is this the lady?" he asked.

"Yes; this is the lady," answered Potter.

There was another period of silence.

"Well," said Wilson at last, slowly, "I s'pose it's all off now."

"It's all off if you say so, Scratchy. You know I didn't make the trouble." Potter lifted his valise.

"Well, I 'low it's off, Jack," said Wilson. He was looking at the ground. "Married!" He was not a student of chivalry; it was merely that in the presence of this foreign condition he was a simple child of the earlier plains. He picked up his starboard revolver, and, placing both weapons in their holsters, he went away. His feet made funnel-shaped tracks in the heavy sand.

INTERPRETATION

1. What pattern, or patterns, do you discover in the plot of this story? Does the kind of patterning used have any relation to the fact that the story is divided into parts? What relation does the patterning have to suspense?

2. What is the attitude of the narrator toward his characters? How would you describe the tone of the story?

3. What do you take to be the theme of the story? What relation does the theme of the story have to the last line: "His feet made funnel-shaped tracks in the heavy sand"? Why doesn't Crane write: "The high heels of his boots made funnel-shaped tracks in the heavy sand"?

4. With the foregoing questions in mind, write an interpretative essay on "The Bride Comes to Yellow Sky."

What Character Reveals

■ THE stories in this section can be usefully considered with a special view to the problem of character in fiction. But as we have had occasion to observe several times before this, fiction never deals with character in isolation, for what a man is determines what he does, and it is primarily through what he does that we who observe him know what he is.

The proof of the inextricable interweaving of character and action may be most readily seen by a glance back at the stories in the preceding section. Though our attention was focused there upon problems of plot, we found that we could not discuss these stories without going into the problems of character. We had constantly to ask whether the actions performed were "in character"; that is, whether they were psychologically credible. We had to ask too whether the actions performed were significant in terms of character.

Though plot and character interpenetrate each other, there is some justification for stressing one problem at a time: let us consider here some of the problems of characterization. One may begin with the problem of exposition. In some fundamental sense, every character in fiction must resemble ourselves; that is, he must be recognizably human even as we are human. But some characters are obviously much more special than others, and require much fuller descriptive characterization. In "The Lottery" the characters are simple village types. Though the modern American suburbanite may consider these people a bit archaic, still he will have no real difficulty in understanding them. They are ordinary and typical, rather than special, and the author needs no elaborate techniques in presenting them. But Dravot in "The Man Who Would Be King" is a man quite outside the average reader's common acquaintance—in many ways a most unusual man—and if he is to seem real, he must be convincingly presented. The fact that Dravot is a man of action, not a meditative and introspective man, makes the author's task easier. If the character's inward life is more complicated and significant than his outer, more special problems of presentation may arise. Walter Mitty is a fairly simple instance of this kind of introverted character. Or, consider Ruby Fisher, the heroine of "A Piece of News," who would be regarded by most people as a rather simple character. Certainly she is an unsophisticated and even primitive character. Yet the "action" of this story has to do almost entirely with her interior life, and part of the charm of this story is its revelation of the unsuspected introspective depths of a "simple" person.

How shall the author present his character? Directly, with a summary of his traits and characteristics; or dramatically, through dialogue and action? The very nature of fiction suggests that the latter is its characteristic means and yet a more direct presentation is constantly used in fiction, and frequently effectively used. Much depends upon the underlying purpose of the story and much depends upon matters of scope and scale. If the author made every presentation of character indirect, insisting that each character gradually unfold himself through natural talk and gesture and action, the procedure might become intolerably boring. "The Necklace" will indicate how direct presentation—and even summary presentation—may be properly and effectively used. (Look back at the first three paragraphs of this story, p. 80.) But when he comes to the significant scenes of the story, the author of "The Necklace" discards summary in favor of dramatic presentation.

The danger of a direct presentation is that it tends to forfeit the vividness of drama and the reader's imaginative participation. Direct presentation works best, therefore, with rather flat and typical characters, or as a means to get rapidly over more perfunctory materials. When the direct presentation of character becomes also a direct commentary on the character, the author may find himself "telling" us what to feel and think rather than "rendering" a scene for our imaginative participation. O. Henry's "The Furnished Room" will illustrate. The author tends to "editorialize" on the hero's motives and beliefs, and the author's constant plucking at the reader's sleeve and nudging him to sympathize with the hero's plight may become so irritating that the whole scene seems falsified. Yet a story later to be read in this section, D. H. Lawrence's "Tickets, Please," will indicate how direct commentary—and even explicit interpretation of the characters' motives—may on occasion be effectively used by the author.

The contrast between rather ordinary characters and out-of-the-way characters can be used to suggest the opposing extremes that bound the domain of fiction. The ordinary and typical characters tend to be secondary in a story. If they are its most prominent characters, then the story is probably tilted toward the fable or the parable. (*Completely* flat characters, mere types, of course, would probably take us out of fiction altogether: even if every hero does at some level represent all of us, still no story can be about that pure abstraction, common humanity as such.)

At the opposite extreme, we find the fictional character who is so eccentric, so much out of the way, so perverse, that he ceases to be humanly credible. Fiction at this point passes off imperceptibly into the psychiatrist's case study. This is not to put narrow limits upon what the artist can do. If one looks deep enough, any character reveals complexities and eccentricities. The great and interesting personalities are indeed in a sense unique and unpredictable. Even madness is not to be automatically ruled out of the subject matter of fiction. In a story to be read later in this text, William Faulkner's "A Rose for Emily," the author tells us the story of a character perverted to the point of madness, and yet many people will feel that the story has a large human significance, and is not merely a clinician's report. (See also the comments on "An Occurrence at Owl Creek Bridge," pp. 102–103, and "A Good Man is Hard to Find," pp. 319–320.)

The domain of fiction is, then, the world of credible human beings, admittedly an amazingly diverse and varied world. Since it is the world of human beings, it can be presented concretely and dramatically. What it excludes at either end is the world of pure abstraction: economic man, Mrs. Average Housewife, the typical American, *homo sapiens;* and at the other extreme, the mere freak, the psychological monster, the report from the psychiatrist's casebook. (But of course an artist may be able to put Mrs. Average Housewife or the young man with the classic Oedipus complex into a successful story. To do so, of course, he must satisfy more than a scientific and statistical interest: the abstraction must be made credible and significant, which means it ceases to be a mere abstraction.)

From what has been said already, it is plain that the author's selection of modes of character presentation will depend upon a number of things. His decision on when to summarize traits or events, on when to describe directly, and on when to allow the character to express his feelings through dialogue and action, will depend upon the general end of the story and upon the way in which the action of the story is to be developed from a beginning, through a complicating middle, to an inevitable end.

One of the most important modes for character revelation is of course the way in which characters talk. The laconic soldier, the querulous charwoman, the shy convent-school girl, the garrulous barkeep, the pedantic professor—all have their own vocabularies and their ways of putting words together. The artist in order to be convincing must have his characters speak "in character," and his normal way of presenting the unusual character is to give us the flavor of his peculiar dialect and idiom.

This use of speech is a rich resource for dramatic presentation. But again, if used incessantly it might kill the story by making it too talky. Indirect discourse, like character summary and character description, is a quicker way of getting over the ground, and in fiction has its very important uses. Notice, for example, in "War" (pp. 132–133) that the husband's speech in which he explains why his wife and he are to be pitied is very properly put into indirect discourse: "And he felt it his duty to explain . . . that the poor woman was to be pitied, for the war was taking away . . . her only son, . . ." But the speeches of the "fat, red-faced man" who argues for the sublimity of sacrificing one's son for one's country have to be given as direct discourse. The importance of those speeches to the story, the need for dramatic vividness, the very pace of the story—all call for direct discourse. Thus we have: " 'Nonsense,' interrupted another traveler," etc.

So important is character to fiction that one way in which to approach the basic pattern of a story is to ask: "Whose story is this?" In other words, it usually is of first importance to see whose fortunes are at stake—whose situation is settled by the events that are described. Sometimes the answer is quite obvious. In "The Secret Life of Walter Mitty," for example, it is very easy to see that this is Mr. Mitty's story and not Mrs. Mitty's. Her only function is to throw light upon her husband's situation. Mrs. Mitty undoubtedly has a story—who of us has not?—and James Thurber might have elected to tell it. But he has not done so here. It is easy to see that this is Mr. Mitty's story, but it is not so easy to see whose story it is that is related in "The Man Who Would Be King." One is inclined to say that it is Dravot's story. He is pictured as the dominant member of the pair; it is he who rises to the heroic gesture at the end and who dies like a king. Yet one could at least argue that this is Peachey's story since he too learns the nature of kingship through witnessing Dravot's heroic action, and since, magnificently loyal to the memory of Dravot, he acts out a heroic role himself. But even when it is not easy to say—or even important to determine—precisely whose story it is, the question is usually worth putting. For to entertain the question is to throw light upon the relation of character with character.

One further word about the Dravot-Peachey relationship: we shall encounter in this text stories in which the story primarily belongs to "Peachey"—that is, to the observer of the action rather than to the most prominent actor himself (see pp. 126–128). For what "happens" in the story is not necessarily some external thing. An internal thing—a shifted relationship, a change of heart—may decisively change the life of a man.

When we ask of "The Lottery" whose story this is, we find ourselves in real difficulties. For if we say that it is Mrs. Hutchinson's story because it is Mrs. Hutchinson who draws the black spot and is stoned to death, we realize that in the terms of the story itself, it might just as easily have been one of a hundred other people. One is driven finally to say that this is the story of the community itself, or to put the same thing in a slightly different way, this is the story of Man—of any human being living in a community—its supporter and its victim. But this kind of answer simply draws attention again to the fact that "The Lottery" is a rather special kind of story, tilted over toward parable.

In our earlier discussion of plot we had a good deal to say about conflict in fiction. Conflict has the closest relation to character, for we cannot remain long interested in conflicts between impersonal forces. If conflicts between animals are more interesting, that is because we can rather easily project ourselves into them. We actually make some such projection even in the instance of a man's conflict with the elements or with some other inanimate force. A man who is fighting a fire or trying to beat his way through a great storm, or who is trying to hold out against hunger and pain is likely to treat the impersonal force as if it were another being—the Enemy.

Man's contest with external forces is the simplest kind of struggle and finally the least interesting. Few stories deal with it in purity. The great and typical human conflict is one human being's conflict with other human beings. This is the material out of which most of our fiction is made. Here we find the typical story of the hero defeating the villain, of the true lover winning out over the wealthy roué, of the amateur detective outwitting the Machiavellian murderer. These are the standard contests of our more popular fiction. But in this general category of one human being against another, we also find stories of greater sensitivity and depth and penetration. For human beings, being the mixture of good and bad that they are, frequently find themselves at cross purposes and in conflict—not only with outsiders but with aspects of their own natures. Indeed, the more mature examples of conflict between character and character shade off into the third category which has to do with man's conflict with himself.

One can illustrate this last statement by referring to some of the stories that we have already read. "The Man Who Would Be King" is an "action" story and we think of the conflict as primarily a conflict between Dravot and the wild tribesmen upon whom he means to impose his will. But even in this story, a more important and significant conflict occurs within Dravot himself. The conflict between his appetites and his sense of statesmanship costs Dravot his kingdom. But it is through another inward event, Dravot's conquest of himself, that his final spiritual victory comes. One can also illustrate the importance of inward conflict from Pirandello's story "War." Ostensibly the conflict is between the fervent old man's attitude toward dying for one's country and the attitudes of his frightened and apprehensive, all-too-human companions in the railway compartment. The old man's passionate arguments prevail over the minds of the others; but in convincing them, he discovers for the first time that he has never really convinced himself.

Throughout this book we have suggested the importance of the truth of coherence as distinguished from the truth of correspondence. Since a work of literature does not pretend to be a factual document of actual events, but a typical and representative "action," the demands of truth of correspondence tend to be limited to correspondence to human nature and to the human norms. Within the story or poem itself we are primarily and unremittingly concerned with truth of coherence—with how the parts cohere into a total meaningful pattern. (In this connection the student may want to reread pp. 1–2, 54–56.)

Nowhere are the claims for coherence asserted more plainly than in the matter of character presentation. A character must be credible—must make sense, must be able to command our belief. True, the character in question may be an eccentric; he may be brutally criminal; he may even be mad. But his thoughts and actions must ultimately be coherent. If the characters in a story simply don't make sense, we have to reject the story. But we must remember that the kind of sense a character must make is his own kind, not our kind. For example, a more sensible, less proud woman than Madame Loisel in "The Necklace" (p. 80) might have made a clean breast of things to her friend and been spared the terrible and unnecessary consequences, but it is the coherence of Madame Loisel's character that Maupassant must convince us of. If he does not convince us that his Madame Loisel is really capable of accepting, and persisting through, the life of hardship that comes with the loss of the necklace, then the story itself is incredible. Unless Eudora Welty has convinced us that Ruby Fisher is capable of entertaining the fantasy which the chance-read newspaper suggests to her, then her story makes no sense. An obvious test of fiction then is that the motives and actions of its characters are rendered coherent. It is the glory of fiction that the great artists have been able to render coherent so many strange and out-of-the-way, often apparently self-contradictory, examples of human nature.

BRET HARTE

Tennessee's Partner

I DO not think that we ever knew his real name. Our ignorance of it certainly never gave us any social inconvenience, for at Sandy Bar in 1854 most men were christened anew. Sometimes these appellatives were derived from some distinctiveness of dress, as in the case of "Dungaree Jack"; or from some peculiarity of habit, as shown in "Saleratus Bill," so called from an undue proportion of that chemical in his daily bread; or from some unlucky slip, as exhibited in "The Iron Pirate," a mild, inoffensive man, who earned that baleful title by his unfortunate mispronunciation of the term "iron pyrites." Perhaps this may have been the beginning of a rude heraldry; but I am constrained to think that it was because a man's real name in that day rested solely upon his own unsupported statement. "Call yourself Clifford, do you?" said Boston, addressing a timid newcomer with infinite scorn; "hell is full of such Cliffords!" He then introduced the unfortunate man, whose name happened to be really Clifford, as "Jay-bird Charley"—an unhallowed inspiration of the moment that clung to him ever after.

But to return to Tennessee's Partner, whom we never knew by any other than this relative title. That he had ever existed as a separate and distinct individuality we only learned later. It seems that in 1853 he left Poker Flat to go to San Francisco, ostensibly to procure a wife. He never got any farther than Stockton. At that place he was attracted by a young person who waited upon the table at the hotel where he took his meals. One morning he said something to her which caused her to smile not unkindly, to somewhat coquettishly break a plate of toast over his upturned, serious, simple face, and to retreat to the kitchen. He followed her, and emerged a few moments later, covered with more toast and victory. That day week they were married by a justice of the peace, and returned to Poker Flat. I am aware that something more might be made of this episode, but I prefer to tell it as it was current at Sandy Bar—in the gulches and barrooms—where all sentiment was modified by a strong sense of humor.

Of their married felicity but little is known, perhaps for the reason that Tennessee, then living with his partner, one day took occasion to say something to the bride on his own account, at which, it is said, she smiled not unkindly and chastely retreated—this time as far as Marysville, where

Tennessee followed her, and where they went to housekeeping without the aid of a justice of the peace. Tennessee's Partner took the loss of his wife simply and seriously, as was his fashion. But to everybody's surprise, when Tennessee one day returned from Marysville, without his partner's wife—she having smiled and retreated with somebody else—Tennessee's Partner was the first man to shake his hand and greet him with affection. The boys who had gathered in the cañon to see the shooting were naturally indignant. Their indignation might have found vent in sarcasm but for a certain look in Tennessee's Partner's eye that indicated a lack of humorous appreciation. In fact, he was a grave man, with a steady application to practical detail which was unpleasant in a difficulty.

Meanwhile a popular feeling against Tennessee had grown up on the Bar. He was known to be a gambler; he was suspected to be a thief. In these suspicions Tennessee's Partner was equally compromised; his continued intimacy with Tennessee after the affair above quoted could only be accounted for on the hypothesis of a copartnership of crime. At last Tennessee's guilt became flagrant. One day he overtook a stranger on his way to Red Dog. The stranger afterward related that Tennessee beguiled the time with interesting anecdote and reminiscence, but illogically concluded the interview in the following words: "And now, young man, I'll trouble you for your knife, your pistols, and your money. You see your weppings might get you into trouble at Red Dog, and your money's a temptation to the evilly disposed. I think you said your address was San Francisco. I shall endeavor to call." It may be stated here that Tennessee had a fine flow of humor, which no business preoccupation could wholly subdue.

This exploit was his last. Red Dog and Sandy Bar made common cause against the highwayman. Tennessee was hunted in very much the same fashion as his prototype, the grizzly. As the toils closed around him, he made a desperate dash through the Bar, emptying his revolver at the crowd before the Arcade Saloon, and so on up Grizzly Cañon; but at its farther extremity he was stopped by a small man on a gray horse. The men looked at each other a moment in silence. Both were fearless, both self-possessed and independent; and both types of a civilization that in the seventeenth century would have been called heroic, but in the nineteenth simply "reckless."

"What have you got there?—I call," said Tennessee, quietly.

"Two bowers and an ace," said the stranger, as quietly, showing two revolvers and a bowie knife.

"That takes me," returned Tennessee; and, with this gambler's epigram, he threw away his useless pistol, and rode back with his captor.

It was a warm night. The cool breeze which usually sprang up with the going down of the sun behind the chaparral-crested mountain was that evening withheld from Sandy Bar. The little cañon was stifling with heated resinous odors, and the decaying driftwood on the Bar sent forth faint, sickening exhalations. The feverishness of day and its fierce passions still filled the camp. Lights moved restlessly along the bank of the river, striking no answering reflection from its tawny current. Against the blackness of the pines the windows of the old loft above the express office stood out staringly bright; and through their curtainless panes the loungers below could see the forms of those who were even then deciding the fate of Tennessee. And above all this, etched on the dark firmament, rose the Sierra, remote and passionless, crowned with remoter passionless stars.

The trial of Tennessee was conducted as fairly as was consistent with a judge and jury who felt themselves to some extent obliged to justify, in their verdict, the previous irregularities of arrest and indictment. The law of Sandy Bar was implacable, but not vengeful. The excitement and personal feeling of the chase were over; with Tennessee safe in their hands, they were ready to listen patiently to any defense, which they were already satisfied was insufficient. There being no doubt in their own minds, they were willing to give the prisoner the benefit of any that might exist. Secure in the hypothesis that he ought to be hanged on general principles, they indulged him with more latitude of defense than his reckless hardihood seemed to ask. The judge appeared to be more anxious than the prisoner, who, otherwise unconcerned, evidently took a grim pleasure in the responsibility he had created. "I don't take any hand in this yer game," had been his invariable, but good-humored reply to all questions. The judge—who was also his captor—for a moment vaguely regretted that he had not shot him "on sight" that morning, but presently dismissed this human weakness as unworthy of the judicial mind. Nevertheless, when there was a tap at the door, and it was said that Tennessee's Partner was there on behalf of the prisoner, he was admitted at once without question. Perhaps the younger members of the jury, to whom the proceedings were becoming irksomely thoughtful, hailed him as a relief.

For he was not, certainly, an imposing figure. Short and stout, with a square face, sunburned into a preternatural redness, clad in a loose duck "jumper" and trousers streaked and splashed with red soil, his aspect under any circumstances would have been quaint, and was now even ridiculous. As he stooped to deposit at his feet a heavy carpetbag he was carrying, it became obvious, from partially developed legends and inscriptions, that the material with which his trousers had been patched had been originally intended for a less ambitious covering. Yet he advanced with great gravity, and after having shaken the hand of each person in the room with labored cordiality, he wiped his serious perplexed face on a red bandana handkerchief, a shade lighter than his complexion, laid his powerful hand upon the table to steady himself, and thus addressed the judge:

"I was passin' by," he began, by way of apology, "and I thought I'd just step in and see how things was gittin' on with Tennessee thar—my pardner. It's a hot night. I disremember any sich weather before on the Bar."

He paused a moment, but nobody volunteering any other meteorological recollection, he again had recourse to his pocket handkerchief, and for some moments mopped his face diligently.

"Have you anything to say on behalf of the prisoner?" said the judge finally.

"Thet's it," said Tennessee's Partner, in a tone of relief. "I come yar as Tennessee's pardner—knowing him nigh on four year, off and on, wet and dry, in luck and out o' luck. His ways ain't aller my ways, but thar ain't any p'ints in that young man, thar ain't any liveliness as he's been up to, as I don't know. And you sez to me, sez you—confidential-like, and between man and man—sez you, 'Do you know anything in his behalf?' and I sez to you, sez I—confidential-like, as between man and man—'What should a man know of his pardner?'"

"Is this all you have to say?" asked the judge impatiently, feeling, perhaps, that a dangerous sympathy of humor was beginning to humanize the court.

"Thet's so," continued Tennessee's Partner. "It ain't for me to say anything agin' him. And now, what's the case? Here's Tennessee wants money, wants it bad, and doesn't like to ask it of his old pardner. Well, what does Tennessee do? He lays for a stranger, and he fetches that stranger; and you lays for *him*, and you fetches *him*; and the honors is easy. And I put it to you, bein' a fa'r-minded man, and to you, gentlemen all, as fa'r-minded men, ef this isn't so."

"Prisoner," said the judge, interrupting, "have you any questions to ask this man?"

"No! no!" continued Tennessee's Partner, hastily. "I play this yer hand alone. To come down to the bedrock, it's just this: Tennessee, thar, has played it pretty rough and expensive-like on a stranger, and on this yer camp. And now, what's the fair thing? Some would say more, some would say less. Here's seventeen hundred dollars in coarse gold and a watch,—it's about all my pile,—and call it square!" And before a hand could be raised to prevent him, he had emptied the contents of the carpet-bag upon the table.

For a moment his life was in jeopardy. One or two men sprang to their feet, several hands groped for hidden weapons, and a suggestion to "throw him from the window" was only overridden by a gesture from the judge. Tennessee laughed. And apparently oblivious of the excitement, Tennessee's Partner improved the opportunity to mop his face again with his handkerchief.

When order was restored, and the man was made to understand, by the use of forcible figures and rhetoric, that Tennessee's offense could not be condoned by money, his face took a more serious and sanguinary hue, and those who were nearest to him noticed that his rough hand trembled slightly on the table. He hesitated a moment as he slowly returned the gold to the carpetbag, as if he had not yet entirely caught the elevated sense of justice which swayed the tribunal, and was perplexed with the belief that he had not offered enough. Then he turned to the judge, and saying, "This yer is a lone hand, played alone, and without my pardner," he bowed to the jury and was about to withdraw, when the judge called him back:

"If you have anything to say to Tennessee, you had better say it now."

For the first time that evening the eyes of the prisoner and his strange advocate met. Tennessee smiled, showed his white teeth, and saying, "Euchred, old man!" held out his hand. Tennessee's Partner took it in his own, and saying, "I just dropped in as I was passin' to see how things was gettin' on," let the hand passively fall, and adding that "it was a warm night," again mopped his face with his handkerchief, and without another word withdrew.

The two men never again met each other alive. For the unparalleled insult of a bribe offered to Judge Lynch—who, whether bigoted, weak, or narrow, was at least incorruptible—firmly fixed in the mind of that mythical personage any wavering determination of Tennessee's fate; and at the break of day he was marched, closely guarded, to meet it at the top of Marley's Hill.

How he met it, how cool he was, how he refused to say anything, how perfect were the arrangements of the committee, were all duly reported, with the addition of a warning moral and example to all future evil-doers, in the *Red Dog Clarion*, by its editor, who was present, and to whose vigorous English I cheerfully refer the reader. But the beauty of that midsummer morning, the blessed amity of earth and air and sky, the awakened life of the free woods and hills, the joyous renewal and promise of Nature, and above all, the infinite serenity that thrilled through each, was not reported, as not being a part of the social lesson. And yet, when the weak and foolish deed was done, and a life, with its possibilities and responsibilities, had passed out of the misshapen thing that dangled between earth and sky, the birds sang, the flowers bloomed, the sun shone, as cheerily as before; and possibly the *Red Dog Clarion* was right.

Tennessee's Partner was not in the group that surrounded the ominous tree. But as they turned to disperse, attention was drawn to the singular appearance of a motionless donkey cart halted at the side of the road. As they approached, they at once recognized the venerable Jenny and the two-wheeled cart as the property of Tennessee's Partner, used by him in carrying dirt from his claim; and a few paces distant the owner of the equipage himself, sitting under a buckeye tree, wiping the perspiration from his glowing face. In answer to an inquiry, he said he had come for the body of the "diseased," "if it was all the same to the committee." He didn't wish to "hurry anything"; he could "wait." He was not working that day; and when the gentlemen were done with the "diseased," he would take him. "Ef thar is any present," he added, in his simple, serious way, "as would care to jine in the fun'l, they kin come." Perhaps it was from a sense of humor, which I have already intimated was a feature of Sandy Bar—perhaps it was from something even better than that, but two thirds of the loungers accepted the invitation at once.

It was noon when the body of Tennessee was delivered into the hands of his partner. As the cart drew up to the fatal tree, we noticed that it contained a rough oblong box,—apparently made from a section of sluicing,—and half filled with bark and the tassels of pine. The cart was further decorated with slips of willow, and made fragrant with buckeye blossoms. When the body was deposited in the box, Tennessee's Partner drew over it a piece of tarred canvas, and gravely mounting the narrow seat in front, with his feet upon the shafts, urged the little donkey forward. The equipage moved slowly on, at that decorous pace which was habitual with Jenny even under less solemn circumstances. The men—half curiously, half jestingly, but all good-humoredly—strolled along beside the cart, some in advance, some a little in the rear of the homely catafalque. But whether from the narrowing of the road or some present sense of decorum, as the cart passed on, the company fell to the rear in couples, keeping step, and otherwise assuming the external show of a formal procession. Jack Folinsbee, who had at the outset played a funeral march in dumb show upon an imaginary trombone, desisted from a lack of sympathy and appreciation—not having, perhaps, your true humorist's capacity to be content with the enjoyment of his own fun.

The way led through Grizzly Cañon, by this time clothed in funereal drapery and shadows. The redwoods, burying their moccasined feet in the red soil, stood in Indian file along the track, trailing an uncouth benediction from their bending boughs upon the passing bier. A hare, surprised into helpless inactivity, sat upright and pulsating in the ferns by the roadside, as the cortège went by. Squirrels hastened to gain a secure outlook from higher boughs; and the bluejays, spreading their wings, fluttered before them like outriders, until the outskirts of Sandy Bar were reached, and the solitary cabin of Tennessee's Partner.

Viewed under more favorable circumstances, it would not have been a cheerful place. The unpicturesque site, the rude and unlovely outlines, the unsavory details, which distinguish the nest-building of the California miner, were all here, with the dreariness of decay superadded. A few paces from the cabin there was a rough enclosure, which, in the brief days of Tennessee's Partner's matrimonial felicity, had been used as a garden, but was now overgrown with fern. As we approached it, we were surprised to find that what we had taken for a recent attempt at cultivation was the broken soil about an open grave.

The cart was halted before the enclosure, and rejecting the offers of assistance with the same air of simple self-reliance he had displayed throughout, Tennessee's Partner lifted the rough coffin on his back, and deposited it unaided within the shallow grave. He then nailed down the board which served as a lid, and mounting the little mound of earth beside it, took off his hat and slowly mopped his face with his handkerchief. This the crowd felt was a preliminary to speech, and they disposed themselves variously on stumps and boulders, and sat expectant.

"When a man," began Tennessee's Partner slowly, "has been running free all day, what's the natural thing for him to do? Why, to come home. And if he ain't in a condition to go home, what can his best friend do? Why, bring him home. And here's Tennessee has been running free, and we brings him home from his wandering." He paused and picked up a fragment of quartz, rubbed it thoughtfully on his sleeve and went on: "It ain't the first time I've packed him on my back, as you see'd me now. It ain't the first time that I brought him to this yer cabin when he couldn't help himself; it ain't the first time that I and Jinny have waited for him on yon hill, and picked him up and so fetched him home, when he couldn't speak and didn't know me. And now that it's the last time, why"—he paused, and rubbed the quartz gently on his sleeve—"you see it's sort of rough on his pardner. And now, gentlemen," he added abruptly, picking up his long-handled shovel, "the fun'l's over; and my thanks, and Tennessee's thanks, to you for your trouble."

Resisting any proffers of assistance, he began to fill in the grave, turning his back upon the crowd, that after a few moments' hesitation gradually withdrew. As they crossed the little ridge that hid Sandy Bar from view, some, looking back, thought they could see Tennessee's Partner, his work done, sitting upon the grave, his shovel between his knees, and his face buried in his red bandana handkerchief. But it was argued by others that you couldn't tell his face from his handkerchief at that distance, and this point remained undecided.

In the reaction that followed the feverish excitement of that day, Tennessee's Partner was not forgotten. A secret investigation had cleared him of any complicity in Tennessee's guilt, and left only a suspicion of his general sanity. Sandy Bar made a point of calling on him, and proffering various uncouth but well-meant kindnesses. But from that day his rude health and great strength seemed visibly to decline; and when the rainy season fairly set in, and the tiny grass blades were beginning to peep from the rocky mound above Tennessee's grave, he took to his bed.

One night, when the pines beside the cabin were swaying in the storm and trailing their slender fingers over the roof, and the roar and rush of the swollen river were heard below, Tennessee's Partner lifted his head from the pillow, saying, "It is time to go for Tennessee; I must put Jinny in the cart"; and would have risen from his bed but for the restraint of his attendant. Struggling, he still pursued his singular fancy: "There, now, steady, Jinny—steady, old girl. How dark it is! Look out for the ruts—and look out for him, too, old gal. Sometimes, you know, when he's blind drunk, he drops down right in the trail. Keep on straight up to the pine on the top of the hill. Thar! I told you so!—thar he is—coming this way, too—all by himself, sober, and his face a-shining. Tennessee! Pardner!"

And so they met.

INTERPRETATION

This is the story of a man's intense loyalty to his friend. The man Tennessee actually steals his partner's wife, but the friendship of the men survives even this severe test: they become reconciled, and later after Tennessee has been executed for highway robbery, his partner claims the body, buries it with such rites of decency as he can contrive, and soon himself wastes away and dies. What makes this display of loyalty even more remarkable, and perhaps, therefore, all the more moving, is that Tennessee's partner is not a man to whom we would ordinarily ascribe much delicacy of feeling. Not that this latter point invalidates the story. Other writers have remarked upon the intensity and rightness of the feelings of simple and "unliterary" persons. William Wordsworth makes this point over and over again in poetry. Or, to take an instance from a contemporary writer, Ernest Hemingway frequently allows his "tough" and "hard-boiled" characters to reveal a sensitivity that belies their apparent callousness (see pp. 271–272).

The difficulty with this story has to do with the credibility of the actions of Tennessee's partner. Do we really believe that he would act so magnanimously? That will depend upon our understanding of his character; and that in turn will have to do with Bret Harte's presentation of the psychological steps by which Tennessee's partner arrives at the actions in question. In any case, the episode of the wife-stealing will be the hardest to accept.

The community in this instance certainly expected trouble: according to the primitive code the loss of honor that Tennessee's partner has suffered definitely demands blood-letting. Moreover, the partner is a man who evidently sees everything in very concrete and personal terms—witness his conduct at the trial in which he shows that he has no conception of abstract justice, and the relation of a man to his wife is a very personal and concrete relation. How could this man forgive Tennessee? (If, of course, he regarded his wife as a mere chattel, then the whole meaning of his act of forgiveness is lost, for the conflict—between affection for his friend on the one hand and affection for his wife on the other—disappears from the situation.)

The problems that we raise are not insuperable. A skillful writer of fiction could presumably make thoroughly credible the reconciliation between Tennessee and his partner. But Bret Harte has really dodged this psychological problem. Even though it is plain that for Bret Harte it is the burial scene and not the wife-stealing episode that is the climax of the story, we still have a right to ask that the wife-stealing episode be credibly developed. In fact, if it is not made credible, the whole story loses its point.

We have said that the burial scene is the climax of the story. What else does Bret Harte give us in preparation for this climax? He gives us the scene of the attempted bribery. The purpose of this scene seems to be to indicate the partner's naïveté with regard to the conventions of society, to the nature of law, and even to the concept of abstract justice itself. Apparently, he honestly sees the situation into which Tennessee has fallen as one which can be settled by a money payment. The stranger will be compensated for his losses and will be given something for his trouble. Perhaps there is the implication that he is attempting to bribe the court; certainly, the violent reaction of the bystanders would support this assumption, though the judge apparently realizes the childlike nature of the man's mind. Indeed, the judge proceeds to give the man a lecture on the nature of law: "the man was made to understand . . . that Tennessee's offense could not be condoned by money." But another purpose of the scene is to develop the idea of the partner's dog-like devotion: he is willing to sacrifice his "pile" for his friend.

For what, after all, does this court incident intend to prepare us? It is, of course, not merely for the incident of the burial, as such. For someone among the rough citizenry would have buried the hanged man in any case, and perhaps with a kind of elemental pity. (Tennessee, has, for instance, certain qualities which would extort special admiration in this primitive community—a courage and coolness, which are dramatized several times in the story.) The intended high point in the story is the funeral oration, which Tennessee's partner delivers to the camp. It is here that our full sense of the pathos is supposed to emerge.

But if such pathos is to emerge to the full, and is to be meaningful, the author must have convinced us (1) that it is logical for this particular character to deliver the oration under the circumstances and (2) that this oration brings to focus elements of interpretation and meaning implicit in previous incidents.

But there are more difficulties. First, would the partner, as his character has been prepared for in earlier pages of the story, have made such a speech to the members of the community who had turned out, purely from curiosity, to see what he would do? A man whose life had been dominated by a merely personal attachment to his friend and who had been completely incapable of understanding why his friend had to be hanged (as indicated by the bribery scene), would more probably have felt a sullen resentment against the men who had done his friend to death for, in his eyes, no good reason. At least, he would probably have wanted privacy for his sorrow. (He can be under no illusion that the spectators have come out of love for Tennessee.)

Second, assuming that the partner would have delivered the oration, would he have said what Bret Harte makes him say? For example, would he have apologized to the spectators and have thanked them for their trouble? (Notice that Bret Harte does not intend for us to take this as the bitter irony of a hurt man, but as a manifestation of a kind of Christlike forgiveness. The partner is almost too good to be true.) And notice, further, in this connection, what Bret Harte has the partner say in his delirium as he dies of a broken heart. Here, even the language becomes unrealistic; it is entirely out of the partner's idiom. For example, would he have said: "There, now, steady, Jinny—steady, old girl. How dark it is!" Isn't it more likely that he would have said: "It's dark as hell." Or: "God-a-mighty, it's dark!" Why does Bret Harte break out of the partner's idiom? Because Bret Harte is straining for a highly emotional effect, and feeling that the realistic language is not good enough, he resorts to "poeticizing" the character. In other words, he is not willing to let the case rest on its own merits. The same thing is true of the symbolic reference, in the dying speech, to the pine tree on the top of the hill.

But other examples of such strain are to be found earlier in the story— take, for example, the description of nature as the partner carries the body to the place of burial: "The way led through Grizzly Cañon, by this time clothed in funereal drapery and shadows. The redwoods, burying their moccasined feet in the red soil, stood in Indian file along the track, trailing an uncouth benediction from their bending boughs upon the passing bier." Nature, apparently, is sympathetic with the partner's grief. Like him, it can give only an "uncouth benediction," but it expresses its brooding sympathy as best it can. One recognizes that a writer may legitimately use description of nature as a device for defining the atmosphere of a piece of fiction, or may even use it as specific symbolism. But it should be quite clear that Bret Harte here is not using it legitimately. It is used here to give a false heightening to the pathos of the scene, and the language in which the description is couched is as "poeticized" as is the language of the partner's dying speech. For example, the description of the redwoods "burying their moccasined feet in the red soil" is completely irrelevant and represents an attempt at fanciful decoration; it is another instance of the author's straining for effects which, he seems to feel, are not adequately supported by the situation in itself.*

The presence of this straining for an emotional effect is one of the surest symptoms that one is dealing with a case of sentimentality. In its

---

* Compare Bret Harte's use of nature here with the use made of the references to the storm in "A Piece of News," p. 104, or to the use of nature made by Chekhov in "The Lament," p. 183.

general sense, as we have seen, sentimentality may be defined as an emotional response in excess of the occasion. We speak of a person who weeps at some trivial occurrence as being sentimental. Such a person lacks a sense of proportion and gets a morbid enjoyment from an emotional debauch for its own sake. When we apply the term to a piece of literature, a story, for instance, we usually mean that the author intends for the reader to experience an intense emotion which is actually not justified by the materials of the story.

One symptom of sentimentality is, as we have said, the author's straining to heighten and prettify and poeticize his language quite apart from the dramatic issues involved in the story.

A second symptom frequently to be found is "editorializing" on the part of the author—pointing out to the reader what he should feel, nudging the reader to respond—devices which would not be necessary if the story could make its own case. (For example, Bret Harte comments on the hanging of Tennessee as follows: "And yet, when the weak and foolish deed was done, and a life, with its possibilities and responsibilities, had passed out of the misshapen thing that dangled between earth and sky, the birds sang, the flowers bloomed, the sun shone, as cheerily as before. . . .")

A third symptom is the tendency to dodge the real issues which should prepare for the final effect of a story. That is, an author who is primarily concerned with giving the emotional effect may not be too scrupulous about the means adopted to that end. For example, in this story Bret Harte is so thoroughly obsessed with the pathos of the partner's loyalty that he has devoted no thought to the precise nature of the basis of that loyalty. As has already been pointed out, he does not bring the wife-stealing episode into real focus. Psychologically and dramatically, the wife-stealing scene, as material, is the most interesting thing in the story. By skimping it and moving away from it toward the final effort at pathos, Bret Harte has made the whole story seem anticlimactic and illogical. Either he was so little interested in the psychology of the situation that he did not investigate it, or he was aware that the issues involved were too complicated for him to handle.

The reading of this story raises such questions as this: Has not Bret Harte taken a theme which, perhaps, he had seen successfully employed for pathetic effects in other fiction, and attempted to trick it out with a new romantic setting, touches of local color (such as descriptions of the community and bits of dialect), and poeticized writing, without ever grounding the story in a presentation of the real psychological issues involved—without, in other words, trying to understand his main character?

1. Compare the relation of Tennessee and his partner with that of Dravot and Peachey in "The Man Who Would Be King." How does Kipling avoid sentimentality?

2. Is O. Henry's "The Furnished Room" guilty of sentimentality? Compare the "editorializing" of O. Henry with that of Bret Harte. What is the function of the "editorializing" in each case?

JAMES JOYCE

Araby

NORTH Richmond Street, being blind, was a quiet street except at the hour when the Christian Brothers' School set the boys free. An uninhabited house of two stories stood at the blind end, detached from its neighbors in a square ground. The other houses of the street, conscious of decent lives within them, gazed at one another with brown imperturbable faces.

The former tenant of our house, a priest, had died in the back drawing room. Air, musty from having been long enclosed, hung in all the rooms, and the waste room behind the kitchen was littered with old useless papers. Among these I found a few paper-covered books, the pages of which were curled and damp: *The Abbot*, by Walter Scott, *The Devout Communicant*, and *The Memoirs of Vidocq*. I liked the last best because its leaves were yellow. The wild garden behind the house contained a central apple tree and a few straggling bushes under one of which I found the late tenant's rusty bicycle pump. He had been a very charitable priest; in his will he had left all his money to institutions and the furniture of his house to his sister.

When the short days of winter came dusk fell before we had well eaten our dinners. When we met in the street the houses had grown somber. The space of sky above us was the color of ever-changing violet and towards it the lamps of the street lifted their feeble lanterns. The cold air stung us and we played till our bodies glowed. Our shouts echoed in the silent street. The career of our play brought us through the dark muddy lanes behind the houses where we ran the gauntlet of the rough tribes from the cottages, to the back doors of the dark dripping gardens where odors arose from the ashpits, to the dark odorous stables where a coachman smoothed and combed the horse or shook music from the buckled harness. When we returned to the street, light from the kitchen windows had filled the areas. If my uncle was seen turning the corner we hid in the shadow until we had seen him safely housed. Or if Mangan's sister came out on the doorstep to call her brother in to his tea we watched her from our shadow peer up and down the street. We waited to see whether she would remain or go in and, if she remained, we left our shadow and walked up to Mangan's steps resignedly. She was waiting for us, her figure defined by the light from the half-opened door. Her brother always teased her before he obeyed and I stood by the railings looking at her. Her dress swung as she moved her body and the soft rope of her hair tossed from side to side.

Every morning I lay on the floor in the front parlor watching her door. The blind was pulled down to within an inch of the sash so that I could not be seen. When she came out on the doorstep my heart leaped. I ran to the hall, seized my books and followed her. I kept her brown figure always in my eye and, when we came near the point at which our ways diverged, I quickened my pace and passed her. This happened morning after morning. I had never spoken to her, except for a few casual words, and yet her name was like a summons to all my foolish blood.

Her image accompanied me even in places the most hostile to romance. On Saturday evenings when my aunt went marketing I had to go to carry some of the parcels. We walked through the flaring streets, jostled by drunken men and bargaining women, amid the curses of laborers, the shrill litanies of shop boys who stood on guard by the barrels of pigs' cheeks, the nasal chanting of street singers, who sang a *come-all-you* about O'Donovan Rossa, or a ballad about the troubles in our native land. These noises converged in a single sensation of life for me: I imagined that I bore my chalice safely through a throng of foes. Her name sprang to my lips at moments in strange prayers and praises which I myself did not understand. My eyes were often full of tears (I could not tell why) and at times a flood from my heart seemed to pour itself out into my bosom. I thought little of the future. I did not know whether I would ever speak to her or not or, if I spoke to her, how I could tell her of my confused adoration. But my body was like a harp and her words and gestures were like fingers running upon the wires.

One evening I went into the back drawing room in which the priest had died. It was a dark rainy evening and there was no sound in the house. Through one of the broken panes I heard the rain impinge upon the earth, the fine incessant needles of water playing in the sodden beds. Some distant lamp or lighted window gleamed below me. I was thankful that I could see so little. All my senses seemed to desire to veil themselves and, feeling that I was about to slip from them, I pressed the palms of my hands together until they trembled, murmuring: "*O love! O love!*" many times.

At last she spoke to me. When she addressed the first words to me I was so confused that I did not know what to answer. She asked me was I going to *Araby*. I forgot whether I answered yes or no. It would be a splendid bazaar, she said; she would love to go.

"And why can't you?" I asked.

While she spoke she turned a silver bracelet round and round her wrist. She could not go, she said, because there would be a retreat that week in her convent. Her brother and two other boys were fighting for their caps and I was alone at the railings. She held one of the spikes, bowing her head towards me. The light from the lamp opposite our door caught the white curve of her neck, lit up her hair that rested there and, falling, lit up the hand upon the railing. It fell over one side of her dress and caught the white border of a petticoat, just visible as she stood at ease.

"It's well for you," she said.

"If I go," I said, "I will bring you something."

What innumerable follies laid waste my waking and sleeping thoughts after that evening! I wished to annihilate the tedious intervening days. I chafed against the work of school. At night in my bedroom and by day in the classroom her image came between me and the page I strove to read. The syllables of the word *Araby* were called to me through the silence in which my soul luxuriated and cast an Eastern enchantment over me. I asked for leave to go to the bazaar on Saturday night. My aunt was surprised and hoped it was not some Freemason affair. I answered few questions in class. I watched my master's face pass from amiability to sternness; he hoped I was not beginning to idle. I could not call my wandering thoughts together. I had hardly any patience with the serious work of life which, now that it stood between me and my desire, seemed to me child's play, ugly monotonous child's play.

On Saturday morning I reminded my uncle that I wished to go to the bazaar in the evening. He was fussing at the hall stand, looking for the hat brush, and answered me curtly:

"Yes, boy, I know."

As he was in the hall I could not go into the front parlor and lie at the window. I left the house in bad humor and walked slowly towards the school. The air was pitilessly raw and already my heart misgave me.

When I came home to dinner my uncle had not yet been home. Still it was early. I sat staring at the clock for some time and, when its ticking began to irritate me, I left the room. I mounted the staircase and gained the upper part of the house. The high cold empty gloomy rooms liberated me and I went from room to room singing. From the front window I saw my companions playing below in the street. Their cries reached me weakened and indistinct and, leaning my forehead against the cool glass, I looked over at the dark house where she lived. I may have stood there for an hour, seeing nothing but the brown-clad figure cast by my imagination, touched discreetly by the lamplight at the curved neck, at the hand upon the railings and at the border below the dress.

When I came downstairs again I found Mrs. Mercer sitting at the fire. She was an old garrulous woman, a pawnbroker's widow, who collected used stamps for some pious purpose. I had to endure the gossip of the tea table. The meal was prolonged beyond an hour and still my uncle did not come. Mrs. Mercer stood up to go: she was sorry she couldn't wait any longer, but it was after eight o'clock and she did not like to be out late, as the night air was bad for her. When she had gone I began to walk up and down the room, clenching my fists. My aunt said:

"I'm afraid you may put off your bazaar for this night of Our Lord."

At nine o'clock I heard my uncle's latchkey in the hall door. I heard him talking to himself and heard the hall stand rocking when it had received the weight of his overcoat. I could interpret these signs. When he was midway through his dinner I asked him to give me the money to go to the bazaar. He had forgotten.

"The people are in bed and after their first sleep now," he said.

I did not smile. My aunt said to him energetically:

"Can't you give him the money and let him go? You've kept him late enough as it is."

My uncle said he was very sorry he had forgotten. He said he believed in the old saying: "All work and no play makes Jack a dull boy." He asked me where I was going and, when I had told him a second time he asked me did I know *The Arab's Farewell to His Steed*. When I left the kitchen he was about to recite the opening lines of the piece to my aunt.

I held a florin tightly in my hand as I strode down Buckingham Street towards the station. The sight of the streets thronged with buyers and glaring with gas recalled to me the purpose of my journey. I took my seat in a third-class carriage of a deserted train. After an intolerable delay the train moved out of the station slowly. It crept onward among ruinous houses and over the twinkling river. At Westland Row Station a crowd of people pressed to the carriage doors; but the porters moved them back, saying that it was a special train for the bazaar. I remained alone in the bare carriage. In a few minutes the train drew up beside an improvised wooden platform. I passed out on to the road and saw by the lighted dial of a clock that it was ten minutes to ten. In front of me was a large building which displayed the magical name.

I could not find any sixpenny entrance and, fearing that the bazaar would be closed, I passed in quickly through a turnstile, handing a shilling to a weary-looking man. I found myself in a big hall girdled at half its height by a gallery. Nearly all the stalls were closed and the greater part of the hall was in darkness. I recognized a silence like that which pervades a church after a service. I walked into the center of the bazaar timidly. A few people were gathered about the stalls which were still open. Before a curtain, over which the words *Café Chantant* were written in colored lamps, two men were counting money on a salver. I listened to the fall of the coins.

Remembering with difficulty why I had come I went over to one of stalls and examined porcelain vases and flowered tea sets. At the door of the stall a young lady was talking and laughing with two young gentle-

men. I remarked their English accents and listened vaguely to their conversation.

"O, I never said such a thing!"

"O, but you did!"

"O, but I didn't!"

"Didn't she say that?"

"Yes. I heard her."

"O, there's a . . . fib!"

Observing me, the young lady came over and asked me did I wish to
buy anything. The tone of her voice was not encouraging; she seemed to
have spoken to me out of a sense of duty. I looked humbly at the great jars
that stood like eastern guards at either side of the dark entrance to the stall
and murmured:

"No, thank you."

The young lady changed the position of one of the vases and went
back to the two young men. They began to talk of the same subject. Once
or twice the young lady glanced at me over her shoulder.

I lingered before her stall, though I knew my stay was useless, to make
my interest in her wares seem the more real. Then I turned away slowly
and walked down the middle of the bazaar. I allowed the two pennies
to fall against the sixpence in my pocket. I heard a voice call from one
end of the gallery that the light was out. The upper part of the hall was
now completely dark.

Gazing up into the darkness I saw myself as a creature driven and
derided by vanity; and my eyes burned with anguish and anger.

INTERPRETATION

On what may be called the simplest level this is a story of a boy's
disappointment. A great part of the story, however, does not directly concern itself with the boy's love affair, but with the world in which he lives—
the description of his street, the information about the dead priest and the
priest's abandoned belongings, the relations with the aunt and uncle. These
matters seem to come very naturally into the story; that is, they may be
justified individually in the story on realistic grounds. But if such elements
merely serve as "setting" or as mere atmosphere, then the story is obviously
overloaded with nonfunctional material. Obviously, for any reader except
the most casual, these items do have a function. If we find in what way
these apparently irrelevant items in "Araby" are related to each other and
to the disappointment of the boy, we shall have defined the theme of the
story.

What, then, is the relation of the boy's disappointment to such matters
as the belongings of the dead priest, the fact that he stands apart talking to
the girl while his friends are quarreling over the cap, the gossip over the

tea table, the uncle's lateness, and so on? One thing that is immediately suggested by the mention of these things is the boy's growing sense of isolation, the lack of sympathy between him and his friends, teachers, and family. He says, "I imagined that I bore my chalice safely through a throng of foes." For instance, when the uncle is standing in the hall, the boy could not go into the front parlor and lie at the window; or at school his ordinary occupations began to seem "ugly monotonous child's play." But this sense of isolation has, also, moments which are almost triumphant, as for example, is implied when the porters at the station wave the crowds back, "saying that it was a special train for the bazaar" and was not for them. The boy is left alone in the bare carriage, but he is going to "Araby," moving triumphantly toward some romantic and exotic fulfillment. The metaphor of the chalice implies the same kind of precious secret triumph. It is not only the ordinary surrounding world, however, from which he is cruelly or triumphantly isolated. He is also isolated from the girl herself. He talks to her only once, and then is so confused that he does not know how to answer her. But the present which he hopes to bring her from Araby would somehow serve as a means of communicating his feelings to her, a symbol for their relationship in the midst of the inimical world.

In the last scene at the bazaar, there is a systematic, though subtle, preparation for the final realization on the part of the boy. There is the "improvised wooden platform" in contrast with the "magical name" displayed above the building. Inside, most of the stalls are closed. The young lady and young men who talk together are important in the preparation. They pay the boy no mind, except in so far as the young lady is compelled by her position as clerk to ask him what he wants. But her tone is not "encouraging." She, too, belongs to the inimical world. But she, also, belongs to a world into which he is trying to penetrate: she and her admirers are on terms of easy intimacy—an intimacy in contrast to his relation to Mangan's sister. It is an exotic, rich world into which he cannot penetrate: he can only look "humbly at the great jars that stood like eastern guards at either side of the dark entrance to the stall. . . ." But, ironically, the young lady and her admirers, far from realizing that they are on holy, guarded ground, indulge in a trivial, easy banter, which seems to defile and cheapen the secret world from which the boy is barred. How do we know this? It is not stated, but the contrast between the conversation of the young lady and her admirers, and the tone of the sentence quoted just above indicates such an interpretation.

This scene, then, helps to point up and particularize the general sense of isolation suggested by the earlier descriptive materials, and thereby to prepare for the last sentence of the story, in which, under the sudden darkness of the cheap and barnlike bazaar, the boy sees himself as "a creature driven and derided by vanity," while his eyes burn with anguish and anger.

We have seen how the apparently casual incidents and items of description do function in the story to build up the boy's sense of intolerable isolation. But this is only part of the function of this material. The careful reader will have noticed how many references, direct or indirect, there are to religion and the ritual of the church. We have the dead priest, the Christian Brothers' School, the aunt's hope that the bazaar is not "some Freemason affair," her remark when the uncle has been delayed, to "this night of Our Lord." At one level, these references merely indicate the type of community in which the impressionable boy is growing up. But there are other, less obvious, references, which relate more intimately to the boy's experience. Even the cries of the shop boys for him are "shrill litanies." He imagines that he bears a "chalice safely through a throng of foes." When he is alone the name of Mangan's sister springs to his lips "in strange prayers and praises." For this reason, when he speaks of his "confused adoration," we see that the love of the girl takes on, for him, something of the nature of a mystic, religious experience. The use of the very word *confused* hints of the fact that romantic love and religious love are mixed up in his mind.

It has been said that the boy is isolated from a world which seems ignorant of, and even hostile to, his love. In a sense he knows that his aunt and uncle are good and kind, but they do not understand him. He had once found satisfaction in the society of his companions and in his school work, but he has become impatient with both. But there is also a sense in which he accepts his isolation and is even proud of it. The world not only does not understand his secret but would cheapen and contaminate it. The metaphor of the chalice borne through a throng of foes, supported as it is by the body of the story, suggests a sort of consecration like that of the religious devotee. The implications of the references to religion, then, help define the boy's attitude and indicate why, for him, so much is staked upon the journey to the bazaar. It is interesting to note, therefore, that the first overt indication of his disillusionment and disappointment is expressed in a metaphor involving a church: "Nearly all the stalls were closed and the greater part of the hall was in darkness. I recognized a silence like that which pervades a church after a service. . . . Two men were counting money on a salver. I listened to the fall of the coins." So, it would seem, here we have the idea that the contamination of the world has invaded the very temple of love—there are, as it were, money-changers in the very temple. (The question may arise as to whether this is not reading too much into the passage. Perhaps it is. But whatever interpretation is to be made of the particular incident, it is by just such suggestion and implication that closely wrought stories, such as this one, are controlled by the author and embody their fundamental meaning.)

Is this a sentimental story? It is about an adolescent love affair, about "calf love," a subject which usually is not to be taken seriously and is often an occasion for amusement. The boy of the story is obviously investing casual incidents with a meaning which they do not deserve; and himself admits, in the end, that he has fallen into self-deception. How does the author avoid the charge that he has taken the matter over-seriously?

The answer to this question would involve a consideration of the point of view from which the story is told. It is told by the hero himself, but after a long lapse of time, after he has reached maturity. This fact, it is true, is not stated in the story, but the style itself is not that of an adolescent boy. It is a formal and complicated style, rich, as has already been observed, in subtle implications. In other words, the man is looking back upon the boy, detached and judicial. For instance, the boy, in the throes of the experience, would never have said of himself: "I had never spoken to her, except for a few casual words, and yet her name was like a summons to all my foolish blood." The man knows, as it were, that the behavior of the boy was, in a sense, foolish. The emotions of the boy are confused, but the person telling the story, the boy grown up, is not confused. He has unraveled the confusion long after, knows that it existed and why it existed.

If the man has unraveled the confusions of the boy, why is the event still significant to him? Is he merely dwelling on the pathos of adolescent experience? It seems, rather, that he sees in the event, as he looks back on it, a kind of parable of a problem which has run through later experience. The discrepancy between the real and the ideal scarcely exists for the child, but it is a constant problem, in all sorts of terms, for the adult. This story is about a boy's first confrontation of that problem—that is, about his growing up. The man may have made adjustments to this problem, and may have worked out certain provisional solutions, but, looking back, he still recognizes it as a problem, and an important one. The sense of isolation and disillusion which, in the boy's experience, may seem to spring from a trivial situation, becomes not less, but more aggravated and fundamental in the adult's experience. So, the story is not merely an account of a stage in the process of growing up—it does not merely represent a clinical interest in the psychology of growing up—but is a symbolic rendering of a central conflict in mature experience.

1. What does the boy have in common with the dead priest? Suppose that the dead man had been a shopkeeper, a lawyer, or anyone else who did not "carry a chalice." Would that have made any difference in the story?

2. Children are supposed to have more imagination than adults. What has happened when, for the boy, his previous occupations seem to be "ugly monotonous child's play"?

3. There is in this story a relatively small amount of dramatically rendered material. Can you say why? Is this fact consistent with the general tone and meaning of the story?

FRANK O'CONNOR

The Drunkard

IT was a terrible blow to Father when Mr. Dooley on the terrace died. Mr. Dooley was a commercial traveller with two sons in the Dominicans and a car of his own, so socially he was miles ahead of us, but he had no false pride. Mr. Dooley was an intellectual, and, like all intellectuals the thing he loved best was conversation, and in his own limited way Father was a well-read man and could appreciate an intelligent talker. Mr. Dooley was remarkably intelligent. Between business acquaintances and clerical contacts, there was very little he didn't know about what went on in town, and evening after evening he crossed the road to our gate to explain to Father the news behinds the news. He had a low, palavering voice and a knowing smile, and Father would listen in astonishment, giving him a conversational lead now and again, and then stump triumphantly in to Mother with his face aglow and ask: "Do you know what Mr. Dooley is after telling me?" Ever since, when somebody has given me some bit of information off the record I have found myself on the point of asking: "Was it Mr. Dooley told you that?"

Till I actually saw him laid out in his brown shroud with the rosary beads entwined between his waxy fingers I did not take the report of his death seriously. Even then I felt there must be a catch and that some summer evening Mr. Dooley must reappear at our gate to give us the lowdown on the next world. But Father was very upset, partly because Mr. Dooley was about one age with himself, a thing that always gives a distinctly personal turn to another man's demise; partly because now he would have no one to tell him what dirty work was behind the latest scene at the Corporation. You could count on your fingers the number of men in Blarney Lane who read the papers as Mr. Dooley did, and none of these would have overlooked the fact that Father was only a laboring man. Even Sullivan, the carpenter, a mere nobody, thought he was a cut above Father. It was certainly a solemn event.

"Half past two to the Curragh," Father said meditatively, putting down the paper.

"But you're not thinking of going to the funeral?" Mother asked in alarm.

"'Twould be expected," Father said, scenting opposition. "I wouldn't give it to say to them."

"I think," said Mother with suppressed emotion, "it will be as much as anyone will expect if you go to the chapel with him."

("Going to the chapel," of course, was one thing, because the body was removed after work, but going to a funeral meant the loss of a half-day's pay.)

"The people hardly know us," she added.

"God between us and all harm," Father replied with dignity, "we'd be glad if it was our own turn."

To give Father his due, he was always ready to lose a half day for the sake of an old neighbor. It wasn't so much that he liked funerals as that he was a conscientious man who did as he would be done by; and nothing could have consoled him so much for the prospect of his own death as the assurance of a worthy funeral. And, to give Mother her due, it wasn't the half-day's pay she begrudged, badly as we could afford it.

Drink, you see, was Father's great weakness. He could keep steady for months, even for years, at a stretch, and while he did he was as good as gold. He was first up in the morning and brought the mother a cup of tea in bed, stayed at home in the evenings and read the paper; saved money and bought himself a new blue serge suit and bowler hat. He laughed at the folly of men who, week in and week out, left their hard-earned money with the publicans; and sometimes, to pass an idle hour, he took pencil and paper and calculated precisely how much he saved each week through being a teetotaller. Being a natural optimist he sometimes continued this calculation through the whole span of his prospective existence and the total was breathtaking. He would die worth hundreds.

If I had only known it, this was a bad sign; a sign he was becoming stuffed up with spiritual pride and imagining himself better than his neighbors. Sooner or later, the spiritual pride grew till it called for some form of celebration. Then he took a drink—not whisky, of course; nothing like that—just a glass of some harmless drink like lager beer. That was the end of Father. By the time he had taken the first he already realized that he had made a fool of himself, took a second to forget it and a third to forget that he couldn't forget, and at last came home reeling drunk. From this on it was "The Drunkard's Progress," as in the moral prints. Next day he stayed in from work with a sick head while Mother went off to make his excuses at the works, and inside a fortnight he was poor and savage and despondent again. Once he began he drank steadily through everything down to the kitchen clock. Mother and I knew all the phases and dreaded all the dangers. Funerals were one.

"I have to go to Dunphy's to do a half-day's work," said Mother in distress. "Who's to look after Larry?"

"I'll look after Larry," Father said graciously. "The little walk will do him good."

There was no more to be said, though we all knew I didn't need anyone to look after me, and that I could quite well have stayed at home and looked after Sonny, but I was being attached to the party to act as a brake on Father. As a brake I had never achieved anything, but Mother still had great faith in me.

Next day, when I got home from school, Father was there before me and made a cup of tea for both of us. He was very good at tea, but too heavy in the hand for anything else; the way he cut bread was shocking. Afterwards, we went down the hill to the church. Father wearing his best blue serge and a bowler cocked to one side of his head with the least suggestion of the masher. To his great joy he discovered Peter Crowley among the mourners. Peter was another danger signal, as I knew well from certain experiences after Mass on Sunday morning: a mean man, as Mother said, who only went to funerals for the free drinks he could get at them. It turned out that he hadn't even known Mr. Dooley! But Father had a sort of contemptuous regard for him as one of the foolish people who wasted their good money in public-houses when they could be saving it. Very little of his own money Peter Crowley wasted!

It was an excellent funeral from Father's point of view. He had it all well studied before we set off after the hearse in the afternoon sunlight.

"Five carriages!" he exclaimed. "Five carriages and sixteen covered cars! There's one alderman, two councillors and 'tis unknown how many priests. I didn't see a funeral like this from the road since Willie Mack, the publican, died."

"Ah, he was well liked," said Crowley in his husky voice.

"My goodness, don't I know that?" snapped Father. "Wasn't the man my best friend? Two nights before he died—only two nights—he was over telling me the goings-on about the housing contract. Them fellows in the Corporation are night and day robbers. But even I never imagined he was as well connected as that."

Father was stepping out like a boy, pleased with everything: the other mourners, and the fine houses along Sunday's Well. I knew the danger signals were there in full force: a sunny day, a fine funeral, and a distinguished company of clerics and public men were bringing out all the natural vanity and flightiness of Father's character. It was with something like genuine pleasure that he saw his old friend lowered into the grave; with the sense of having performed a duty and the pleasant awareness that however much he would miss poor Mr. Dooley in the long summer evenings, it was he and not poor Mr. Dooley who would do the missing.

"We'll be making tracks before they break up," he whispered to Crowley as the gravediggers tossed in the first shovelfuls of clay, and away he went, hopping like a goat from grassy hump to hump. The drivers, who were probably in the same state as himself, though without months of abstinence to put an edge on it, looked up hopefully.

"Are they nearly finished, Mick?" bawled one.

"All over now bar the last prayers," trumpeted Father in the tone of one who brings news of great rejoicing.

The carriages passed us in a lather of dust several hundred yards from the public-house, and Father, whose feet gave him trouble in hot weather, quickened his pace, looking nervously over his shoulder for any sign of the main body of mourners crossing the hill. In a crowd like that a man might be kept waiting.

When we did reach the pub the carriages were drawn up outside, and solemn men in black ties were cautiously bringing out consolation to mysterious females whose hands reached out modestly from behind the drawn blinds of the coaches. Inside the pub there were only the drivers and a couple of shawly women. I felt if I was to act as a brake at all, this was the time, so I pulled Father by the coattails.

"Dadda, can't we go home now?" I asked.

"Two minutes now," he said, beaming affectionately. "Just a bottle of lemonade and we'll go home."

This was a bribe, and I knew it, but I was always a child of weak character. Father ordered lemonade and two pints. I was thirsty and swallowed my drink at once. But that wasn't Father's way. He had long months of abstinence behind him and an eternity of pleasure before. He took out his pipe, blew through it, filled it, and then lit it with loud pops, his eyes bulging above it. After that he deliberately turned his back on the pint, leaned one elbow on the counter in the attitude of a man who did not know there was a pint behind him, and deliberately brushed the tobacco from his palms. He had settled down for the evening. He was steadily working through all the important funerals he had ever attended. The carriages departed and the minor mourners drifted in till the pub was half full.

"Dadda," I said, pulling his coat again, "can't we go home now?"

"Ah, your mother won't be in for a long time yet," he said benevolently enough. "Run out in the road and play, can't you?"

It struck me as very cool, the way grown-ups assumed that you could play all by yourself on a strange road. I began to get bored as I had so often been bored before. I knew Father was quite capable of lingering there till nightfall. I knew I might have to bring him home, blind drunk, down Blarney Lane, with all the old women at their doors, saying: "Mick Delaney is on it again." I knew that my mother would be half crazy with anxiety; that next day Father wouldn't go out to work; and before the end of the week she would be running down to the pawn with the clock under her shawl. I could never get over the lonesomeness of the kitchen without a clock.

I was still thirsty. I found if I stood on tiptoe I could just reach Father's glass, and the idea occurred to me that it would be interesting to know what the contents were like. He had his back to it and wouldn't notice. I took down the glass and sipped cautiously. It was a terrible disappointment. I was astonished that he could even drink such stuff. It looked as if he had never tried lemonade.

I should have advised him about lemonade but he was holding forth himself in great style. I heard him say that bands were a great addition to a funeral. He put his arms in the position of someone holding a rifle in reverse and hummed a few bars of Chopin's Funeral March. Crowley nodded reverently. I took a longer drink and began to see that porter might have its advantages. I felt pleasantly elevated and philosophic. Father hummed a few bars of the Dead March in *Saul*. It was a nice pub and a very fine funeral, and I felt sure that poor Mr. Dooley in Heaven must be highly gratified. At the same time I thought they might have given him a band. As Father said, bands were a great addition.

But the wonderful thing about porter was the way it made you stand aside, or rather float aloft like a cherub rolling on a cloud, and watch yourself with your legs crossed, leaning against a bar counter, not worrying about trifles but thinking deep, serious, grown-up thoughts about life and death. Looking at yourself like that, you couldn't help thinking after a while how funny you looked, and suddenly you got embarrassed and wanted to giggle. But by the time I had finished the pint, that phase too had passed; I found it hard to put back the glass, the counter seemed to have grown so high. Melancholia was supervening again.

"Well," Father said reverently, reaching behind him for his drink, "God rest the poor man's soul, wherever he is!" He stopped, looked first at the glass, and then at the people round him. "Hello," he said in a fairly good-humoured tone, as if he were just prepared to consider it a joke, even if it was in bad taste, "who was at this?"

There was silence for a moment while the publican and the old women looked first at Father and then at his glass.

"There was no one at it, my good man," one of the women said with an offended air. "Is it robbers you think we are?"

"Ah, there's no one here would do a thing like that, Mick," said the publican in a shocked tone.

"Well, someone did it," said Father, his smile beginning to wear off.

"If they did, they were them that were nearer it," said the woman darkly, giving me a dirty look; and at the same moment the truth began to dawn on Father. I suppose I must have looked a bit starry-eyed. He bent and shook me.

"Are you all right, Larry?" he asked in alarm.

Peter Crowley looked down at me and grinned.

"Could you beat that?" he exclaimed in a husky voice.

I could, and without difficulty. I started to get sick. Father jumped back in holy terror that I might spoil his good suit, and hastily opened the back door.

"Run! run! run!" he shouted.

I saw the sunlit wall outside with the ivy overhanging it, and ran. The intention was good but the performance was exaggerated, because I lurched right into the wall, hurting it badly, as it seemed to me. Being always very polite, I said "Pardon" before the second bout came on me. Father, still concerned for his suit, came up behind and cautiously held me while I got sick.

"That's a good boy!" he said encouragingly. "You'll be grand when you get that up."

Begor, I was not grand! Grand was the last thing I was. I gave one unmerciful wail out of me as he steered me back to the pub and put me sitting on the bench near the shawlies. They drew themselves up with an offended air, still sore at the suggestion that they had drunk his pint.

"God help us!" moaned one, looking pityingly at me, "isn't it the likes of them would be fathers?"

"Mick," said the publican in alarm, spraying sawdust on my tracks, "that child isn't supposed to be in here at all. You'd better take him home quick in case a bobby would see him."

"Merciful God!" whimpered Father, raising his eyes to heaven and clapping his hands silently as he only did when distraught, "what misfortune was on me? Or what will his mother say? . . . If women might stop at home and look after their children themselves!" he added in a snarl for the benefit of the shawlies. "Are them carriages all gone, Bill?"

"The carriages are finished long ago, Mick," replied the publican.

"I'll take him home," Father said despairingly. . . . "I'll never bring you out again," he threatened me. "Here," he added, giving me the clean handkerchief from his breast pocket, "put that over your eyes."

The blood on the handkerchief was the first indication I got that I was cut, and instantly my temple began to throb and I set up another howl.

"Whisht, whisht, whisht!" Father said testily, steering me out the door. "One'd think you were killed. That's nothing. We'll wash it when we get home."

"Steady now, old scout!" Crowley said, taking the other side of me. "You'll be all right in a minute."

I never met two men who knew less about the effects of drink. The first breath of fresh air and the warmth of the sun made me groggier than ever and I pitched and rolled between wind and tide till Father started to whimper again.

"God Almighty, and the whole road out! What misfortune was on me didn't stop at my work! Can't you walk straight?"

I couldn't. I saw plain enough that, coaxed by the sunlight, every woman old and young in Blarney Lane was leaning over her half-door or sitting on her doorstep. They all stopped gabbling to gape at the strange spectacle of two sober, middle-aged men bringing home a drunken small boy with a cut over his eye. Father, torn between the shamefast desire to get me home as quick as he could, and the neighborly need to explain that it wasn't his fault, finally halted outside Mrs. Roche's. There was a gang of old women outside a door at the opposite side of the road. I didn't like the look of them from the first. They seemed altogether too interested in me. I leaned against the wall of Mrs. Roche's cottage with my hands in my trousers pockets, thinking mournfully of poor Mr. Dooley in his cold grave on the Curragh, who would never walk down the road again, and, with great feeling, I began to sing a favorite song of Father's.

> *Though lost to Mononia and cold in the grave*
> *He returns to Kincora no more.*

"Wisha, the poor child!" Mrs. Roche said. "Haven't he a lovely voice, God bless him!"

That was what I thought myself, so I was the more surprised when Father said "Whisht!" and raised a threatening finger at me. He didn't seem to realize the appropriateness of the song, so I sang louder than ever.

"Whisht, I tell you!" he snapped, and then tried to work up a smile for Mrs. Roche's benefit. "We're nearly home now. I'll carry you the rest of the way."

But, drunk and all as I was, I knew better than to be carried home ignominiously like that.

"Now," I said severely, "can't you leave me alone? I can walk all right. 'Tis only my head. All I want is a rest."

"But you can rest at home in bed," he said viciously, trying to pick me up, and I knew by the flush on his face that he was very vexed.

"Ah, Jasus," I said crossly, "what do I want to go home for? Why the hell can't you leave me alone?"

For some reason the gang of old women at the other side of the road thought this very funny. They nearly split their sides over it. A gassy fury began to expand in me at the thought that a fellow couldn't have a drop taken without the whole neighborhood coming out to make game of him.

"Who are ye laughing at?" I shouted, clenching my fists at them. "I'll make ye laugh at the other side of yeer faces if ye don't let me pass."

They seemed to think this funnier still; I had never seen such ill-mannered people.

"Go away, ye bloody bitches!" I said.

"Whisht, whisht, whisht, I tell you!" snarled Father, abandoning all pretence of amusement and dragging me along behind him by the hand. I was maddened by the women's shrieks of laughter. I was maddened by Father's bullying. I tried to dig in my heels but he was too powerful for me, and I could only see the women by looking back over my shoulder.

"Take care or I'll come back and show ye!" I shouted. "I'll teach ye to let decent people pass. Fitter for ye to stop at home and wash yeer dirty faces."

" 'Twill be all over the road," whimpered Father. "Never again, never again, not if I lived to be a thousand!"

To this day I don't know whether he was forswearing me or the drink. By way of a song suitable to my heroic mood I bawled "The Boys of Wexford," as he dragged me in home. Crowley, knowing he was not safe, made off and Father undressed me and put me to bed. I couldn't sleep because of the whirling in my head. It was very unpleasant, and I got sick again. Father came in with a wet cloth and mopped up after me. I lay in a fever, listening to him chopping sticks to start a fire. After that I heard him lay the table.

Suddenly the front door banged open and Mother stormed in with Sonny in her arms, not her usual gentle, timid self, but a wild, raging woman. It was clear that she had heard it all from the neighbors.

"Mick Delaney," she cried hysterically, "what did you do to my son?"

"Whisht, woman, whisht, whisht!" he hissed, dancing from one foot to the other. "Do you want the whole road to hear?"

"Ah," she said with a horrifying laugh, "the road knows all about it by this time. The road knows the way you filled your unfortunate innocent child with drink to make sport for you and that other rotten, filthy brute."

"But I gave him no drink," he shouted, aghast at the horrifying interpretation the neighbors had chosen to give his misfortune. "He took it while my back was turned. What the hell do you think I am?"

"Ah," she replied bitterly, "everyone knows what you are now. God forgive you, wasting our hard-earned few ha'pence on drink, and bringing up your child to be a drunken corner-boy like yourself."

Then she swept into the bedroom and threw herself on her knees by the bed. She moaned when she saw the gash over my eye. In the kitchen Sonny set up a loud bawl on his own, and a moment later Father appeared in the bedroom door with his cap over his eyes, wearing an expression of the most intense self-pity.

"That's a nice way to talk to me after all I went through," he whined. "That's a nice accusation, that I was drinking. Not one drop of drink crossed my lips the whole day. How could it when he drank it all? I'm the one that ought to be pitied, with my day ruined on me, and I after being made a show for the whole road."

But next morning, when he got up and went out quietly to work with his dinner-basket, Mother threw herself on me in the bed and kissed me. It seemed it was all my doing, and I was being given a holiday till my eye got better.

"My brave little man!" she said with her eyes shining. "It was God did it you were there. You were his guardian angel."

INTERPRETATION

In this amusing story, there is a reversal of roles: it is not the father who comes reeling down the street, the scandal of the family and the talk of the neighbors, as the appalled little son tries to lead him home and put him mercifully out of sight. It is the little boy who is unsteady on his feet, singing off key, calling the neighbor women "bloody bitches"—to the horror of the appalled father. If the story simply presented us with this topsy-turvy situation and let it go at that, it would amount to no more than a joke that was momentarily amusing. It would not be very much of a story and it would not even wear well as a joke. For even a joke, if it is to continue to seem funny, must be rooted in a true perception of human nature.

The reversal of the roles of father and son in this story is not a momentary trick. If we think back a bit, we shall see that the reversal is assumed throughout the story. On the important matter of his father's weakness for drink, Larry, the little boy, takes his mother's viewpoint. His is the adult concern for an essentially good but childishly weak character who must be protected from himself. Larry is apprehensive and worried. He knows what "signs" are ominous. He knows all too well what the consequences of the first drink will be. His consciousness continues to be suffused with this kind of concern for his father until the beer finally takes effect upon *him*, and for the first time in the story, his apprehensions melt away.

Throughout the story it is the father who has the childlike guilelessness —and the charm that frequently accompanies such guilelessness. Consider his delight in the funeral: "It was an excellent funeral from Father's point of view." He exclaims that there are "Five carriages and sixteen covered cars!" Later, as Larry remarks, "It was with something like genuine pleasure that he saw his old friend lowered into the grave; with the sense of having performed a duty and the pleasant awareness that however much he would miss poor Mr. Dooley in the long summer evenings, it was he and not Mr. Dooley who would do the missing." Later still, he tells the waiting coachmen that the service at the grave is nearly over: " 'All over now bar the last prayers,' trumpeted Father in the tone of one who brings news of great rejoicing." And how happily a few minutes later he settles down in the pub as he gets ready to break his long drought!

If Larry's father were a more calculating man, or even a more self-conscious man, the special quality of the humor would be lost, for we would have to take a different attitude toward him. If it is his simplicity and his naïveté that cause his troubles, they go far toward relieving him of adult responsibility for them. He is a man more sinned against than sinning —and nowhere more so than when he has to face the protests of the neighborwomen that he has got his own son drunk. The character of the father thus has everything to do with the point of the story and even with the matter of whether or not we find the story genuinely funny. Though "all occasions inform against him," he has the consciousness of outraged innocence.

The most amusing instance of the general reversal of roles occurs on the way home from the pub, when the father does not forcibly shut up the noisy, tipsy little boy, but pleads with him to be reasonable and quiet just as Larry himself might have pleaded with the drunken father—if our normal expectations about this particular expedition had been realized. But this most amusing of the reversals is also rooted in the father's character: a more cruel man, a more brutal man, would have forced the boy to hush. He would thus have eliminated the humorous exchanges, and the suppression of these—and perhaps also the harshness by which they were suppressed—would have deprived the scene of its humor.

The most startling of the reversals (and that which caps the story) is the twist at the end in which the episode of juvenile delinquency becomes Providential and the little boy drunkenly weaving down the street becomes in the mother's grateful eyes a "guardian angel" guiding aright the steps of the weak father. We laugh at the mother—the way in which she has expressed her commendation is almost as startling as the phrasings of Mrs. Malaprop—and yet what she says is, from her point of view, quite right: Larry has been a little "man." He has saved the family one of the usual visits to the pawnbroker.

1. Is the episode in which Larry drinks his father's pint of beer made plausible? Is this the sort of thing that Larry usually does? Is it credible that the father should have neglected his pint long enough for the child to drink it?

2. Are the observations made by Larry upon his father too sophisticated for a child to make? Is this story being told by Larry soon after the events described, or long after, when Larry has become a man?

3. The exposition in this story is managed very skillfully. Comment upon it. What is gained by deferring for over a page the matter of the father's propensity to drink?

4. What is the importance of the fact that Larry gets a little nick over his eye? Does the fact of the blood and the wound help account for certain reactions to the incident?

ANTON CHEKHOV

The Lament

IT is twilight. A thick wet snow is twirling around the newly lighted street lamps, and lying in soft thin layers on roofs, on horses' backs, on people's shoulders and hats. The cabdriver Iona Potapov is quite white, and looks like a phantom; he is bent double as far as a human body can bend double; he is seated on his box; he never makes a move. If a whole snowdrift fell on him, it seems as if he would not find it necessary to shake it off. His little horse is also quite white, and remains motionless; its immobility, its angularity, and its straight wooden-looking legs, even close by, give it the appearance of a ginger-bread horse worth a *kopek*. It is, no doubt, plunged in deep thought. If you were snatched from the plow, from your usual gray surroundings, and were thrown into this slough full of monstrous lights, unceasing noise, and hurrying people, you too would find it difficult not to think.

Iona and his little horse have not moved from their place for a long while. They left their yard before dinner, and up to now, not a fare. The evening mist is descending over the town, the white lights of the lamps replacing brighter rays, and the hubbub of the street getting louder. "Cabby for Viborg way!" suddenly hears Iona. "Cabby!"

Iona jumps, and through his snow-covered eyelashes sees an officer in a greatcoat, with his hood over his head.

"Viborg way!" the officer repeats. "Are you asleep, eh? Viborg way!"

With a nod of assent Iona picks up the reins, in consequence of which layers of snow slip off the horse's back and neck. The officer seats himself in the sleigh, the cabdriver smacks his lips to encourage his horse, stretches out his neck like a swan, sits up, and, more from habit than necessity, brandishes his whip. The little horse also stretches its neck, bends its wooden-looking legs, and makes a move undecidedly.

"What are you doing, werewolf!" is the exclamation Iona hears from the dark mass moving to and fro, as soon as they have started.

"Where the devil are you going? To the r-r-right!"

"You do not know how to drive. Keep to the right!" calls the officer angrily.

A coachman from a private carriage swears at him; a passerby, who has run across the road and rubbed his shoulder against the horse's nose, looks at him furiously as he sweeps the snow from his sleeve. Iona shifts about on his seat as if he were on needles, moves his elbows as if he were trying to keep his equilibrium, and gapes about like someone suffocating, who does not understand why and wherefore he is there.

"What scoundrels they all are!" jokes the officer; "one would think they had all entered into an agreement to jostle you or fall under your horse."

Iona looks round at the officer, and moves his lips. He evidently wants to say something, but the only sound that issues is a snuffle.

"What?" asks the officer.

Iona twists his mouth into a smile, and with an effort says hoarsely:

"My son, *barin*, died this week."

"Hm! What did he die of?"

Iona turns with his whole body toward his fare, and says:

"And who knows! They say high fever. He was three days in the hospital, and then died. . . . God's will be done."

"Turn round! The devil!" sounds from the darkness. "Have you popped off, old doggie, eh? Use your eyes!"

"Go on, go on," says the officer, "otherwise we shall not get there by tomorrow. Hurry up a bit!"

The cabdriver again stretches his neck, sits up, and, with a bad grace, brandishes his whip. Several times again he turns to look at his fare, but the latter has closed his eyes, and apparently is not disposed to listen. Having deposited the officer in the Viborg, he stops by the tavern, doubles himself up on his seat, and again remains motionless, while the snow once more begins to cover him and his horse. An hour, and another. . . . Then, along the footpath, with a squeak of galoshes, and quarreling, come three young men, two of them tall and lanky, the third one short and hump-backed.

"Cabby, to the Police Bridge!" in a cracked voice calls the humpback. "The three of us for two *griveniks!*"

Iona picks up his reins, and smacks his lips. Two *griveniks* is not a fair price, but he does not mind whether it is a *rouble* or five *kopeks*—to him it is all the same now, so long as they are fares. The young men, jostling each other and using bad language, approach the sleigh, and all three at once try to get onto the seat; then begins a discussion as to which two shall sit and who shall be the one to stand. After wrangling, abusing each other, and much petulance, it is at last decided that the humpback shall stand, as he is the smallest.

"Now then, hurry up!" says the humpback in a twanging voice, as he takes his place and breathes in Iona's neck. "Old furry! Here, mate, what a cap you have! There is not a worse one to be found in all Petersburg! . . ."

"He-he!—he-he!" giggles Iona. "Such a . . ."

"Now you, 'such a,' hurry up, are you going the whole way at this pace? Are you? . . . Do you want it in the neck?"

"My head feels like bursting," says one of the lanky ones. "Last night at the Donkmasovs, Vaska and I drank the whole of four bottles of cognac."

"I don't understand what you lie for," says the other lanky one angrily; "you lie like a brute."

"God strike me, it's the truth!"

"It's as much the truth as that a louse coughs!"

"He, he," grins Iona, "what gay young gentlemen!"

"Pshaw, go to the devil!" says the humpback indignantly.

"Are you going to get on or not, you old pest? Is that the way to drive? Use the whip a bit! Go on, devil, go on, give it to him well!"

Iona feels at his back the little man wriggling, and the tremble in his voice. He listens to the insults hurled at him, sees the people, and little by little the feeling of loneliness leaves him. The humpback goes on swearing until he gets mixed up in some elaborate six-foot oath, or chokes with coughing. The lankies begin to talk about a certain Nadejda Petrovna. Iona looks round at them several times; he waits for a temporary silence, then, turning round again, he murmurs:

"My son . . . died this week."

"We must all die," sighs the humpback, wiping his lips after an attack of coughing. "Now, hurry up, hurry up! Gentlemen, I really cannot go any farther like this! When will he get us there?"

"Well, just you stimulate him a little in the neck!"

"You old pest, do you hear, I'll bone your neck for you! If one treated the like of you with ceremony one would have to go on foot! Do you hear, old serpent Gorinytch! Or do you not care a spit?"

Iona hears rather than feels the blows they deal him.

"He, he," he laughs. "They are gay young gentlemen, God bless 'em!"

"Cabby, are you married?" asks a lanky one.

"I? He, he, gay young gentlemen! Now I have only a wife and the moist ground. . . . He, ho, ho . . . that is to say, the grave. My son has died, and I am alive. . . . A wonderful thing, death mistook the door . . . instead of coming to me, it went to my son. . . ."

Iona turns round to tell them how his son died, but at this moment, the humpback, giving a little sigh, announces, "Thank God, we have at last reached our destination," and Iona watches them disappear through the dark entrance. Once more he is alone, and again surrounded by silence. . . . His grief, which has abated for a short while, returns and rends his heart with greater force. With an anxious and hurried look, he searches among the crowds passing on either side of the street to find whether there may be just one person who will listen to him. But the crowds hurry by without noticing him or his trouble. Yet it is such an immense, illimitable grief. Should his heart break and the grief pour out, it would flow over the whole earth, so it seems, and yet no one sees it. It has managed to conceal itself in such an insignificant shell that no one can see it even by day and with a light.

Iona sees a hall porter with some sacking, and decides to talk to him.

"Friend, what sort of time is it?" he asks.

"Past nine. What are you standing here for? Move on."

Iona moves on a few steps, doubles himself up, and abandons himself to his grief. He sees it is useless to turn to people for help. In less than five minutes he straightens himself, holds up his head as if he felt some sharp pain, and gives a tug at the reins; he can bear it no longer. "The stables," he thinks, and the little horse, as if it understood, starts off at a trot.

About an hour and a half later Iona is seated by a large dirty stove. Around the stove, on the floor, on the benches, people are snoring; the air is thick and suffocatingly hot. Iona looks at the sleepers, scratches himself, and regrets having returned so early.

"I have not even earned my fodder," he thinks. "That's what's my trouble. A man who knows his job, who has had enough to eat, and his horse too, can always sleep peacefully."

A young cabdriver in one of the corners half gets up, grunts sleepily, and stretches towards a bucket of water.

"Do you want a drink?" Iona asks him.

"Don't I want a drink!"

"That's so? Your good health! But listen, mate—you know, my son is dead. . . . Did you hear? This week, in the hospital. . . . It's a long story."

Iona looks to see what effect his words have, but sees none—the young man has hidden his face and is fast asleep again. The old man sighs, and scratches his head. Just as much as the young one wants to drink, the old man wants to talk. It will soon be a week since his son died, and he has not been able to speak about it properly to anyone. One must tell it slowly and carefully; how his son fell ill, how he suffered, what he said before he died, how he died. One must describe every detail of the funeral, and the journey to the hospital to fetch the dead son's clothes. His daughter Anissia has remained in the village—one must talk about her too. Is it nothing he has to tell? Surely the listener would gasp and sigh, and sympathize with him? It is better, too, to talk to women; although they are stupid, two words are enough to make them sob.

"I'll go and look after my horse," thinks Iona; "there's always time to sleep. No fear of that!"

He puts on his coat, and goes to the stables to his horse; he thinks of the corn, the hay, the weather. When he is alone, he dares not think of his son; he can speak about him to anyone, but to think of him, and picture him to himself, is unbearably painful.

"Are you tucking in?" Iona asks his horse, looking at its bright eyes; "go on, tuck in, though we've not earned our corn, we can eat hay. Yes!

I am too old to drive—my son could have, not I. He was a first-rate cab-driver. If only he had lived!"

Iona is silent for a moment, then continues:

"That's how it is, my old horse. There's no more Kuzma Ionitch. He has left us to live, and he went off pop. Now let's say, you had a foal, you were the foal's mother, and suddenly, let's say, that foal went and left you to live after him. It would be sad, wouldn't it?"

The little horse munches, listens, and breathes over its master's hand. . . .

Iona's feelings are too much for him, and he tells the little horse the whole story.

INTERPRETATION

This story, like "Tennessee's Partner," deals with a pathetic situation. An old cabdriver, who has lost his son, can find no one in the world to whom he can confide his grief, and in the end goes out to the stable to tell his horse. In writing this story an author would almost certainly run the risk of sentimentality. In considering this story, particularly after having read "Tennessee's Partner," one is interested in seeing what means Chekhov uses to avoid sentimentalizing his material.

One of the most obvious things which the reader notices in looking back on this story is the objective and neutral presentation. The author seems to be presenting scenes and actions to us without weighting them in favor of one interpretation or another.

For instance, consider his use of nature. In "Tennessee's Partner," as has been pointed out, Bret Harte uses nature to set a mood. But the use here—say in the first paragraph of "The Lament"—is different on two counts. First, Chekhov gives us the picture of the lonely scene on the street corner at evening, with the snow falling on the old cabdriver and the little horse. The fact of isolation is suggested, but there is no appeal to our sympathies either by poeticized language, as is the case in "Tennessee's Partner," or by editorial comment. Indeed, when Chekhov does depart from the straight, neutral, objective description, the effect is to play down the appeal to our sympathy rather than to insist upon it. For example, the suggestion is that the scene is scarcely real: "The cabdriver . . . is quite white, and looks like a phantom." And the "little horse is also quite white, and remains motionless; its immobility, its angularity, and its straight wooden-looking legs, even close by, give it the appearance of a gingerbread horse worth a *kopek*." The comparisons to the phantom and to the gingerbread horse serve to make the scene vivid and particular. But phantoms and gingerbread horses are fantastic things which do not feel or suffer and can make no appeal to sympathy. In other words, the scene, though it does give a sense of isolation, an effect which is important in the story of the cab-driver, is ostensibly pointed *away* from the appeal for sympathy and not *toward* it; Chekhov seems to say that he will be willing to rest his case on its own merits. The second way in which Chekhov's use of nature differs from that of Bret Harte in "Tennessee's Partner" is this: the function of the scene in "The Lament" is purely preparatory; the function in "Tennessee's Partner" is to seduce the reader into a proper response when he comes to the crucial point in the story.

The objective and neutral presentation, of which we have spoken in connection with the first paragraph of the story, continues through the various incidents which constitute the action.

The cabman picks up a fare who seems to be friendly and conversational. Apparently the cabman is sufficiently encouraged by the friendliness of the officer to make a remark that his son has just died. But Chekhov does not indicate at this point the true meaning of the son's death to the cabman. Chekhov merely tells us that he "twists his mouth into a smile, and with an effort says hoarsely" that the boy is dead. This description of how the cabman says the words is our first revelation of his feelings, but we notice that the description is objective, and, indeed, somewhat ambiguous. What does the smile mean? Obviously, we can take it to be, in part, a response of gratitude for the officer's friendliness which comes in contrast to the isolation of the original scene. But the smile, like the comparisons to the phantom and the gingerbread horse in the first scene, tends to play down, rather than up, any direct appeal to our sympathy with the cabman as a grief-stricken man. At any rate, when the cabman, further encouraged by the officer's perfunctory expression of curiosity, takes his attention from his driving and begins to give some details of the son's death, he is interrupted by an irate protest from the darkness. And the officer then tells him to hurry, and forbids further conversation by leaning back and shutting his eyes.

It is worth noting that such information as we have been given about the cabman's feelings has come to us *dramatically*—that is, we have had it only in terms of his speech and not by commentary. By the same token, our information is incomplete. The basic motivation of the cabman has only been hinted at; it has not been fully revealed. Thus the dramatic presentation and the development of the reader's suspense here go hand in hand.

The motivation is further developed in the next scene, when the cabman tries, with unfriendly and boisterous passengers, to open the same subject. Their attitude toward him, too, emphasizes his own isolation. He tries to humor them in their drunkenness, and flatter them. In part, this behavior, no doubt, may be taken as an effort to get on good terms with his fares and as an indication of his humble position in society: but in part it may be taken as an indication of his willingness to accept any humiliation in order to tell his story. Thus, his behavior dramatically suggests the over-powering necessity which compels him to tell his story. (One should notice how, even here, Chekhov continues to play down the pathos of Iona: the young men are not necessarily cruel, but may be merely drunken and thoughtless.)

After the young men get out and the cabman is again left alone, Chekhov introduces his first explicit statement of the situation: "His grief, which has abated for a short while, returns and rends his heart with greater force. With an anxious and hurried look, he searches among the crowds passing on either side of the street to find if there may be just one person who will listen to him." In other words, Chekhov has been cunning enough to validate the situation dramatically, before he commits himself to the overt statement. Unlike similar statements in the Bret Harte story, which attempt to prod the reader's sympathies, this statement summarizes what the intelligent reader has already been able to infer. But, of course, it is not merely a summary. It analyzes the state of mind of the cabman: as long as he has had any kind of human contact, even an unpleasant one, as with the drunken youths, his grief has abated, but now that he is completely alone, it returns with added force. Now he is even compelled to get out of the cab and seek conversation.

But the attempt to engage the porter in conversation fails, and the cabman finally returns to the stables. There, at least, one would expect him to be able to find some sympathy among his own kind and class. But even here he is forced back upon himself.

This sets the stage for the second piece of analysis of the cabman's state of mind. Chekhov now, for the first time, gives us some of the details of the son's death. But not merely as information. He gives them as preparation for the question which is wrung from the heart of the old man by the realization that no one will listen to him: "Is it nothing he has to tell?"

This seems to be the summary of the old man's feelings—his incom-prehension of the world, and his loneliness in it. If this were all, however, the story could come to a proper close after the old man's next thought: "I'll go and look after my horse . . . there's always time to sleep. No fear of that!"

But the situation is a little more complicated than this. Therefore, we have the last bit of analysis, which is now fully prepared for. Iona tries to think of the corn, the hay, and the weather. Presumably, he is go-ing out to see about his horse, but really, we learn, he thinks of these things and goes out to his horse, simply because he cannot bear to be alone with the thought of his loss. The impulse to go to the stable does not depend on any conscious decision to tell the horse his troubles. He is fulfilling an un-conscious need. This need is unconscious, but it colors even the way in which he begins to talk to the horse: "Are you tucking in?" He talks as if the horse were a child. But the unconscious need is so great that before he has uttered more than a sentence or two, he is back to the subject of his son. And once he has started talking with the horse, he begins to explain to the horse what he had been unable to explain to anyone else. But we may note that not only what he says to the horse is important, but the way in which he speaks: he adopts the careful, patient tone of explanation which a father might take to a young child: "Now, let's say, you had a foal, you were the foal's mother . . ."

This whole episode, though it has been prepared for by all preceding incidents and by the psychological analysis in the story, comes with an *ironical* shock of surprise. It is a surprise because the cabman's decision to go out to the stables is presented, on the surface at least, as a routine matter: the good cabman goes out to look after his horse. It is ironical, because it offers a commentary on a world in which one human being can find human sympathy only from a beast. Furthermore, this irony itself is shocking, for Chekhov has so presented the world of the story that it does not seem entirely vindictive and cruel. Some of the people who do not listen are simply preoccupied with their own affairs, or worn out with their own work. Yet this apparently normal world, in which there is a mixture of attitudes, turns out to be a world which does drive the man, seeking human sympathy, to the beast in the stable. And this turns out to be the theme of the story.

1. Comment on the use of the comparison of the old man to a swan in the fifth paragraph.

2. Comment on the function of these lines in helping supply preparation for the last scene: ". . . he can bear it no longer. 'The stables,' he thinks . . . starts off at a trot" (p. 186).

3. In the last scene, Chekhov gives us Iona, a simple man, speaking in his full simplicity. This is a device for pathetic effect. Bret Harte uses a similar device in the funeral speech and in the dying speech of the partner. Why is the device successful in one instance, and unsuccessful in the other?

D. H. LAWRENCE

Tickets, Please

THERE is in the Midlands a single-line tramway system which boldly leaves the country town and plunges off into the black, industrial countryside, up hill and down dale, through the long, ugly villages of workmen's houses, over canals and railways, past churches perched high and nobly over the smoke and shadows, through stark, grimy, cold little market-places, tilting away in a rush past cinemas and shops down to the hollow where the collieries are, then up again, past a little rural church, under the ash trees, on in a rush to the terminus, the last little ugly place of industry, the cold little town that shivers on the edge of the wild, gloomy country beyond. There the green and creamy colored tram-car seems to pause and purr with curious satisfaction. But in a few minutes—the clock on the turret of the Co-operative Wholesale Society's Shops gives the time—away it starts once more on the adventure. Again there are the reckless swoops downhill, bouncing the loops: again the chilly wait in the hill-top market-place: again the breathless slithering round the precipitous drop under the church: again the patient halts at the loops, waiting for the outcoming car: so on and on, for two long hours, till at last the city looms beyond the fat gas-works, the narrow factories draw near, we are in the sordid streets of the great town, once more we sidle to a standstill at our terminus, abashed by the great crimson and cream-coloured city cars, but still perky, jaunty, somewhat dare-devil, green as a jaunty sprig of parsley out of a black colliery garden.

To ride on these cars is always an adventure. Since we are in war-time, the drivers are men unfit for active service: cripples and hunchbacks. So they have the spirit of the devil in them. The ride becomes a steeple-chase. Hurray! we have leapt in a clear jump over the canal bridges—now for the four-lane corner. With a shriek and a trail of sparks we are clear again. To be sure, a tram often leaps the rails—but what matter! It sits in a ditch till other trams come to haul it out. It is quite common for a car, packed with one solid mass of living people, to come to a dead halt in the midst of unbroken blackness, the heart of nowhere on a dark night, and for the driver and the girl conductor to call, "All get off—car's on fire!" Instead, however, of rushing out in a panic, the passengers stolidly reply: "Get on—get on! We're not coming out. We're stopping where we are. Push on, George." So till flames actually appear.

The reason for this reluctance to dismount is that the nights are howlingly cold, black, and windswept, and a car is a haven of refuge. From village to village the miners travel, for a change of cinema, of girl, of pub. The trams are desperately packed. Who is going to risk himself in the black gulf outside, to wait perhaps an hour for another tram, then to see the forlorn notice "Depot Only," because there is something wrong! or to greet a unit of three bright cars all so tight with people that they sail past with a howl of derision. Trams that pass in the night.

This, the most dangerous tram-service in England, as the authorities themselves declare, with pride, is entirely conducted by girls, and driven by rash young men, a little crippled, or by delicate young men, who creep forward in terror. The girls are fearless young hussies. In their ugly blue uniform, skirts up to their knees, shapeless old peaked caps on their heads, they have all the sang-froid of an old non-commissioned officer. With a tram packed with howling colliers, roaring hymns downstairs and a sort of antiphony of obscenities upstairs, the lasses are perfectly at their ease. They pounce on the youths who try to evade their ticket-machine. They push off the men at the end of their distance. They are not going to be done in the eye—not they. They fear nobody—and everybody fears them.

"Hello, Annie!"

"Hello, Ted!"

"Oh, mind my corn, Miss Stone. It's my belief you've got a heart of stone, for you've trod on it again."

"You should keep it in your pocket," replies Miss Stone, and she goes sturdily upstairs in her high boots.

"Tickets, please."

She is peremptory, suspicious, and ready to hit first. She can hold her own against ten thousand. The step of that tram-car is her Thermopylæ.

Therefore, there is a certain wild romance aboard these cars—and in the sturdy bosom of Annie herself. The time for soft romance is in the morning, between ten o'clock and one, when things are rather slack: that is, except market-day and Saturday. Thus Annie has time to look about her. Then she often hops off her car and into a shop where she has spied something, while the driver chats in the main road. There is very good feeling between the girls and the drivers. Are they not companions in peril, shipments aboard this careering vessel of a tram-car, for ever rocking on the waves of a stormy land.

Then, also, during the easy hours, the inspectors are most in evidence. For some reason, everybody employed in this tram-service is young: there are no grey heads. It would not do. Therefore the inspectors are of the right age, and one, the chief, is also good-looking. See him stand on a wet, gloomy morning, in his long oilskin, his peaked cap well down over his eyes, waiting to board a car. His face is ruddy, his small brown moustache is weathered, he has a faint impudent smile. Fairly tall and agile, even in his waterproof, he springs aboard a car and geets Annie.

"Hello, Annie! Keeping the wet out?"

"Trying to."

There are only two people in the car. Inspecting is soon over. Then for a long and impudent chat on the footboard, a good, easy, twelve-mile chat.

The inspector's name is John Thomas Raynor—always called John Thomas, except sometimes, in malice, Coddy. His face sets in fury when he is addressed, from a distance, with this abbreviation. There is considerable scandal about John Thomas in half a dozen villages. He flirts with the girl conductors in the morning and walks out with them in the dark night, when they leave their tram-car at the depot. Of course, the girls quit the service frequently. Then he flirts and walks out with the newcomer: always providing she is sufficiently attractive, and that she will consent to walk. It is remarkable, however, that most of the girls are quite comely, they are all young, and this roving life aboard the car gives them a sailor's dash and recklessness. What matter how they behave when the ship is in port. Tomorrow they will be aboard again.

Annie, however, was something of a Tartar, and her sharp tongue had kept John Thomas at arm's length for many months. Perhaps, therefore, she liked him all the more: for he always came up smiling, with impudence. She watched him vanquish one girl, then another. She could tell by the movement of his mouth and eyes, when he flirted with her in the morning, that he had been walking out with this lass, or the other, the night before. A fine cock-of-the-walk he was. She could sum him up pretty well.

In this subtle antagonism they knew each other like old friends, they were as shrewd with one another almost as man and wife. But Annie had always kept him sufficiently at arm's length. Besides, she had a boy of her own.

The Statutes fair, however, came in November, at Bestwood. It happened that Annie had the Monday night off. It was a drizzling ugly night, yet she dressed herself up and went to the fair ground. She was alone, but she expected soon to find a pal of some sort.

The roundabouts were veering round and grinding out their music, the side shows were making as much commotion as possible. In the cocoanut shies there were no cocoanuts, but artificial war-time substitutes, which the lad declared were fastened into the irons. There was a sad decline in brilliance and luxury. None the less, the ground was muddy as ever, there was the same crush, the press of faces lighted up by the flares and the electric lights, the same smell of naphtha and a few fried potatoes, and of electricity.

Who should be the first to greet Miss Annie, on the show ground, but John Thomas. He had a black overcoat buttoned up to his chin, and a tweed cap pulled down over his brows, his face between was ruddy and smiling and handy as ever. She knew so well the way his mouth moved.

She was very glad to have a "boy." To be at the Statutes without a fellow was no fun. Instantly, like the gallant he was, he took her on the Dragons, grim-toothed, roundabout switchbacks. It was not nearly so exciting as a tram-car actually. But, then, to be seated in a shaking green dragon, uplifted above the sea of bubble faces, careering in a rickety fashion in the lower heavens, whilst John Thomas leaned over her, his cigarette in his mouth, was after all the right style. She was a plump, quick, alive little creature. So she was quite excited and happy.

John Thomas made her stay on for the next round. And therefore she could hardly for shame repulse him when he put his arm round her and drew her a little nearer to him, in a very warm and cuddly manner. Besides, he was fairly discreet, he kept his movement as hidden as possible. She looked down and saw that his red, clean hand was out of sight of the crowd. And they knew each other so well. So they warmed up to the fair.

After the dragons they went on the horses. John Thomas paid each time, so she could but be complaisant. He, of course, sat astride on the outer horse—named "Black Bess"—and she sat sideways, towards him, on the inner horse—named "Wildfire." But of course John Thomas was not going to sit discreetly on "Black Bess," holding the brass bar. Round they spun and heaved, in the light. And round he swung on his wooden steed, flinging one leg across her mount, and perilously tipping up and down, across the space, half lying back, laughing at her. He was perfectly happy; she was afraid her hat was on one side, but she was excited.

He threw quoits on a table and won for her two large, pale-blue hatpins. And then, hearing the noise of the cinemas, announcing another performance, they climbed the boards and went in.

Of course, during these performances pitch darkness falls from time to time, when the machine goes wrong. Then there is a wild whooping, and a loud smacking of simulated kisses. In these moments John Thomas drew Annie towards him. After all, he had a wonderfully warm, cosy way of holding a girl with his arm, he seemed to make such a nice fit. And after all, it was pleasant to be so held: so very comforting and cosy and nice. He leaned over her and she felt his breath on her hair; she knew he wanted to kiss her on the lips. And after all, he was so warm and she fitted in to him so softly. After all, she wanted him to touch her lips.

But the light sprang up; she also started electrically, and put her hat straight. He left his arm lying nonchalantly behind her. Well, it was fun, it was exciting to be at the Statutes with John Thomas.

When the cinema was over they went for a walk across the dark, damp fields. He had all the arts of love-making. He was especially good at holding a girl, when he sat with her on a stile in the black, drizzling darkness. He seemed to be holding her in space, against his own warmth and gratification. And his kisses were soft and slow and searching.

So Annie walked out with John Thomas, though she kept her own boy dangling in the distance. Some of the tram-girls chose to be huffy. But there, you must take things as you find them, in this life.

There was no mistake about it, Annie liked John Thomas a good deal. She felt so rich and warm in herself whenever he was near. And John Thomas really liked Annie more than usual. The soft, melting way in which she could flow into a fellow, as if she melted into his very bones, was something rare and good. He fully appreciated this.

But with a developing acquaintance there began a developing intimacy. Annie wanted to consider him a person, a man; she wanted to take an intelligent interest in him, and to have an intelligent response. She did not want a mere nocturnal presence, which was what he was so far. And she prided herself that he could not leave her.

Here she made a mistake. John Thomas intended to remain a nocturnal presence; he had no idea of becoming an all-round individual to her. When she started to take an intelligent interest in him and his life and his character, he sheered off. He hated intelligent interest. And he knew that the only way to stop it was to avoid it. The possessive female was aroused in Annie. So he left her.

It is no use saying she was not surprised. She was at first startled, thrown out of her count. For she had been so *very* sure of holding him. For a while she was staggered, and everything became uncertain to her. Then she wept with fury, indignation, desolation, and misery. Then she had a spasm of despair. And then, when he came, still impudently, on to her car, still familiar, but letting her see by the movement of his head that he had gone away to somebody else for the time being and was enjoying pastures new, then she determined to have her own back.

She had a very shrewd idea what girls John Thomas had taken out. She went to Nora Purdy. Nora was a tall, rather pale, but well-built girl, with beautiful yellow hair. She was rather secretive.

"Hey!" said Annie, accosting her; then softly, "Who's John Thomas on with now?"

"I don't know," said Nora.

"Why tha does," said Annie, ironically lapsing into dialect. "Tha knows as well as I do."

"Well, I do, then," said Nora. "It isn't me, so don't bother."

"It's Cissy Meakin, isn't it?"

"It is, for all I know."

"Hasn't he got a face on him!" said Annie. "I don't half like his cheek. I could knock him off the footboard when he comes round at me."

"He'll get dropped-on one of these days," said Nora.

"Ay, he will when somebody makes up their mind to drop it on him. I should like to see him taken down a peg or two, shouldn't you?"

"I shouldn't mind," said Nora.

"You've got quite as much cause to as I have," said Annie. "But we'll drop on him one of these days, my girl. What? Don't you want to?"

"I don't mind," said Nora.

But as a matter of fact, Nora was much more vindictive than Annie.

One by one Annie went the round of the old flames. It so happened that Cissy Meakin left the tramway service in quite a short time. Her mother made her leave. Then John Thomas was on the qui-vive. He cast his eyes over his old flock. And his eyes lighted on Annie. He thought she would be safe now. Besides, he liked her.

She arranged to walk home with him on Sunday night. It so happened that her car would be in the depot at half-past nine: the last car would come in at ten-fifteen. So John Thomas was to wait for her there.

At the depot the girls had a little waiting-room of their own. It was quite rough, but cosy, with a fire and an oven and a mirror, and table and wooden chairs. The half dozen girls who knew John Thomas only too well had arranged to take service this Sunday afternoon. So, as the cars began to come in, early, the girls dropped into the waiting-room. And instead of hurrying off home, they sat around the fire and had a cup of tea. Outside was the darkness and lawlessness of war-time.

John Thomas came on the car after Annie, at about a quarter to ten. He poked his head easily into the girls' waiting-room.

"Prayer-meeting?" he asked.

"Ay," said Laura Sharp. "Ladies only."

"That's me!" said John Thomas. It was one of his favourite exclamations.

"Shut the door, boy," said Muriel Baggaley.

"On which side of me?" said John Thomas.

"Which tha likes," said Polly Birkin.

He had come in and closed the door behind him. The girls moved in their circle, to make a place for him near the fire. He took off his greatcoat and pushed back his hat.

"Who handles the teapot?" he said.

Nora Purdy silently poured him out a cup of tea.

"Want a bit o' my bread and drippin'?" said Muriel Baggaley to him.

"Ay, give us a bit."

And he began to eat his piece of bread.

"There's no place like home, girls," he said.

They all looked at him as he uttered this piece of impudence. He seemed to be sunning himself in the presence of so many damsels.

"Especially if you're not afraid to go home in the dark," said Laura Sharp.

"Me! By myself I am."

They sat till they heard the last tram come in. In a few minutes Emma Houselay entered.

"Come on, my old duck!" cried Polly Birkin.

"It *is* perishing," said Emma, holding her fingers to the fire.

"But—I'm afraid to, go home in, the dark," sang Laura Sharp, the tune having got into her mind.

"Who're you going with tonight, John Thomas?" asked Muriel Baggaley, coolly.

"Tonight?" said John Thomas. "Oh, I'm going home by myself tonight—all on my lonely-O."

"That's me!" said Nora Purdy, using his own ejaculation.

The girls laughed shrilly.

"Me as well, Nora," said John Thomas.

"Don't know what you mean," said Laura.

"Yes, I'm toddling," said he, rising and reaching for his overcoat.

"Nay," said Polly. "We're all here waiting for you."

"We've got to be up in good time in the morning," he said in the benevolent official manner.

They all laughed.

"Nay," said Muriel. "Don't leave us all lonely, John Thomas. Take one!"

"I'll take the lot, if you like," he responded gallantly.

"That you won't, either," said Muriel. "Two's company; seven's too much of a good thing."

"Nay—take one," said Laura. "Fair and square, all above board, and say which."

"Ay," cried Annie, speaking for the first time. "Pick, John Thomas; let's hear thee."

"Nay," he said. "I'm going home quiet tonight. Feeling good, for once."

"Whereabouts?" said Annie. "Take a good un, then. But tha's got to take one of us!"

"Nay, how can I take one," he said, laughing uneasily. "I don't want to make enemies."

"You'd only make *one*," said Annie.

"The chosen *one*," added Laura.

"Oh, my! Who said girls!" exclaimed John Thomas, again turning, as if to escape. "Well—good-night."

"Nay, you've got to make your pick," said Muriel. "Turn your face to the wall and say which one touches you. Go on—we shall only just touch your back—one of us. Go on—turn your face to the wall, and don't look, and say which one touches you."

He was uneasy, mistrusting them. Yet he had not the courage to break away. They pushed him to a wall and stood him there with his face to it. Behind his back they all grimaced, tittering. He looked so comical. He looked around uneasily.

"Go on!" he cried.

"You're looking—you're looking!" they shouted.

He turned his head away. And suddenly, with a movement like a swift cat, Annie went forward and fetched him a box on the side of the head that set his cap flying, and himself staggering. He started round.

But at Annie's signal they all flew at him, slapping him, pinching him, pulling his hair, though more in fun than in spite or anger. He, however, saw red. His blue eyes flamed with strange fear as well as fury, and he butted through the girls to the door. It was locked. He wrenched at it. Roused, alert, the girls stood round and looked at him. He faced them, at bay. At that moment they were rather horrifying to him, as they stood in their short uniforms. He was distinctly afraid.

"Come on, John Thomas! Come on! Choose!" said Annie.

"What are you after? Open the door," he said.

"We sha'n't—not till you've chosen!" said Muriel.

"Chosen what?" he said.

"Chosen the one you're going to marry," she replied.

He hesitated a moment.

"Open the blasted door," he said, "and get back to your senses." He spoke with official authority.

"You've got to choose!" cried the girls.

"Come on!" cried Annie, looking him in the eye. "Come on! Come on!"

He went forward, rather vaguely. She had taken off her belt, and swinging it, she fetched him a sharp blow over the head with the buckle end. He sprang and seized her. But immediately the other girls rushed upon him, pulling and tearing and beating him. Their blood was now thoroughly up. He was their sport now. They were going to have their own back, out of him. Strange, wild creatures, they hung on him and rushed at him to bear him down. His tunic was torn right up the back, Nora had hold at the back of his collar, and was actually strangling him. Luckily the button burst. He struggled in a wild frenzy of fury and terror, almost mad terror. His tunic was simply torn off his back, his shirt-sleeves were torn away, his arms were naked. The girls rushed at him, clenched their hands on him and pulled at him: or they rushed at him and pushed him, butted him with all their might: or they struck him wild blows. He ducked and cringed and struck sideways. They became more intense.

At last he was down. They rushed on him, kneeling on him. He had neither breath nor strength to move. His face was bleeding with a long scratch, his brow was bruised.

Annie knelt on him, the other girls knelt and hung on to him. Their faces were flushed, their hair wild, their eyes were all glittering strangely. He lay at last quite still, with face averted, as an animal lies when it is defeated and at the mercy of the captor. Sometimes his eye glanced back at the wild faces of the girls. His breast rose heavily, his wrists were torn.

"Now, then, my fellow!" gasped Annie at length. "Now then—now——"

At the sound of her terrifying, cold triumph, he suddenly started to struggle as an animal might, but the girls threw themselves upon him with unnatural strength and power, forcing him down.

"Yes—now, then!" gasped Annie at length.

And there was a dead silence, in which the thud of heart-beating was to be heard. It was a suspense of pure silence in every soul.

"Now you know where you are," said Annie.

The sight of his white, bare arm maddened the girls. He lay in a kind of trance of fear and antagonism. They felt themselves filled with supernatural strength.

Suddenly Polly started to laugh—to giggle wildly—helplessly—and Emma and Muriel joined in. But Annie and Nora and Laura remained the same, tense, watchful, with gleaming eyes. He winced away from these eyes.

"Yes," said Annie, in a curious low tone, secret and deadly. "Yes! You've got it now! You know what you've done, don't you? You know what you've done."

He made no sound nor sign, but lay with bright, averted eyes, and averted, bleeding face.

"You ought to be *killed*, that's what you ought," said Annie tensely. "You ought to be *killed*." And there was a terrifying lust in her voice.

Polly was ceasing to laugh, and giving long-drawn oh-h-hs and sighs as she came to herself.

"He's got to choose," she said vaguely.

"Oh, yes, he has," said Laura, with vindictive decision.

"Do you hear—do you hear?" said Annie. And with a sharp movement that made him wince, she turned his face to her.

"Do you hear?" she repeated, shaking him.

But he was quite dumb. She fetched him a sharp slap on the face. He started, and his eyes widened. Then his face darkened with defiance, after all.

"Do you hear?" she repeated.

He only looked at her with hostile eyes.

"Speak!" she said, putting her face devilishly near his.

"What?" he said, almost overcome.

"You've got to *choose*!" she cried, as if it were some terrible menace, and as if it hurt her that she could not exact more.

"What?" he said in fear.

"Choose your girl, Coddy. You've got to choose her now. And you'll get your neck broken if you play any more of your tricks, my boy. You're settled now."

There was a pause. Again he averted his face. He was cunning in his overthrow. He did not give in to them really—no, not if they tore him to bits.

"All right, then," he said, "I choose Annie." His voice was strange and full of malice. Annie let go of him as if he had been a hot coal.

"He's chosen Annie!" said the girls in chorus.

"Me!" cried Annie. She was still kneeling, but away from him. He was still lying prostrate, with averted face. The girls grouped uneasily around.

"Me!" repeated Annie, with a terrible bitter accent.

Then she got up, drawing away from him with strange disgust and bitterness.

"I wouldn't touch him," she said.

But her face quivered with a kind of agony, she seemed as if she would fall. The other girls turned aside. He remained lying on the floor, with his torn clothes and bleeding, averted face.

"Oh, if he's chosen——" said Polly.

"I don't want him—he can choose again," said Annie, with the same rather bitter hopelessness.

"Get up," said Polly, lifting his shoulder. "Get up."

He rose slowly, a strange, ragged, dazed creature. The girls eyed him from a distance, curiously, furtively, dangerously.

"Who wants him?" cried Laura roughly.

"Nobody," they answered with contempt. Yet each one of them waited for him to look at her, hoped he would look at her. All except Annie, and something was broken in her.

He, however, kept his face closed and averted from them all. There was a silence of the end. He picked up the torn pieces of his tunic, without knowing what to do with them. The girls stood about uneasily, flushed, panting, tidying their hair and their dress unconsciously, and watching him. He looked at none of them. He espied his cap in a corner and went and picked it up. He put it on his head, and one of the girls burst into a shrill, hysteric laugh at the sight he presented. He, however, took no heed but went straight to where his overcoat hung on a peg. The girls moved away from contact with him as if he had been an electric wire. He put on his coat and buttoned it down. Then he rolled his tunic-rags into a bundle, and stood before the locked door, dumbly.

"Open the door, somebody," said Laura.

"Annie's got the key," said one.

Annie silently offered the key to the girls. Nora unlocked the door.

"Tit for tat, old man," she said. "Show yourself a man, and don't bear a grudge."

But without a word or sign he had opened the door and gone, his face closed, his head dropped.

"That'll learn him," said Laura.

"Coddy!" said Nora.

"Shut up, for God's sake!" cried Annie fiercely, as if in torture.

"Well, I'm about ready to go, Polly. Look sharp!" said Muriel.

The girls were all anxious to be off. They were tidying themselves hurriedly, with mute, stupefied faces.

INTERPRETATION

The plot of this story is quite simple. One of the young inspectors of the tram line, John Thomas, begins to go out with Annie, one of the girl conductors. He drops her when he realizes that she is taking his attentions seriously. Annie plans to revenge herself by having the other girls whom he has treated in this fashion join her in roughing him up. They do not hurt him, though they get in some blows and they tear his tunic. John Thomas leaves, and the girls find themselves nonplussed at what they have done, a little dazed, and even a little frightened.

Though the story presents a good deal of action, even violent action, not very much has been resolved. Presumably John Thomas and Annie will continue to go their separate ways. Indeed, the story ends on a note of uneasy irresolution. The superficial reader may even feel baffled by the ending of the story and so dismiss it.

Other readers, however, may feel that the internal action is important. Indeed, the very debacle of the ending points toward an exciting psychological development. The girls have got in over their depth and find that their emotions toward John Thomas are in excess of, and indeed widely different from, the rather tomboyish triumph of their revenge. As the author tells us in the last sentence, after John Thomas's departure, the girls wear "mute, stupified faces."

The story derives much of its richness from the fact that it succeeds in dramatizing what may be called the "doubleness" of love—its strange mixture of aggressiveness and passivity, of cruelty and tenderness, of possessiveness and surrender. All the characters in the story experience something of these contradictory feelings, but the author has properly kept the focus upon one particular character, Annie, who is more deeply involved than the others, and who therefore not only feels the experience more intensely but is also the more intensely subject to the contradictory impulses within the experience.

The point comes out clearly when we see that nobody knows just how to end the joke. Once they have got into it, their actions are emotional and compulsive. Annie hits John Thomas a box on the side of the head that is probably much harder than she had first meant to strike. At this signal the girls fly at John Thomas "more in fun than in spite or anger." But soon they have their "blood . . . up," and are attacking in frenzy. When John Thomas stops resisting, the girls find themselves waiting for something to happen, not knowing what to do next, and repeating illogically and "vaguely" that he has "got to choose." Indeed, some of the girls, beginning "to giggle wildly," are obviously on the verge of hysteria.

There is, of course, no way for the episode to end satisfactorily for any of the girls—least of all for the leader of the prank, Annie, whose relation to John Thomas is so emotionally ambiguous. The only satisfactory ending for such a mixture of feelings—and of feelings waked to such intensity by the physical struggle—is possession and marriage. But this is the solution that the tomboy prank has made impossible. (To Annie at least it will now *seem* so.) It is as if Annie's revenge has made John Thomas more desirable, and yet that the forcing of his admission that, having to choose, he would indeed choose her, has made that choice in fact impossible. The very frustration of the prank she has engineered has revealed to her things about herself that she had not surmised.

1. Why is it with a "bitter hopelessness" that Annie says "I don't want him"?

2. What is meant by the author's saying of Annie that "something was broken in her"?

3. How would you describe Annie's feelings toward John Thomas at the end of the story?

4. How would you characterize John Thomas's feelings toward Annie?

5. Has the author put too much emphasis upon John Thomas's emotions, particularly in the last half of the story? Or too little emphasis?

6. Note that the author is constantly telling us what the characters think and what certain of their actions mean: for example, "He was uneasy, mistrusting them," or, "Yet each one of them . . . hoped he would look at her." Even so, the story is vivid in its presentation and remains "dramatic." Why do not the author's comments and interpretations "kill" the immediacy of this story?

JAMES PURDY

Eventide

MAHALA had waited as long as she thought she could; after all, Plumy had left that morning and now here it was going on four o'clock. It was hardly fair if she was loitering, but she knew that certainly Plumy would never loiter on a day like this when Mahala wanted so to hear. It was in a way the biggest day of her whole life, bigger than any day she had ever lived through as a girl or young woman. It was the day that decided whether her son would come back to live with her or not.

And just think, a whole month had rolled past since he left home. Two months ago if anyone would have said that Teeboy would leave home, she would have stopped dead in her tracks, it would have been such a terrible thing even to say, and now here she was, talking over the telephone about how Teeboy had gone.

"My Teeboy is gone," that is what Mahala said for a long time after the departure. These words announced to her mind what had happened, and just as an announcement they gave some mild comfort, like a pain-killer with a fatal disease.

"My Teeboy," she would say, like the mother of a dead son, like the mother of a son who had died in battle, because it hurt as much to have a son missing in peacetime as to have lost him through war.

The room seemed dark even with the summer sunshine outside, and close, although the window was open. There was a darkness all over the city. The fire department had been coming and going all afternoon. There were so many fires in the neighborhood—that is what she was saying to Cora on the telephone, too many fires: the fire chief had just whizzed past again. No, she said to Cora, she didn't know if it was in the white section of town or theirs, she couldn't tell, but oh it was so hot to have a fire.

Talking about the fires seemed to help Mahala more than anything. She called several other old friends and talked about the fires and she mentioned that Teeboy had not come home. The old friends did not say much about Teeboy's not having returned, because, well, what was there to say about a boy who had been practicing to leave home for so long. Everyone had known it but her blind mother love.

"What do you suppose can be keeping my sister Plumy?" Mahala said to herself as she walked up and down the hall and looked out from behind the screen in the window. "She would have to fail me on the most important errand in the world."

Then she thought about how much Plumy hated to go into white neighborhoods, and how the day had been hot and she thought of the fires and how perhaps Plumy had fallen under a fire truck and been crushed. She thought of all the possible disasters and was not happy, and always in the background there was the fresh emotion of having lost Teeboy.

"People don't know," she said, "that I can't live without Teeboy."

She would go in the clothes closet and look at his dirty clothes just as he had left them; she would kiss them and press them to her face, smelling them; the odors were especially dear to her. She held his rayon trousers to her bosom and walked up and down the small parlor. She had not prayed; she was waiting for Plumy to come home first, then maybe they would have prayer.

"I hope I ain't done anything I'll be sorry for," she said.

It was then, though, when she felt the worst, that she heard the steps on the front porch. Yes, those were Plumy's steps, she was coming with the news. But whatever the news was, she suddenly felt, she could not accept it.

As she came up the steps, Plumy did not look at Mahala with any particular kind of meaning on her face. She walked unsteadily, as if the heat had been too much for her.

"Come on in now, Plumy, and I will get you something cool to drink."

Inside, Plumy watched Mahala as if afraid she was going to ask her to begin at once with the story, but Mahala only waited, not saying anything, sensing the seriousness of Plumy's knowledge and knowing that this knowledge could be revealed only when Plumy was ready.

While Mahala waited patiently there in the kitchen, Plumy arranged herself in the easy chair, and when she was once settled, she took up the straw fan which lay on the floor.

"Well, I seen him!" Plumy brought the words out.

This beginning quieted the old mother a little. She closed her mouth and folded her hands, moving now to the middle of the parlor, with an intentness on her face as if she was listening to something high up in the sky, like a plane which is to drop something, perhaps harmless and silver, to the ground.

"I seen him!" Plumy repeated, as if to herself. "And I seen all the white people!" she finished, anger coming into her voice.

"Oh, Plumy," Mahala whined. Then suddenly she made a gesture for her sister to be quiet because she thought she heard the fire department going again, and then when there was no sound, she waited for her to go on, but Plumy did not say anything. In the slow afternoon there was nothing, only a silence a city sometimes has within itself.

Plumy was too faint from the heat to go on at once; her head suddenly shook violently and she slumped in the chair.

"Plumy Jackson!" Mahala said, going over to her. "You didn't *walk* here from the white district! You didn't walk them forty-seven blocks in all this August heat!"

Plumy did not answer immediately. Her hand caressed the worn upholstery of the chair.

"You know how nervous white folks make me," she said at last.

Mahala made a gesture of disgust. "Lord, to think you walked it in this hot sun. Oh, I don't know why God wants to upset me like this. As if I didn't have enough to make me wild already, without havin' you come home in this condition."

Mahala watched her sister's face for a moment with the same figuring expression of the man who comes to read the water meter. She saw everything she really wanted to know there, yet she pretended she didn't know the verdict; she brought the one question out:

"You did see Teeboy, honey?" she said, her voice changed from her tears. She waited a few seconds, and then as Plumy did not answer but only sank deeper into the chair, she continued: "What word did he send?"

"It's the way I told you before," Plumy replied crossly. "Teeboy ain't coming back. I thought you knowed from the way I looked at you that he ain't coming back."

Mahala wept quietly into a small handkerchief.

"Your pain is realer to me sometimes than my own," Plumy said, watching her cry. "That's why I hate to say to you he won't never come back, but it's true as death he won't."

"When you say that to me I got a feeling inside myself like everything had been busted and taken; I got the feeling like I don't have nothing left inside of me."

"Don't I know that feeling!" Plumy said, almost angrily, resting the straw fan on the arm of the chair, and then suddenly fanning herself violently so that the strokes sounded like those of a small angry whip. "Didn't I lose George Watson of sleeping sickness and all 'cause doctor wouldn't come?"

Plumy knew that Mahala had never shown any interest in the death of her own George Watson and that it was an unwelcome subject, especially tonight, when Teeboy's never coming back had become final, yet she could not help mentioning George Watson just the same. In Mahala's eyes there really had never been any son named George Watson; there was only a son named Teeboy and Mahala was the only mother.

"It ain't like there bein' no way out to your troubles: it's the way out that kills you," Mahala said. "If it was good-bye for always like when someone dies, I think I could stand it better. But this kind of parting ain't like the Lord's way!"

Plumy continued fanning herself, just letting Mahala run on.

"So he ain't never coming back!" Mahala began beating her hands together as if she were hearing music for a dance.

Plumy looked away as the sound of the rats downstairs caught her attention; there seemed to be more than usual tonight and she wondered why they were running so much, for it was so hot everywhere.

Her attention strayed back to Mahala standing directly in front of her now, talking about her suffering: "You go through all the suffering and the heartache," she said, "and then they go away. The only time children is nice is when they're babies and you know they can't get away from you. You got them then and your love is all they crave. They don't know who you are exactly, they just know you are the one to give them your love, and they ask you for it until you're worn out giving it."

Mahala's speech set Plumy to thinking of how she had been young and how she had had George Watson, and how he had died of sleeping sickness when he was four.

"My only son died of sleeping sickness," Plumy said aloud, but not really addressing Mahala. "I never had another. My husband said it was funny. He was not a religious man, but he thought it was queer."

"Would you like a cooling drink?" Mahala said absently.

Plumy shook her head and there was a silence of a few minutes in which the full weight of the heat of evening took possession of the small room.

"I can't get used to that idea of him *never* comin' back!" Mahala began again. "I ain't never been able to understand that word *never* anyhow. And now it's like to drive me wild."

There was another long silence, and then, Mahala suddenly rousing herself from drowsiness and the heat of the evening, began eagerly: "How did he look, Plumy? Tell me how he looked, and what he was doing. Just describe."

"He wasn't doin' nothin'!" Plumy said flatly. "He looked kind of older, though, like he had been thinking about new things."

"Don't keep me waiting," Mahala whined. "I been waitin' all day for the news, don't keep me no more, when I tell you I could suicide over it all. I ain't never been through such a hell day. Don't you keep me waitin'."

"Now hush," Plumy said. "Don't go frettin' like this. Your heart won't take a big grief like this if you go fret so."

"It's *so* unkind of you not to tell," she muffled her lips in her handkerchief.

Plumy said: "I told you I talked to him, but I didn't tell you where. It was in a drinking place called the Music Box. He called to me from inside. The minute I looked at him I knew there was something wrong. There was something wrong with his hair."

"With his hair!" Mahala cried.

"Then I noticed he had had it all made straight! That's right," she said looking away from Mahala's eyes. "He had had his hair straightened. 'Why ain't you got in touch with your mother,' I said. 'If you only knowed how she was carryin' on.'

"Then he told me how he had got a tenor sax and how he was playing it in the band at the Music Box and that he had begun a new life, and it was all on account of his having the tenor sax and being a musician. He said the players didn't have time to have homes. He said they were playing all the time, they never went home, and that was why he hadn't been."

Plumy stopped. She saw the tenor sax only in her imagination because he had not shown it to her, she saw it curved and golden and heard it playing far-off melodies. But the real reason she stopped was not on account of the tenor sax but because of the memory of the white woman who had come out just then. The white woman had come out and put her arm around Teeboy. It had made her get creepy all over. It was the first time that Plumy had realized that Teeboy's skin was nearly as light as the white people's.

Both Teeboy and the woman had stood there looking at Plumy, and Plumy had not known how to move away from them. The sun beat down on her in the street but she could not move. She saw the streetcars going by with all the white people pushing one another around and she looked around on the scorched pavements and everyone was white, with Teeboy looking just as white as the rest of them, looking just as white as if he had come out of Mahala's body white, and as if Mahala had been a white woman and not her sister, and as if Mahala's mother and hers had not been black.

Then slowly she had begun walking away from Teeboy and the Music Box, almost without knowing she was going herself, walking right on through the streets without knowing what was happening, through the big August heat, without an umbrella or a hat to keep off the sun; she could see no place to stop, and people could see the circles of sweat that were forming all over her dress. She was afraid to stop and she was afraid to go on walking. She felt she would fall down eventually in the afternoon sun and it would be like the time George Watson had died of sleeping sickness, nobody would help her to an easy place.

Would George Watson know her now? That is what she was thinking as she walked through the heat of that afternoon. Would he know her—

because when she had been his mother she had been young and her skin, she was sure, had been lighter; and now she was older looking than she remembered her own mother ever being, and her skin was very black.

It was Mahala's outcries which brought her back to the parlor, now full of the evening twilight.

"Why can't God call me home?" Mahala was asking. "Why can't He call me to His Throne of Grace?"

Then Mahala got up and wandered off into her own part of the house. One could hear her in her room there, faintly kissing Teeboy's soiled clothes and speaking quietly to herself.

"Until you told me about his having his hair straightened, I thought maybe he would be back," Mahala was saying from the room. "But when you told me that, I knew. He won't never be back."

Plumy could hear Mahala kissing the clothes after she had said this.

"He was so dear to her," Plumy said aloud. It was necessary to speak aloud at that moment because of the terrible feeling of evening in the room. Was it the smell of the four o'clocks, which must have just opened to give out their perfume, or was it the evening itself which made her uneasy? She felt not alone, she felt someone else had come, uninvited and from far away.

Plumy had never noticed before what a strong odor the four o'clocks had, and then she saw the light in the room, growing larger, a light she had not recognized before, and then she turned and saw *him*, George Watson Jackson, standing there before her, large as life. Plumy wanted to call out, she wanted to say *No* in a great voice, she wanted to brush the sight before her all away, which was strange because she was always wanting to see her baby and here he was, although seventeen years had passed since she had laid him away.

She looked at him with unbelieving eyes because really he was the same, the same except she did notice that little boys' suits had changed fashion since his day, and how that everything about him was slightly different from the little children of the neighborhood now.

"Baby!" she said, but the word didn't come out from her mouth, it was only a great winged thought that could not be made into sound. "George Watson, honey!" she said still in her silence.

He stood there, his eyes like they had been before. Their beauty stabbed at her heart like a great knife; the hair looked so like she had just pressed the wet comb to it and perhaps put a little pomade on the sides; and the small face was clean and sad. Yet her arms somehow did not ache to hold him like her heart told her they should. Something too far away and too strong was between her and him; she only saw him as she had always seen resurrection pictures, hidden from us as in a wonderful mist that will not let us see our love complete.

There was this mist between her and George Watson like the dew that will be on the four o'clocks when you pick one of them off the plant.

It was her baby come home, and at such an hour.

Then as she came slowly to herself, she began to raise herself slightly, stretching her arms and trying to get the words to come out to him:

"George Watson, baby!"

This time the words did come out, with a terrible loudness, and as they did so the light began to go from the place where he was standing: the last thing she saw of him was his bright forehead and hair, then there was nothing at all, not even the smell of flowers.

Plumy let out a great cry and fell back in the chair. Mahala heard her and came out of her room to look at her.

"What you got?" Mahala said.

"I seen *him!* I seen *him!* Big as life!"

"Who?" Mahala said.

"George Watson, just like I laid him away seventeen years ago!"

Mahala did not know what to say. She wiped her eyes dry, for she had quit crying.

"You was exposed too long in the sun," Mahala said vaguely.

As she looked at her sister she felt for the first time the love that Plumy had borne all these years for a small son Mahala had never seen, George Watson. For the first time she dimly recognized Plumy as a mother, and she had suddenly a feeling of intimacy for her that she never had before.

She walked over to the chair where Plumy was and laid her hand on her. Somehow the idea of George Watson's being dead so long and yet still being a baby a mother could love had a kind of perfect quality that she liked. She thought then, quietly and without shame, how nice it would be if Teeboy could also be perfect in death, so that he would belong to her in the same perfect way as George Watson belonged to Plumy. There was comfort in tending the grave of a dead son, whether he was killed in war or peace, and it was so difficult to tend the memory of a son who just went away and never came back. Yet somehow she knew as she looked at Plumy, somehow she would go on with the memory of Teeboy Jordan even though he still lived in the world.

As she stood there considering the lives of the two sons Teeboy Jordan and George Watson Jackson, the evening which had for some time been moving slowly into the house entered now as if in one great wave, bringing the small parlor into the heavy summer night until you would have believed daylight would never enter there again, the night was so black and secure.

INTERPRETATION

The most interesting questions about this story may be put as follows:

1. What is the action? (Since it is obviously internal and psychologi-

cal rather than some overt thing "done" by one of the characters, the definition may not be easy.)

2. What are we to make of the vision that appears to Plumy? Can we believe that she would have this particular hallucination and just at this time?

3. What is the meaning of Plumy's vision? For Plumy herself? For Mahala? For the story?

Even a cursory inspection of the questions makes it plain that we need to know a good deal about the characters of the two women and their relationship to each other. The author has nowhere given us full-dress "discussions" of his characters; what we know about them comes largely from their conversation when Plumy returns to Mahala to tell her about having seen Teeboy. The method of character presentation is thus "dramatic": the characters are not "explained" to us abstractly but are revealed through what they do and say—that is, they are made to "act out" their relationship.

The method is effective: before the story ends we have learned a great deal about these sisters. For one thing, there is a very close rapport between them. When Plumy comes in, her sister, in spite of her agony of suspense, waits, "not saying anything, sensing the seriousness of Plumy's knowledge and knowing that this knowledge could be revealed only when Plumy was ready." Later, before Plumy says a word, her sister knows the answer to her question: "She saw everything she really wanted to know" on Plumy's face. Plumy herself is well aware of the fact that she does not need really to tell her sister Teeboy's answer in so many words. She says to Mahala: "I thought you knowed from the way I looked at you that he ain't coming back."

Yet there are other matters in which the sisters are not in rapport at all. Mahala seems to lack full confidence in her sister's sympathy. She has a bad moment when she actually murmurs to herself: "She would have to fail me on the most important errand in the world." Specifically, her inability to believe that Plumy is really able to sympathize with her in her grief stems from the fact that she cannot think of Plumy as ever having had the experience of motherhood. As the author tells us, "In Mahala's eyes there really had never been any son named George Watson; there was only a son named Teeboy and Mahala was the only mother."

This then is in brief the relationship that exists between the sisters as Plumy, exhausted after the long afternoon, recovers herself in Mahala's parlor and tries to tell her sister about Teeboy's refusal to come home. There is a further point that might be added. Plumy, one surmises, has all along been aware of the hopelessness of her mission, for apparently all of Mahala's friends had known that Teeboy for a long time "had been practising to leave home." She says at one point to her sister: "It's the way I told you before" as if this were an old issue about which she has more than once tried to convince her sister.

With this in mind, we can say that this story is not primarily concerned with Teeboy's decision. The attentive reader has from the beginning probably been aware that Mahala's son will not return. What "happens" in this story—if indeed anything happens—must concern some other issue. We may be sure that it bears upon—perhaps has chiefly to do with—the relation of the sisters themselves.

As for Plumy, something indeed does "happen": she has a vision of her four-year old son. The problem is to see whether the vision has been made plausible to us who are the readers, and if so, what bearing it has upon the import of the story.

The most important fact, of course, is the obvious one: Plumy has just talked to Mahala's son, she is worried about Mahala, and she wonders how her sister will take the news that Teeboy will not come back. What is more natural than that she should suddenly find herself thinking about her own son and the way in which she has lost him. Her general emotional state is also very important. She is a rather primitive and unsophisticated person, and she is now experiencing the letdown after a period of sustained excitement. She has seen Teeboy, she has made the long journey back through the white neighborhood that always makes her nervous, and she has gone through the difficult business of telling her sister the depressing truth. There is her physical state to be considered too: she has taken a long walk through the hot sun and she is now very tired. Mahala refers to Plumy's having "come home in this condition," and a little later, when Plumy cries out to tell her sister about the vision, Mahala says "You was exposed too long in the sun."

Perhaps Plumy has experienced a touch of the sun, but the significance of the experience is not to be measured by what may have been one of its contributing causes. Plumy has been exposed, we might say, to life as well as to the sun. So Mahala finds herself at last profoundly moved by her sister's vision. She goes over to lay her hand upon her sister, and as she does she feels for the first time that Plumy also has been a mother and with this realization, there comes "a feeling of intimacy for her that she never had before."

What happens in the story, then, is a change in the relation between the two sisters. In the last three paragraphs of the story, Purdy handles skillfully and very delicately their concordant movement into sympathy and understanding. The student should ponder these concluding paragraphs carefully. In order to see just what they accomplish and how, he might consider the following questions:

1. What is the meaning, in this context, of "perfect quality" and "perfect in death" and "perfect way"? Is the adjective *perfect* used vaguely and sentimentally?

2. Is the phrasing of these paragraphs too literary and highfalutin for a description of what is going on in Mahala's mind? If not, why not?

3. Does an appreciation of Plumy's experience help to modify Mahala's own experience of loss? How?

4. What, if anything, is accomplished by the last sentence with its description of the surging into the parlor of the night and darkness? What does darkness usually signify? Is that significance modified here by the phrase "so black and *secure*"?

The student may want to put to himself some further questions that have to do with earlier sections of the story or the story as a whole.

5. Would you agree that exposition is well handled in the opening paragraphs? Is it also mingled with a forward movement—the setting up of expectations in the reader's mind? How specifically is this done?

6. Does Mahala have to be regarded as in reality a selfish, possessive mother? Is there any evidence for this interpretation of her character? If you think that there is evidence for it, how, if at all, is the meaning of the story affected?

7. How is sentimentality avoided in this story as it is *not* avoided in the Bret Harte story?

CARSON McCULLERS

A Domestic Dilemma

ON Thursday Martin Meadows left the office early enough to make the first express bus home. It was the hour when the evening lilac glow was fading in the slushy streets, but by the time the bus had left the Mid-town terminal the bright city night had come. On Thursdays the maid had a half-day off and Martin liked to get home as soon as possible, since for the past year his wife had not been—well. This Thursday he was very tired and, hoping that no regular commuter would single him out for conversation, he fastened his attention to the newspaper until the bus had crossed the George Washington Bridge. Once on 9-W Highway Martin always felt that the trip was halfway done, he breathed deeply, even in cold weather when only ribbons of draught cut through the smoky air of the bus, confident that he was breathing country air. It used to be that at this point he would relax and begin to think with pleasure of his home. But in this last year nearness brought only a sense of tension and he did not anticipate the journey's end. This evening Martin kept his face close to the window and watched the barren fields and lonely lights of passing townships. There was a moon, pale on the dark earth and areas of late, porous snow; to Martin the countryside seemed vast and somehow desolate that evening. He took his hat from the rack and put his folded newspaper in the pocket of his overcoat a few minutes before time to pull the cord.

The cottage was a block from the bus stop, near the river but not directly on the shore; from the living-room window you could look across the street and opposite yard and see the Hudson. The cottage was modern, almost too white and new on the narrow plot of yard. In summer the grass was soft and bright and Martin carefully tended a flower border and a rose trellis. But during the cold, fallow months the yard was bleak and the cottage seemed naked. Lights were on that evening in all the rooms in the little house and Martin hurried up the front walk. Before the steps he stopped to move a wagon out of the way.

The children were in the living room, so intent on play that the opening of the front door was at first unnoticed. Martin stood looking at his safe, lovely children. They had opened the bottom drawer of the secretary and taken out the Christmas decorations., Andy had managed to plug in the Christmas tree lights and the green and red bulbs glowed with out-of-season festivity on the rug of the living room. At the moment he was trying to trail the bright cord over Marianne's rocking horse. Marianne sat on the floor pulling off an angel's wings. The children wailed a startling welcome. Martin swung the fat little baby girl up to his shoulder and Andy threw himself against his father's legs.

"Daddy, Daddy, Daddy!"

Martin sat down the little girl carefully and swung Andy a few times like a pendulum. Then he picked up the Christmas tree cord.

"What's all this stuff doing out? Help me put it back in the drawer. You're not to fool with the light socket. Remember I told you that before. I mean it, Andy."

The six-year-old child nodded and shut the secretary drawer. Martin stroked his fair soft hair and his hand lingered tenderly on the nape of the child's frail neck.

"Had supper yet, Bumpkin?"

"It hurt. The toast was hot."

The baby girl stumbled on the rug and, after the first surprise of the fall, began to cry; Martin picked her up and carried her in his arms back to the kitchen.

"See, Daddy," said Andy. "The toast——"

Emily had laid the children's supper on the uncovered porcelain table. There were two plates with the remains of cream-of-wheat and eggs and silver mugs that had held milk. There was also a platter of cinnamon toast, untouched, except for one tooth-marked bite. Martin sniffed the bitten piece and nibbled gingerly. Then he put the toast into the garbage pail.

"Hoo—phui—What on earth!"

Emily had mistaken the tin of cayenne for the cinnamon.

"I like to have burnt up," Andy said. "Drank water and ran outdoors and opened my mouth. Marianne didn't eat none."

"Any," corrected Martin. He stood helpless, looking around the walls of the kitchen. "Well, that's that, I guess," he said finally. "Where is your mother now?"

"She's up in you alls' room."

Martin left the children in the kitchen and went up to his wife. Outside the door he waited for a moment to still his anger. He did not knock and once inside the room he closed the door behind him.

Emily sat in the rocking chair by the window of the pleasant room. She had been drinking something from a tumbler and as he entered she put the glass hurriedly on the floor behind the chair. In her attitude there was confusion and guilt which she tried to hide by a show of spurious vivacity.

"Oh, Marty! You home already? The time slipped up on me. I was just going down——" She lurched to him and her kiss was strong with sherry. When he stood unresponsive she stepped back a pace and giggled nervously.

"What's the matter with you? Standing there like a barber pole. Is anything wrong with you?"

"Wrong with *me?*" Martin bent over the rocking chair and picked up the tumbler from the floor. "If you could only realize how sick I am—how bad it is for all of us."

Emily spoke in a false, airy voice that had become too familiar to him. Often at such times she affected a slight English accent copying perhaps some actress she admired. "I haven't the vaguest idea what you mean. Unless you are referring to the glass I used for a spot of sherry. I had a finger of sherry—maybe two. But what is the crime in that, pray tell me? I'm quite all right. Quite all right."

"So anyone can see."

As she went into the bedroom Emily walked with careful gravity. She turned on the cold water and dashed some on her face with her cupped hands, then patted herself dry with the corner of a bath towel. Her face was delicately featured and young, unblemished.

"I was just going down to make dinner." She tottered and balanced herself by holding to the door frame.

"I'll take care of dinner. You stay up here. I'll bring it up."

"I'll do nothing of the sort. Why, whoever heard of such a thing?"

"Please," Martin said.

"Leave me alone. I'm quite all right. I was just on the way down——"

"Mind what I say."

"Mind your grandmother."

She lurched toward the door, but Martin caught her by the arm. "I don't want the children to see you in this condition. Be reasonable."

"Condition!" Emily jerked her arm. Her voice rose angrily. "Why, because I drink a couple of sherries in the afternoon you're trying to make me out a drunkard. Condition! Why, I don't even touch whiskey. As well you know. *I* don't swill liquor at bars. And that's more than you can say. I don't even have a cocktail at dinnertime. I only sometimes have a glass of sherry. What, I ask you, is the disgrace of that? Condition!"

Martin sought words to calm his wife. "We'll have a quiet supper by ourselves up here. That's a good girl." Emily sat on the side of the bed and he opened the door for a quick departure.

"I'll be back in a jiffy."

As he busied himself with the dinner downstairs he was lost in the familiar question as to how this problem had come upon his home. He himself had always enjoyed a good drink. When they were still living in Alabama they had served long drinks or cocktails as a matter of course. For years they had drunk one or two—possibly three drinks before dinner, and at bedtime a long nightcap. Evenings before holidays they might get a buzz on, might even become a little tight. But alcohol had never seemed a problem to him, only a bothersome expense that with the increase in the family they could scarcely afford. It was only after his company had transferred him to New York that Martin was aware that certainly his wife was drinking too much. She was tippling, he noticed, during the day.

The problem acknowledged, he tried to analyze the source. The change from Alabama to New York had somehow disturbed her; accustomed to the idle warmth of a small Southern town, the matrix of the family and cousinship and childhood friends, she had failed to accommodate herself to the stricter, lonelier mores of the North. The duties of motherhood and housekeeping were onerous to her. Homesick for Paris City, she had made no friends in the suburban town. She read only magazines and murder books. Her interior life was insufficient without the artifice of alcohol.

The revelations of incontinence insidiously undermined his previous conceptions of his wife. There were times of unexplainable malevolence, times when the alcoholic fuse caused an explosion of unseemly anger. He encountered a latent coarseness in Emily, inconsistent with her natural simplicity. She lied about drinking and deceived him with unsuspected stratagems.

Then there was an accident. Coming home from work one evening about a year ago, he was greeted with screams from the children's room. He found Emily holding the baby, wet and naked from her bath. The baby had been dropped, her frail, frail skull striking the table edge, so that a thread of blood was soaking into the gossamer hair. Emily was sobbing and intoxicated. As Martin cradled the hurt child, so infinitely precious at that moment, he had an affrighted vision of the future.

The next day Marianne was all right. Emily vowed that never again would she touch liquor, and for a few weeks she was sober, cold and downcast. Then gradually she began—not whiskey or gin—but quantities of beer, or sherry, or outlandish liqueurs; once he had come across a hatbox of empty crème de menthe bottles. Martin found a dependable maid who managed the household competently. Virgie was also from Alabama and Martin had never dared tell Emily the wage scale customary in New York. Emily's drinking was entirely secret now, done before he reached the house. Usually the effects were almost imperceptible—a looseness of movement or the heavy-lidded eyes. The times of irresponsibilities, such as the cayenne-pepper toast were rare, and Martin could dismiss his worries when Virgie was at the house. But, nevertheless, anxiety was always latent, a threat of undefined disaster that underlaid his days.

"Marianne!" Martin called, for even the recollection of that time brought the need for reassurance. The baby girl, no longer hurt, but no less precious to her father, came into the kitchen with her brother. Martin went on with the preparations for the meal. He opened a can of soup and put two chops in the frying pan. Then he sat down by the table and took Marianne on his knees for a pony ride. Andy watched them, his fingers wobbling the tooth that had been loose all that week.

"Andy-the-candyman!" Martin said. "Is that old critter still in your mouth? Come closer, let Daddy have a look."

"I got a string to pull it with." The child brought from his pocket a tangled thread. "Virgie said to tie it to the tooth and tie the other end to the doorknob and shut the door real suddenly."

Martin took out a clean handkerchief and felt the loose tooth carefully. "That tooth is coming out of my Andy's mouth tonight. Otherwise I'm awfully afraid we'll have a tooth tree in the family."

"A what?"

"A tooth tree," Martin said. "You'll bite into something and swallow that tooth. And the tooth will take root in poor Andy's stomach and grow into a tooth tree with sharp little teeth insead of leaves."

"Shoo, Daddy," Andy said. But he held the tooth firmly between his grimy little thumb and forefinger. "There ain't any tree like that. I never seen one."

"There *isn't* any tree like that and I never *saw* one."

Martin tensed suddenly. Emily was coming down the stairs. He listened to her fumbling footsteps, his arm embracing the little boy with dread. When Emily came into the room he saw from her movements and her sullen face that she had again been at the sherry bottle. She began to yank open drawers and set the table.

"Condition!" she said in a furry voice. "You talk to me like that. Don't think I'll forget. I remember every dirty lie you say to me. Don't you think for a minute that I forget."

"Emily!" he begged. "The children——"

"The children—yes! Don't think I don't see through your dirty plots and schemes. Down here trying to turn my own children against me. Don't think I don't see and understand."

"Emily! I beg you—please go upstairs."

"So you can turn my children—my very own children——" Two large tears coursed rapidly down her cheeks. "Trying to turn my little boy, my Andy, against his own mother."

With drunken impulsiveness Emily knelt on the floor before the startled child. Her hands on his shoulders balanced her. "Listen, my Andy— you wouldn't listen to any lies your father tells you? You wouldn't believe what he says? Listen, Andy, what was your father telling you before I came downstairs?" Uncertain, the child sought his father's face. "Tell me. Mama wants to know."

"About the tooth tree."

"What?"

The child repeated the words and she echoed them with unbelieving terror. "The tooth tree!" She swayed and renewed her grasp on the child's shoulder. "I don't know what you're talking about. But listen, Andy, Mama is all right, isn't she?" The tears were spilling down her face and Andy drew back from her, for he was afraid. Grasping the table edge, Emily stood up.

"See! You have turned my child against me."

Marianne began to cry, and Martin took her in his arms.

"That's all right, you can take *your* child. You have always shown partiality from the very first. I don't mind, but at least you can leave me my little boy."

Andy edged close to his father and touched his leg. "Daddy," he wailed.

Martin took the children to the foot of the stairs. "Andy, you take up Marianne and Daddy will follow you in a minute."

"But Mama?" the child asked, whispering.

"Mama will be all right. Don't worry."

Emily was sobbing at the kitchen table, her face buried in the crook of her arm. Martin poured a cup of soup and set it before her. Her rasping sobs unnerved him; the vehemence of her emotion, irrespective of the source, touched in him a strain of tenderness. Unwillingly he laid his hand on her dark hair. "Sit up and drink the soup." Her face as she looked up at him was chastened and imploring. The boy's withdrawal or the touch of Martin's hand had turned the tenor of her mood.

"Ma-Martin," she sobbed. "I'm so ashamed."

"Drink the soup."

Obeying him, she drank between gasping breaths. After a second cup she allowed him to lead her up to their room. She was docile now and more restrained. He laid her nightgown on the bed and was about to leave the room when a fresh round of grief, the alcoholic tumult, came again.

"He turned away. My Andy looked at me and turned away."

Impatience and fatigue hardened his voice, but he spoke warily. "You forget that Andy is still a little child—he can't comprehend the meaning of such scenes."

"Did I make a scene? Oh, Martin, did I make a scene before the children?"

Her horrified face touched and amused him against his will. "Forget it. Put on your nightgown and go to sleep."

"My child turned away from me. Andy looked at his mother and turned away. The children——"

She was caught in the rhythmic sorrow of alcohol. Martin withdrew from the room saying: "For God's sake go to sleep. The children will forget by tomorrow."

As he said this he wondered if it was true. Would the scene glide so easily from memory—or would it root in the unconscious to fester in the after-years? Martin did not know, and the last alternative sickened him. He thought of Emily, foresaw the morning-after humiliation: the shards of memory, the lucidities that glared from the obliterating darkness of shame. She would call the New York office twice—possibly three or four times. Martin anticipated his own embarrassment, wondering if the others at the office could possibly suspect. He felt that his secretary had divined the trouble long ago and that she pitied him. He suffered a moment of rebellion against his fate, he hated his wife.

Once in the children's room he closed the door and felt secure for the first time that evening. Marianne fell down on the floor, picked herself up and calling: "Daddy, watch me," fell again, got up, and continued the falling-calling routine. Andy sat in the child's low chair, wobbling the tooth. Martin ran the water in the tub, washed his own hands in the lavatory, and called the boy into the bathroom.

"Let's have another look at that tooth." Martin sat on the toilet, holding Andy between his knees. The child's mouth gaped and Martin grasped the tooth. A wobble, a quick twist and the nacreous milk tooth was free. Andy's face was for the first moment split between terror, astonishment, and delight. He mouthed a swallow of water and spat into the lavatory.

"Look, Daddy! It's blood. Marianne!"

Martin loved to bathe his children, loved inexpressibly the tender, naked bodies as they stood in the water so exposed. It was not fair of Emily to say that he showed partiality. As Martin soaped the delicate boy-body of his son he felt that further love would be impossible. Yet he admitted the difference in the quality of his emotions for the two children. His love for his daughter was graver, touched with a strain of melancholy, a gentleness that was akin to pain. His pet names for the little boy were the absurdities of daily inspiration—he called the little girl always Marianne, and his voice as he spoke it was a caress. Martin patted dry the fat baby stomach and the sweet little genital fold. The washed child faces were radiant as flower petals, equally loved.

"I'm putting the tooth under my pillow. I'm supposed to get a quarter."

"What for?"

"*You* know, Daddy. Johnny got a quarter for his tooth."

"Who puts the quarter there?" asked Martin. "I used to think the fairies left it in the night. It was a dime in my day, though."

"That's what they say in kindergarten."

"Who does put it there?"

"Your parents," Andy said. "You!"

Martin was pinning the cover on Marianne's bed. His daughter was already asleep. Scarcely breathing, Martin bent over and kissed her forehead, kissed again the tiny hand that lay palm-upward, flung in slumber beside her head.

"Good night, Andy-man."

The answer was only a drowsy murmur. After a minute Martin took out his change and slid a quarter underneath the pillow. He left a night light in the room.

As Martin prowled about the kitchen making a late meal, it occurred to him that the children had not once mentioned their mother or the scene that must have seemed to them incomprehensible. Absorbed in the instant— the tooth, the bath, the quarter—the fluid passage of child-time had borne these weightless episodes like leaves in the swift current of a shallow stream while the adult enigma was beached and forgotten on the shore. Martin thanked the Lord for that.

But his own anger, repressed and lurking, rose again. His youth was being frittered by a drunkard's waste, his very manhood subtly undermined. And the children, once the immunity of incomprehension passed— what would it be like in a year or so? With his elbows on the table he ate his food brutishly, untasting. There was no hiding the truth—soon there would be gossip in the office and in the town; his wife was a dissolute woman. Dissolute. And he and his children were bound to a future of degradation and slow ruin.

Martin pushed away from the table and stalked into the living room. He followed the lines of a book with his eyes but his mind conjured miserable images: he saw his children drowned in the river, his wife a disgrace on the public street. By bedtime the dull, hard anger was like a weight upon his chest and his feet dragged as he climbed the stairs.

The room was dark except for the shafting light from the half-opened bathroom door. Martin undressed quietly. Little by little, mysteriously, there came in him a change. His wife was asleep, her peaceful respiration sounding gently in the room. Her high-heeled shoes with the carelessly dropped stockings made to him a mute appeal. Her underclothes were flung in disorder on the chair. Martain picked up the girdle and the soft, silk brassière and stood for a moment with them in his hands. For the first time that evening he looked at his wife. His eyes rested on the sweet forehead, the arch of the fine brow. The brow had descended to Marianne, and the tilt at the end of the delicate nose. In his son he could trace the high cheekbones and pointed chin. Her body was full-bosomed, slender and undulant. As Martin watched the tranquil slumber of his wife the ghost of anger vanished. All thoughts of blame or blemish were distant from him now. Martin put out the bathroom light and raised the window. Careful not to awaken Emily he slid into the bed. By moonlight he watched his wife for the last time. His hand sought the adjacent flesh and sorrow paralleled desire in the immense complexity of love.

INTERPRETATION

This story has to do with a not too eventful evening in Suburbia. An office worker comes home to find his wife a little befuddled with drink, his children neglected, and dinner still to cook. The story recounts his reactions through the rest of the evening from his attending to the children to his final turning in for the night. What happens in this story has to do primarily with his shifting emotions: his exasperation at the disordered house, his anger at his wife, his anxiety for his children, his hurt and despair as he thinks of the future, and his final state of mind as he slips into bed. We shall suggest a little later that the story does more than to describe these feelings. If it did no more than to describe the sequence of them, then it might be a sound psychological account, but we could hardly call it a piece of fiction. The claim that it is fiction requires that we raise the question of its significance—its presenting some kind of theme, however indirectly and concretely it may do so.

In any case, the character of Martin Meadows is of first importance in this story. We are not led to think of Martin as a highly sensitive and imaginative man. Our impression is that he is an ordinary man. Yet though we do not associate Martin with intense introspection or with the cultivated sensitivity of the professional artist, the author probably convinces us of the intensity and even delicacy of his feelings. The special quality of the story inheres in this revelation of the range of feelings to be found in an ordinary man. Martin loves his wife, but love is often a very complex thing.

The character of his wife, Emily, is of course also very important in this story. We see her as she appears on this particular evening. But the author has gone further and sketched in a little account of her background with some specific comments on what has happened to her and what has caused her to take refuge in alcohol. But Emily, important as she is for the story, constituting as she does Martin's problem, is still a subordinate character. The focus is kept steadily on Martin himself.

If the story is successful, we must be made to feel that Martin and Emily are believable and that their actions and thoughts, including Martin's final shift in feeling toward his wife, are true to what this pair of people would do and think and feel. Yet, as has been remarked earlier, if the story involves nothing more than this kind of psychological plausibility, it would not be a piece of fiction. What is the story "about"? Does it have any larger significance than the presentation of these two people? This is a question which the student should ponder and for which he should try to devise an answer. But before attempting this larger question, he might try to answer some of the following questions about the development and technique of the story.

1. How do the first two paragraphs of this story point ahead to what is to come? What details suggest Martin's apprehension? Are there any suggestions as to what kind of man he is?

2. Our first direct view of Emily comes only when Martin, having come into the house and having greeted his children, climbs the stairs to speak to his wife. Since the reader begins with Martin in the city, this is a normal sequence. But what advantages, if any, accrue from this postponement. How are we "prepared" for our first sight of Emily?

3. Can you justify the author's summary account of what ails Emily? Is it adequate? Why did she not work it out dramatically and concretely?

4. Is Martin a weak and indulgent man? A strong and competent man? How would you characterize him?

5. We have already read one story that has to do with the return of a husband to his wife in the evening, "A Piece of News." Does "A Domestic Dilemma" have *anything* in common with "A Piece of News"? Does a comparison of the two stories—admittedly so different—throw any light on either of them?

6. Can you justify the ending of the story? Has Martin's final state of mind been sufficiently prepared for? How does the ending affect the total meaning of the story? What, in your opinion, is the meaning?

KATHERINE ANNE PORTER

Theft

SHE had the purse in her hand when she came in. Standing in the middle of the floor, holding her bathrobe around her and trailing a damp towel in one hand, she surveyed the immediate past and remembered everything clearly. Yes, she had opened the flap and spread it out on the bench after she had dried the purse with her handkerchief.

She had intended to take the Elevated, and naturally she looked in her purse to make certain she had the fare, and was pleased to find forty cents in the coin envelope. She was going to pay her own fare, too, even if Camilo did have the habit of seeing her up the steps and dropping a nickel in the machine before he gave the turnstile a little push and sent her through it with a bow. Camilo by a series of compromises had managed to make effective a fairly complete set of smaller courtesies, ignoring the larger and more troublesome ones. She had walked with him to the station in a pouring rain, because she knew he was almost as poor as she was, and when he insisted on a taxi, she was firm and said, "You know it simply will not do." He was wearing a new hat of a pretty biscuit shade, for it never occurred to him to buy anything of a practical color; he had put it on for the first time and the rain was spoiling it. She kept thinking, "But this is dreadful, where will he get another?" She compared it with Eddie's hats that always seemed to be precisely seven years old and as if they had been quite purposely left out in the rain, and yet they sat with a careless and incidental rightness on Eddie. But Camilo was far different; if he wore a shabby hat it would be merely shabby on him, and he would lose his spirits over it. If she had not feared Camilo would take it badly, for he insisted on the practice of his little ceremonies up to the point he had fixed for them, she would have said to him as they left Thora's house, "Do go home. I can surely reach the station by myself."

"It is written that we must be rained upon tonight," said Camilo, "so let it be together."

At the foot of the platform stairway she staggered slightly—they were both nicely set up on Thora's cocktails—and said: "At least, Camilo, do me the favor not to climb these stairs in your present state, since for you it is only a matter of coming down again at once, and you'll certainly break your neck."

He made three quick bows, he was Spanish, and leaped off through the rainy darkness. She stood watching him, for he was a very graceful young man, thinking that tomorrow morning he would gaze soberly at his spoiled hat and soggy shoes and possibly associate her with his misery. As she watched, he stopped at the far corner and took off his hat and hid it under his overcoat. She felt she had betrayed him by seeing, because he would have been humiliated if he thought she even suspected him of trying to save his hat.

Roger's voice sounded over her shoulder above the clang of the rain falling on the stairway shed, wanting to know what she was doing out in the rain at this time of night, and did she take herself for a duck? His long, imperturbable face was streaming with water, and he tapped a bulging spot on the breast of his buttoned-up overcoat: "Hat," he said. "Come on, let's take a taxi."

She settled back against Roger's arm which he laid around her shoulders, and with the gesture they exchanged a glance full of long amiable associations, then she looked through the window at the rain changing the shapes of everything, and the colors. The taxi dodged in and out between the pillars of the Elevated, skidding slightly on every curve, and she said: "The more it skids the calmer I feel, so I really must be drunk."

"You must be," said Roger. "This bird is a homicidal maniac, and I could do with a cocktail myself this minute."

They waited on the traffic at Fortieth Street and Sixth Avenue, and three boys walked before the nose of the taxi. Under the globes of light they were cheerful scarecrows, all very thin and all wearing very seedy snappy-cut suits and gay neckties. They were not very sober either, and they stood for a moment wobbling in front of the car, and there was an argument going on among them. They leaned toward each other as if they were getting ready to sing, and the first one said: "When I get married it won't be jus' for getting married, I'm gonna marry for *love*, see?" and the second one said, "Aw, gwan and tell that stuff to *her*, why n't yuh?" and the third one gave a kind of hoot, and said, "Hell, dis guy? Wot the hell's he got?" and the first one said: "Aaah, shurrup yuh mush, I got plenty." Then they all squealed and scrambled across the street beating the first one on the back and pushing him around.

"Nuts," commented Roger, "pure nuts."

Two girls went skittering by in short transparent raincoats, one green, one red, their heads tucked against the drive of the rain. One of them was saying to the other, "Yes, I know all about *that*. But what about me? You're always so sorry for *him* . . ." and they ran on with their little pelican legs flashing back and forth.

The taxi backed up suddenly and leaped forward again, and after a while Roger said: "I had a letter from Stella today, and she'll be home on the twenty-sixth, so I suppose she's made up her mind and it's all settled."

"I had a sort of letter today too," she said, "making up my mind for me. I think it is time you and Stella to do something definite."

When the taxi stopped on the corner of West Fifty-third Street, Roger said, "I've just enough if you'll add ten cents," so she opened her purse and gave him a dime, and he said, "That's beautiful, that purse."

"It's a birthday present," she told him, "and I like it. How's your show coming?"

"Oh, still hanging on, I guess. I don't go near the place. Nothing sold yet. I mean to keep right on the way I'm going and they can take it or leave it. I'm through with the argument."

"It's absolutely a matter of holding out, isn't it?"

"Holding out's the tough part."

"Good night, Roger."

"Good night, you should take aspirin and push yourself into a tub of hot water, you look as though you're catching cold."

"I will."

With the purse under her arm she went upstairs, and on the first landing Bill heard her step and poked his head out with his hair tumbled and his eyes red, and he said: "For Christ's sake, come in and have a drink with me. I've had some bad news."

"You're perfectly sopping," said Bill, looking at her drenched feet. They had two drinks, while Bill told how the director had thrown his play out after the cast had been picked over twice, and had gone through three rehearsals. "I said to him, 'I didn't say it was a masterpiece, I said it would make a good show.' And he said, 'It just doesn't *play*, do you see? It needs a doctor.' So I'm stuck, absolutely stuck," said Bill, on the edge of weeping again. "I've been crying," he told her, "in my cups." And he went on to ask her if she realized his wife was ruining him with her extravagance. "I send her ten dollars every week of my unhappy life, and I don't really have to. She threatens to jail me if I don't, but she can't do it. God, let her try it after the way she treated me! She's no right to alimony and she knows it. She keeps on saying she's got to have it for the baby and I keep on sending it because I can't bear to see anybody suffer. So I'm way behind on the piano and the victrola, both—"

"Well, this is a pretty rug, anyhow," she said.

Bill stared at it and blew his nose. "I got it at Ricci's for ninety-five dollars," he said. "Ricci told me it once belonged to Marie Dressler, and cost fifteen hundred dollars, but there's a burnt place on it, under the divan. Can you beat that?"

"No," she said. She was thinking about her empty purse and that she could not possibly expect a check for her latest review for another three days, and her arrangement with the basement restaurant could not last much longer if she did not pay something on account. "It's no time to speak of it," she said, "but I've been hoping you would have by now that fifty dollars you promised for my scene in the third act. Even if it doesn't play. You were to pay me for the work anyhow out of your advance."

"Weeping Jesus," said Bill, "you, too?" He gave a loud sob, or hiccough, in his moist handkerchief. "Your stuff was no better than mine, after all. Think of that."

"But you got something for it," she said. "Seven hundred dollars."

Bill said, "Do me a favor, will you? Have another drink and forget about it. I can't, you know I can't, I would if I could, but you know the fix I'm in."

"Let it go, then," she found herself saying almost in spite of herself. She had meant to be quite firm about it. They drank again without speaking, and she went to her apartment on the floor above.

There, she now remembered distinctly, she had taken the letter out of the purse before she spread the purse out to dry.

She had sat down and read the letter over again: but there were phrases that insisted on being read many times, they had a life of their own separate from the others, and when she tried to read past and around them, they moved with the movement of her eyes, and she could not escape them . . . "thinking about you more than I mean to . . . yes, I even talk about you . . . why were you so anxious to destroy . . . even if I could see you now I would not . . . not worth all this abominable . . . the end . . ."

Carefully she tore the letter into narrow strips and touched a lighted match to them in the coal grate.

Early the next morning she was in the bathtub when the janitress knocked and then came in, calling out that she wished to examine the radiators before she started the furnace going for the winter. After moving about the room for a few minutes, the janitress went out, closing the door very sharply.

She came out of the bathroom to get a cigarette from the package in the purse. The purse was gone. She dressed and made coffee, and sat by the window while she drank it. Certainly the janitress had taken the purse, and certainly it would be impossible to get it back without a great deal of ridiculous excitement. Then let it go. With this decision of her mind, there rose coincidentally in her blood a deep almost murderous anger. She set the cup carefully in the center of the table, and walked steadily downstairs, three long flights and a short hall and a steep short flight into the basement, where the janitress, her face streaked with coal dust, was shaking up the furnace. "Will you please give me back my purse? There isn't any money in it. It was a present, and I don't want to lose it."

The janitress turned without straightening up and peered at her with hot flickering eyes, a red light from the furnace reflected in them. "What do you mean, your purse?"

"The gold cloth purse you took from the wooden bench in my room," she said. "I must have it back."

"Before God I never laid eyes on your purse, and that's the holy truth," said the janitress.

"Oh, well then, keep it," she said, but in a very bitter voice; "keep it if you want it so much." And she walked away.

She remembered how she had never locked a door in her life, on some principle of rejection in her that made her uncomfortable in the ownership of things, and her paradoxical boast before the warnings of her friends, that she had never lost a penny by theft; and she had been pleased with the bleak humility of this concrete example designed to illustrate and justify a certain fixed, otherwise baseless and general faith which ordered the movements of her life without regard to her will in the matter.

In this moment she felt that she had been robbed of an enormous number of valuable things, whether material or intangible: things lost or broken by her own fault, things she had forgotten and left in houses when she moved: books borrowed from her and not returned, journeys she had planned and had not made, words she had waited to hear spoken to her and had not heard, and the words she had meant to answer with; bitter alternatives and intolerable substitutes worse than nothing, and yet inescapable: the long patient suffering of dying friendships and the dark inexplicable death of love—all that she had had, and all that she had missed, were lost together, and were twice lost in this landslide of remembered losses.

The janitress was following her upstairs with the purse in her hand and the same deep red fire flickering in her eyes. The janitress thrust the purse towards her while they were still a half dozen steps apart, and said: "Don't never tell on me. I musta been crazy. I get crazy in the head sometimes, I swear I do. My son can tell you."

She took the purse after a moment, and the janitress went on: "I got a niece who is going on seventeen, and she's a nice girl and I thought I'd give it to her. She needs a pretty purse. I musta been crazy; I thought maybe you wouldn't mind, you leave things around and don't seem to notice much."

She said: "I missed this because it was a present to me from some-one..."

The janitress said: "He'd get you another if you lost this one. My niece is young and needs pretty things, we oughta give the young ones a chance. She's got young men after her maybe will want to marry her. She oughta have nice things. She needs them bad right now. You're a grown woman, you've had your chance, you ought to know how it is!"

She held the purse out to the janitress saying: "You don't know what you're talking about. Here, take it, I've changed my mind. I really don't want it."

The janitress looked up at her with hatred and said: "I don't want it either now. My niece is young and pretty, she don't need fixin' up to be pretty, she's young and pretty anyhow! I guess you need it worse than she does!"

"It wasn't really yours in the first place," she said, turning away. "You mustn't talk as if I had stolen it from you."

"It's not from me, it's from her you're stealing it," said the janitress, and went back downstairs.

She laid the purse on the table and sat down with the cup of chilled coffee, and thought: I was right not to be afraid of any thief but myself, who will end by leaving me nothing.

INTERPRETATION

This is the story of a woman who comes suddenly to a realization of something in her own character—the realization that she herself is the thief who will leave her nothing. With this in mind, review the episodes of the story, and try to see how they make a pattern leading up to a revelation. What does each add to the progression? Think, also, of the conversations overheard on the street while the main character is with Roger. What significance does this have? Now write an interpretation of the story.

■ SECTION IV

What Theme Reveals

■ IN discussing the stories we have read thus far we have continually referred to the theme, the idea, the meaning. This is natural and inevitable. We cannot very long consider the action or the characters of a story without coming to some concern with theme, for, as we have already insisted, a story, in so far as it is a good story, is an organic unity in which all the elements have vital interrelations. Each element implies the other elements, and implies them in movement toward a significant end.

Now as we turn to a more systematic treatment of theme in fiction, let us review some of our notions. For one thing, the theme of a piece of fiction is not to be thought of as merely the topic with which the story may be taken to concern itself—though the word is sometimes loosely used in this sense. For instance, we can say that two stories soon to be encountered, "The Killers," by Ernest Hemingway, and "I Want to Know Why," by Sherwood Anderson, have the same topic—the topic of growing up, the initiation into manhood. But in the two stories the meaning of the initiation is very different. Or to take another pair, when we come to "Love," by Maupassant, and "Love," by Jesse Stuart, even though the titles proclaim the same topic, and even though there is considerable similarity in treatment, we shall still find significant differences in meaning and differences indeed in the very "feel" of the stories. The theme is what is made of the topic. It is the comment on the topic that is implied in the process of the story.

The theme, furthermore, is not to be confused with any ideas or pieces of information, however interesting or important, which we may happen to take away from our reading of a piece of fiction. For instance, Herman Melville's novel *Moby Dick* gives a full and fascinating account of whaling, but that information is not to be confused with either the topic or the theme. The life of whaling is simply the world in which—the background against which—the human experience works itself out meaningfully. Though "The Man Who Would be King" tells us much about life in India in the late nineteenth century, that information is not to be confused with the theme.

The theme is what a piece of fiction stacks up to. It is the idea, the significance, the interpretation of persons and events, the pervasive and unifying view of life which is embodied in the total narrative. It is, as we have said in our general remarks on plot (pp. 54–55), what we are to make of the human experience rendered in the story. And what we make of such human experience always involves, directly or indirectly, some comment on values in human nature and human conduct, on good and bad, on the true and the false, some conception of what the human place is in the world.

This last remark may provoke two objections. Some may feel that it makes fiction merely a kind of moralizing, with illustrations. And some may feel that it gives no accommodation to stories that are gay, light-hearted, and comic. Both of these objections are well taken, and deserve discussion.

Let us take a somewhat indirect approach to the first objection. When we read a good piece of fiction, we may be caught by any of a number of things, in different degrees. We may simply find a character attractive, and relish that company much as one would relish the company of a person in real life, for humor, for kindliness, for wit, for wisdom, for any number of possible qualities. Or we may find our curiosity stimulated by the strange world of the story—the kind of curiosity evoked by travel books, or travel. Or we may be held by the suspense of the plot, our anxiety to know what will come next and who does what. We may, even, be caught by the writer's own personality, his charm of style and sprightliness of observation on life and character, or his poetic perceptions. Or we may enjoy daydreaming into experiences that we can never have in our own humdrum and conventional lives. We may, in fact, be caught by any number of things or combination of things.

But in the end there is always the question: What does it add up to? What does it mean? If we do not feel that things have worked themselves out to that moment of significant stability which we spoke on in connection with plot (p. 52–55), we are left feeling defrauded and dissatisfied.

One reason for such a feeling of dissatisfaction is our simple human craving to have things put in order. We like to observe a story working itself out to a unity. Just as we instinctively demand the logic of cause and effect, the logic of motivation, in fiction, so we demand that there be a logic of theme—a thematic structure into which the various elements are fitted and in terms of which they achieve unity. It is not, in other words, any moralizing aspect of theme that comes first to mind; it is the structural necessity. If there is no satisfactorily developed theme, all our other interests, no matter how intense they may be, tend to evaporate. If we want a story, we are forced by our very psychological make-up to demand a theme: *No theme, no story.*

That is one approach to the objection that our discussion of theme tends to make fiction seem like mere moralizing, with illustrations, like a Sunday School lesson with colored lantern slides. But there is another approach, related but dissimilar. It is best understood by examining the word *illustration* in the sentence above.

Fiction is not illustration, even though sometimes it pretends to be—as "The Man Who Would Be King" pretends to be an illustration of its motto: "Brother to a Prince and fellow to a beggar if he be found worthy." Fiction is not illustration, because with illustration we are always aware that the idea being illustrated comes first, that the content of the illustration is being dictated by the nature of the thing being illustrated. The illustration is an explanation, not a discovery. The illustration has no independent life. It tends to be *abstract.*

With fiction, in so far as it is successful, the imagination creates a world, characters and events which exist, as it were, in their own right. They live in our imagination. With great masterpieces, this reality is so compelling that it is often closer to us than things we know to be hard, cold facts. Hamlet, as a person, is more vivid to us than George Washington, Herbert Hoover, or the man next door. But even fiction that is merely good, not great, carries with it some degree of this illusion of independent existence.

How does this impression of an independent existence bear on our question of theme? In a manner as simple as this: In a successful piece of fiction, out of this sense of an independent world, as the characters act and are acted upon, as one event leads to another, we become more and more aware of the significance of the whole. That is, we gradually sense a developing theme. We *seem* * to be caught up in a vital process in which meaning emerges from experience—and that is what, in the end, makes our own lives, in so far as we live above the brute level, interesting to us: the sense of deepening discovery, the satisfaction of learning and achieving, the growth of awareness and appreciation, the fuller understanding of our own experience. Fiction, then, is never the "illustration" of an idea. It is a created image of our very life process by which significance emerges from experience.

Let us turn, at long last, to the second objection, the objection that our

* We must say *seem* because we are speaking of the finished story, not of the process of writing it, which may have involved a good deal of cold calculation.

emphasis on the serious place of theme in fiction leaves little play for stories that are gay or comic. A full discussion of this objection would take us into a study of the nature of comedy, but it should be enough here to say that we are aware of the gay only by an implied contrast, however remote, with the serious, that the laughter of comedy always has in it some element of escape from the urgency—even the pain—of life, and that even burlesque and slapstick depend on some acceptance of the thing that is being abused and made sport of.

If we look back at the comic stories we have read thus far—say, "De Mortuis" or "The Drunkard"—we shall readily see that always a slight shift of emphasis would plunge us into a world of an entirely different order from that of the present story. Comedy, including even warm humor as well as savage satire, has to do with disappointment and surprises, confusions and miscarriages, the criticism and defeat of aspirations, contrasts of pretensions and reality, failure of expectations, inability to adjust to the changing demands of life. The man with his head in the clouds and a top hat on his head stepping on the banana peel is the image behind all comedy— but the fall that rebukes his vanity may sometimes also break his neck. The distance between the good laugh and the need to call the ambulance is not very great.

The fact of comedy itself, generally considered, implies a view of life—the notion that an awareness of the rough edges of things may lead to laughter, not tears, that the shrewd observation of human frailty may end in tolerance and enjoyment, not anger and disappointment. The comic story starts with a certain bias of interpretation, but that bias does not deny either the structural importance of theme or its importance as a comment on human values. In its own way, the comic story affirms them.

At this point another question may be asked. Since theme is a comment on human values, how can we appreciate a story that has a theme which we cannot accept? There is no use in trying to evade this question by taking refuge in nice generalities, and no use in minimizing its importance or the difficulty of giving an honest and useful answer.

It may be that a roundabout approach gives us the quickest path to an answer. Let us forget fiction altogether, and think of our relations with other people. We live with a variety of people, and with most of them we have, at some point or other, serious differences of opinion, tastes, and values. With Susie Jones we disagree violently on literary matters, and every time we go to a movie with her we have an argument. With John Jacobs we disagree on politics; with Alfred Kobeck, on how to play a hand of bridge; with Jim Simmons, on religion. And we take a very dim view of Mary Moffett's intelligence. But—and here is the point—we may be good friends with all of them. We may recognize in any one of them some particular qualities which we value and enjoy despite disagreements. More importantly, we may recognize an underlying good will, and an honest attempt to make sense of things and to achieve decency. In recognizing these things, we may discover in ourselves some tolerance and some power of sympathetic imagination that enables us to feel ourselves into another person's skin and to understand how the world looks to him. In this process of recognition through imaginative sympathy, we realize that the world is complicated, and that it is the richer for its very complication. We realize too that opinions, tastes, and values which are opposed to each other may each have a place, that there may be more than one answer to a question, and that our own private convictions and dogmatic beliefs may have to be modified.

This is not to be taken as saying that one thing is as good as another. We each have to work out our own scale of values and try to justify it and live by it. But it does mean that when we encounter differences, we must try to understand their nature and then try to find the underlying common ground that makes human respect possible.

But how does this apply to fiction? In this way: We can think of the authors of stories as we think of our friends and associates. We can try to recognize the values that they offer us even when we disagree with them. We can make the effort of imagination necessary to realize the variety and richness of experience which they offer, and in so doing modify our own dogmatisms. We can try to recognize the logic by which a theme unfolds even in a story that at first glance seems antipathetic to us.

What, then, of the common ground? The common ground is the understanding of the fact that, in so far as a theme is coherently developed through a story, we are witnessing and taking part in the great human effort to achieve meaning through experience. And a story, as we have said, gives us an image of our life process—and in that, an enlightening image of ourselves.

We must here be prepared to make a concession. We must simply recognize that some writers, and some stories, offend us at too deep a level. They embody some attitude toward life, some set of values, which denies our own very basis of life. Sometimes we simply may not be able to find the common ground. In a situation like that we are bound to acknowledge the fact and deal with it. We reject the story, just as we would reject a person in real life. But always we should be very careful that we have made the imaginative effort to understand what values may be there, and what common ground might, with more effort, be found.

Furthermore, in the end, we may find that we have rejected the story not because of its theme as such, but because we have found the story unconvincing. The story failed in its logic of motivation, or in its presentation of character, or in the attempt to make the theme develop from the action. Or perhaps we have found the story guilty of sentimentality; that is, the emotional response demanded by the story is not really justified by the events in the story. In other words, we have rejected the story, not because of the theme, taken as a thing in itself, but because the story is incoherent as a story.

This leads us back to the organic nature of fiction. On this basis we distinguish truth of correspondence and truth of coherence (p. 153). If we reject a story because the theme offends us, we are appealing to the truth of correspondence: the theme does not correspond to what we take to be the truth about life and human values. If we reject a story because it is, as we ordinarily say, unconvincing, we are appealing to the truth of coherence: the story does not hang together in its own terms, and therefore whatever meaning it may claim to possess does not really come out of the experience of the story. Most of our problems with stories have to do with offences against the truth of coherence—against the organic structure.

The mention of coherence leads us to the notion that the meaning of a good story is general and pervasive. If a story possesses an organic unity, then all the parts are significant and have some bearing on the total significance. All contribute to the total meaning. We live, of course, in an imperfect world, and no doubt few stories are free of defects. Even many of the best stories reveal some undigested material. Nevertheless, the principle of organic unity is to be stressed in our reading. We ought to assume that a story is coherent until it is proved otherwise. Assuming this coherence, we then try to find what idea, what feeling, what attitude, is consistently developing throughout the story.

We can look at what kind of characters and what kind of world is presented. That is a starting point, for it tells us something of the interest of the writer and his range of experience. We can ask what problems the characters confront, what is at stake for them—or, if the story is one of developing awareness, what discovery is being made. We can look at the pattern of plot and try to see what significant repetitions appear. We can look at the end and ask, first, if it logically follows from the body of the story; and second, what is the intended significance. We can ask what is the tone of the story? Is it comic, ironical, cold and reportorial, pathetic, or what? We can ask if the author has tried to evoke emotional responses for which there is no justification. We can ask about the speech of the characters and the style of the author—are they in keeping with the rest of the story? All in all, we ask how fully and deeply coherent is the story. As we try to answer these questions, we usually find that we have defined the theme, and have accepted or rejected it.

Our examination of the stories to follow is not to be taken as an exercise in moral-hunting. It is not even to be taken, primarily, as an exercise in giving a general statement to the various themes of the stories—though, of course, the attempt to make such general statements is a necessary part of our study. More important than framing general statements are these two considerations:

First, to see how the theme of a story, if it is a good story, *necessarily* develops from the experience as rendered in the story. To do this means that we must inspect the coherence of the story.

Second, to see how the theme is *uniquely* developed, and to do this means that we must try to see how a theme—even though we suppose we may be able to state it in general terms—is, in fact, qualified and modified by the actual treatment in the story, so that what the story "says" finally becomes something more or less unique.

The stories to follow in this section employ various methods in the presentation of their themes. There may be general statement. There may be allegory and symbolism and parable. There may be a realistic dramatic situation. But always we must remember that the total story, including the general atmosphere, is the embodiment of the theme. As we have said in discussing plot (pp. 55–56), we must think of the whole story as an image, however shadowy, of the meaning of experience.

HONORÉ DE BALZAC

Christ in Flanders

AT a time somewhat indeterminate in Brabantine history, connection between the island of Cadzant and the coast of Flanders was kept up by a boat used for passengers to and fro. The capital of the island, Middleburg, afterward so celebrated in the annals of Protestantism, counted then hardly two or three hundred hearths. Rich Ostend was then an unknown harbor, flanked by a village thinly peopled by a few fisherfolk, and poor dealers, and pirates who plied their trade with impunity. Nevertheless, the borough of Ostend, composed of about twenty houses and three hundred cottages, cabins, and hovels—made with the remains of wrecked ships—rejoiced in a governor, a militia, a gallows, a convent, and a burgomaster, in fact, all the institutions of advanced civilization. Who was reigning at that time in Brabant, Belgium, and Flanders? On this point tradition is mute.

Let us admit that this story is strangely imbued with that vagueness, indefiniteness, and love of the marvelous which the favorite orators of Flemish vigils love to intermingle in their legends, as varied in poetry as they are contradictory in detail. Told from age to age, repeated from hearth to hearth, by grandmothers and by storytellers night and day, this chronicle has received each century a different coloring. Like those buildings planned according to the architectural caprice of each epoch, whose dark, crumbling masses are a pleasure to poets alone, this legend would drive commentators, and wranglers over facts, words, and dates, to desperation. The narrator believes in it, as all superstitious souls in Flanders have believed in it, without being for that reason either more learned or more weak-minded. Admitting the impossibility of harmonizing all the different versions, here is the story, stripped perhaps of its romantic naïveté—for this it is impossible to reproduce—but still, with its daring statements disproved by history, and its morality approved by religion, its fantastic flowers of imagination, and hidden sense which the wise can interpret each to his own liking. Let each one seek his pasture herein and take the trouble to separate the good grain from the tares.

The boat which served to carry over the passengers from the island of Cadzant to Ostend was just about to leave the village. Before undoing the iron chain which held his boat to a stone on the little jetty where people embarked, the skipper blew his horn several times to call the loiterers, for this journey was his last. Night was coming on, the last fires of the setting sun scarcely gave enough light to distinguish the coast of Flanders or the tardy passengers on the island wandering along the earthen walls which surrounded the fields or among the tall reeds of the marshes. The boat was full. "What are you waiting for? Let us be off!" they cried. Just then a man appeared a few steps from the jetty. The pilot, who had neither heard nor seen him approaching, was somewhat surprised. The passenger seemed to have risen from the earth on a sudden. He might have been a peasant sleeping in a field, waiting for the hour for starting, whom the horn had wakened up. Was it a thief, or was it someone from the Customs House or police? When he arrived on the jetty to which the boat was moored, seven persons who were standing in the stern hastened to sit down on the benches, in order to have them to themselves and prevent the stranger from seating himself among them. It was a sudden instinctive feeling, one of those aristocratic instincts which suggest themselves to rich people. Four of these personages belonged to the highest nobility of Flanders.

First of all, there was a young cavalier, with two beautiful greyhounds, wearing over his long hair a cap decked with jewels. He clinked his gilded spurs, and now and again curled his mustache, as he cast disdainful looks at the rest of the freight.

Then there was a proud damosel, who carried a falcon on her wrist and spoke only to her mother or to an ecclesiastic of high rank, a relative, no doubt. These persons made as much noise talking together as if they were the only people on the boat. All the same, next to them sat a man of great importance in the country, a fat merchant from Bruges, enveloped in a large mantle. His servant, armed to the teeth, kept by his side two bags full of money. Beside them was a man of science, a doctor of the University of Louvain, with his clerk. These people, who all despised one another, were separated from the bows by the rower's bench.

When the late passenger put his foot into the boat he gave a swift look at the stern, but when he saw no room there he went to seek a place among the people in the bows. It was the poor who sat there. At the sight of a man bareheaded, whose brown cloth coat and fine linen shirt had no ornament, who held in his hand neither hat nor cap, with neither purse nor rapier at his girdle, all took him for a burgomaster—a good and gentle man, like one of those old Flemings whose nature and simple character have been so well rendered by the painters of their country. The poor passengers welcomed the stranger with a respectful demeanor, which excited mocking whispers among the people in the stern. An old soldier, a man of toil and trouble, gave him his place on the bench, and sat himself at the end of the boat, keeping himself steady by putting his feet against one of the transverse beams which knit the planks together like the backbone of a fish.

A young woman, a mother with her little child, who seemed to belong to the working class of Ostend, moved back to make room for the newcomer. In this movement there was no trace either of servility or disdain. It was merely a mark of that kindliness by which the poor, who know so well how to appreciate a service, show their frank and natural disposition—so simple and obvious in the expression of all their qualities, good or bad.

The stranger thanked them with a gesture full of nobility, and sat down between the young mother and the old soldier. Behind him was a peasant with his son, ten years old. A poor old woman, with a wallet almost empty, old and wrinkled, and in rags—a type of misery and neglect—lay in the prow, crouched upon a coil of ropes. One of the rowers, an old sailor, who had known her when she was rich and beautiful, had let her get in for what the people so beautifully call "the love of God." "Thank you kindly, Thomas," the old woman had said; "I will say two *Paters* and two *Aves* for you in my prayers this evening."

The skipper blew his horn once more, looked at the silent country, cast the chain into his boat, ran along the side to the helm, took the tiller, and stood erect; then, having looked at the sky, called out in a loud voice to the rowers, when they were well in the open sea, "Row hard, make haste; the sea smiles evilly—the witch! I feel the swell at the helm and the storm at my wound." These words, spoken in the language of the sea—a tongue only understood of those accustomed to the sound of the waves—gave to the oars a hastened but ever-cadenced movement, as different from the former manner of rowing as the gallop of a horse from its trot. The fine people sitting at the stern took pleasure in seeing the sinuous arms, the bronzed faces with eyes of fire, the distended muscles, and the different human forms working in unison, just to get *them* the quicker over this narrow strait. So far from being sorry for their labor, they pointed out the rowers to each other, and laughed at the grotesque expressions which their exertion printed on their anxious faces. In the prow the soldier, the peasant, and the old woman regarded the mariners with that kind of compassion natural to people who, living by toil, know its hard anguish and feverish fatigue. Besides, being accustomed to life in the open air, they all divined by the look of the sky the danger which threatened them; so *they* were serious. The young mother was rocking her child to sleep, singing to it some old hymn of the church.

"If we *do* get over," said the old soldier to the peasant, "God will have taken a deal of trouble to keep us alive."

"Ah! He is master," said the old woman; "but I think it is His good pleasure to call us to Himself. Do you see that light, there?" and by a gesture of the head she pointed out the setting sun. Bands of fire streaked vividly the brown-red tinted clouds, which seemed just about to unchain a furious wind. The sea gave forth a suppressed murmur, a sort of internal groan, something like the growling of a dog whose anger will not be appeased.

After all Ostend was not far off. Just now the sky and the sea showed one of those sights to which it is impossible for words or painting to give longer duration than they have in reality. Human creations like powerful contrasts, so artists generally demand from nature its most brilliant aspects, despairing perhaps to be able to render the great and beautiful poetry of her ordinary appearance, although the human soul is often as profoundly moved by calm as by motion, by the silence as much as by the storm.

There was one moment when everyone on the boat was silent and gazed on the sea and sky, whether from presentiment or in obedience to that religious melancholy which comes over nearly all of us at the hour of prayer, at the fall of day, at the moment when nature is silent and the bells speak. The sea cast up a faint, white glimmer, but changing like the color of steel; the sky was mostly gray; in the west, long, narrow spaces looked like waves of blood, whereas in the east, glittering lines, marked as by a fine pencil, were separated from one another by clouds, folded like the wrinkles on an old man's forehead. Thus the sea and the sky formed a neutral background, everything in half tints, which made the fires of the setting sun glare ominously. The face of nature inspired a feeling of terror. If it is allowable to interweave the daring hyperboles of the people into the written language, one might repeat what the soldier said, "Time is rolling away," or what the peasant answered, that the sky had the look of a hangman. All of a sudden the wind rose in the west, and the skipper, who never ceased to watch the sea, seeing it swell toward the horizon, cried, "Ho, ho!"

At this cry the sailors stopped immediately, and let their oars float.

"The skipper is right," said Thomas. The boat, borne on the top of a huge wave, seemed to be descending to the bottom of the gaping sea. At this extraordinary movement and this sudden rage of the ocean the people in the stern turned pale, and gave a terrible cry, "We perish!"

"Not yet," answered the skipper quietly. At this moment the clouds were rent in twain by the force of the wind exactly above the boat. The gray masses spread out with ominous quickness from east to west, and the twilight, falling straight down through a rent made by the storm wind, rendered visible every face. The passengers, the rich and the noble, the sailors and the poor, all stopped one moment in astonishment at the aspect of the last comer. His golden hair, parted in the middle on his tranquil, serene forehead, fell in many curls on his shoulders, and outlined against the gray sky a face sublime in its gentleness, radiant with divine love. He did not despise death; he was certain not to perish. But if at first the people at the stern had forgotten for an instant the tempest whose implacable fury menaced them, they soon returned to their selfish sentiments and life-long habits.

"It's lucky for him, that dolt of a burgomaster, that he does not know the danger we are all in. There he stands like a dog, and doesn't seem to mind dying," said the doctor.

Hardly had he completed this judicious remark when the tempest unchained its legions; wind blew from every side, the boat spun round like a top, and the sea swamped it.

"Oh, my poor child! my child! who will save my child?" cried the mother, in a heartrending voice.

"You yourself," replied the stranger. The sound of this voice penetrated the heart of the young woman and put hope therein. She heard this sweet word, in spite of the raging of the storm, in spite of the shrieks of the passengers.

"Holy Virgin of Perpetual Succor, who are at Antwerp, I promise you twenty pounds of wax and a statue if you will only get me out of this," cried the merchant, falling on his knees upon his bags of gold.

"The Virgin is no more at Antwerp than she is here," replied the doctor.

"She is in heaven," said a voice, which seemed to come forth from the sea.

"Who spoke?"

"The devil," said the servant; "he's mocking the Virgin of Antwerp."

"Shut up with your blessed Virgin," said the skipper to the passengers; "take hold of the bowls and help me get the water out of the boat. As to you," he continued, addressing the sailors, "row hard, we have a moment's grace, and in the devil's name, who has left you in this world until now, let us be our own Providence. This little strip of water is horribly dangerous, I know from thirty years' experience. Is this evening the first time I have had a storm to deal with?" Then standing at the helm, the skipper continued to look alternately at the boat, the sea, and the sky.

"The skipper mocks at everything," said Thomas in a low voice.

"Will God let *us* die with these wretched people?" asked the proud damosel of the handsome cavalier.

"No! no! Noble damsel, listen to me." He put his arm round her waist, and spoke in her ear. "I can swim—don't say anything about it; I will take you by your beautiful hair and bring you safely to the shore; but I can save you only."

The damosel looked at her old mother; the dame was on her knees asking absolution from the bishop, who was not listening to her. The cavalier read in the eyes of his beautiful mistress some faint sentiment of filial piety, so he said to her in a low voice, "Submit yourself to the will of God; if He wishes to call your mother to Himself, it will doubtless be for her happiness—in the other world," he added, in a voice still lower, "and for ours in this."

The dame Rupelmonde possessed seven fiefs, besides the barony of Gâvres. The damosel listened to the voice of life, to the interests of love, speaking through the mouth of the handsome adventurer, a young miscreant, who haunted churches, seeking for prey—either a girl to marry or else good ready money.

The bishop blessed the waves and ordered them to be calm, not knowing exactly what to do; he was thinking of his concubine awaiting him with a delicate feast, perhaps at this moment in her bath perfuming herself, or arraying herself in velvet, and fastening on her necklaces and jewels. So far from thinking of the powers of the Church, and consoling these Christians, and exhorting them to trust in God, the perverse bishop mingled worldly regrets and words of lust with the sacred words of the Breviary.

The light, which lit up the pale faces, showed all their varying expressions, when the boat was borne up into the air by a wave, or cast down to the bottom of the abyss; then, shaken like a frail leaf, a plaything of the autumn wind, it cracked its shell, and seemed nigh to break altogether. Then there were horrible cries alternating with awful silence.

The demeanor of the people seated in the prow of the boat contrasted singularly with that of the rich and powerful in the stern. The young mother strained her child to her bosom every time that the waves threatened to engulf the frail bark; but she held to the hope with which the words of the stranger had filled her heart: each time she turned her eyes toward this man she drank in from his face a new faith, the strong faith of a weak woman, the faith of a mother. Living by the divine word, the word of love, which had gone forth from this man, the simple creature awaited trustfully the fulfillment of the sort of promise he had given her, and scarcely feared the tempest any more. Sticking to the side of the boat, the soldier ceased not to contemplate this singular being, on whose impassibility he sought to model his own rough, tanned face, bringing into play all his intelligence and strength of will, whose powerful springs had not been vitiated in the course of a passive mechanical life. He was emulous to show himself tranquil and calm, after the manner of this superior courage; he ended by identifying himself in some measure with the secret principle of its interior power. Then his imagination became an instinctive fanaticism, a love without limit, a faith in this man, like that enthusiasm which soldiers have for their commander when he is a man of power, surrounded with the glory of victories, marching in the midst of the splendid prestige of genius. The poor old woman said in a low voice, "Ah! what a miserable sinner I am! Have I not suffered enough to expiate the pleasures of my youth? Miserable one, why hast thou led the gay life of a Frenchwoman? Why hast thou consumed the goods of God with the people of the Church, the goods of the poor 'twixt the drink shop and the pawn shop? Ah! how wicked I was! Oh! my God! my God! let me finish my hell in this world of misery. Holy Virgin, Mother of God, take pity on me."

"Console yourself, mother, God is not a Lombard; although I have killed here and there good people and wicked, I do not fear for the resurrection."

"Ah! Sir, how happy they are, those beautiful ladies who are near the bishop, holy man!" the old woman went on; "they will have absolution from their sins. Oh! if I could only hear the voice of a priest saying to me, 'Your sins are forgiven you,' I could believe him."

The stranger turned toward her, and his look, full of charity, made her tremble. "Have faith," he said, "and you will be saved."

"May God reward you, good sir," she answered. "If you speak truly, I will go for you and for me on a pilgrimage to Our Lady of Loretto, barefooted."

The two peasants, father and son, remained silent, resigned, and submitting to the will of God, as people accustomed to follow instinctively, like animals, the convulsions of nature.

So on one side there were riches, pride, knowledge, debauchery, crime, all human society such as it is made by arts, thought, and education, the world and its laws; but also on this side, only shrieks, terror, the struggles of a thousand conflicting feelings, with horrible doubt—naught but the anguish of fear. And, towering above these, one powerful man, the skipper of the boat, doubting nothing, the chief, the fatalist king, making his own Providence, crying out for bailing bowls and not on the Virgin to save him, defying the storm, and wrestling with the sea, body to body.

At the other end of the boat, the weak: The mother, holding to her bosom a little child, who smiled at the storm. A wanton once gay, now given over to horrible remorse. A soldier, scarred with wounds, without other reward than his mutilated life, as a price for indefatigable devotion— he had hardly a morsel of bread, steeped in tears; all the same, he laughed at everything, and marched on without care, happy when he could drown his glory at the bottom of a pot of beer, or was telling stories thereof to wondering children; he commended gaily to God the care of his future. Lastly, two peasants, people of toil and weariness, labor incarnate, the work on which the world lives; these simple creatures were guileless of thought and its treasures, but ready to lose themselves utterly in a belief; having a more robust faith, in that they had never discussed or analyzed it; virgin natures, in whom conscience had remained pure and feeling strong. Contrition, misery, love, work had exercised, purified, concentrated, disculpated their will, the only thing which in man resembles that which sages call the soul.

When the boat, piloted by the marvelous dexterity of the skipper, came almost in view of Ostend, fifty paces from the shore, it was driven back by the convulsion of the storm, and suddenly began to sink. The stranger with the light upon his face then said to this little world of sorrow, "Those who have faith shall be saved; let them follow me." This man stood up and walked with a firm step on the waves. At once the young mother took her child in her arms and walked with him on the sea. The soldier suddenly stood at attention, saying in his rough language, "By my pipe! I follow you to the devil." Then, without seeming astonished, he marched on the sea.

The old prostitute, believing in the omnipotence of God, followed the man, and walked on the sea. The two peasants said, "As they are walking on the sea, why should not *we?*" So they got up and hastened after the others, walking on the sea.

Thomas wished to do likewise; but his faith wavered, and he fell several times into the sea, but got out again; and after three failures he too walked upon the sea.

The daring pilot stuck like a leech to the bottom of his boat. The merchant had faith, and had risen, but he wanted to take his gold with him, and his gold took him to the bottom of the sea. Mocking at the charlatan and the imbeciles who listened to him, at the moment when he saw the stranger proposing to the passengers to walk on the sea, the man of science began to laugh, and was swallowed up in the ocean. The damosel was drawn down into the abyss by her lover. The bishop and the old lady went to the bottom, heavy with sin perhaps, heavier still with unbelief and confidence in false images; heavy with devotional practices, light of alms and true religion.

The faithful troop, who trod with firm, dry feet on the plain of the raging waters, heard around them the horrible howling of the storm; great sheets of water broke in their path; irresistible force rent the ocean in twain. Through the mist these faithful ones perceived on the shore a little feeble light, which flickered in the window of a fisherman's cabin. Each one as he marched bravely toward this light seemed to hear his neighbor crying through the roaring sea, "Courage!" Nevertheless, absorbed each in his own danger, no one said a single word. And so they reached the shore. When they were all seated at the hearth of the fisherman, they sought in vain the guide who had a light upon his face. From his seat upon the summit of a rock, at the base of which the hurricane had cast the pilot clinging to his plank with all the strength of a sailor in the throes of death, the MAN descended, picked up the shipwrecked man almost dashed to pieces; then he said, as he held out a helping hand over his head, "It is well this once, but do as thou *hast* done no more; the example would be too bad." He took the mariner on his shoulders, and carried him to the fisherman's cottage. He knocked for the unfortunate man, so that someone would open the door of this humble refuge to him; then the Savior disappeared.

In this place the sailors built the Convent of Mercy, where were long to be seen the prints that the feet of JESUS CHRIST had, it was said, left on the sand.

Afterward, when the French entered Belgium, some monks took away with them this precious relic, the testimony of the last visit JESUS ever paid to the earth.

INTERPRETATION

In previous sections, we have already read stories which illustrate a variety of ways in which fiction may embody its idea, or theme. The present story shows one of the simplest of all methods. It is a method similar to that found in fables and parables. In a parable, for instance, the idea, or truth, is presented by a simple narrative in which the events, persons, and the like, of the narrative are understood as being directly equivalent to elements involved in the statement of the truth. At this point it might be well to turn back to p. 47 and reread the parable of the sower which we quoted there from St. Mark's Gospel. The events in such a parable are, as we saw, summarized as economically as possible. Actually the parable is a kind of metaphor or image, of a basic truth which in reality may assume many forms. For example, the "affliction or persecution" which "ariseth for the word's sake" might assume many forms, and the reaction of the person whose heart, like the stony ground, could give no deep root to the seed, might take many different forms. Ordinarily, fiction is concerned with these specific, individual forms—character, event, experience—and does not content itself with presenting merely the basic image as detached from the details of the particular instance. The story of a man whose heart was like stony ground and whose faith withered under the scorching sun of persecution would be presented as the story of a particular man, living in a particular place and time. The psychological stages in the struggle between faith and persecution would be indicated.

But despite the fact that ordinary fiction, as contrasted with parable or fable, is intensely concerned with specific persons and the circumstantiality of experience, all fiction implies a meaningfulness beyond the particular instances which it presents. The meanings involved in characters and events can be extended to apply to other characters and events. The problems and issues and decisions involved in a particular piece of fiction are not limited to that situation and those persons. For example, in "War," by Pirandell, the conflict between the attitude of the fat woman and that of the old man does not appear, in life, merely in the case of persons whose sons are in an army. It appears in all cases of grief and bereavement. And the pathetic isolation of the cabdriver in "The Lament" can be observed in all sorts and conditions of people.

But the way in which fiction embodies its meaning will vary from story to story. Some stories, like "The Lottery," will approach the method of the parable, in that only the aspect of the characters and events which is directly involved in the meaning will be presented; there will not be, in such cases, much circumstantiality, for the character, or event, tends to "stand for something," for an idea, rather than to be fully developed as an individual person or as a particular event with its own complications. Such a story tends to be *allegorical* (see Glossary). Usually, such stories are relatively simple, because the complexities of individual character and particular event are purged away; once one has grasped the key idea everything falls into its pattern. But in some stories of this general type, there is great complication and obscurity because the idea behind the allegory is a complicated one and because the "key" is difficult to come by.

In "Christ in Flanders," however, we have a story which approaches the method of the parable. The persons are presented only in so far as some one aspect of character is involved in the meaning. For instance, the merchant is fat and has two large money bags guarded by an armed servant. The man of science laughs at the stranger's preposterous suggestion that the passengers walk on the sea. The pretty damosel, with the falcon on her wrist, hearkens to the whispered temptation of the cavalier. The old soldier is a little more fully presented, but even in his case we know merely the central fact, the "key" trait, of the character. We are given, in each case, just the aspect of character which means salvation or damnation in the shipwreck, the crucial trait. Thus, the representation of character is simplified to a point where we have little more than a series of equivalents, almost as strict as in allegory: the man of science is pride of intellect; the soldier, fidelity and courage; the damosel and cavalier, pleasure; the merchant, avarice; and so on. Finally, the boatload of people seems to be an image of the world, the high and the low, all confronted by the fact of death.

1. What is the significance of the first two paragraphs of the story? What does the author gain, if anything, by not plunging immediately into the narrative with the third paragraph?

2. What is the basic theme of the story? What are the subsidiary themes associated with this basic theme?

3. Why does Jesus save the skipper, who had not obeyed His command?

GUY DE MAUPASSANT

Love: Three Pages from a Sportsman's Book

I HAVE just read among the general news in one of the papers a drama of passion. He killed her and then he killed himself, so he must have loved her. What matters He or She? Their love alone matters to me, and it does not interest me because it moves me or astonishes me or because it softens me or makes me think, but because it recalls to my mind a remembrance of my youth, a strange recollection of a hunting adventure where Love appeared to me, as the Cross appeared to the early Christians, in the midst of the heavens.

I was born with all the instincts and the senses of primitive man, tempered by the arguments and the restraints of a civilized being. I am passionately fond of shooting, yet the sight of the wounded animal, of the blood on its feathers and on my hands, affects my heart so as almost to make it stop.

That year the cold weather set in suddenly toward the end of autumn, and I was invited by one of my cousins, Karl de Rauville, to go with him and shoot ducks on the marshes at daybreak.

My cousin was a jolly fellow of forty with red hair, very stout and bearded, a country gentleman, an amiable semibrute of a happy disposition and endowed with that Gallic wit which makes even mediocrity agreeable. He lived in a house, half farmhouse, half chateau, situated in a broad valley through which a river ran. The hills right and left were covered with woods, old manorial woods where magnificent trees still remained and where the rarest feathered game in that part of France was to be found. Eagles were shot there occasionally, and birds of passage, such as rarely venture into our overpopulated part of the country, invariably lighted amid these giant oaks as if they knew or recognized some little corner of a primeval forest which had remained there to serve them as a shelter during these short nocturnal halts.

In the valley there were large meadows watered by trenches and separated by hedges; then, further on, the river, which up to that point had been kept between banks, expanded into a vast marsh. That marsh was the best shooting ground I ever saw. It was my cousin's chief care, and he kept it as a preserve. Through the rushes that covered it, and made it rustling and rough, narrow passages had been cut, through which the flat-bottomed boats, impelled and steered by poles, passed along silently over dead water, brushing up against the reeds and making the swift fish take refuge in the weeds and the wild fowl, with their pointed black heads, dive suddenly.

I am passionately fond of the water: of the sea, though it is too vast, too full of movement, impossible to hold; of the rivers which are so beautiful but which pass on and flee away; and above all of the marshes, where the whole unknown existence of aquatic animals palpitates. The marsh is an entire world in itself on the world of earth—a different world which has its own life, its settled inhabitants and its passing travelers, its voices, its noises and above all its mystery. Nothing is more impressive, nothing more disquieting, more terrifying occasionally, than a fen. Why should a vague terror hang over these low plains covered with water? Is it the low rustling of the rushes, the strange will-o'-the-wisp lights, the silence which prevails on calm nights, the still mists which hang over the surface like a shroud; or is it the almost inaudible splashing, so slight and so gentle, yet sometimes more terrifying than the cannons of men or the thunders of the skies, which make these marshes resemble countries one has dreamed of, terrible countries holding an unknown and dangerous secret?

No, something else belongs to it—another mystery, perhaps the mystery of the creation itself! For was it not in stagnant and muddy water, amid the heavy humidity of moist land under the heat of the sun, that the first germ of life pulsated and expanded to the day?

I arrived at my cousin's in the evening. It was freezing hard enough to split the stones.

During dinner, in the large room whose sideboards, walls and ceiling were covered with stuffed birds with wings extended or perched on branches to which they were nailed—hawks, herons, owls, nightjars, buzzards, tercels, vultures, falcons—my cousin, who, dressed in a sealskin jacket, himself resembled some strange animal from a cold country, told me what preparations he had made for that same night.

We were to start at half-past three in the morning so as to arrive at the place which he had chosen for our watching place at about half-past four. On that spot a hut had been built of lumps of ice so as to shelter us somewhat from the trying wind which precedes daybreak, a wind so cold as to tear the flesh like a saw, cut it like the blade of a knife, prick it like a poisoned sting, twist it like a pair of pincers, and burn it like fire.

My cousin rubbed his hands. "I have never known such a frost," he said; "it is already twelve degrees below zero at six o'clock in the evening."

I threw myself onto my bed immediately after we had finished our meal and went to sleep by the light of a bright fire burning in the grate.

At three o'clock he woke me. In my turn I put on a sheepskin and found my cousin Karl covered with a bearskin. After having each swallowed two cups of scalding coffee, followed by glasses of liqueur brandy, we started, accompanied by a gamekeeper and our dogs, Plongeon and Pierrot.

From the first moment that I got outside I felt chilled to the very marrow. It was one of those nights on which the earth seems dead with cold. The frozen air becomes resisting and palpable, such pain does it cause; no breath of wind moves it, it is fixed and motionless; it bites you, pierces through you, dries you, kills the trees, the plants, the insects, the small birds themselves, who fall from the branches onto the hard ground and become stiff themselves under the grip of the cold.

The moon, which was in her last quarter and was inclining all to one side, seemed fainting in the midst of space, so weak that she was unable to wane, forced to stay up yonder, seized and paralyzed by the severity of the weather. She shed a cold mournful light over the world, that dying and wan light which she gives us every month at the end of her period.

Karl and I walked side by side, our backs bent, our hands in our pockets and our guns under our arms. Our boots, which were wrapped in wool so that we might be able to walk without slipping on the frozen river, made no sound, and I looked at the white vapor which our dogs' breath made.

We were soon on the edge of the marsh and entered one of the lanes of dry rushes which ran through the low forest.

Our elbows, which touched the long ribbonlike leaves, left a slight noise behind us, and I was seized, as I had never been before, by the powerful and singular emotion which marshes cause in me. This one was dead,

dead from cold, since we were walking on it in the middle of its population of dried rushes.

Suddenly, at the turn of one of the lanes, I perceived the ice hut which had been constructed to shelter us. I went in, and as we had nearly an hour to wait before the wandering birds would awake I rolled myself up in my rug in order to try and get warm. Then, lying on my back, I began to look at the misshapen moon, which had four horns through the vaguely transparent walls of this polar house. But the frost of the frozen marshes, the cold of these walls, the cold from the firmament penetrated me so terribly that I began to cough. My cousin Karl became uneasy.

"No matter if we do not kill much today," he said. "I do not want you to catch cold; we will light a fire." And he told the gamekeeper to cut some rushes.

We made a pile in the middle of our hut, which had a hole in the middle of the roof to let out the smoke, and when the red flames rose up to the clear crystal blocks, they began to melt, gently, imperceptibly, as if they were sweating. Karl, who had remained outside, called out to me: "Come and look here!" I went out of the hut and remained struck with astonishment. Our hut, in the shape of a cone, looked like an enormous diamond with a heart of fire which had been suddenly planted there in the midst of the frozen water of the marsh. And inside we saw two fantastic forms, those of our dogs, who were warming themselves at the fire.

But a peculiar cry, a lost, a wandering cry, passed over our heads, and the light from our hearth showed us the wild birds. Nothing moves one so much as the first clamor of a life which one does not see, which passes through the somber air so quickly and so far off, just before the first streak of a winter's day appears on the horizon. It seems to me, at this glacial hour of dawn, as if that passing cry which is carried away by the wings of a bird is the sigh of a soul from the world!

"Put out the fire," said Karl; "it is getting daylight."

The sky was, in fact, beginning to grow pale, and the flights of ducks made long rapid streaks which were soon obliterated on the sky.

A stream of light burst out into the night; Karl had fired, and the two dogs ran forward.

And then nearly every minute now he, now I, aimed rapidly as soon as the shadow of a flying flock appeared above the rushes. And Pierrot and Plongeon, out of breath but happy, retrieved the bleeding birds whose eyes still, occasionally, looked at us.

The sun had risen, and it was a bright day with a blue sky, and we were thinking of taking our departure, when two birds with extended necks and outstretched wings glided rapidly over our heads. I fired, and one of them fell almost at my feet. It was a teal with a silver breast, and then, in the blue space above me, I heard a voice, the voice of a bird. It was a short, repeated heart-rending lament; and the bird, the little animal that had been spared, began to turn round in the blue sky over our heads, looking at its dead companion which I was holding in my hand.

Karl was on his knees, his gun to his shoulder, watching it eagerly until it should be within shot. "You have killed the duck," he said, "and the drake will not fly away."

He certainly did not fly away; he circled over our heads continually and continued his cries. Never have any groans of suffering pained me so much as that desolate appeal, as that lamentable reproach of this poor bird which was lost in space.

Occasionally he took flight under the menace of the gun which followed his movements and seemed ready to continue his flight alone, but as he could not make up his mind to this he returned to find his mate.

"Leave her on the ground," Karl said to me; "he will come within shot by and by." And he did indeed come near us, careless of danger, infatuated by his animal love, by his affection for his mate which I had just killed.

Karl fired, and it was as if somebody had cut the string which held the bird suspended. I saw something black descend, and I heard the noise of a fall among the rushes. And Pierrot brought it to me.

I put them—they were already cold—into the same gamebag, and I returned to Paris the same evening.

INTERPRETATION

1. State the theme of this story.

2. Now that you have read the story, what do you make of the first paragraph? Why does the story interest the narrator?

3. What is the significance of the second paragraph? What conflict is there in the story?

4. Does the characterization of the cousin serve any purpose in relation to the theme?

5. What is the value, if any, of the long atmospheric description of the marshes?

6. What do you make of the last sentence of the story?

JESSE STUART

Love

YESTERDAY when the bright sun blazed down on the wilted corn my father and I walked around the edge of the new ground to plan a fence. The cows kept coming through the chestnut oaks on the cliff and running over the young corn. They bit off the tips of the corn and trampled down the stubble.

My father walked in the cornbalk. Bob, our Collie, walked in front of my father. We heard a ground squirrel whistle down over the bluff among the dead treetops at the clearing's edge. "Whoop, take him, Bob," said my father. He lifted up a young stalk of corn, with wilted dried roots, where the ground squirrel had dug it up for the sweet grain of corn left on its tender roots. This has been a dry spring and the corn has kept well in the earth where the grain has sprouted. The ground squirrels love this corn. They dig up rows of it and eat the sweet grains. The young corn stalks are killed and we have to replant the corn.

I can see my father keep sicking Bob after the ground squirrel. He jumped over the corn rows. He started to run toward the ground squirrel. I, too, started running toward the clearing's edge where Bob was jumping and barking. The dust flew in tiny swirls behind our feet. There was a cloud of dust behind us.

"It's a big bull blacksnake," said my father. "Kill him, Bob! Kill him, Bob!"

Bob was jumping and snapping at the snake so as to make it strike and throw itself off guard. Bob had killed twenty-eight copperheads this spring. He knows how to kill a snake. He doesn't rush to do it. He takes his time and does the job well.

"Let's don't kill the snake," I said. "A blacksnake is a harmless snake. It kills poison snakes. It kills the copperhead. It catches more mice from the fields than a cat."

I could see the snake didn't want to fight the dog. The snake wanted to get away. Bob wouldn't let it. I wondered why it was crawling toward a heap of black loamy earth at the bench of the hill. I wondered why it had come from the chestnut oak sprouts and the matted greenbriars on the cliff. I looked as the snake lifted its pretty head in response to one of Bob's jumps. "It's not a bull blacksnake," I said. "It's a she-snake. Look at the white on her throat."

"A snake is an enemy to me," my father snapped. "I hate a snake. Kill it, Bob. Go in there and get that snake and quit playing with it!"

Bob obeyed my father. I hated to see him take this snake by the throat. She was so beautifully poised in the sunlight. Bob grabbed the white patch on her throat. He cracked her long body like an ox whip in the wind. He cracked it against the wind only. The blood spurted from her fine-curved throat. Something hit against my legs like pellets. Bob threw the snake down. I looked to see what had struck my legs. It was snake eggs. Bob had slung them from her body. She was going to the sand heap to lay her eggs, where the sun is the setting-hen that warms them and hatches them.

Bob grabbed her body there on the earth where the red blood was running down on the gray-piled loam. Her body was still writhing in pain. She acted like a greenweed held over a new-ground fire. Bob slung her viciously many times. He cracked her limp body against the wind. She was now limber as a shoestring in the wind. Bob threw her riddled body back on the sand. She quivered like a leaf in the lazy wind, then her riddled body lay perfectly still. The blood colored the loamy earth around the snake.

"Look at the eggs, won't you?" said my father. We counted thirty-seven eggs. I picked an egg up and held it in my hand. Only a minute ago there was life in it. It was an immature seed. It would not hatch. Mother sun could not incubate it on the warm earth. The egg I held in my hand was almost the size of a quail's egg. The shell on it was thin and tough and the egg appeared under the surface to be a watery egg.

"Well, Bob, I guess you see now why this snake couldn't fight," I said. "It is life. Weaker devour the stronger even among human beings. Dog kills snake. Snake kills birds. Birds kill the butterflies. Man conquers all. Man, too, kills for sport."

Bob was panting. He walked ahead of us back to the house. His tongue was out of his mouth. He was tired. He was hot under his shaggy coat of hair. His tongue nearly touched the dry dirt and white flecks of foam dripped from it. We walked toward the house. Neither my father nor I spoke. I still thought about the dead snake. The sun was going down over the chestnut ridge. A lark was singing. It was late for a lark to sing. The red evening clouds floated above the pine trees on our pasture hill. My father stood beside the path. His black hair was moved by the wind. His face was red in the blue wind of day. His eyes looked toward the sinking sun.

"And my father hates a snake," I thought.

I thought about the agony women know of giving birth. I thought about how they will fight to save their children. Then, I thought of the snake. I thought it was silly for me to think such thoughts.

This morning my father and I got up with the chickens. He says one has to get up with the chickens to do a day's work. We got the posthole digger, ax, spud, measuring pole and the mattock. We started for the clearing's edge. Bob didn't go along.

The dew was on the corn. My father walked behind with the posthole digger across his shoulder. I walked in front. The wind was blowing. It was a good morning wind to breathe and a wind that makes one feel like he can get under the edge of a hill and heave the whole hill upside down.

I walked out the corn row where we had come yesterday afternoon. I looked in front of me. I saw something. I saw it move. It was moving like a huge black rope winds around a windlass. "Steady," I says to my father. "Here is the bull blacksnake." He took one step up beside me and stood. His eyes grew wide apart.

"What do you know about this," he said.

"You have seen the bull blacksnake now," I said. "Take a good look at him! He is lying beside his dead mate. He has come to her. He, perhaps, was on her trail yesterday."

The male snake had trailed her to her doom. He had come in the night, under the roof of stars, as the moon shed rays of light on the quivering clouds of green. He had found his lover dead. He was coiled beside her, and she was dead.

The bull blacksnake lifted his head and followed us as we walked around the dead snake. He would have fought us to his death. He would have fought Bob to his death. "Take a stick," said my father, "and throw him over the hill so Bob won't find him. Did you ever see anything to beat that? I've heard they'd do that. But this is my first time to see it." I took a stick and threw him over the bank into the dewy sprouts on the cliff.

INTERPRETATION

1. This story is clearly very similar to "Love," by Maupassant, but the general "feel" of the treatment is different. What difference do you think this makes in the meaning?

2. Wherein does the conflict lie in this story?

3. What change, if any, comes about in the story?

4. Is there any value in having the narrator? If the story were told in the third person what problems of exposition might arise that do not now appear?

MARCEL AYMÉ

Dermuche

HE had murdered a family of three in order to get possession of a gramophone record which he had coveted for several years. The fiery eloquence of counsel for the prosecution was unnecessary, and that of the defending counsel unavailing. He was unanimously condemned to have his head cut off, and not a voice was raised in sympathy, in the courtroom or elsewhere. Heavy-shouldered and bull-necked, he had a huge, flat face, all jaw and no forehead, with small, half-closed, dull-staring eyes. Even had there been a doubt as to his guilt, his brutish aspect would have caused any sensitive jury to condemn him. Throughout the trial he stayed motionless, seemingly indifferent and uncomprehending.

"Dermuche," asked the presiding judge, "are you sorry for what you did?"

"Well, yes and no, your Honor," said Dermuche. "I am, and then again, I'm not."

"Try to make yourself more clear. Do you feel any remorse?"

"Pardon, your Honor?"

"Don't you know what the word 'remorse' means? Have you no feeling of distress when you think of your victims?"

"I feel all right, your Honor, thanking you all the same."

Only at one moment during the trial did Dermuche display any interest, and this was when the prosecution produced the gramophone record. Leaning over the edge of the dock he gazed at it steadfastly, and when the gramophone, set in motion by the clerk, ground out the refrain, a smile of great gentleness passed over his dull, heavy face.

In the condemned cell he waited calmly for the day of execution, seemingly untroubled by the prospect. He never spoke of it to the warders entering the cell. Indeed, he had no desire to talk to them, and merely replied politely to the questions put to him. His sole occupation was to hum the magical refrain that had driven him to murder, and he knew it badly. His was a very slow memory, and perhaps it was his exasperation at being unable to recapture it which had taken him, on a September evening, to the modest villa in Nogent-sur-Mare. Three persons of small independent means lived in the villa, two old maids and an uncle, decorated with the Legion of Honor, who felt the cold. Every Sunday, at the end of the midday meal, the elder of the two sisters wound up the gramophone. In fine weather they kept the dining-room window open, and for three years Dermuche had known enchanted summers. Crouched at the foot of the villa wall he listened to that Sunday melody which during the ensuing week he sought to fix wholly in his memory, without ever being completely successful in doing so. But with the onset of autumn the uncle who felt the cold caused the window to be shut, and thereafter the music sounded only for persons of independent means. For three years in succession Dermuche had lived through the long months of deprivation, without music and without rapture. Little by little the refrain escaped him, diminishing day by day, until by the end of winter nothing was left of it but the longing. The fourth year he could not endure the thought of that long period of waiting, and so he broke into the villa. The police found him there next morning, listening to the song of the gramophone record in company with the three dead bodies.

For a month he had it by heart, but by the time the trial came on he had forgotten it again. Now, in the condemned cell, he gathered together the fragments restored to him by the playing of the record during the trial, but which every day became more uncertain. *Tum-tum-ti-tum*, hummed the condemned man from morning till night.

The prison chaplain visited Dermuche and found him filled with good will. He would have liked it better, however, if the poor wretch had shown himself more receptive, so that the words of consolation entered his heart. Dermuche listened with the docility of a tree, but neither his brief replies nor his expressionless face afforded any evidence that he was interested in his soul's salvation, or even that he possessed a soul. Nevertheless, one day in December, when he was talking of the Holy Virgin and the angels, the chaplain thought he caught a little gleam of light in those dull eyes—so fugitive, however, that he was not sure if he had really seen it. At the end of the interview Dermuche asked abruptly: "And the little Jesus, is he still alive?" The chaplain did not hesitate. No doubt he should have replied that the infant Jesus had once lived, but that, since he had died on the cross at the age of thirty-three, it was not possible to speak of him in the present tense. But Dermuche was so thick-headed that it was difficult to get him to understand. The fable of the infant Jesus was more within his range and might open his heart to the light of the sacred truths. The chaplain told the story of how the Son of God had elected to be born in a stable, between the ox and the ass.

"You see, Dermuche, it was to show that he loved the poor and had come for their sake. He might equally well have chosen to be born in a prison, among the most unhappy of men."

"Yes, sir, I see. In fact, Jesus might have been born in this cell I'm in, but he wouldn't have wanted to be born in a villa."

The chaplain contented himself with a wag of the head. Dermuche's logic was unassailable, but it was related rather too narrowly to his own particular case, and seemed unlikely to lead him into the way of repentance. Having thus nodded non-committally, the chaplain went on to tell him about the magi, the slaughter of innocents, the flight, and finally how the infant Jesus, when his beard was grown, had died crucified between two thieves to open the gates of heaven to mankind.

"Only think, Dermuche. The soul of the good thief must have been the first of all human souls to enter Paradise, and that was not due to accident, it was because God wished to show us what every sinner may expect of His mercy. For Him even the greatest crimes are no more than the accidents of life. . . ."

But for some time past Dermuche had not been following the chaplain's narrative, and the story of the good thief seemed to him as obscure as the miracle of the loaves and fishes.

"And so then little Jesus went back to his manger?"

He could think only of the infant Jesus. The chaplain left the cell reflecting that this murderer possessed no more understanding than a child. He even questioned whether Dermuche could be held responsible for his crime, and he prayed God to have mercy on him.

"A child's soul in a laborer's body. . . . He killed those three old people without malice, just as a child cuts open its doll, or pulls off its legs. A child that doesn't know its own strength. An unhappy child and nothing more. And the proof is that he believes in the infant Jesus."

A few days later, paying Dermuche another visit, the chaplain asked the warder who opened the cell door:

"What's that he's singing?"

The male voice of Dermuche, like a deep-toned bell, could be heard incessantly repeating, *tum-tum-ti-tum*.

"He never stops that *tum-tum-tum* of his," said the warder. "If only it sounded like something it wouldn't be so bad, but it isn't even a tune."

This apparent lightness of heart, on the part of a condemned man who had not yet come to terms with Heaven, was disturbing to the chaplain. He found Dermuche livelier than usual. His brutish face had an expression of gentle alertness, and through the half-closed lids there shone a gleam of laughter. Moreover, he was almost talkative.

"What's the weather like outside today, sir?"

"It's snowing, my son."

"Well, that doesn't matter. The snow won't stop him. A fat lot he cares about the snow."

Once again the chaplain talked of God's mercy and the light of repentance, but the condemned man constantly interrupted him with questions about the infant Jesus, so that his exhortations were without effect.

"Does little Jesus know everybody? Is little Jesus the boss in Paradise? Would you say, sir, that little Jesus likes music?"

The chaplain finally found himself unable to get a word in edgeways. As he turned towards the door Dermuche thrust into his hand a sheet of paper folded in four.

"It's my letter to little Jesus," he said with a smile.

The chaplain took it and read it a few minutes later.

"Dear little Jesus," the letter ran. "This is asking you a favor. My name is Dermuche. It will soon be Christmas. I know you don't mind about me doing those three old geezers in Nogent. You wouldn't have wanted to be born in the house of people like that. I'm not asking for anything here on earth, seeing it won't be long before I have my chips. All I ask is when I get to Heaven can I have my gramophone record? Thanking you in advance, and good luck to you—Dermuche."

The priest was horrified by the letter, which revealed all too clearly how impervious the murderer was to the idea of repentance.

"It is true," he reflected, "that the man is an innocent possessing no more discernment than a newborn babe. The trust he places in the infant Jesus bears sufficient witness to his childlike simplicity. But when he appears at the Seat of Judgment with three murders on his conscience, and no vestige of repentance, even God will be able to do nothing for him. Yet his small soul is as pure as the waters of a spring."

That evening he went to the prison chapel, and after having prayed for Dermuche, placed his letter in the plaster cradle of the infant Jesus.

At dawn on the 24th December, Christmas Eve, a party of well-dressed gentlemen accompanied the warders into the condemned cell. Their eyes still heavy with sleep, stomachs rumbling and mouths suppressing yawns, they paused at a short distance from the bed, seeking in the pallid early light to make out the shape of a body stretched beneath the coverings. The blankets moved feebly and a faint wail came from the bed. The Public Prosecutor felt a shiver pass down his spine. The Governor of the prison straightened his black tie and moved apart from the group. Shooting his cuffs he sought a posture appropriate to the occasion, and with his head inclined forward, shoulders rounded and hands clasped in front of his fly-buttons, he said in a theatrical voice:

"You must be brave, Dermuche. Your appeal has failed."

Another wail answered him, louder and more insistent than the first, but Dermuche did not move. He seemed to be buried even to his hair, and nothing of him emerged from the blankets.

"Come, Dermuche, you mustn't keep us waiting," said the Governor. "Do show a little co-operation, just for once."

A warder moved forward to shake the condemned man. He bent over the bed, then straightened himself and turned to the Governor with an air of astonishment.

"Why, what's the matter?"

"I don't know, sir. The bedclothes are moving, and yet . . ."

A long wail of heart-rending poignancy came from the blankets. With an abrupt movement the warder stripped them off the bed and then uttered a sharp exclamation. The others, who had pressed forward, in their turn uttered a cry of stupefaction. In place of Dermuche, on the uncovered bed, lay an infant a few months old. It seemed pleased to find itself in the light, and gazed placidly smiling at the visitors.

"What does this mean?" shouted the Governor, turning to the chief warder. "Have you let the prisoner escape?"

"It's impossible, sir. I made my last round three-quarters of an hour ago, and I'm positive I saw Dermuche in his bed."

Purple with fury, the Governor abused his subordinates, threatening them with the direst sanctions. The chaplain, meanwhile, had sunk to his knees and was offering thanks to God, the Holy Virgin, St. Joseph, Providence and the infant Jesus. But no one paid any attention to him.

"God almighty," cried the Governor, bending over the child, "will you look at that? It's got the same tattoo-marks as Dermuche on its chest!"

The others leaned over in their turn. The child had two pictures tattooed on either side of is chest, a woman's head on one side and a dog's head on the other. Dermuche had had exactly the same, even to their relative size. The warders all confirmed it. There was a long silence.

"I am perhaps mistaken," said M. Leboeuf, the Public Prosecutor, "but the child seems to me to be as much like Dermuche as a child that age can be like a man of thirty-three. Look at the big head, the flat face, the low forehead, the small, slit-eyes and even the shape of the nose. Don't you agree?" And he turned to M. Bridon, counsel for the defense.

"There does certainly seem to be a resemblance," said M. Bridon.

"Dermuche had a brown birthmark on the back of one thigh," the chief warder said.

They examined the child's leg and found the same thing.

"Fetch me the condemned man's finger-prints," said the Governor. "We'll see how those compare."

The chief warder went off at the double. While they awaited his return the others sought to find some rational explanation for the metamorphosis of Dermuche, which none could any longer doubt. The Governor alone took no part in the conversation but paced nervously up and down the cell. When the infant, alarmed by the sound of voices, began to cry, he advanced to the bedside and said in a threatening voice:

"You wait, my lad. I'll give you something to cry about!"

M. Leboeuf, who had seated himself beside the child, looked up at him with an intrigued expression.

"Do you really think this is your murderer?" he asked.

"I hope so. In any case, we shall soon know."

Confronted by this exquisite miracle, the chaplain continued to give thanks to God, his eyes damp with tenderness as he gazed at the virtually divine infant lying between Leboeuf and the Governor. He wondered a little anxiously what was to happen now, but concluded with confidence, "It will be as if the infant Jesus decides."

When the comparison of finger-prints had confirmed the extraordinary metamorphosis the Governor gave a sigh of relief and rubbed his hands.

"Well, now let's get on with it," he said. "We've simply been wasting time. Come along, Dermuche. Come along."

A murmur of protest arose in the cell, and M. Bridon cried indignantly:

"You surely can't intend to execute a babe in arms! It would be a hideous thing to do, utterly monstrous. Even if we admit the fact of Dermuche's guilt, and that he deserved the death sentence, we have surely no need to plead the innocence of a newly born infant."

"I can't go into those details," answered the Governor. "Is this Dermuche, or isn't it? Did he murder three people in Nogent-sur-Marne? Was he condemned to death? The law applies to everyone and I don't want any trouble. The scaffold has been erected and the guillotine was set up more than an hour ago. This talk about the innocence of the newly born is merely tiresome. At that rate anyone could escape justice simply by turning themselves into an infant. It would be a bit too easy!"

The defending counsel, with a maternal gesture, had drawn the covers back over the dimpled body of his client. The infant, responding to the warmth, laughed and crowed with pleasure, and the Governor looked coldly at it, finding this manifestation of gaiety out of place.

"You note the cynicism," he said. "He means to brazen it out to the end."

"My dear Governor," said the chaplain, "is it possible that you cannot see in this episode the hand of God?"

"Perhaps, but that makes no difference. It's certainly nothing to do with me. It isn't God who gave me my job or who is responsible for my advancement. I've had my instructions, and I intend to carry them out." The Governor turned to the Public Prosecutor. "Don't you agree that I'm entirely right?"

M. Leboeuf took time for thought before giving his opinion.

"Undoubtedly your position is logically sound. It would be profoundly unjust for a murderer to be privileged to begin his life again instead of paying the just penalty of his crime. On the other hand, the execution of an infant is a rather ticklish matter. I think you would be wise to consult your superiors."

"I know them," said the Governor. "They'll be annoyed with me for putting them in an embarrassing position. However, I'll ring them up."

The high officials concerned had not yet arrived at the Ministry. The Governor had to ring up their homes. Being still only half awake they were not in the best of tempers. The metamorphosis of Dermuche seemed to them a treacherous stratagem aimed directly at themselves, and they were highly indignant. The fact remained, none the less, that the condemned man was now a babe in arms. But the times were harsh, and they feared for their advancement if they should be suspected of lenience. Having agreed among themselves they resolved that—"the fact that the murderer has somewhat shrunk beneath the burden of remorse, or from no matter what cause, can in no way be allowed to divert the course of Justice."

Accordingly the condemned man's toilet was proceeded with—that is to say, he was wrapped in one of the bed coverings and the soft down on the back of his neck was shaved off. The chaplain then took the precaution of baptising him. It was he who carried him in his arms to the machine erected in the prison courtyard.

As they returned from the place of execution he told counsel for the defense of Dermuche's letter to the infant Jesus.

"God could not allow a murderer entirely untouched by remorse to enter Paradise. But Dermuche had hope on his side, and his love of the infant Jesus. So God effaced his life as a sinner and restored him to the age of innocence."

"But if his life as a sinner was effaced, then Dermuche committed no crime and those people in Nogent were never murdered."

Wanting to be quite sure on this point, the Counsel immediately went to Nogent-sur-Marne. Upon arriving there he asked to be directed to the house where the crime had been committed, but no one had heard of any crime. He had no difficulty, however, in finding the house where the two Mademoiselles Bridaine lived with their uncle who suffered from the cold. The three old people received him at first with mistrust, and after being reassured, complained to him that that very night someone had stolen a gramophone record lying on the dining-room table.

INTERPRETATION

This story, like those that have come before it in this section, is essentially a parable. What are the main points needing discussion? Write a short essay of explanation.

ERNEST HEMINGWAY

The Killers

THE door of Henry's lunchroom opened and two men came in. They sat down at the counter.

"What's yours?" George asked them.

"I don't know," one of the men said. "What do you want to eat, Al?"

"I don't know," said Al. "I don't know what I want to eat."

Outside it was getting dark. The street light came on outside the window. The two men at the counter read the menu. From the other end of the counter Nick Adams watched them. He had been talking to George when they came in.

"I'll have a roast pork tenderloin with apple sauce and mashed pota-toes," the first man said.

"It isn't ready yet."

"What the hell do you put it on the card for?"

"That's the dinner," George explained. "You can get that at six o'clock."

George looked at the clock on the wall behind the counter.

"It's five o'clock."

"The clock says twenty minutes past five," the second man said.

"It's twenty minutes fast."

"Oh, to hell with the clock," the first man said. "What have you got to eat?"

"I can give you any kind of sandwiches," George said. "You can have ham and eggs, bacon and eggs, liver and bacon, or a steak."

"Give me chicken croquettes with green peas and cream sauce and mashed potatoes."

"That's the dinner."

"Everything we want's the dinner, eh? That's the way you work it."

"I can give you ham and eggs, bacon and eggs, liver—"

"I'll take ham and eggs," the man called Al said. He wore a derby hat and a black overcoat buttoned across the chest. His face was small and white and he had tight lips. He wore a silk muffler and gloves.

"Give me bacon and eggs," said the other man. He was about the same size as Al. Their faces were different, but they were dressed like twins. Both wore overcoats too tight for them. They sat leaning forward, their elbows on the counter.

"Got anything to drink?" Al asked.

"Silver beer, bevo, ginger ale," George said.

"I mean you got anything to *drink?*"

"Just those I said."

"This is a hot town," said the other. "What do they call it?"

"Summit."

"Ever hear of it?" Al asked his friend.

"No," said the friend.

"What do you do here nights?" Al asked.

"They eat the dinner," his friend said. "They all come here and eat the big dinner."

"That's right," George said.

"So you think that's right?" Al asked George.

"Sure."

"You're a pretty bright boy, aren't you?"

"Sure," said George.

"Well, you're not," said the other little man. "Is he, Al?"

"He's dumb," said Al. He turned to Nick. "What's your name?"

"Adams."

"Another bright boy," Al said. "Ain't he a bright boy, Max?"

"The town's full of bright boys," Max said.

George put the two platters, one of ham and eggs, the other of bacon and eggs, on the counter. He set down two side dishes of fried potatoes and closed the wicket into the kitchen.

"Which is yours?" he asked Al.

"Don't you remember?"

"Ham and eggs."

"Just a bright boy," Max said. He leaned forward and took the ham and eggs. Both men ate with their gloves on. George watched them eat.

"What are *you* looking at?" Max looked at George.

"Nothing."

"The hell you were. You were looking at me."

"Maybe the boy meant it for a joke, Max," Al said.

George laughed.

"*You* don't have to laugh," Max said to him. "*You* don't have to laugh at all, see?"

"All right," said George.

"So he thinks it's all right." Max turned to Al. "He thinks it's all right. That's a good one."

"Oh, he's a thinker," Al said. They went on eating.

"What's the bright boy's name down the counter?" Al asked Max.

"Hey, bright boy," Max said to Nick. "You go around on the other side of the counter with your boy friend."

"What's the idea?" Nick asked.

"There isn't any idea."

"You better go around, bright boy," Al said. Nick went around behind the counter.

"What's the idea?" George asked.

"None of your damn business," Al said. "Who's out in the kitchen?"

"The nigger."

"What do you mean the nigger?"

"The nigger that cooks."

"Tell him to come in."

"What's the idea?"

"Tell him to come in."

"Where do you think you are?"

"We know damn well where we are," the man called Max said, "Do we look silly?"

"You talk silly," Al said to him. "What the hell do you argue with this kid for? Listen," he said to George, "tell the nigger to come out here."

"What are you going to do to him?"

"Nothing. Use your head, bright boy. What would we do to a nigger?"

George opened the slit that opened back into the kitchen. "Sam," he called. "Come in here a minute."

The door to the kitchen opened and the nigger came in. "What was it?" he asked. The two men at the counter took a look at him.

"All right, nigger. You stand right there," Al said.

Sam, the nigger, standing in his apron, looked at the two men sitting at the counter. "Yes, sir," he said. Al got down from his stool.

"I'm going back to the kitchen with the nigger and bright boy," he said. "Go on back to the kitchen, nigger. You go with him, bright boy." The little man walked after Nick and Sam, the cook, back into the kitchen. The door shut after them. The man called Max sat at the counter opposite George. He didn't look at George but looked in the mirror that ran along back of the counter. Henry's had been made over from a saloon into a lunch counter.

"Well, bright boy," Max said, looking into the mirror, "why don't you say something?"

"What's it all about?"

"Hey, Al," Max called, "bright boy wants to know what it's all about."

"Why don't you tell him?" Al's voice came from the kitchen.

"What do you think it's all about?"

"I don't know."

"What do you think?"

Max looked into the mirror all the time he was talking.

"I wouldn't say."

"Hey, Al, bright boy says he wouldn't say what he thinks it's all about."

"I can hear you, all right," Al said from the kitchen. He had propped open the slit that dishes passed through into the kitchen with a catsup bottle. "Listen, bright boy," he said from the kitchen to George. "Stand a little further along the bar. You move a little to the left, Max." He was like a photographer arranging for a group picture.

"Talk to me, bright boy," Max said. "What do you think's going to happen?"

George did not say anything.

"I'll tell you," Max said. "We're going to kill a Swede. Do you know a big Swede named Ole Andreson?"

"Yes."

"He comes here to eat every night, don't he?"

"Sometimes he comes here."

"He comes here at six o'clock, don't he?"

"If he comes."

"We know all that, bright boy," Max said. "Talk about something else. Ever go to the movies?"

"Once in a while."

"You ought to go to the movies more. The movies are fine for a bright boy like you."

"What are you going to kill Ole Andreson for? What did he ever do to you?"

"He never had a chance to do anything to us. He never even seen us."

"And he's only going to see us once," Al said from the kitchen.

"What are you going to kill him for, then?" George asked.

"We're killing him for a friend. Just to oblige a friend, bright boy."

"Shut up," said Al from the kitchen. "You talk too goddamn much."

"Well, I got to keep bright boy amused. Don't I, bright boy?"

"You talk too damn much," Al said. "The nigger and my bright boy are amused by themselves. I got them tied up like a couple of girl friends in a convent."

"I suppose you were in a convent."

"You never know."

"You were in a kosher convent. That's where you were."

George looked up at the clock.

"If anybody comes in you tell them the cook is off, and if they keep after it, you tell them you'll go back and cook yourself. Do you get that, bright boy?"

"All right," George said. "What you going to do with us afterward?"

"That'll depend," Max said. "That's one of those things you never know at the time."

George looked up at the clock. It was a quarter past six. The door from the street opened. A street-car motorman came in.

"Hello, George," he said. "Can I get supper?"

"Sam's gone out," George said. "He'll be back in about half an hour."

"I'd better go up the street," the motorman said. George looked at the clock. It was twenty minutes past six.

"That was nice, bright boy," Max said. "You're a regular little gentleman."

"He knew I'd blow his head off," Al said from the kitchen.

"No," said Max. "It ain't that. Bright boy is nice. He's a nice boy. I like him."

At six-fifty-five George said: "He's not coming."

Two other people had been in the lunchroom. Once George had gone out to the kitchen and made a ham-and-egg sandwich "to go" that a man wanted to take with him. Inside the kitchen he saw Al, his derby hat tipped back, sitting on a stool beside the wicket with the muzzle of a sawed-off shotgun resting on the ledge. Nick and the cook were back to back in the corner, a towel tied in each of their mouths. George had cooked the sand-wich, wrapped it up in oiled paper, put it in a bag, brought it in, and the man had paid for it and gone out.

"Bright boy can do everything," Max said. "He can cook and every-thing. You'd make some girl a nice wife, bright boy."

"Yes?" George said. "Your friend, Ole Andreson, isn't going to come."

"We'll give him ten minutes," Max said.

Max watched the mirror and the clock. The hands of the clock marked seven o'clock, and then five minutes past seven.

"Come on, Al," said Max. "We better go. He's not coming."

"Better give him five minutes," Al said from the kitchen.

In the five minutes a man came in, and George explained that the cook was sick.

"Why the hell don't you get another cook?" the man asked. "Aren't you running a lunch counter?" He went out.

"Come on, Al," Max said.

"What about the two bright boys and the nigger?"

"They're all right."

"You think so?"

"Sure. We're through with it."

"I don't like it," said Al. "It's sloppy. You talk too much."

"Oh, what the hell," said Max. "We got to keep amused, haven't we?"

"You talk too much, all the same," Al said. He came out from the kitchen. The cut-off barrels of the shotgun made a slight bulge under the waist of his too tight-fitting overcoat. He straightened his coat with his gloved hands.

"So long, bright boy," he said to George. "You got a lot of luck."

"That's the truth," Max said. "You ought to play the races, bright boy."

The two of them went out the door. George watched them, through the window, pass under the arc light and cross the street. In their tight overcoats and derby hats they looked like a vaudeville team. George went back through the swinging door into the kitchen and untied Nick and the cook.

"I don't want any more of that," said Sam, the cook. "I don't want any more of that."

Nick stood up. He had never had a towel in his mouth before.

"Say," he said. "What the hell?" He was trying to swagger it off.

"They were going to kill Ole Andreson," George said. "They were going to shoot him when he came in to eat."

"Ole Andreson?"

"Sure."

The cook felt the corners of his mouth with his thumbs.

"They all gone?" he asked.

"Yeah," said George. "They're gone now."

"I don't like it," said the cook. "I don't like any of it at all."

"Listen," George said to Nick. "You better go see Ole Andreson."

"All right."

"You better not have anything to do with it at all," Sam, the cook, said. "You better stay way out of it."

"Don't go if you don't want to," George said.

"Mixing up in this ain't going to get you anywhere," the cook said. "You stay out of it."

"I'll go see him," Nick said to George. "Where does he live?"

The cook turned away.

"Little boys always know what they want to do," he said.

"He lives up at Hirsch's rooming house," George said to Nick.

"I'll go up there."

Outside the arc light shone through the bare branches of a tree. Nick walked up the street beside the car tracks and turned at the next arc light down a side street. Three houses up the street was Hirsch's rooming house. Nick walked up the two steps and pushed the bell. A woman came to the door.

"Is Ole Andreson here?"

"Do you want to see him?"

"Yes, if he's in."

Nick followed the woman up a flight of stairs and back to the end of a corridor. She knocked on the door.

"Who is it?"

"It's somebody to see you, Mr. Andreson," the woman said.

"It's Nick Adams."

"Come in."

Nick opened the door and went into the room. Ole Andreson was lying on the bed with all his clothes on. He had been a heavyweight prize-fighter and he was too long for the bed. He lay with his head on two pillows. He did not look at Nick.

"What was it?" he asked.

"I was up at Henry's," Nick said, "and two fellows came in and tied up me and the cook, and they said they were going to kill you."

It sounded silly when he said it. Ole Andreson said nothing.

"They put us out in the kitchen," Nick went on. "They were going to shoot you when you came in to supper."

Ole Andreson looked at the wall and did not say anything.

"George thought I better come and tell you about it."

"There isn't anything I can do about it," Ole Andreson said.

"I'll tell you what they were like."

"I don't want to know what they were like," Ole Andreson said. He looked at the wall. "Thanks for coming to tell me about it."

"That's all right."

Nick looked at the big man lying on the bed.

"Don't you want me to go and see the police?"

"No," Ole Andreson said. "That wouldn't do any good."

"Isn't there something I could do?"

"No. There ain't anything to do."

"Maybe it was just a bluff."

"No. It ain't just a bluff."

Ole Andreson rolled over toward the wall.

"The only thing is," he said, talking toward the wall, "I just can't make up my mind to go out. I been in here all day."

"Couldn't you get out of town?"

"No," Ole Andreson said. "I'm through with all that running around."

He looked at the wall.

"There ain't anything to do now."

"Couldn't you fix it up some way?"

"No. I got in wrong." He talked in the same flat voice. "There ain't anything to do. After a while I'll make up my mind to go out."

"I better go back and see George," Nick said.

"So long," said Ole Andreson. He did not look toward Nick. "Thanks for coming around."

Nick went out. As he shut the door he saw Ole Andreson with all his clothes on, lying on the bed looking at the wall.

"He's been in his room all day," the landlady said downstairs. "I guess he don't feel well. I said to him: 'Mr. Andreson, you ought to go out and take a walk on a nice fall day like this,' but he didn't feel like it."

"He doesn't want to go out."

"I'm sorry he don't feel well," the woman said. "He's an awfully nice man. He was in the ring, you know."

"I know it."

"You'd never know it except from the way his face is," the woman said. They stood talking just inside the street door. "He's just as gentle."

"Well, good-night, Mrs. Hirsch," Nick said.

"I'm not Mrs. Hirsch," the woman said. "She owns the place. I just look after it for her. I'm Mrs. Bell."

"Well, good-night, Mrs. Bell," Nick said.

"Good-night," the woman said.

Nick walked up the dark street to the corner under the arc light, and then along the car tracks to Henry's eating house. George was inside, back of the counter.

"Did you see Ole?"

"Yes," said Nick. "He's in his room and he won't go out."

The cook opened the door from the kitchen when he heard Nick's voice.

"I don't even listen to it," he said and shut the door.

"Did you tell him about it?" George asked.

"Sure. I told him but he knows what it's all about."

"What's he going to do?"

"Nothing."

"They'll kill him."

"I guess they will."

"He must have got mixed up in something in Chicago."

"I guess so," said Nick.

"It's a hell of a thing."

"It's an awful thing," Nick said.

They did not say anything. George reached down for a towel and wiped the counter.

"I wonder what he did?" Nick said.

"Double-crossed somebody. That's what they kill them for."

"I'm going to get out of this town," Nick said.

"Yes," said George. "That's a good thing to do."

"I can't stand to think about him waiting in the room and knowing he's going to get it. It's too damned awful."

"Well," said George, "you better not think about it."

INTERPRETATION

There are certain fairly obvious points to be made about the technique of this story. It breaks up into one long scene and three short scenes. Indeed, the method is so thoroughly scenic that not over three or four sentences are required to make the transitions. The focus of narration is objective throughout, practically all information being conveyed in simple realistic dialogue. In the first scene the revelation of the mission of the gangsters is accomplished through a few significant details—the fact that the gangsters eat with gloves (to avoid leaving fingerprints), the fact that they keep their eyes on the mirror behind the bar, the fact that, after Nick and the cook have been tied up, the gangster who has the shotgun at the service window stations his friend and George out front "like a photographer arranging for a group picture"—all of this before the specific nature of their mission is made clear.

Other observations concerning the technique of the story could be made—the cleverness of composition, the subtlety with which the suspense is maintained in the first scene by the banter of the gangsters, and then is transferred to another level in the second scene. But such observations, though they are worth making, do not answer the first question which, to the reader, usually presents itself, or should be allowed to present itself. That question is: what is the story about?

The importance of giving an early answer to this question is indicated by the fact that a certain kind of reader, upon first acquaintance with the story, is inclined to feel that the story is exhausted in the first scene, and in fact that the first scene itself does not come to focus—does not have a "point." Another kind of reader sees that the first scene, with its lack of resolution, is really being used to "charge" the second scene. He finds his point in Ole Andreson's decision not to try to escape the gangsters—to stop "all that running around." This reader feels that the story should end here. He sees no relevance in the last several pages of the story, and wonders why the author has flattened out his effect. The first reader we may say, feels that "The Killers" is the gangsters' story—a story of action which does not come off. The second and more sophisticated reader interprets it as Andreson's story, though perhaps with some wonder that Andreson's story has been approached so indirectly and is allowed to trail off so irrelevantly. In other words, the reader is inclined to transpose the question, What is the story? into the question, Whose story is it? When he states the question in this way, he confronts the fact that Hemingway has left the story focused not on the gangsters, nor on Andreson, but on the boys at the lunchroom. Consider the last sentences of the story:

"I'm going to get out of this town," Nick said.
"Yes," said George. "That's a good thing to do."
"I can't stand to think about him waiting in the room and knowing he's going to get it. It's too damned awful."
"Well," said George, "you better not think about it."

So, of the two boys, it is obviously Nick on whom the impression has been made. George has managed to come to terms with the situation. By this line of reasoning, it is Nick's story. And the story is about the discovery of evil. The theme, in a sense, is the Hamlet theme, or the theme of Sherwood Anderson's "I Want to Know Why" (p. 279).

This definition of the theme of the story, even if it appears acceptable, must, of course, be tested against the detail structure. In evaluating the story, as well as in understanding it, the skill with which the theme has been assimilated must be taken into account. For instance, to put a concrete question: does the last paragraph of the story illuminate for the reader certain details which had, at their first appearance, seemed to be merely casual, realistic items? If we take the theme to be the boy's discovery of evil, several such details do find their fulfillment and meaning. Nick had been bound and gagged by the gangsters, and has been released by George. To quote, "Nick stood up. He had never had a towel in his mouth before. 'Say,' he said. 'What the hell?' He was trying to swagger it off." Being gagged was something you read about in a thriller and not something which happened to you; and the first effect is one of excitement, almost pleasurable, certainly an excuse for a manly pose. (It may be worth noting in this connection that Hemingway uses the specific word *towel* and not the general word *gag*. It is true that the word *towel* has a certain sensory advantage over the word *gag*—because it suggests the coarseness of the fabric and the unpleasant drying effect on the membranes of the mouth. But this advantage in immediacy is probably overshadowed by another: the towel is sanctified in the thriller as the gag, and here that cliché of the thriller has come true.) The way the whole incident is given—"He had *never* had a towel in his mouth *before*"—charges the apparently realistic detail as a pointer to the final discovery.

Another pointer appears in the gangster's wisecrack about the movies: "You ought to go to the movies more. The movies are fine for a bright boy like you." In one sense, of course, the iterated remarks about the movies, coming just after the gangsters have made their arrangements in the lunchroom, serve as a kind of indirect exposition: the reader knows the standard reason and procedure for gang killings. But at another level, these remarks emphasize the discovery that the unreal clichés of horror have a reality.

The boy to whom the gangster speaks understands the allusion to the movies, or he immediately asks: "What are you going to kill Ole Andreson for? What did he ever do to you?"

"He never had a chance to do anything to us. He never even seen us," the gangster replies. The gangster accepts, and even glories a little in, the terms by which he lives—terms which transcend the small-town world. He lives, as it were, by a code, which lifts him above questions of personal likes or personal animosities. This unreal code—unreal because it denies the ordinary personal elements of life—has, like the gag, suddenly been discovered as real. This unreal and theatrical quality is reflected in the description of the gangsters as, after leaving the lunchroom, they go out under the arc light and cross the street: "In their tight overcoats and derby hats they looked like a vaudeville team." It even permeates their dialogue. The dialogue itself has the sleazy quality of mechanized gag and wisecrack, a kind of inflexible and stereotyped banter that is always *a priori* to the situation and overrides the situation. On this level the comparison to the vaudeville team is a kind of explicit summary of details which have been presented more indirectly and dramatically. On another level, the weary and artificial quality of their wit has a grimmer implication. It is an index to the professional casualness with which they accept a situation which to the boys is shocking. They are contemptuous and even bored, with the contempt and boredom of the initiated when confronted by callow lay observers. This code, which has suddenly been transferred from the artificial world of the thriller and movie into reality, is shocking enough, but even more shocking to Nick is the fact that Ole Andreson, the hunted man, accepts the code too. Confronted by the news which Nick brings, he rejects all the responses which the boy would have considered normal: he will not call the police; he will not regard the thing as a mere bluff; he will not leave town. "Couldn't you fix it up some way?" the boy asks. "No. I got in wrong."

As we observed earlier, for a certain type of reader this is the high point of the story, and the story should end here. If one is to convince such a reader that the author is right in proceeding, one is obligated to answer his question: What is the significance of the rather tame, and apparently irrelevant, little incident which follows, the conversation with Mrs. Bell? It is sometimes said that Mrs. Bell serves to give a bit of delayed exposition or even to point the story by gaining sympathy for Andreson, who is, to her, "an awfully nice man," not at all like her idea of a pugilist. But this is not enough to satisfy the keen reader, and he is right in refusing to be satisfied with this. Mrs. Bell is, really, the Porter at Hell Gate in *Macbeth*. She is the world of normality, which is shocking now from the very fact that it continues to flow on in its usual course. To her, Ole Andreson is just a nice man, despite the fact that he has been in the ring; he ought to go out and take his walk on such a nice day. She points to his ordinary individuality, which is in contrast to the demands of the mechanical code. Even if the unreal horror of the movie thriller has become real, even if the hunted man lies upstairs on his bed trying to make up his mind to go out, Mrs Bell is still Mrs. Bell. She is not Mrs. Hirsch. Mrs. Hirsch owns the place, she just looks after it for Mrs. Hirsch. She is Mrs. Bell.

At the door of the rooming house Nick has met Mrs. Bell—normality unconscious of the ironical contrast it presents. Back at the lunchroom, Nick returns to the normal scene, but the normal scene conscious of the impingement of horror. It is the same old lunchroom, with George and the cook going about their business. But they, unlike Mrs. Bell, know what has happened. Yet even they are scarcely deflected from their ordinary routine. George and the cook represent two different levels of response to the situation. The cook, from the first, has wanted no part of it. When he hears Nick's voice, on his return, he says, "I don't even listen to it." And he shuts the door. But George had originally suggested that Nick go see Andreson, telling him, however, "Don't go if you don't want to." After Nick has told his story, George can comment, "It's a hell of a thing," but George, in one sense at least, has accepted the code, too. When Nick says: "I wonder what he did?" George replies, with an echo of the killers' own casualness: "Double-crossed somebody. That's what they kill them for." In other words, the situation is shocking to the cook only in so far as it involves his own safety. George is aware of other implications but can dismiss them. For neither of them, does the situation mean the discovery of evil. But for Nick, it is the discovery, for he has not yet learned to take George's adult advice: "Well, you better not think about it."

To this point the discussion of "The Killers" has been concerned with the structure of the story with regard to the relations among incidents and with regard to the attitudes of the characters. But there remain as important questions such items as the following: What is Hemingway's attitude toward his material? How does this attitude find its expression?

Perhaps the simplest approach to these questions may be through a consideration of the situations and characters which interest Hemingway. These situations are usually violent ones: the hard-drinking and sexually promiscuous world of *The Sun Also Rises;* the chaotic and brutal world of war as in *A Farewell to Arms, For Whom the Bell Tolls,* or "A Way You'll Never Be"; the dangerous and exciting world of the bull ring or the prize ring as in *The Sun Also Rises, Death in the Afternoon,* "The Undefeated," "Fifty Grand"; the world of crime, as in "The Killers," *To Have and to Have Not,* or "The Gambler, the Nun, and the Radio." Hemingway's typical characters are usually tough men, experienced in the hard worlds they inhabit, and apparently insensitive: Lieutenant Henry in *A Farewell to Arms,* the big-game hunter in "The Snows of Kilimanjaro," Robert Jordan in *For Whom the Bell Tolls,* or even Ole Andreson. They are, also, usually defeated men. Out of their practical defeat, however, they have managed to salvage something. And here we come upon Hemingway's basic interest in such situations and such characters. They are not defeated except upon their own terms; some of them have even courted defeat; certainly, they have maintained, even in the practical defeat, an ideal of themselves, formulated or unformulated, by which they have lived. Hemingway's attitude is, in a sense, like that of Robert Louis Stevenson, as Stevenson states it in one of his essays, "Pulvis et Umbra":

"Poor soul, here for so little, cast among so many hardships, filled with desires so incommensurate and so inconsistent, savagely surrounded, savagely descended, irremediably condemned to prey upon his fellow lives: who should have blamed him had he been of a piece with his destiny and a being merely barbarous? And we look and behold him instead filled with imperfect virtues: . . . an ideal of decency, to which he would rise if it were possible; a limit of shame, below which, if it be possible, he will not stoop. . . . Man is indeed marked for failure in his efforts to do right. But where the best consistently miscarry, how tenfold more remarkable that all should continue to strive; and surely we should find it both touching and inspiriting, that in a field from which success is banished, our race should not cease to labor. . . . It matters not where we look, under what climate we observe him, in what stage of society, in what depth of ignorance, burthened with what erroneous morality; by campfires in Assiniboia, the snow powdering his shoulders, the wind plucking his blanket, as he sits, passing the ceremonial calumet and uttering his grave opinions like a Roman senator; in ships at sea, a man inured to hardship and vile pleasures, his brightest hope a fiddle in a tavern and a bedizened trull who sells herself to rob him, and he for all that, simple, innocent, cheerful, kindly like a child, constant to toil, brave to drown, for others; . . . in the brothel, the discard of society, living mainly on strong drink, fed with affronts, a fool, a thief, the comrade of thieves, and even here keeping the point of honor and the touch of pity, often repaying the world's scorn with service, often standing firm upon a scruple, and at a certain cost, rejecting riches;— everywhere some virtue cherished or affected, everywhere some decency of thought and carriage, everywhere the ensign of man's ineffectual goodness! . . . under every circumstance of failure, without hope, without health, without thanks, still obscurely fighting the lost fight of virtue, still clinging, in the brothel or on the scaffold, to some rag of honor, the poor jewel of their souls! They may seek to escape, and yet they cannot; it is not alone their privilege and glory, but their doom, they are condemned to some nobility . . ."

For Stevenson, the world in which this drama is played out is, objectively considered, a violent and meaningless world—"our rotary island loaded with predatory life and more drenched with blood . . . than ever mutinied ship, scuds through space." This is Hemingway's world, too. But its characters, at least those whose story Hemingway cares to tell, make one gallant effort to redeem the incoherence and meaninglessness of this world: they attempt to impose some form upon the disorder of their lives, the technique of the bullfighter or sportsman, the discipline of the soldier, the code of the gangster, which, even though brutal and dehumanizing, has its own ethic. (Ole Andreson is willing to take his medicine without whining. Or the dying Mexican in "The Gambler, the Nun, and the Radio" refuses to squeal, despite the detective's argument: "One can, with honor, denounce one's assailant.") The form is never quite adequate to subdue the world, but the fidelity to it is part of the gallantry of defeat.

It has been said above that the typical Hemingway character is tough and, apparently, insensitive. But only apparently, for the fidelity to a code, to a discipline, may be an index to a sensitivity which allows the characters to see, at moments, their true plight. At times, and usually at times of stress, it is the tough man, for Hemingway, the disciplined man, who actually is aware of pathos or tragedy. The individual toughness (which may be taken to be the private discipline demanded by the world), may find itself in conflict with some more natural and spontaneous human emotion; in contrast with this the discipline may, even, seem to be inhuman; but the Hemingway hero, though he is aware of the claims of this spontaneous human emotion, is afraid to yield to those claims because he has learned that the only way to hold on to "honor," to individuality, to, even, the human order as against the brute chaos of the world, is to live by his code. This is the irony of the situation in which the hero finds himself. Hemingway's heroes are aristocrats in the sense that they are the initiate, and practice a lonely virtue.

Hemingway's heroes utter themselves, not in rant and bombast, but in terms of ironic understatement. This understatement, stemming from the contrast between the toughness and the sensitivity, the violence and the sensitivity, is a constant aspect of Hemingway's method, an aspect which was happily caught in a cartoon in the *New Yorker* some years ago. The cartoonist showed a brawny, hairy forearm and a muscled hand clutching a little rose. The cartoon was entitled "The Soul of Ernest Hemingway." Just as there is a margin of victory in the defeat of the Hemingway characters, so there is a little margin of sensibility in their brutal and violent world. The revelation arises from the most unpromising circumstances and from the most unpromising people—the little streak of poetry or pathos in "The Pursuit Race," "The Undefeated," "My Old Man," and, let us say, "The Killers."

It has already been pointed out that Ole Andreson fits into this pattern. Andreson won't whimper. He takes his medicine quietly. But Ole Andreson's story is buried in the larger story, which is focused on Nick. How does Nick Adams fit into the pattern? Hemingway, as a matter of fact, is accustomed to treat his basic situation at one or the other of two levels. There is the story of the person who is already initiated, who already has adopted his appropriate code, or discipline, in the world which otherwise he cannot cope with. (One finds examples in Jake and Brett in *The Sun Also Rises*, Jordan and Pilar in *For Whom the Bell Tolls*, the bullfighter in "The Undefeated," and many other stories.) There is also the story of the process of the initiation, the discovery of evil and disorder, and the first step toward the mastery of the discipline. This is Nick's story. (But the same basic situation occurs in many other stories by Hemingway, for example, "Up In Michigan," "Indian Camp," and "The Three-Day Blow.") The underlying attitude in Hemingway's work may be stated like this: pity is only valid when it is wrung from a man who has been seasoned by experience, and is only earned by a man who never demands it, a man who takes his chances.

A further question suggests itself. How is Hemingway's *style* (see Glossary) related to his basic fictional concerns. In "The Killers," as in many of his other stories, the style is simple even to the point of monotony. The characteristic sentence is simple, or compound; and if compound, there is no implied subtlety in the co-ordination of the clauses. The paragraph structure is, characteristically, based on simple sequence.* First, we can observe that there is an obvious relation between this style and the characters and situations with which the author is concerned: unsophis-

---

* In some of Hemingway's work, especially in the novels, there are examples of a more fluent, lyrical style than is found in "The Killers." But even in such examples, one can observe that the fluency and the lyrical effect is based on the conjunction *and*—that there is no process of subordination but rather a process of sequence in terms of direct perceptions. The lyrical quality of such examples is to be taken as a manifestation of the "marginal sensibility," as can be demonstrated by an analysis of the situations in which the lyrical passages occur.

ticated characters and simple, fundamental situations are rendered in an uncomplicated style. But there is another, and more interesting, aspect of the question which involves, not the sensibility of the characters, but the sensibility of the author himself. The short simple rhythms, the succession of co-ordinate clauses, and the general lack of subordination—all suggest a dislocated and ununified world. Hemingway is apparently trying to suggest in his style the direct experience—things as seen and felt, one after another, and not as the mind arranges and analyzes them. A style which involves subordination and complicated shadings of emphasis—a style which tends toward complex sentences with many qualifying clauses and phrases —implies an exercise of critical discrimination—the sifting of experience through the intellect. But Hemingway, apparently, is primarily concerned with giving the immediate impact of experience rather than with analyzing and evaluating it in detail. (We can notice, in this connection, that in his work he rarely indulges in any psychological analysis, and is rarely concerned with the detailed development of a character.) His very style, then, seems to imply that the use of the intellect, with its careful discriminations, may blur the rendering of experience and may falsify it; and this style, in connection with his basic concern for the character of marginal sensibility, may be taken as implying a distrust of the intellect in solving man's basic problems. It is as though he should say: despite the application of the human intellect to the problems of the world, the world is still a disorderly and brutal mess, in which it is hard to find any sure scale of values; therefore, it is well for one to remember the demands of fundamental situations —those involving sex, love, danger, and death, in which the instinctive life is foremost—which are frequently glossed over or falsified by social conventions or sterile intellectuality, and to remember the simple virtues of courage, honesty, fidelity, discipline.

But is all of this a way of saying that Hemingway is really writing innocently, without calculation, crudely? Now, as a matter of fact, his style is a result of calculation, and is not, strictly speaking, spontaneous and naïve at all. His style is, then, a dramatic device, developed because of its appropriateness to the total effect which he intends to give. A writer who was in point of fact uninstructed and spontaneous would probably not be able to achieve the impression of spontaneity and immediacy which is found in Hemingway's best work, the work in which his basic attitude and subject matter can be truly and functionally co-ordinated.

In our comment on this story we have tried, among other and more obvious concerns, to relate the style of the story to the theme and then to relate the various qualities of this story to the general body of Hemingway's work and his attitude toward his world. Ordinarily we have been studying stories taken individually, but it is time for us to realize that the various (and often quite different) stories done by a good writer always have some fundamental unifying attitudes—for a man can be only himself.

Since this is true, we can nearly always enter more deeply into a piece of fiction and understand it more fully when we are prepared to relate it to the writer's other work. A good writer does not offer us, for instance, a glittering variety of themes. He probably treats, over and over, those few themes that seem to him most important in his actual living and observation of life. For we can remember, too, that a good writer is not merely playing a game to amuse his readers or to make a living—though quite properly he may do these things in addition to what else he may do. The good writer is trying in his personal way to find and to say something that he regards as true about life.

1. Either one of the men who are characters in "The Bride Comes to Yellow Sky" (p. 138) is a type that might appear in a story by Hemingway. But is it likely that Hemingway would take the same attitude toward them? How could you state the difference in tone between "The Bride Comes to Yellow Sky" and such stories by Hemingway as you have read?

2. Suppose you had read "A Piece of News" or "The Drunkard" without knowing the author and had been told it was by Hemingway. Would you have believed this? If not, why not?

KATHERINE MANSFIELD

The Fly

"Y'ARE very snug in here," piped old Mr. Woodifield, and he peered out of the great, green leather armchair by his friend, the boss's desk, as a baby peers out of its pram. His talk was over; it was time for him to be off. But he did not want to go. Since he had retired, since his . . . stroke, the wife and the girls kept him boxed up in the house every day of the week except Tuesday. On Tuesday he was dressed up and brushed and allowed to cut back to the City for the day. Though what he did there the wife and girls couldn't imagine. Made a nuisance of himself to his friends, they supposed. . . . Well, perhaps so. All the same, we cling to our last pleasures as the tree clings to its last leaves. So there sat old Woodifield, smoking a cigar and staring almost greedily at the boss, who rolled in his office chair, stout, rosy, five years older than he, and still going strong, still at the helm. It did one good to see him.

Wistfully, admiringly, the old voice added, "It's snug in here, upon my word!"

"Yes, it's comfortable enough," agreed the boss, and he flipped *The Financial Times* with a paper knife. As a matter of fact he was proud of his room; he liked to have it admired, especially by old Woodifield. It gave him a feeling of deep, solid satisfaction to be planted there in the midst of it in full view of that frail old figure in the muffler.

"I've had it done up lately," he explained, as he had explained for the past—how many?—weeks. "New carpet," and he pointed to the bright red carpet with a pattern of large white rings. "New furniture," and he nodded towards the massive bookcase and the table with legs like twisted treacle. "Electric heating!" He waved almost exultantly towards the five transparent, pearly sausages glowing so softly in the tilted copper pan.

But he did not draw old Woodifield's attention to the photograph over the table of a grave-looking boy in uniform standing in one of those spectral photographers' parks with photographers' storm clouds behind him. It was not new. It had been there for over six years.

"There was something I wanted to tell you," said old Woodifield, and his eyes grew dim remembering. "Now what was it? I had it in mind when I started out this morning." His hands began to tremble, and patches of red showed above his beard.

Poor old chap, he's on his last pins, thought the boss. And, feeling kindly, he winked at the old man, and said jokingly, "I tell you what. I've got a little drop of something here that'll do you good before you go out into the cold again. It's beautiful stuff. It wouldn't hurt a child." He took a key off his watch-chain, unlocked a cupboard below his desk, and drew forth a dark, squat bottle. "That's the medicine," said he. "And the man from whom I got it told me on the strict Q.T. it came from the cellars at Windsor Castle."

Old Woodifield's mouth fell open at the sight. He couldn't have looked more surprised if the boss had produced a rabbit.

"It's whisky, ain't it?" he piped, feebly.

The boss turned the bottle and lovingly showed him the label. Whisky it was.

"D'you know," said he, peering up at the boss wonderingly, "they won't let me touch it at home." And he looked as though he was going to cry.

"Ah, that's where we know a bit more than the ladies," cried the boss, swooping across for two tumblers that stood on the table with the water bottle, and pouring a generous finger into each. "Drink it down. It'll do you good. And don't put any water with it. It's sacrilege to tamper with stuff like this. Ah!" He tossed off his, pulled out his handkerchief, hastily wiped his mustaches, and cocked an eye at old Woodifield, who was rolling his in his chaps.

The old man swallowed, was silent a moment, and then said faintly, "It's nutty!"

But it warmed him; it crept into his chill old brain—he remembered.

"That was it," he said, heaving himself out of his chair. "I thought you'd like to know. The girls were in Belgium last week having a look at poor Reggie's grave, and they happened to come across your boy's. They are quite near each other, it seems."

Old Woodifield paused, but the boss made no reply. Only a quiver of his eyelids showed that he heard.

"The girls were delighted with the way the place is kept," piped the old voice. "Beautifully looked after. Couldn't be better if they were at home. You've not been across, have yer?"

"No, no!" For various reasons the boss had not been across.

"There's miles of it," quavered old Woodifield, "and it's all as neat as a garden. Flowers growing on all the graves. Nice broad paths." It was plain from his voice how much he liked a nice broad path.

The pause came again. Then the old man brightened wonderfully.

"D'you know what the hotel made the girls pay for a pot of jam?" he piped. "Ten francs! Robbery, I call it. It was a little pot, so Gertrude says, no bigger than a half-crown. And she hadn't taken more than a spoonful when they charged her ten francs. Gertrude brought the pot away with her to teach 'em a lesson. Quite right, too; it's trading on our feelings. They think because we're over there having a look around we're ready to pay anything. That's what it is." And he turned towards the door.

"Quite right, quite right!" cried the boss, though what was quite right he hadn't the least idea. He came round by his desk, followed the shuffling footsteps to the door, and saw the old fellow out. Woodifield was gone.

For a long moment the boss stayed, staring at nothing, while the gray-haired office messenger, watching him, dodged in and out of his cubbyhole like a dog that expects to be taken for a run: "I'll see nobody for half an hour, Macey," said the boss. "Understand? Nobody at all."

"Very good, sir."

The door shut, the firm, heavy steps recrossed the bright carpet, the fat body plumped down in the spring chair, and leaning forward, the boss covered his face with his hands. He wanted, he intended, he had arranged to weep. . . .

It had been a terrible shock to him when old Woodifield sprang that remark upon him about the boy's grave. It was exactly as though the earth had opened and he had seen the boy lying there with Woodifield's girls staring down at him. For it was strange. Although over six years had passed away, the boss never thought of the boy except as lying unchanged, unblemished in his uniform, asleep for ever. "My son!" groaned the boss. But no tears came yet. In the past, in the first months and even years after the boy's death, he had only to say those words to be overcome by such grief that nothing short of a violent fit of weeping could relieve him. Time, he had declared then, he had told everybody, could make no difference. Other men perhaps might recover, might live their loss down, but not he. How was it possible? His boy was an only son. Ever since his birth the boss had worked at building up this business for him; it had no other meaning if it was not for the boy. Life itself had come to have no other meaning. How on earth could he have slaved, denied himself, kept going all these years without the promise for ever before him of the boy's stepping into his shoes and carrying on where he left off?

And that promise had been so near being fulfilled. The boy had been in the office learning the ropes for a year before the war. Every morning they had started off together; they had come back by the same train. And what congratulations he had received as the boy's father! No wonder; he had taken to it marvelously. As to his popularity with the staff, every man jack of them down to old Macey couldn't make enough of the boy. And he wasn't in the least spoiled. No, he was just his bright, natural self, with the right word for everybody, with that boyish look and his habit of saying, "Simply splendid!"

But all that was over and done with as though it never had been. The day had come when Macey had handed him the telegram that brought the whole place crashing about his head. "Deeply regret to inform you . . ." And he had left the office a broken man, with his life in ruins.

Six years ago, six years . . . How quickly time passed! It might have happened yesterday. The boss took his hands from his face; he was puzzled. Something seemed to be wrong with him. He wasn't feeling as he wanted to feel. He decided to get up and have a look at the boy's photograph. But it wasn't a favorite photograph of his; the expression was unnatural. It was cold, even stern-looking. The boy had never looked like that.

At that moment the boss noticed that a fly had fallen into his broad inkpot, and was trying feebly but desperately to clamber out again. Help! help! said those struggling legs. But the sides of the inkpot were wet and slippery; it fell back again and began to swim. The boss took up a pen, picked the fly out of the ink, and shook it on to a piece of blotting paper. For a fraction of a second it lay still on the dark patch that oozed round it. Then the front legs waved, took hold, and, pulling its small sodden body up it began the immense task of cleaning the ink from its wings. Over and under, over and under, went a leg along a wing, as the stone goes over and under the scythe. Then there was a pause, while the fly, seeming to stand on the tips of its toes, tried to expand first one wing and then the other. It succeeded at last, and, sitting down, it began, like a minute cat, to clean its face. Now one could imagine that the little front legs rubbed against each other lightly, joyfully. The horrible danger was over; it had escaped; it was ready for life again.

But just then the boss had an idea. He plunged his pen back into the ink, leaned his thick wrist on the blotting paper, and as the fly tried its wings down came a great heavy blot. What would it make of that? What indeed! The little beggar seemed absolutely cowed, stunned, and afraid to move because of what would happen next. But then, as if painfully, it dragged itself forward. The front legs waved, caught hold, and, more slowly this time, the task began from the beginning.

"He's a plucky little devil," thought the boss, and he felt a real admiration for the fly's courage. That was the way to tackle things; that was the right spirit. Never say die; it was only a question of . . . But the fly had again finished its laborious task, and the boss had just time to refill his pen, to shake fair and square on the new-cleaned body yet another dark drop. What about it this time? A painful moment of suspense followed. But behold, the front legs were again waving; the boss felt a rush of relief. He leaned over the fly and said to it tenderly, "You artful little b. . . ." And he actually had the brilliant notion of breathing on it to help the drying process. All the same, there was something timid and weak about its efforts now, and the boss decided that this time should be the last, as he dipped the pen into the inkpot.

It was. The last blot fell on the soaked blotting paper, and the draggled fly lay in it and did not stir. The back legs were stuck to the body; the front legs were not to be seen.

"Come on," said the boss. "Look sharp!" And he stirred it with his pen—in vain. Nothing happened or was likely to happen. The fly was dead.

The boss lifted the corpse on the end of the paper knife and flung it into the wastepaper basket, but such a grinding feeling of wretchedness seized him that he felt positively frightened. He started forward and pressed the bell for Macey.

"Bring me some fresh blotting paper," he said, sternly, "and look sharp about it." And while the old dog padded away he fell to wondering what it was he had been thinking about before. What was it? It was . . . He took out his handkerchief and passed it inside his collar. For the life of him he could not remember.

INTERPRETATION

1. Before attempting to define the theme of this story one should consider several preliminary questions. (a) It is obvious that the function of old Woodifield is to provide information—to serve as a device for exposition—and to focus attention on the problem of the boss's relation to the dead son. But other functions are served by the introduction of this character, functions which involve the very meaning of the story. What are they? (b) What purpose is served beyond the purpose of mere exposition by the cutback following Woodifield's departure? Is the main conflict of the story presented here? The boss has been accustomed to give way to

his grief, and has expected to give way to it now, but he cannot weep. Why? (*c*) It is obvious that the introduction of the incident of the fly is used to indicate the boss's distraction from his grief, from his intention to weep, but does the incident have a further function? Can the struggling fly be regarded as a symbol? If so, of what?

2. The boss had felt that time would never dull his grief. Relate this fact to the mention of new carpet and new furniture in the office, to the general atmosphere of well-being in the office of the firm, and to the boss's attitude of pity and patronage toward the broken old employee of the firm. The boss's interest in the fly's struggle to maintain its life, to survive somehow, and his final testing of the fly's strength, a test which kills the fly and leaves the boss confused and ashamed, is intended to tell the reader something about the boss's own situation. What is that "something"?

3. What, then, is the theme of the story? Does the end of the story simply mean that the boss has ceased to be sentimental? Has he gained something, or has he lost something at the end? Or has he done both?

4. In the analysis of the story "War," by Pirandello, the question is raised as to when the son of the patriotic father actually "dies"—dies, that is, for the father. Discuss the present story with the same consideration in mind.

SHERWOOD ANDERSON

I Want to Know Why

WE got up at four in the morning, that first day in the east. On the evening before we had climbed off a freight train at the edge of town, and with the true instinct of Kentucky boys had found our way across town and to the racetrack and the stables at once. Then we knew we were all right. Hanley Turner right away found a nigger we knew. It was Bildad Johnson who in the winter works at Ed Becker's livery barn in our home town, Beckersville. Bildad is a good cook as almost all our niggers are and of course he, like everyone in our part of Kentucky who is anyone at all, likes the horses. In the spring Bildad begins to scratch around. A nigger from our country can flatter and wheedle anyone into letting him do most anything he wants. Bildad wheedles the stable men and the trainers from the horse farms in our country around Lexington. The trainers come into town in the evening to stand around and talk and maybe get into a poker game. Bildad gets in with them. He is always doing little favors and telling about things to eat, chicken browned in a pan, and how is the best way to cook sweet potatoes and corn bread. It makes your mouth water to hear him.

When the racing season comes on and the horses go to the races and there is all the talk on the streets in the evenings about the new colts, and everyone says when they are going over to Lexington or to the spring meeting at Churchill Downs or to Latonia, and the horsemen that have been down to New Orleans or maybe at the winter meeting at Havana in Cuba come home to spend a week before they start out again, at such a time when everything talked about in Beckersville is just horses and nothing else and the outfits start out and horse racing is in every breath of air you breathe, Bildad shows up with a job as cook for some outfit. Often when I think about it, his always going all season to the races and working in the livery barn in the winter where horses are and where men like to come and talk about horses, I wish I was a nigger. It's a foolish thing to say, but that's the way I am about being around horses, just crazy. I can't help it.

Well, I must tell you about what we did and let you in on what I'm talking about. Four of us boys from Beckersville, all whites and sons of men who live in Beckersville regular, made up our minds we were going to the races, not just to Lexington or Louisville, I don't mean, but to the big eastern track we were always hearing our Beckersville men talk about, to Saratoga. We were all pretty young then. I was just turned fifteen and I was the oldest of the four. It was my scheme. I admit that and I talked the others into trying it. There was Hanley Turner and Henry Rieback and Tom Tumberton and myself. It had thirty-seven dollars I had earned during the winter working nights and Saturdays in Enoch Myer's grocery. Henry Rieback had eleven dollars and the others, Hanley and Tom, had only a dollar or two each. We fixed it all up and laid low until the Kentucky spring meetings were over and some of our men, the sportiest ones, the ones we envied the most, had cut out—then we cut out too.

I won't tell you the trouble we had beating our way on freights and all. We went through Cleveland and Buffalo and other cities and saw Niagara Falls. We bought things there, souvenirs and spoons and cards and shells with pictures of the Falls on them for our sisters and mothers, but thought we had better not send any of the things home. We didn't want to put the folks on our trail and maybe be nabbed.

We got into Saratoga as I said at night and went to the track. Bildad fed us up. He showed us a place to sleep in hay over a shed and promised to keep still. Niggers are all right about things like that. They won't squeal on you. Often a white man you might meet, when you had run away from home like that, might appear to be all right and give you a quarter or a half dollar or something, and then go right and give you away. White men will do that, but not a nigger. You can trust them. They are squarer with kids. I don't know why.

At the Saratoga meeting that year there were a lot of men from home. Dave Williams and Arthur Mulford and Jerry Myers and others. Then there was a lot from Louisville and Lexington Henry Rieback knew but I didn't. They were professional gamblers and Henry Rieback's father is one too. He is what is called a sheet writer and goes away most of the year to tracks. In the winter when he is home in Beckersville he don't stay there much but goes away to cities and deals faro. He is a nice man and generous, is always sending Henry presents, a bicycle and a gold watch and a boy scout suit of clothes and things like that.

My own father is a lawyer. He's all right, but don't make much money and can't buy me things and anyway I'm getting so old now I don't expect it. He never said nothing to me against Henry, but Hanley Turner and Tom Tumberton's fathers did. They said to their boys that money so come by is no good and they didn't want their boys brought up to hear gamblers' talk and be thinking about such things and maybe embrace them.

That's all right and I guess the men know what they are talking about, but I don't see what it's got to do with Henry or horses either. That's what I'm writing this story about. I'm puzzled. I'm getting to be a man and want to think straight and be O.K., and there's something I saw at the race meeting at the eastern track I can't figure out.

I can't help it, I'm crazy about thoroughbred horses. I've always been that way. When I was ten years old and saw I was growing to be big and couldn't be a rider I was so sorry I nearly died. Harry Hellinfinger in Beckersville, whose father is Postmaster, is grown up and too lazy to work, but likes to stand around in the street and get up jokes on boys like sending them to a hardware store for a gimlet to bore square holes and other jokes like that. He played one on me. He told me that if I would eat a half a cigar I would be stunted and not grow any more and maybe could be a rider. I did it. When father wasn't looking I took a cigar out of his pocket and gagged it down some way. It made me awful sick and the doctor had to be sent for, and then it did no good. I kept right on growing. It was a joke. When I told what I had done and why most fathers would have whipped me but mine didn't.

Well, I didn't get stunted and didn't die. It serves Harry Hellinfinger right. Then I made up my mind I would like to be a stable boy, but had to give that up too. Mostly niggers do that work and I knew father wouldn't let me go into it. No use to ask him.

If you've never been crazy about thoroughbreds it's because you've never been around where they are much and don't know any better. They're beautiful. There isn't anything so lovely and clean and full of spunk and honest and everything as some race horses. On the big horse farms that are all around our town Beckersville there are tracks and the horses run in the early morning. More than a thousand times I've got out of bed before daylight and walked two or three miles to the tracks. Mother wouldn't of let me go but father always says, "Let him alone." So I got some bread out of the bread box and some butter and jam, gobbled it and lit out.

At the tracks you sit on the fence with men, whites and niggers, and they chew tobacco and talk, and then the colts are brought out. It's early and the grass is covered with shiny dew and in another field a man is plowing and they are frying things in a shed where the track niggers sleep, and you know how a nigger can giggle and laugh and say things that make you laugh. A white man can't do it and some niggers can't but a track nigger can every time.

And so the colts are brought out and some are just galloped by stable boys, but almost every morning on a big track owned by a rich man who lives maybe in New York, there are always, nearly every morning, a few colts and some of the old race horses and geldings and mares that are cut loose.

It brings a lump up into my throat when a horse runs. I don't mean all horses but some. I can pick them nearly every time. It's in my blood like in the blood of race-track niggers and trainers. Even when they just go slop-jogging along with a little nigger on their backs I can tell a winner. If my throat hurts and it's hard for me to swallow, that's him. He'll run like Sam Hill when you let him out. If he don't win every time it'll be a wonder and because they've got him in a pocket behind another or he was pulled or got off bad at the post or something. If I wanted to be a gambler like Henry Rieback's father I could get rich. I know I could and Henry says so too. All I would have to do is to wait 'til that hurt comes when I see a horse and then bet every cent. That's what I would do if I wanted to be a gambler, but I don't.

When you're at the tracks in the morning—not the race tracks but the training tracks around Beckersville—you don't see a horse, the kind I've been talking about, very often, but it's nice anyway. Any thoroughbred, that is sired right and out of a good mare and trained by a man that knows how, can run. If he couldn't what would he be there for and not pulling a plow?

Well, out of the stables they come and the boys are on their backs and it's lovely to be there. You hunch down on top of the fence and itch inside you. Over in the sheds the niggers giggle and sing. Bacon is being fried and coffee made. Everything smells lovely. Nothing smells better than coffee and manure and horses and niggers and bacon frying and pipes being smoked out of doors on a morning like that. It just gets you, that's what it does.

But about Saratoga. We was there six days and not a soul from home seen us and everything came off just as we wanted it to, fine weather and horses and races and all. We beat our way home and Bildad gave us a basket with fried chicken and bread and other eatables in, and I had eighteen dollars when we got back to Beckersville. Mother jawed and cried but Pop didn't say much. I told everything we done except one thing. I did and saw that alone. That's what I'm writing about. It got me upset. I think about it at night. Here it is.

At Saratoga we laid up nights in the hay in the shed Bildad had showed us and ate with the niggers early and at night when the race people had all gone away. The men from home stayed mostly in the grandstand and betting field, and didn't come out around the places where the horses are kept except to the paddocks just before a race when the horses are saddled. At Saratoga they don't have paddocks under an open shed as at Lexington and Churchill Downs and other tracks down in our country, but saddle the horses right out in an open place under trees on a lawn as smooth and nice as Banker Bohon's front yard here in Beckersville. It's lovely. The horses are sweaty and nervous and shine and the men come out and smoke cigars and look at them and the trainers are there and the owners, and your heart thumps so you can hardly breathe.

Then the bugle blows for post and the boys that ride come running out with their silk clothes on and you run to get a place by the fence with the niggers.

I always am wanting to be a trainer or owner, and at the risk of being seen and caught and sent home I went to the paddocks before every race. The other boys didn't but I did.

We got to Saratoga on a Friday and on Wednesday the next week the big Mullford Handicap was to be run. Middlestride was in it and Sunstreak. The weather was fine and the track fast. I couldn't sleep the night before.

What had happened was that both these horses are the kind it makes my throat hurt to see. Middlestride is long and looks awkward and is a gelding. He belongs to Joe Thompson, a little owner from home who only has a half-dozen horses. The Mullford Handicap is for a mile and Middlestride can't untrack fast. He goes away slow and is always way back at the half, then he begins to run and if the race is a mile and a quarter he'll just eat up everything and get there.

Sunstreak is different. He is a stallion and nervous and belongs on the biggest farm we've got in our country, the Van Riddle place that belongs to Mr. Van Riddle of New York. Sunstreak is like a girl you think about sometimes but never see. He is hard all over and lovely too. When you look at his head you want to kiss him. He is trained by Jerry Tillford who knows me and has been good to me lots of times, lets me walk into a horse's stall to look at him close and other things. There isn't anything as sweet as that horse. He stands at the post quiet and not letting on, but he is just burning up inside. Then when the barrier goes up he is off like his name, Sunstreak. It makes you ache to see him. It hurts you. He just lays down and runs like a bird dog. There can't anything I ever see run like him except Middlestride when he gets untracked and stretches himself.

Gee! I ached to see that race and those two horses run, ached and dreaded it too. I didn't want to see either of our horses beaten. We had never sent a pair like that to the races before. Old men in Beckersville said so and the niggers said so. It was a fact.

Before the race I went over to the paddocks to see. I looked a last look at Middlestride, who isn't such a much standing in a paddock that way, then I went to see Sunstreak.

It was his day. I knew when I seen him. I forgot all about being seen myself and walked right up. All the men from Beckersville were there and no one noticed me except Jerry Tillford. He saw me and something happened. I'll tell you about that.

I was standing looking at that horse and aching. In some way, I can't tell how, I knew just how Sunstreak felt inside. He was quiet and letting the niggers rub his legs and Mr. Van Riddle himself put the saddle on, but he was just a raging torrent inside. He was like the water in the river at Niagara Falls just before it goes plunk down. That horse wasn't thinking about running. He don't have to think about that. He was just thinking about holding himself back 'til the time for the running came. I knew that. I could just in a way see right inside him. He was going to do some awful running and I knew it. He wasn't bragging or letting on much or prancing or making a fuss, but just waiting. I knew it and Jerry Tillford his trainer knew. I looked up and then that man and I looked into each other's eyes. Something happened to me. I guess I loved the man as much as I did the horse because he knew what I knew. Seemed to me there wasn't anything in the world but that man and the horse and me. I cried and Jerry Tillford had a shine in his eyes. Then I came away to the fence to wait for the race. The horse was better than me, more steadier, and now I know better than Jerry. He was the quietest and he had to do the running.

Sunstreak ran first of course and he busted the world's record for a mile. I've seen that if I never see anything more. Everything came out just as I expected. Middlestride got left at the post and was way back and closed up to be second, just as I knew he would. He'll get a world's record too some day. They can't skin the Beckersville country on horses.

I watched the race calm because I knew what would happen. I was sure. Hanley Turner and Henry Rieback and Tom Tumberton were all more excited than me.

A funny thing had happened to me. I was thinking about Jerry Tillford the trainer and how happy he was all through the race. I liked him that afternoon even more than I ever liked my own father. I almost forgot the horses thinking that way about him. It was because of what I had seen in his eyes as he stood in the paddocks beside Sunstreak before the race started. I knew he had been watching and working with Sunstreak since the horse was a baby colt, had taught him to run and be patient and when to let himself out and not to quit, never. I knew that for him it was like a mother seeing her child do something brave or wonderful. It was the first time I ever felt for a man like that.

After the race that night I cut out from Tom and Hanley and Henry. I wanted to be by myself and I wanted to be near Jerry Tillford if I could work it. Here is what happened.

The track in Saratoga is near the edge of town. It is all polished up and trees around, the evergreen kind, and grass and everything painted and nice. If you go past the track you get to a hard road made of asphalt for automobiles, and if you go along this for a few miles there is a road turns off to a little rummy-looking farmhouse set in a yard.

That night after the race I went along that road because I had seen Jerry and some other men go that way in an automobile. I didn't expect to find them. I walked for a ways and then sat down by a fence to think. It was the direction they went in. I wanted to be as near Jerry as I could. I felt close to him. Pretty soon I went up the side road—I don't know why— and came to the rummy farmhouse. I was just lonesome to see Jerry, like wanting to see your father at night when you are a young kid. Just then an automobile came along and turned in. Jerry was in it and Henry Rieback's father, and Arthur Bedford from home, and Dave Williams and two other men I didn't know. They got out of the car and went into the house, all but Henry Rieback's father who quarreled with them and said he wouldn't go. It was only about nine o'clock, but they were all drunk and the rummy-looking farmhouse was a place for bad women to stay in. That's what it was. I crept up along a fence and looked through a window and saw.

It's what give me the fantods. I can't make it out. The women in the house were all ugly mean-looking women, not nice to look at or be near. They were homely too, except one who was tall and looked a little like the gelding Middlestride, but not clean like him, but with a hard ugly mouth. She had red hair. I saw everything plain. I got up by an old rose-bush by an open window and looked. The women had on loose dresses and sat around in chairs. The men came in and some sat on the women's laps. The place smelled rotten and there was rotten talk, the kind a kid hears around a livery stable in a town like Beckersville in the winter but don't ever expect to hear talked when there are women around. It was rotten. A nigger wouldn't go into such a place.

I looked at Jerry Tillford. I've told you how I had been feeling about him on account of his knowing what was going on inside of Sunstreak in the minute before he went to the post for the race in which he made a world's record.

Jerry bragged in that bad-woman house as I know Sunstreak wouldn't never have bragged. He said that he made that horse, that it was him that won the race and made the record. He lied and bragged like a fool. I never heard such silly talk.

And then, what do you suppose he did! He looked at the woman in there, the one that was lean and hard-mouthed and looked a little like the gelding Middlestride, but not clean like him, and his eyes began to shine just as they did when he looked at me and at Sunstreak in the paddocks at the track in the afternoon. I stood there by the window—gee!—but I wished I hadn't gone away from the tracks, but had stayed with the boys and the niggers and the horses. The tall rotten-looking woman was between us just as Sunstreak was in the paddocks in the afternoon.

Then, all of a sudden, I began to hate that man. I wanted to scream and rush in the room and kill him. I never had such a feeling before. I was so mad clean through that I cried and my fists were doubled up so my finger-nails cut my hands.

And Jerry's eyes kept shining and he waved back and forth, and then he went and kissed that woman and I crept away and went back to the tracks and to bed and didn't sleep hardly any, and then next day I got the other kids to start home with me and never told them anything I seen.

I been thinking about it ever since. I can't make it out. Spring has come again and I'm nearly sixteen and go to the tracks mornings same as always, and I see Sunstreak and Middlestride and a new colt named Strident I'll bet will lay them all out, but no one thinks so but me and two or three niggers.

But things are different. At the tracks the air don't taste as good or smell as good. It's because a man like Jerry Tillford, who knows what he does, could see a horse like Sunstreak run, and kiss a woman like that the same day. I can't make it out. Darn him, what did he want to do like that for? I keep thinking about it and it spoils looking at horses and smelling things and hearing niggers laugh and everything. Sometimes I'm so mad about it I want to fight someone. It gives me the fantods. What did he do it for? I want to know why.

INTERPRETATION

This story, like "The Killers," by Hemingway, is a story of the "initiation." That is, the hero—a boy, as in "The Killers"—discovers something about the nature of evil, and tries to find some way of coming to terms with his discovery. Let us try to trace the stages by which the "discovery" is arrived at in the story.

The story is a first-person account of what happens to a boy who runs away to the races at Saratoga. But the boy has a special motive in telling the story. The incident which he narrates raises a problem which he finds difficult to cope with. He does not tell us this in so many words as he begins his account, but as the story develops we get hints as to the nature of the problem, long before it is specified at the climax. These hints are not merely important as a means of providing mechanical preparation for the problem. They do accomplish this, but they also, more importantly, accomplish three other things. First, they suggest the nature of the boy to whom the final incident comes with such impact. To some boys this incident would have been almost meaningless; therefore, the story must provide some dramatic probability for the effect on this particular boy. The boy in his first-person narration can give us the details of his experience, but he cannot tell us in so many words what he himself is like; that, too, must be conveyed by hints which the reader can interpret. Second, the hints, arising from many different circumstances, imply that the final problem is an all-pervasive one and is not to be associated merely with the incident at the climax. Three, the series of hints provides, structurally, the pattern for the telling of the story.

The boy starts off in boy fashion by trying to tell us something about himself, where he lives, how he likes horses, how he wishes he were a Negro so he could be around horses all the time, how Negroes are "squarer" with kids than white men are, how he can't understand how the father of his friend, Henry Rieback, is "a nice man and generous," even though he is a gambler. These details seem merely casual, but we suddenly discover that to the boy they are not casual. They have a bearing on his problem. "That's all right and I guess the men know what they are talking about," he says in commenting on the fact that some families don't want their sons to associate with Henry Rieback because his father is a gambler or don't permit them to hang around the horses because there is gambling at the tracks. But he goes on to say, "I don't see what it's got to do with Henry or with horses either. That's what I'm writing this story about. I'm puzzled. I'm getting to be a man and want to think straight and be O.K."

This pronouncement comes with a little dramatic shock after the apparently casual description of himself and of his home town. How do these details about Negroes and horses and Henry Rieback and gambling have a bearing on thinking straight and being O.K.? We see that the boy has begun to question some of the accepted values and codes of the society in which he lives. (Is the boy's attitude simply one of unthinking rebellion, or are his questions real questions?) He feels that the Negroes, who hold an inferior position in the community in which he lives, have certain points of superiority over the white people; the Negroes love the horses, while many of the white people see the horses only as something associated with the vice of gambling, and the Negroes are, in a sense, more honest, they are "squarer with kids." He feels that the community is unfair in condemning Henry Rieback's father, who, even though he is a gambler, is a "nice man and generous," and is even more unfair in condemning Henry simply because his father is not acceptable. And, furthermore, he feels that something is wrong with people who cannot love horses simply because gambling goes on at race tracks. All of this means that he is beginning to understand that ordinarily accepted standards of inferiority and superiority, of right and wrong, of good and bad, of ugliness and beauty, may really work out unjustly when they are applied by a sort of rule of thumb to particular cases. He is puzzled, because this private discovery is in contradiction to the things he has been taught. So he says: "I guess the men know what they are talking about, but I don't see what it's got to do with Henry or with horses either."

We see, at this point in the story, that the Negroes, the Rieback boy, and the horses are all involved in the problem which puzzles the boy. At first glance, it may seem strange that human beings and horses are bracketed together in his mind. But then the boy begins to develop more fully for us exactly what the horses mean to him. It is not merely the excitement of the race track which attracts him. It is something about the horses themselves. "They're beautiful," he says. And he continues: "There isn't anything so lovely and clean and full of spunk and honest and everything as some race horses." If we examine this sentence, we see that all of the qualities which he admires in the horses, except the first one, are qualities which are specifically human, which have to do with human character—cleanliness, courage, honesty, and "everything." He is reading the human traits into the horses, and he cannot understand why other people cannot see and admire those same traits just as he cannot see why other people cannot give credit to the Negro for being warm-hearted and square with kids or to Henry Rieback's father for being nice and generous.

From this point, which may be said to conclude the preparatory and expository part of the story, the narrative moves rather rapidly to the scene in which the boy finds Sunstreak and the trainer in the paddock. This scene sums up in dramatic form all that the boy has previously said about his feeling for horses. Again, his admiration for the horse is cast in terms which are essentially human. The horse doesn't brag. The horse is "better" than the boy, "steadier." It is implied that the horse is courageous, confident, and ready to do to the utmost what he has to do, but he will do it for nothing, win or lose.

The boy simply "knows" this as a sort of mystical revelation. Here is something which is fine and beautiful and which is beyond perplexing questions. The horse, for him, stands for all that is most valuable and admirable in life. Jerry Tillford, the boy feels, also knows this. In fact, at the moment, because Jerry Tillford does know it, the boy feels that Jerry shares these same qualities with the horse.

After the race has been won by Sunstreak, the boy feels impelled to stay as close to Jerry Tillford as possible. "I liked him that afternoon," the boy says, "even more than I ever liked my own father." In other words, because he has shared the mystical revelation with Jerry Tillford, he finds a tie which is even stronger than the tie of family affection. That evening, he follows Jerry, not even expecting to find him; he is filled with the exaltation which, he is sure, Jerry still shares with him. But in the scene at the "rummy farmhouse," he discovers another Jerry. This Jerry "lied and bragged like a fool," and we see the implied contrast to the horse, which is "honest" and does not "brag." We see another contrast. This scene is filthy and ugly and rotten, whereas the thoroughbreds had attracted the boy because they are "so lovely and clean and full of spunk." But these contrasts, we learn, are merely preliminary contrasts to the key contrast in the scene. Jerry approaches the woman who "looked a little like the gelding Middlestride, but not clean like him." The scene is set as a parallel to the scene in the paddock: "The tall rotten-looking woman was between us just as Sunstreak was in the paddocks in the afternoon." But now, facing the rotten-looking woman, Jerry's eyes have the same gleam which they had had in the afternoon when he had faced Sunstreak. The horror and disgust which the boy feels is emphasized by the very parallelism of the scenes.

The horror does not come from the fact that the boy discovers that evil exists in the world. He knows about bad women, he has heard rotten talk, he understands that there are good and bad people in the world. His discovery is that the good and evil can be so intimately allied—can exist in the same person. Jerry Tillford, who had been capable of sharing the exaltation which the boy felt in the paddock, is also capable of the experience in the rummy farmhouse. Indeed, Jerry enters fully into that world and is at home there.

This discovery, in a sense, is a surprise turn to the story. But we see that it has been prepared for in two ways: first in regard to the boy's psychology, and second, in regard to the structure of the story.

Although the discovery that moral definitions are complicated comes, in the special incident, as a shock to the boy, nevertheless he has been moving toward that discovery through his questioning of the easy, conventional definitions which society had given him. The boy has wanted to "think straight and be O.K." Though in Beckersville Negroes are social outcasts, he sees that they are in many ways superior human beings. Mr. Rieback, though a gambler, is a "nice" man, generous to his son. Though gambling may be an evil, the horses, which are gambled on, are "lovely and clean and full of spunk and honest." To sum up, there has been a logic in the boy's experience, though a logic of which he has been largely unaware. And this logic has provided the logic of the story.

How has the preparation been made in terms of the structure of the story?* We have already said that the series of things the boy wants "to know why" about provides a pattern for the telling of the story. We can now go further. The basic device used by the author to point up the contrast in the rummy farmhouse scene is the symbolism of the horse. Constantly, and for the boy unconsciously, the horse becomes a measure of human values. For the example, Sunstreak "is like a girl you think about sometimes but never see." The woman that Jerry meets in the farmhouse "looks" a little like the gelding Middlestride but not clean like him, and with a hard ugly mouth. (The phrase "hard mouth" works here perhaps in a double sense: a hard mouth, as applied to a human being, tells us something about character, and as applied to a horse, it tells us that the animal is refractory and stubborn, not like the trained thoroughbred. Furthermore, the fact that the woman is compared to a gelding may be significant: a gelding is sterile, and the "love" found in the rummy farmhouse is sterile, too.)

We have seen that the horse symbolism has pointed to the scene in the farmhouse, and has provided certain preparatory items in the course of the story. But what is the full meaning of this symbolism? To answer this question, however, we must take into consideration the last two paragraphs of the story, which follow the actual scene in the farmhouse.

The boy says that he still goes to the track, and enjoys being there, "but things are different." The incident in the farmhouse, now long past, continues to color his attitude and "spoils looking at horses and smelling things and hearing niggers laugh and everything" which he had once enjoyed. It spoils everything, he says, "because a man like Jerry Tillford, who knows what he does, could see a horse like Sunstreak run, and kiss a woman like that the same day." At first glance this seems to be merely a summary of the meaning of the scene in the farmhouse, but on closer inspection we may see that it adds a further interpretation of the scene. For example, the phrase, "who knows what he does," is important. What is the difference in moral terms between a horse and a man? The man is responsible, and the horse is not: the man "knows what he does."

The boy, we have seen, has taken the horse to be the very embodiment of the virtues which he admires most. But virtue is human. The finely bred race horse cannot do other than be "spunky," "honest," and "brave." He is bred that way. With man, however, virtue is a matter of knowledge and choice. A deed is not virtuous in itself; it is only virtuous in terms of a particular man's motivation and awareness. In other words, the horse (nature) is not capable of evil or of goodness, which depend upon human choice. This explains why nature—"looking at horses and smelling things," and the like—has been tainted for the boy. He can no longer lose himself in

* Naturally the items involved in the boy's psychological development are also involved in the structure of the story, but in so far as the items operate merely in terms of the boy's personal psychology, we may permissibly, as a matter of convenience, distinguish them from the others.

the things which merely seem good to him. The horse is no longer a satisfactory symbol for the things he admires.

But the symbol continues to have an ironical significance. Man, because he is capable of choice—because he "knows" what he does—because he is capable of being better than the brute, becomes, when he fails to exercise his capacity, something worse than the brute. We see this implied in the scene in the farmhouse, when the ugly, hard-mouthed woman is compared to Middlestride. A brute is always innocent, but man, because of his capacity for choice, is always either better or worse than the brute. This ironical use of the beast as a symbol is not a new one. We find it, for example, in Gulliver's adventures among the Houyhnhnms and Yahoos in Swift's *Gulliver's Travels.** The Houyhnhnms, the noble horses, which live clean, orderly, "reasonable" lives, are contrasted with filthy, degenerate "men," the Yahoos, who are far worse than beasts.

In the beginning of this analysis it was said that this story is, like Hemingway's "The Killers," the story of an "initiation." The boy discovers something about the nature of evil. Not that evil exists, for he had known for a long time that there are good and bad people—that is, he was acquainted with the ordinary conventional definitions. But he discovers that good and bad are very intimately wedded in the very nature of a man, and, perhaps more important still, that it is man's capacity for choice which makes good and evil meaningful.

Having said this, having extracted what may seem to be a moral "message," one should remind himself that the "message" is, as such, not the story. The story may be said to be the dramatization of the discovery. Now the message is something of which everyone is aware; it is a platitude. But the platitude ceases to be a platitude, it is revitalized and becomes meaningful again, when it is shown to be operating in terms of experience. It is revitalized if we accept its meaning for the boy.

It is obvious that in this story, which is related by a first-person narrator, Anderson has attempted to use a style which is appropriate to that narrator.

What does Anderson gain by this? To start with, we may ask if this boy could be just any boy? Certainly the kind of questions the boy asks cross the mind of any moderately intelligent and moderately decent boy, but here they appear with more than ordinary clarity and vividness. So the boy is, in that degree, special rather than ordinary. In other words, we have to assume a sensitivity. If the writer, however, should insist upon the special sensitivity, the reader might be inclined to resent the story, or at least to refuse it any very broad human application. To avoid this the writer takes the most subtle way of giving us the exposition of the boy's

---

* Swift's use of the horse symbol is much more complicated than is Anderson's, and it is certainly not to be understood that Anderson derives his symbol from that of Swift.

general personality: he lets the boy speak for himself. What the boy says and the way he says it both continuously define him. The questions he asks, as we have said, set him off, and the kind of observations he makes; but his instinctive description of the thoroughbreds as somehow an image of human virtue, and not merely an excuse for excitement, is even more revealing. Again, the boy's appreciation of natural beauty, the freshness of early morning at the training track or the grace and power of a running horse, help to present him to us. So much for what he says; but in the saying we notice a lyrical fluency of style which, appearing at the moments when he is speaking of what excites him, is very significant.

To sum up, we may say that Anderson's choice of the point of view makes it possible for him to give us a sense of the boy's special sensitivity without ever insisting on it. The point of view used here means that the style itself can work as exposition.

We have said that Anderson uses a style appropriate to his narrator, but at least two instances seem to be violations of this appropriateness. The first of these violations occurs in the first paragraph: ". . . and with the true instinct of Kentucky boys had found our way across town and to the racetrack and the stables at once." The second occurs in the sixth paragraph: ". . . and they didn't want their boys brought up to hear gamblers' talk and be thinking about such things and maybe embrace them." One of these instances seems to be a definite lapse from the dramatic appropriateness of the style; one cannot imagine a boy of this sort putting the matter this way. The other instance may be defended. Consider the two passages. What do you think?

THOMAS WOLFE

The Far and the Near

ON the outskirts of a little town upon a rise of land that swept back from the railway there was a tidy little cottage of white boards, trimmed vividly with green blinds. To one side of the house there was a garden neatly patterned with plots of growing vegetables, and an arbor for the grapes which ripened late in August. Before the house there were three mighty oaks which sheltered it in their clean and massive shade in summer, and to the other side there was a border of gay flowers. The whole place had an air of tidiness, thrift, and modest comfort.

Every day, a few minutes after two o'clock in the afternoon, the limited express between two cities passed this spot. At that moment the great train, having halted for a breathing-space at the town near by, was beginning to lengthen evenly into its stroke, but it had not yet reached the full drive of its terrific speed. It swung into view deliberately, swept past with a powerful swaying motion of the engine, a low smooth rumble of its heavy cars upon pressed steel, and then it vanished in the cut. For a moment the progress of the engine could be marked by heavy bellowing puffs of smoke that burst at spaced intervals above the edges of the meadow grass, and finally nothing could be heard but the solid clacking tempo of the wheels receding into the drowsy stillness of the afternoon.

Every day for more than twenty years, as the train had approached this house, the engineer had blown on the whistle, and every day, as soon as she heard this signal, a woman had appeared on the back porch of the little house and waved to him. At first she had a small child clinging to her skirts, and now this child had grown to full womanhood, and every day she, too, came with her mother to the porch and waved.

The engineer had grown old and gray in service. He had driven his great train, loaded with its weight of lives, across the land ten thousand times. His own children had grown up and married, and four times he had seen before him on the tracks the ghastly dot of tragedy converging like a cannon ball to its eclipse of horror at the boiler head—a light spring wagon filled with children, with its clustered row of small stunned faces; a cheap automobile stalled upon the tracks, set with the wooden figures of people paralyzed with fear; a battered hobo walking by the rail, too deaf and old to hear the whistle's warning; and a form flung past his window with a scream—all this the man had seen and known. He had known all the grief, the joy, the peril and the labor such a man could know; he had grown seamed and weathered in his loyal service, and now, schooled by the qualities of faith and courage and humbleness that attended his labor, he had grown old, and had the grandeur and the wisdom these men have.

But no matter what peril or tragedy he had known, the vision of the little house and the women waving to him with a brave free motion of the arm had become fixed in the mind of the engineer as something beautiful and enduring, something beyond all change and ruin, and something that would always be the same, no matter what mishap, grief or error might break the iron schedule of his days.

The sight of the little house and of these two women gave him the most extraordinary happiness he had ever known. He had seen them in a thousand lights, a hundred weathers. He had seen them through the harsh bare light of wintry gray across the brown and frosted stubble of the earth, and he had seen them again in the green luring sorcery of April.

He felt for them and for the little house in which they lived such tenderness as a man might feel for his own children, and at length the picture of their lives was carved so sharply in his heart that he felt that he knew their lives completely, to every hour and moment of the day, and he resolved that one day, when his years of service should be ended, he would go and find these people and speak at last with them whose lives had been so wrought into his own.

That day came. At last the engineer stepped from a train onto the station platform of the town where these two women lived. His years upon the rail had ended. He was a pensioned servant of his company, with no more work to do. The engineer walked slowly through the station and out into the streets of the town. Everything was as strange to him as if he had never seen this town before. As he walked on, his sense of bewilderment and confusion grew. Could this be the town he had passed ten thousand times? Were these the same houses he had seen so often from the high windows of his cab? It was all as unfamiliar, as disquieting as a city in a dream, and the perplexity of his spirit increased as he went on.

Presently the houses thinned into the straggling outposts of the town, and the street faded into a country road—the one on which the women lived. And the man plodded on slowly in the heat and dust. At length he stood before the house he sought. He knew at once that he had found the proper place. He saw the lordly oaks before the house, the flower beds, the garden and the arbor, and farther off, the glint of rails.

Yes, this was the house he sought, the place he had passed so many times, the destination he had longed for with such happiness. But now that he had found it, now that he was here, why did his hand falter on the gate; why had the town, the road, the earth, the very entrance to this place he loved turned unfamiliar as the landscape of some ugly dreams? Why did he now feel this sense of confusion, doubt, and hopelessness?

At length he entered by the gate, walked slowly up the path and in a moment more had mounted three short steps that led up to the porch, and was knocking at the door. Presently he heard steps in the hall, the door was opened, and a woman stood facing him.

And instantly, with a sense of bitter loss and grief, he was sorry he had come. He knew at once that the woman who stood there looking at him with a mistrustful eye was the same woman who had waved to him so many thousand times. But her face was harsh and pinched and meager; the flesh sagged wearily in sallow folds, and the small eyes peered at him with timid suspicion and uneasy doubt. All the brave freedom, the warmth and the affection that he had read into her gesture, vanished in the moment that he saw her and heard her unfriendly tongue.

And now his own voice sounded unreal and ghastly to him as he tried to explain his presence, to tell her who he was and the reason he had come. But he faltered on, fighting stubbornly against the horror of regret, confusion, disbelief that surged up in his spirit, drowning all his former joy and making his act of hope and tenderness seem shameful to him.

At length the woman invited him almost unwillingly into the house, and called her daughter in a harsh shrill voice. Then, for a brief agony of time, the man sat in an ugly little parlor, and he tried to talk while the two women stared at him with a dull, bewildered hostility, a sullen, timorous restraint.

And finally, stammering a crude farewell, he departed. He walked away down the path and then along the road toward town, and suddenly he knew that he was an old man. His heart, which had been brave and confident when it looked along the familiar vista of the rails, was now sick with doubt and horror as it saw the strange and unsuspected visage of an earth which had always been within a stone's throw of him, and which he had never seen or known. And he knew that all the magic of that bright lost way, the vista of that shining line, the imagined corner of that small good universe of hope's desire, was gone forever, could never be got back again.

INTERPRETATION

Here is a story dealing with dream and reality, or expectation and fulfillment. What has the engineer expected? What, in other words, has been the significance of the relationship with the occupants of the house he has daily passed? Or can it be said that the story is, if we take it from the point of view of the people in the house, about a yearning people have for communion which some fear or diffidence prevents their gratifying—a story, then, about isolation and loneliness? Try to develop your own statement for the theme of the story, and then write an essay to justify your interpretation.

WILLIAM FAULKNER

A Rose for Emily

I

WHEN Miss Emily Grierson died, our whole town went to her funeral: the men through a sort of respectful affection for a fallen monument, the women mostly out of curiosity to see the inside of her house, which no one save an old manservant—a combined gardener and cook—had seen in at least ten years.

It was a big, squarish frame house that had once been white, decorated with cupolas and spires and scrolled balconies in the heavily lightsome style of the seventies, set on what had once been our most select street. But garages and cotton gins had encroached and obliterated even the august names of that neighborhood; only Miss Emily's house was left, lifting its stubborn and coquettish decay above the cotton wagons and the gasoline pumps—an eyesore among eyesores. And now Miss Emily had gone to join the representatives of those august names where they lay in the cedar-bemused cemetery among the ranked and anonymous graves of Union and Confederate soldiers who fell at the battle of Jefferson.

Alive, Miss Emily had been a tradition, a duty, and a care; a sort of hereditary obligation upon the town, dating from that day in 1894 when Colonel Sartoris, the mayor—he who fathered the edict that no Negro woman should appear on the streets without an apron—remitted her taxes, the dispensation dating from the death of her father on into perpetuity. Not that Miss Emily would have accepted charity. Colonel Sartoris invented an involved tale to the effect that Miss Emily's father had loaned money to the town, which the town, as a matter of business, preferred this way of repaying. Only a man of Colonel Sartoris' generation and thought could have invented it, and only a woman could have believed it.

When the next generation, with its more modern ideas, became mayors and aldermen, this arrangement created some little dissatisfaction. On the first of the year they mailed her a tax notice. February came, and there was no reply. They wrote her a formal letter, asking her to call at the sheriff's office at her convenience. A week later the mayor wrote her himself, offering to call or to send his car for her, and received in reply a note on paper of an archaic shape, in a thin, flowing calligraphy in faded ink, to the effect that she no longer went out at all. The tax notice was also enclosed, without comment.

They called a special meeting of the Board of Aldermen. A deputation waited upon her, knocked at the door through which no visitor had passed since she ceased giving china-painting lessons eight or ten years earlier. They were admitted by the old Negro into a dim hall from which a stairway mounted into still more shadow. It smelled of dust and disuse—a close, dank smell. The Negro led them into the parlor. It was furnished in heavy, leather-covered furniture. When the Negro opened the blinds of one window, a faint dust rose sluggishly about their thighs, spinning with slow motes in the single sun-ray. On a tarnished gilt easel before the fireplace stood a crayon portrait of Miss Emily's father.

They rose when she entered—a small, fat woman in black, with a thin gold chain descending to her waist and vanishing into her belt, leaning on an ebony cane with a tarnished gold head. Her skeleton was small and spare; perhaps that was why what would have been merely plumpness in another was obesity in her. She looked bloated, like a body long submerged in motionless water, and of that pallid hue. Her eyes, lost in the fatty ridges of her face, looked like two small pieces of coal pressed into a lump of dough as they moved from one face to another while the visitors stated their errand.

She did not ask them to sit. She just stood in the door and listened quietly until the spokesman came to a stumbling halt. Then they could hear the invisible watch ticking at the end of the gold chain.

Her voice was dry and cold. "I have no taxes in Jefferson. Colonel Sartoris explained it to me. Perhaps one of you can gain access to the city records and satisfy yourselves."

"But we have. We are the city authorities, Miss Emily. Didn't you get a notice from the sheriff, signed by him?"

"I received a paper, yes," Miss Emily said. "Perhaps he considers himself the sheriff. . . . I have no taxes in Jefferson."

"But there is nothing on the books to show that, you see. We must go by the—"

"See Colonel Sartoris. I have no taxes in Jefferson."

"But, Miss Emily—"

"See Colonel Sartoris." (Colonel Sartoris had been dead almost ten years.) "I have no taxes in Jefferson. Tobe!" The Negro appeared. "Show these gentlemen out."

II

So she vanquished them, horse and foot, just as she had vanquished their fathers thirty years before about the smell. That was two years after her father's death and a short time after her sweetheart—the one we believed would marry her—had deserted her. After her father's death she went out very little; after her sweetheart went away, people hardly saw her at all. A few of the ladies had the temerity to call, but were not received, and the only sign of life about the place was the Negro man—a young man then— going in and out with a market basket.

"Just as if a man—any man—could keep a kitchen properly," the ladies said; so they were not surprised when the smell developed. It was another link between the gross, teeming world and the high and mighty Griersons.

A neighbor, a woman, complained to the mayor, Judge Stevens, eighty years old.

"But what will you have me do about it, madam?" he said.

"Why, send her word to stop it," the woman said. "Isn't there a law?"

"I'm sure that won't be necessary," Judge Stevens said. "It's probably just a snake or a rat that nigger of hers killed in the yard. I'll speak to him about it."

The next day he received two more complaints, one from a man who came in diffident deprecation. "We really must do something about it, Judge. I'd be the last one in the world to bother Miss Emily, but we've got to do something." That night the Board of Aldermen met—three gray-beards and one younger man, a member of the rising generation.

"It's simple enough," he said. "Send her word to have her place cleaned up. Give her a certain time to do it in, and if she don't . . ."

"Dammit, sir," Judge Stevens said, "will you accuse a lady to her face of smelling bad?"

So the next night, after midnight, four men crossed Miss Emily's lawn and slunk about the house like burglars, sniffing along the base of the brickwork and at the cellar openings while one of them performed a regular sowing motion with his hand out of a sack slung from his shoulder. They broke open the cellar door and sprinkled lime there, and in all the out-buildings. As they recrossed the lawn, a window that had been dark was lighted and Miss Emily sat in it, the light behind her, and her upright torso motionless as that of an idol. They crept quietly across the lawn and into the shadow of the locusts that lined the street. After a week or two the smell went away.

That was when people had begun to feel really sorry for her. People in our town, remembering how old lady Wyatt, her great-aunt, had gone completely crazy at last, believed that the Griersons held themselves a little too high for what they really were. None of the young men were quite good enough for Miss Emily and such. We had long thought of them as a tableau; Miss Emily a slender figure in white in the background, her father a spraddled silhouette in the foreground, his back to her and clutch-ing a horsewhip, the two of them framed by the back-flung front door. So when she got to be thirty and was still single, we were not pleased exactly, but vindicated; even with insanity in the family she wouldn't have turned down all of her chances if they had really materialized.

When her father died, it got about that the house was all that was left to her; and in a way, people were glad. At last they could pity Miss Emily. Being left alone, and a pauper, she had become humanized. Now she too would know the old thrill and the old despair of a penny more or less.

The day after his death all the ladies prepared to call at the house and offer condolence and aid, as is our custom. Miss Emily met them at the door, dressed as usual and with no trace of grief on her face. She told them that her father was not dead. She did that for three days, with the ministers calling on her, and the doctors, trying to persuade her to let them dispose of the body. Just as they were about to resort to law and force, she broke down, and they buried her father quickly.

We did not say she was crazy then. We believed she had to do that. We remembered all the young men her father had driven away, and we knew that with nothing left, she would have to cling to that which had robbed her, as people will.

III

She was sick for a long time. When we saw here again, her hair was cut short, making her look like a girl, with a vague resemblance to those angels in colored church windows—sort of tragic and serene.

The town had just let the contracts for paving the sidewalks, and in the summer after her father's death they began to work. The construction company came with niggers and mules and machinery, and a foreman named Homer Barron, a Yankee—a big, dark, ready man, with a big voice and eyes lighter than his face. The little boys would follow in groups to hear him cuss the niggers, and the niggers singing in time to the rise and fall of picks. Pretty soon he knew everybody in town. Whenever you heard a lot of laughing anywhere about the square, Homer Barron would be in the center of the group. Presently we began to see him and Miss Emily on Sunday afternoons driving in the yellow-wheeled buggy and the matched team of bays from the livery stable.

At first we were glad that Miss Emily would have an interest, because the ladies all said, "Of course a Grierson would not think seriously of a Northerner, a day laborer." But there were still others, older people, who said that even grief could not cause a real lady to forget *noblesse oblige*—without calling it *noblesse oblige*. They just said, "Poor Emily. Her kinsfolk should come to her." She had some kin in Alabama; but years ago her father had fallen out with them over the estate of old lady Wyatt, the crazy woman, and there was no communication between the two families. They had not even been represented at the funeral.

And as soon as the old people said, "Poor Emily," the whispering began. "Do you suppose it's really so?" they said to one another. "Of course it is. What else could . . ." This behind their hands; rustling of craned silk and satin behind jalousies closed upon the sun of Sunday afternoon as the thin, swift clop-clop-clop of the matched team passed: "Poor Emily."

She carried her head high enough—even when we believed that she was fallen. It was as if she demanded more than ever the recognition of her dignity as the last Grierson; as if it had wanted that touch of earthiness to reaffirm her imperviousness. Like when she bought the rat poison, the arsenic. That was over a year after they had begun to say "Poor Emily," and while the two female cousins were visiting her.

"I want some poison," she said to the druggist. She was over thirty then, still a slight woman, though thinner than usual, with cold, haughty black eyes in a face the flesh of which was strained across the temples and about the eyesockets as you imagine a lighthouse-keeper's face ought to look. "I want some poison," she said.

"Yes, Miss Emily. What kind? For rats and such? I'd recom—"

"I want the best you have. I don't care what kind."

The druggist named several. "They'll kill anything up to an elephant. But what you want is—"

"Arsenic," Miss Emily said. "Is that a good one?"

"Is . . . arsenic? Yes ma'am. But what you want—"

"I want arsenic."

The druggist looked down at her. She looked back at him, erect, her face like a strained flag. "Why, of course," the druggist said. "If that's what you want. But the law requires you to tell what you are going to use it for."

Miss Emily just stared at him, her head tilted back in order to look him eye for eye, until he looked away and went and got the arsenic and wrapped it up. The Negro delivery boy brought her the package; the druggist didn't come back. When she opened the package at home there was written on the box, under the skull and bones: "For rats."

IV

So the next day we all said, "She will kill herself"; and we said it would be the best thing. When she had first begun to be seen with Homer Barron, we had said, "She will marry him." Then we said, "She will persuade him yet," because Homer himself had remarked—he liked men, and it was known that he drank with the younger men in the Elk's Club—that he was not a marrying man. Later we said, "Poor Emily," behind the jalousies as they passed on Sunday afternoon in the glittering buggy, Miss Emily with her head high and Homer Barron with his hat cocked and a cigar in his teeth, reins and whip in a yellow glove.

Then some of the ladies began to say that it was a disgrace to the town and a bad example to the young people. The men did not want to interfere, but at last the ladies forced the Baptist minister—Miss Emily's people were Episcopal—to call upon her. He would never divulge what happened during that interview, but he refused to go back again. The next Sunday they again drove about the streets, and the following day the minister's wife wrote to Miss Emily's relations in Alabama.

So she had blood-kin under her roof again and we sat back to watch developments. At first nothing happened. Then we were sure that they were to be married. We learned that Miss Emily had been to the jeweler's and ordered a man's toilet set in silver, with the letters H.B. on each piece. Two days later we learned that she had bought a complete outfit of men's clothing, including a nightshirt, and we said, "They are married." We were really glad. We were glad because the two female cousins were even more Grierson than Miss Emily had ever been.

So we were not surprised when Homer Barron—the streets had been finished some time since—was gone. We were a little disappointed that there was not a public blowing-off, but we believed that he had gone on to prepare for Miss Emily's coming, or to give her a chance to get rid of the cousins. (By that time it was a cabal, and we were all Miss Emily's allies to help circumvent the cousins.) Sure enough, after another week they departed. And, as we had expected all along, within three days Homer Barron was back in town. A neighbor saw the Negro man admit him at the kitchen door at dusk one evening.

And that was the last we saw of Homer Barron. And of Miss Emily for some time. The Negro man went in and out with the market basket, but the front door remained closed. Now and then we would see her at a window for a moment, as the men did that night when they sprinkled the lime, but for almost six months she did not appear on the streets. Then we knew that this was to be expected too; as if that quality of her father which had thwarted her woman's life so many times had been too virulent and too furious to die.

When we next saw Miss Emily, she had grown fat and her hair was turning gray. During the next few years it grew grayer and grayer until it attained an even pepper-and-salt iron-gray, when it ceased turning. Up to the day of her death at seventy-four it was still that vigorous iron-gray, like the hair of an active man.

From that time on her front door remained closed, save for a period of six or seven years, when she was about forty, during which she gave lessons in china-painting. She fitted up a studio in one of the downstairs rooms, where the daughters and granddaughters of Colonel Sartoris' contemporaries were sent to her with the same regularity and in the same spirit that they were sent on Sundays with a twenty-five cent piece for the collection plate. Meanwhile her taxes had been remitted.

Then the newer generation became the backbone and the spirit of the town, and the painting pupils grew up and fell away and did not send their children to her with boxes of color and tedious brushes and pictures cut from the ladies' magazines. The front door closed upon the last one and remained closed for good. When the town got free postal delivery Miss Emily alone refused to let them fasten the metal numbers above her door and attach a mailbox to it. She would not listen to them.

Daily, monthly, yearly we watched the Negro grow grayer and more stooped, going in and out with the market basket. Each December we sent her a tax notice, which would be returned by the post office a week later, unclaimed. Now and then we would see her in one of the downstairs windows—she had evidently shut up the top floor of the house—like the carven torso of an idol in a niche, looking or not looking at us, we could never tell which. Thus she passed from generation to generation—dear, inescapable, impervious, tranquil, and perverse.

And so she died. Fell ill in the house filled with dust and shadows, with only a doddering Negro man to wait on her. We did not even know she was sick; we had long since given up trying to get any information from the Negro. He talked to no one, probably not even to her, for his voice had grown harsh and rusty, as if from disuse.

She died in one of the downstairs rooms, in a heavy walnut bed with a curtain, her gray head propped on a pillow yellow and moldy with age and lack of sunlight.

V

The Negro met the first of the ladies at the front door and let them in, with their hushed, sibilant voices and their quick, curious glances, and then he disappeared. He walked right through the house and out the back and was not seen again.

The two female cousins came at once. They held the funeral on the second day, with the town coming to look at Miss Emily beneath a mass of bought flowers, with the crayon face of her father musing profoundly above the bier and the ladies sibilant and macabre; and the very old men—some in their brushed Confederate uniforms—on the porch and the lawn, talking of Miss Emily as if she had been a contemporary of theirs, believing that they had danced with her and courted her perhaps, confusing time with its mathematical progression, as the old do, to whom all the past is not a diminishing road, but, instead, a huge meadow which no winter ever quite touches, divided from them now by the narrow bottleneck of the most recent decade of years.

Already we knew that there was one room in that region above stairs which no one had seen in forty years, and which would have to be forced. They waited until Miss Emily was decently in the ground before they opened it.

The violence of breaking down the door seemed to fill this room with pervading dust. A thin, acrid pall as of the tomb seemed to lie everywhere upon this room decked and furnished as for a bridal: upon the valance curtains of faded rose color, upon the rose-shaded lights, upon the dressing table, upon the delicate array of crystal and the man's toilet things backed with tarnished silver, silver so tarnished that the monogram was obscured. Among them lay a collar and tie, as if they had just been removed, which, lifted, left upon the surface a pale crescent in the dust. Upon a chair hung the suit, carefully folded; beneath it the two mute shoes and the discarded socks.

The man himself lay in the bed.

For a long while we just stood there, looking down at the profound and fleshless grin. The body had apparently once lain in the attitude of an embrace, but now the long sleep that outlasts love, that conquers even the grimace of love, had cuckolded him. What was left of him, rotted beneath what was left of the nightshirt, had become inextricable from the bed in which he lay; and upon him and upon the pillow beside him lay that even coating of the patient and biding dust.

Then we noticed that in the second pillow was the indentation of a head. One of us lifted something from it, and leaning forward, that faint and invisible dust dry and acrid in the nostrils, we saw a long strand of iron-gray hair.

INTERPRETATION

This is a story of horror. We have a decaying mansion in which the protagonist, shut away from the world, grows into something monstrous, and becomes as divorced from the human as some fungus growing in the dark on a damp wall. Miss Emily Grierson remains in voluntary isolation (or perhaps fettered by some inner compulsion) away from the bustle and dust and sunshine of the human world of normal affairs, and what in the end is found in the upstairs room gives perhaps a sense of penetrating and gruesome horror.

Has this sense of horror been conjured up for its own sake? If not, then why has the author contrived to insert so much of the monstrous into the story? In other words, does the horror contribute to the theme of Faulkner's story? Is the horror meaningful?

In order to answer this question, we shall have to examine rather carefully some of the items earlier in the story. In the first place, why does Miss Emily commit her monstrous act? Is she supplied with a proper motivation? Faulkner has, we can see, been rather careful to prepare for his dénouement. Miss Emily, it becomes obvious fairly early in the story, is one of those persons for whom the distinction between reality and illusion has blurred out. For example, she refuses to admit that she owes any taxes. When the mayor protests, she does not recognize him as mayor. Instead, she refers the committee to Colonel Sartoris, who, as the reader is told, has been dead for nearly ten years. For Miss Emily, apparently, Colonel Sartoris is still alive. Most specific preparation of all, when her father dies, she denies to the townspeople for three days that he is dead: "Just as they were about to resort to law and force, she broke down, and they buried her father quickly."

Miss Emily is obviously a pathological case. The narrator indicates plainly enough that people felt that she was crazy. All of this explanation prepares us for what Miss Emily does in order to hold her lover—the dead lover is in one sense still alive for her—the realms of reality and appearance merge. But having said this, we have got no nearer to justifying the story: for, if Faulkner is merely interested in relating a case history of abnormal psychology, the story lacks meaning and justification as a story and we are back to fiction as "clinical report" which we spoke of in connection with "The Occurrence at Owl Creek Bridge" (p. 103). If the story is to be justified, there must be what may be called a moral significance, a meaning in moral terms—not merely psychological terms.

Incidentally, it is very easy to misread the story as merely a horrible case history, presented in order to titillate the reader. Faulkner has been frequently judged to be doing nothing more than this in his work.

The lapse of the distinction between illusion and reality, between life and death, is important, therefore, in helping to account for Miss Emily's motivation, but merely to note this lapse is not fully to account for the theme of the story.

Suppose we approach the motivation again in these terms: what is

Miss Emily like? What are the mainsprings of her character? What causes the distinction between illusion and reality to blur out for her? She is obviously a woman of tremendous firmness of will. In the matter of the taxes, crazed though she is, she is never at a loss. She is utterly composed. She dominates the rather frightened committee of officers who see her. In the matter of her purchase of the poison, she completely overawes the clerk. She makes no pretense. She refuses to tell him what she wants the poison for. And yet this firmness of will and this iron pride have not kept her from being thwarted and hurt. Her father has run off the young men who came to call upon her, and for the man who tells the story, Miss Emily and her father form a tableau: "Miss Emily a slender figure in white in the background, her father a spraddled silhouette in the foreground, his back to her and clutching a horsewhip, the two of them framed by the back-flung front door." Whether the picture is a remembered scene, or merely a symbolical construct, this is the picture which remains in the storyteller's mind.

We have indicated that her pride is connected with her contempt for public opinion. This comes to the fore, of course, when she rides around about the town with the foreman whom everybody believes is beneath her. And it is her proud refusal to admit an external set of codes, or conventions, or other wills which contradict her own will, which makes her capable at the end of keeping her lover from going away. Confronted with his jilting her, she tries to override not only his will and the opinion of other people, but the laws of death and decay themselves.

But this, still, hardly gives the meaning of the story. For in all that has been said thus far, we are still merely accounting for a psychological aberration—we are still merely dealing with a case history in abnormal psychology. In order to make a case for the story as "meaningful," we shall have to tie Miss Emily's thoughts and actions back into the normal life of the community, and establish some sort of relationship between them. And just here one pervasive element in the narration suggests a clue. The story is told by one of the townspeople. And in it, as a constant factor, is the reference to what the community thought of Miss Emily. Continually through the story is it what "we" said, and then what "we" did, and what seemed true to "us," and so on. The narrator puts the matter even more sharply still. He says, in the course of the story, that to the community Miss Emily seemed "dear, inescapable, impervious, tranquil, and perverse." Each of the adjectives is important and meaningful. In a sense, Miss Emily because of her very fact of isolation and perversity belongs to the whole community. She is even something treasured by it. Ironically, because of Emily's perversion of an aristocratic independence of mores and because of her contempt for "what people say," her life is public, even communal. And various phrases used by the narrator underline this view of her position. For example, her face looks "as you imagine a lighthouse-keeper's face ought to look," like the face of a person who lives in the kind of isolation imposed on a lighthouse-keeper, who looks out into the blackness and whose light serves a public function. Or, again, after her father's death, she becomes very ill, and when she appears after the illness, she has "a vague resemblance to those angels in colored church windows—sort of tragic and serene." Whatever we make of these descriptions, certainly the author is trying to suggest a kind of calm and dignity which is super-mundane, unearthly, or "over-earthly," such as an angel might possess.

Miss Emily, then, is a combination of idol and scapegoat for the community. On the one hand, the community feels admiration for Miss Emily —she represents something in the past of the community which the community is proud of. They feel a sort of awe of her, as is illustrated by the behavior of the mayor and the committee in her presence. On the other hand, her queerness, the fact that she cannot compete with them in their ordinary life, the fact that she is hopelessly out of touch with the modern world—all of these things make them feel superior to her, and also to that past which she represents. It is, then, Miss Emily's complete detachment which gives her actions their special meaning for the community.

Miss Emily, since she is the conscious aristocrat, since she is consciously "better" than other people, since she is above and outside their canons of behavior, can, at the same time, be worse than other people; and she *is* worse, horribly so. She is worse than other people, but at the same time, as the narrator implies, she remains somehow admirable. This raises a fundamental question: why is this true?

Perhaps the horrible and the admirable aspects of Miss Emily's final deed arise from the same basic fact of her character: she insists on meeting the world on her own terms. She never cringes, she never begs for sympathy, she refuses to shrink into an amiable old maid, she never accepts the community's ordinary judgments or values. This independence of spirit and pride can, and does in her case, twist the individual into a sort of monster, but, at the same time, this refusal to accept the herd values carries with it a dignity and courage. The community senses this, as we gather from the fact that the community carries out the decencies of the funeral before breaking in the door of the upper room. There is, as it were, a kind of secret understanding that she has won her right of privacy, until she herself has entered history. Furthermore, despite the fact that, as the narrator says, "already we knew that there was one room in that region above stairs which no one had seen in forty years, and which would have to be forced," her funeral is something of a state occasion, with "the very old men—some in their brushed Confederate uniforms—on the porch and the lawn, talking of Miss Emily as if she had been a contemporary of theirs, believing that they had danced with her and courted her perhaps . . ." In other words, the community accepts her into its honored history. All of this works as a kind of tacit recognition of Miss Emily's triumph of will.

The community, we are told earlier, had wanted to pity Miss Emily when she had lost her money, just as they had wanted to commiserate over her when they believed that she had actually become a fallen woman, but she had triumphed over their pity and commiseration and condemnation, just as she had triumphed over all their other attitudes.

But, as we have indicated earlier, it may be said that Miss Emily is mad. This may be true, but there are two things to consider in this connection. First, one must consider the special terms which her "madness" takes. Her madness is simply a development of her pride and her refusal to submit to ordinary standards of behavior. So, because of this fact, her "madness" is meaningful after all. It involves issues which in themselves are really important and have to do with the world of conscious moral choice. Second, the community interprets her "madness" as meaningful. They admire her, even if they are disappointed by her refusals to let herself be pitied, and the narrator, who is a spokesman for the community, recognizes the last grim revelation as an instance of her having carried her own values to their ultimate conclusion. She would marry the common laborer, Homer Barron, let the community think what it would. She would not be jilted. And she would hold him as a lover. But it would all be on her own terms. She remains completely dominant, and contemptuous of the day-to-day world.

It has been suggested by many critics that tragedy implies a hero who is completely himself, who insists on meeting the world on his own terms, who wants something so intensely, or lives so intensely, that he cannot accept any compromise. It cannot be maintained that this story is comparable to any of the great tragedies, such as *Hamlet* or *King Lear*, but it can be pointed out that this story, in its own way, involves some of the same basic elements. Certainly, Miss Emily's pride, isolation, and independence remind one of factors in the character of the typical tragic hero. And it can be pointed out that, just as the horror of her deed lies outside the ordinary life of the community, so the magnificence of her independence lies outside its ordinary virtues.

1. What difficulties would be raised if one should try to tell this story from the point of view of the third person?

2. Why is it significant that Miss Emily chooses for her lover a man who is scornfully regarded by the community as a "Northerner, a day laborer"?

3. Look back at "The Lottery" and "The Killers" in the light of their general symbolic significance. Can it be argued that the present story, like them, has a more general significance—that it is a symbolic commentary on our society?

FLANNERY O'CONNOR

A Good Man Is Hard to Find

THE grandmother didn't want to go to Florida. She wanted to visit some of her connections in east Tennessee and she was seizing at every chance to change Bailey's mind. Bailey was the son she lived with, her only boy. He was sitting on the edge of his chair at the table, bent over the orange sports section of the *Journal*. "Now look here, Bailey," she said, "see here, read this," and she stood with one hand on her thin hip and the other rattling the newspaper at his bald head. "Here this fellow that calls himself The Misfit is aloose from the Federal Pen and headed toward Florida and you read what it says he did to these people. Just you read it. I wouldn't take my children in any direction with a criminal like that aloose in it. I couldn't answer to my conscience if I did."

Bailey didn't look up from his reading so she wheeled around then and faced the children's mother, a young woman in slacks, whose face was as broad and innocent as a cabbage and was tied around with a green headkerchief that had two points on the top like rabbit's ears. She was sitting on the sofa, feeding the baby his apricots out of a jar. "The children have been to Florida before," the old lady said. "You all ought to take them somewhere else for a change so they would see different parts of the world and be broad. They never have been to east Tennessee."

The children's mother didn't seem to hear her but the eight-year-old boy, John Wesley, a stocky child with glasses, said, "If you don't want to go to Florida, why dontcha stay at home?" He and the little girl, June Star, were reading the funny papers on the floor.

"She wouldn't stay at home to be queen for a day," June Star said without raising her yellow head.

"Yes, and what would you do if this fellow, The Misfit, caught you?" the grandmother asked.

"I'd smack his face," John Wesley said.

"She wouldn't stay at home for a million bucks," June Star said. "Afraid she'd miss something. She has to go everywhere we go."

"All right, Miss," the grandmother said. "Just remember that the next time you want me to curl your hair."

June Star said her hair was naturally curly.

The next morning the grandmother was the first one in the car, ready to go. She had her big black valise that looked like the head of a hippopotamus in one corner, and underneath it she was hiding a basket with Pitty Sing, the cat, in it. She didn't intend for the cat to be left alone in the house for three days because he would miss her too much and she was afraid he might brush against one of the gas burners and accidentally asphyxiate himself. Her son, Bailey, didn't like to arrive at a motel with a cat.

She sat in the middle of the back seat with John Wesley and June Star on either side of her. Bailey and the children's mother and the baby sat in front and they left Atlanta at eight forty-five with the mileage on the car at 55890. The grandmother wrote this down because she thought it would be interesting to say how many miles they had been when they got back. It took them twenty minutes to reach the outskirts of the city.

The old lady settled herself comfortably, removing her white cotton gloves and putting them up with her purse on the shelf in front of the back window. The children's mother still had on slacks and still had her head tied up in a green kerchief, but the grandmother had on a navy blue straw sailor hat with a bunch of white violets on the brim and a navy blue dress with a small white dot in the print. Her collars and cuffs were white organdy trimmed with lace and at her neckline she had pinned a purple spray of cloth violets containing a sachet. In case of an accident, anyone seeing her dead on the highway would know at once that she was a lady.

She said she thought it was going to be a good day for driving, neither too hot nor too cold, and she cautioned Bailey that the speed limit was fifty-five miles an hour and that the patrolmen hid themselves behind billboards and small clumps of trees and sped out after you before you had a chance to slow down. She pointed out interesting details of the scenery: Stone Mountain; the blue granite that in some places came up to both sides of the highway; the brilliant red clay banks slightly streaked with purple; and the various crops that made rows of green lace-work on the ground. The trees were full of silver-white sunlight and the meanest of them sparkled. The children were reading comic magazines and their mother had gone back to sleep.

"Let's go through Georgia fast so we won't have to look at it much," John Wesley said.

"If I were a little boy," said the grandmother, "I wouldn't talk about my native state that way. Tennessee has the mountains and Georgia has the hills."

"Tennessee is just a hillbilly dumping ground," John Wesley said, "and Georgia is a lousy state too."

"You said it," June Star said.

"In my time," said the grandmother, folding her thin veined fingers, "children were more respectful of their native states and their parents and everything else. People did right then. Oh look at the cute little pickaninny!" she said and pointed to a Negro child standing in the door of a shack. "Wouldn't that make a picture, now?" she asked and they all turned and looked at the little Negro out of the back window. He waved.

"He didn't have any britches on," June Star said.

"He probably didn't have any," the grandmother explained. "Little niggers in the country don't have things like we do. If I could paint, I'd paint that picture," she said.

The children exchanged comic books.

The grandmother offered to hold the baby and the children's mother passed him over the front seat to her. She set him on her knee and bounced him and told him about the things they were passing. She rolled her eyes and screwed up her mouth and stuck her leathery thin face into his smooth bland one. Occasionally he gave her a faraway smile. They passed a large cotton field with five or six graves fenced in the middle of it, like a small island. "Look at the graveyard!" the grandmother said, pointing it out. "That was the old family burying ground. That belonged to the plantation."

"Where's the plantation?" John Wesley asked.

"Gone With the Wind," said the grandmother. "Ha. Ha."

When the children finished all the comic books they had brought, they opened the lunch and ate it. The grandmother ate a peanut butter sandwich and an olive and would not let the children throw the box and the paper napkins out the window. When there was nothing else to do they played a game by choosing a cloud and making the other two guess what shape it suggested. John Wesley took one the shape of a cow and June Star guessed a cow and John Wesley said, no, an automobile, and June Star said he didn't play fair, and they began to slap each other over the grandmother.

The grandmother said she would tell them a story if they would keep quiet. When she told a story, she rolled her eyes and waved her head and was very dramatic. She said once when she was a maiden lady she had been courted by a Mr. Edgar Atkins Teagarden from Jasper, Georgia. She said he was a very good-looking man and a gentleman and that he brought her a watermelon every Saturday afternoon with his initials cut in it, E. A. T. Well, one Saturday, she said, Mr. Teagarden brought the watermelon and there was nobody at home and he left it on the front porch and returned in his buggy to Jasper, but she never got the watermelon, she said, because a nigger boy ate it when he saw the initials, E. A. T.! This story tickled John Wesley's funny bone and he giggled and giggled but June Star didn't think it was any good. She said she wouldn't marry a man that just brought her a watermelon on Saturday. The grandmother said she would have done well to marry Mr. Teagarden because he was a gentleman and had bought Coca-Cola stock when it first came out and that he had died only a few years ago, a very wealthy man.

They stopped at The Tower for barbecued sandwiches. The Tower was a part stucco and part wood filling station and dance hall set in a clearing outside of Timothy. A fat man named Red Sammy Butts ran it and there were signs stuck here and there on the building and for miles up and down the highway saying, TRY RED SAMMY'S FAMOUS BARBE-CUE. NONE LIKE FAMOUS RED SAMMY'S! RED SAM! THE FAT BOY WITH THE HAPPY LAUGH. A VETERAN! RED SAMMY'S YOUR MAN!

Red Sammy was lying on the bare ground outside The Tower with his head under a truck while a gray monkey about a foot high, chained to a small chinaberry tree, chattered nearby. The monkey sprang back into the tree and got on the highest limb as soon as he saw the children jump out of the car and run toward him.

Inside, The Tower was a long dark room with a counter at one end and tables at the other and dancing space in the middle. They all sat down at a board table next to the nickelodeon and Red Sam's wife, a tall burnt-brown woman with hair and eyes lighter than her skin, came and took their order. The children's mother put a dime in the machine and played "The Tennessee Waltz," and the grandmother said that tune always made her want to dance. She asked Bailey if he would like to dance but he only glared at her. He didn't have a naturally sunny disposition like she did and trips made him nervous. The grandmother's brown eyes were very bright. She swayed her head from side to side and pretended she was dancing in her chair. June Star said play something she could tap to so the children's mother put in another dime and played a fast number and June Star stepped out onto the dance floor and did her tap routine.

"Ain't she cute?" Red Sam's wife said, leaning over the counter. "Would you like to come be my little girl?"

"No I certainly wouldn't," June Star said. "I wouldn't live in a broken-down place like this for a million bucks!" and she ran back to the table.

"Ain't she cute?" the woman repeated, stretching her mouth politely.

"Aren't you ashamed?" hissed the grandmother.

Red Sam came in and told his wife to quit lounging on the counter and hurry up with these people's order. His khaki trousers reached just to his hip bones and his stomach hung over them like a sack of meal swaying under his shirt. He came over and sat down at a table nearby and let out a combination sigh and yodel. "You can't win," he said. "You can't win," and he wiped his sweating red face off with a gray handkerchief. "These days you don't know who to trust," he said. "Ain't that the truth?"

"People are certainly not nice like they used to be," said the grandmother.

"Two fellers come in here last week," Red Sammy said, "driving a Chrysler. It was a old beat-up car but it was a good one and these boys looked all right to me. Said they worked at the mill and you know I let them fellers charge the gas they bought? Now why did I do that?"

"Because you're a good man!" the grandmother said at once.

"Yes'm, I suppose so," Red Sam said as if he were struck with this answer.

His wife brought the orders, carrying the five plates all at once without a tray, two in each hand and one balanced on her arm. "It isn't a soul in this green world of God's that you can trust," she said. "And I don't count nobody out of that, not nobody," she repeated, looking at Red Sammy.

"Did you read about that criminal, The Misfit, that's escaped?" asked the grandmother.

"I wouldn't be a bit surprised if he didn't attack this place right here," said the woman. "If he hears about it being here, I wouldn't be none surprised to see him. If he hears it's two cent in the cash register, I wouldn't be at all surprised if he . . ."

"That'll do," Red Sam said. "Go bring these people their Co'-Colas," and the woman went off to get the rest of the order.

"A good man is hard to find," Red Sammy said. "Everything is getting terrible. I remember the day you could go off and leave your screen door unlatched. Not no more."

He and the grandmother discussed better times. The old lady said that in her opinion Europe was entirely to blame for the way things were now. She said the way Europe acted you would think we were made of money and Red Sam said it was no use talking about it, she was exactly right. The children ran outside into the white sunlight and looked at the monkey in the lacy chinaberry tree. He was busy catching fleas on himself and biting each one carefully between his teeth as if it were a delicacy.

They drove off again into the hot afternoon. The grandmother took cat naps and woke up every few minutes with her own snoring. Outside of Toombsboro she woke up and recalled an old plantation that she had visited in this neighborhood once when she was a young lady. She said the house had six white columns across the front and that there was an avenue of oaks leading up to it and two little wooden trellis arbors on either side in front where you sat down with your suitor after a stroll in the garden. She recalled exactly which road to turn off to get to it. She knew that Bailey would not be willing to lose any time looking at an old house, but the more she talked about it, the more she wanted to see it once again and find out if the little twin arbors were still standing. "There was a secret panel in this house," she said craftily, not telling the truth but wishing that she were, "and the story went that all the family silver was hidden in it when Sherman came through but it was never found . . ."

"Hey!" John Wesley said. "Let's go see it! We'll find it! We'll poke all the woodwork and find it! Who lives there? Where do you turn off at? Hey Pop, can't we turn off there?"

"We never have seen a house with a secret panel!" June Star shrieked. "Let's go to the house with the secret panel! Hey Pop, can't we go see the house with the secret panel!"

"It's not far from here, I know," the grandmother said. "It wouldn't take over twenty minutes."

Bailey was looking straight ahead. His jaw was as rigid as a horseshoe. "No," he said.

The children began to yell and scream that they wanted to see the house with the secret panel. John Wesley kicked the back of the front seat and June Star hung over her mother's shoulder and whined desperately into her ear that they never had any fun even on their vacation, that they could never do what THEY wanted to do. The baby began to scream and John Wesley kicked the back of the seat so hard that his father could feel the blows in his kidney.

"All right!" he shouted and drew the car to a stop at the side of the road. "Will you all shut up? Will you all just shut up for one second? If you don't shut up, we won't go anywhere."

"It would be very educational for them," the grandmother murmured.

"All right," Bailey said, "but get this: this is the only time we're going to stop for anything like this. This is the one and only time."

"The dirt road that you have to turn down is about a mile back," the grandmother directed. "I marked it when we passed."

"A dirt road," Bailey groaned.

After they had turned around and were headed toward the dirt road, the grandmother recalled other points about the house, the beautiful glass over the front doorway and the candle-lamp in the hall. John Wesley said that the secret panel was probably in the fireplace.

"You can't go inside this house," Bailey said. "You don't know who lives there."

"While you all talk to the people in front, I'll run around behind and get in a window," John Wesley suggested.

"We'll all stay in the car," his mother said.

They turned onto the dirt road and the car raced roughly along in a swirl of pink dust. The grandmother recalled the times when there were no paved roads and thirty miles was a day's journey. The dirt road was hilly and there were sudden washes in it and sharp curves on dangerous embankments. All at once they would be on a hill, looking down over the blue tops of trees for miles around, then the next minute, they would be in a red depression with the dust-coated trees looking down on them.

"This place had better turn up in a minute," Bailey said, "or I'm going to turn around."

The road looked as if no one had traveled on it in months.

"It's not much farther," the grandmother said and just as she said it, a horrible thought came to her. The thought was so embarrassing that she turned red in the face and her eyes dilated and her feet jumped up, upsetting her valise in the corner. The instant the valise moved, the newspaper top she had over the basket under it rose with a snarl and Pitty Sing, the cat, sprang onto Bailey's shoulder.

The children were thrown to the floor and their mother, clutching the baby, was thrown out the door onto the ground; the old lady was thrown into the front seat. The car turned over once and landed right-side-up in a gulch off the side of the road. Bailey remained in the driver's seat with the cat—gray-striped with a broad white face and an orange nose—clinging to his neck like a caterpillar.

As soon as the children saw they could move their arms and legs, they scrambled out of the car, shouting, "We've had an ACCIDENT!" The grandmother was curled up under the dashboard, hoping she was injured so that Bailey's wrath would not come down on her all at once. The horrible thought she had had before the accident was that the house she had remembered so vividly was not in Georgia but in Tennessee.

Bailey removed the cat from his neck with both hands and flung it out the window against the side of a pine tree. Then he got out of the car and started looking for the children's mother. She was sitting against the side of the red gutted ditch, holding the screaming baby, but she only had a cut down her face and a broken shoulder. "We've had an ACCIDENT!" the children screamed in a frenzy of delight.

"But nobody's killed," June Star said with disappointment as the grandmother limped out of the car, her hat still pinned to her head but the broken front brim standing up at a jaunty angle and the violet spray hanging off the side. They all sat down in the ditch, except the children, to recover from the shock. They were all shaking.

"Maybe a car will come along," said the children's mother hoarsely.

"I believe I have an injured organ," said the grandmother, pressing her side, but no one answered her. Bailey's teeth were clattering. He had on a yellow sport shirt with bright blue parrots designed on it and his face was as yellow as the shirt. The grandmother decided that she would not mention that the house was in Tennessee.

The road was about ten feet above and they could see only the tops of the trees on the other side of it. Behind the ditch they were sitting in there were more woods, tall and dark and deep. In a few minutes they saw a car some distance away on top of a hill, coming slowly as if the occupants were watching them. The grandmother stood up and waved both arms dramatically to attract their attention. The car continued to come on slowly, disappeared around a bend and appeared again, moving even slower, on top of the hill they had gone over. It was a big black battered hearse-like automobile. There were three men in it.

It came to a stop just over them and for some minutes, the driver looked down with a steady expressionless gaze to where they were sitting, and didn't speak. Then he turned his head and muttered something to the other two and they got out. One was a fat boy in black trousers and a red sweat shirt with a silver stallion embossed on the front of it. He moved around on the right side of them and stood staring, his mouth partly open in a kind of loose grin. The other had on khaki pants and a blue striped coat and a gray hat pulled down very low, hiding most of his face. He came around slowly on the left side. Neither spoke.

The driver got out of the car and stood by the side of it, looking down at them. He was an older man than the other two. His hair was just beginning to gray and he wore silver-rimmed spectacles that give him a scholarly look. He had a long creased face and didn't have on any shirt or undershirt. He had on blue jeans that were too tight for him and was holding a black hat and a gun. The two boys also had guns.

"We've had an ACCIDENT!" the children screamed.

The grandmother had the peculiar feeling that the bespectacled man was someone she knew. His face was as familiar to her as if she had known him all her life but she could not recall who he was. He moved away from the car and began to come down the embankment, placing his feet carefully so that he wouldn't slip. He had on tan and white shoes and no socks, and his ankles were red and thin. "Good afternoon," he said. "I see you all had you a little spill."

"We turned over twice!" said the grandmother.

"Oncet," he corrected. "We seen it happen. Try their car and see will it run, Hiram," he said quietly to the boy with the gray hat.

"What you got that gun for?" John Wesley asked. "Whatcha gonna do with that gun?"

"Lady," the man said to the children's mother, "would you mind calling them children to sit down by you? Children make me nervous. I want all you to sit down right together there where you're at."

"What are you telling US what to do for?" June Star asked.

Behind them the line of woods gaped like a dark open mouth. "Come here," said their mother.

"Look here now," Bailey began suddenly, "we're in a predicament! We're in . . ."

The grandmother shrieked. She scrambled to her feet and stood staring. "You're The Misfit!" she said. "I recognized you at once!"

"Yes'm," the man said, smiling slightly as if he were pleased in spite of himself to be known, "but it would have been better for all of you, lady, if you hadn't of reckernized me."

Bailey turned his head sharply and said something to his mother that shocked even the children. The old lady began to cry and The Misfit reddened.

"Lady," he said, "don't you get upset. Sometimes a man says things he don't mean. I don't reckon he meant to talk to you thataway."

"You wouldn't shoot a lady, would you?" the grandmother said and removed the clean handkerchief from her cuff and began to slap at her eyes with it.

The Misfit pointed the toe of his shoe into the ground and made a little hole and then covered it up again. "I would hate to have to," he said.

"Listen," the grandmother almost screamed, "I know you're a good man. You don't look a bit like you have common blood. I know you must come from nice people!"

"Yes mam," he said, "finest people in the world." When he smiled he showed a row of strong white teeth. "God never made a finer woman than my mother and my daddy's heart was pure gold," he said. The boy with the red sweat shirt had come around behind them and was standing with his gun at his hip. The Misfit squatted down on the ground. "Watch them children, Bobby Lee," he said. "You know they make me nervous." He looked at the six of them huddled together in front of him and he seemed to be embarrassed as if he couldn't think of anything to say. "Ain't a cloud in the sky," he remarked, looking up at it. "Don't see no sun but don't see no cloud neither."

"Yes, it's a beautiful day," said the grandmother. "Listen," she said, "you shouldn't call yourself The Misfit because I know you're a good man at heart. I can just look at you and tell."

"Hush!" Bailey yelled. "Hush! Everybody shut up and let me handle this!" He was squatting in the position of a runner about to sprint forward but he didn't move.

"I pre-chate that, lady," The Misfit said and drew a little circle in the ground with the butt of his gun.

"It'll take a half a hour to fix this here car," Hiram called, looking over the raised hood of it.

"Well, first you and Bobby Lee get him and that little boy to step over yonder with you," The Misfit said, pointing to Bailey and John Wesley. "The boys want to ask you something," he said to Bailey. "Would you mind stepping back in them woods there with them?"

"Listen," Bailey began, "we're in a terrible predicament! Nobody realizes what this is," and his voice cracked. His eyes were as blue and intense as the parrots on his shirt and he remained perfectly still.

The grandmother reached up to adjust her hat brim as if she were going to the woods with him but it came off in her hand. She stood staring at it and after a second she let it fall on the ground. Hiram pulled Bailey up by the arm as if he were assisting an old man. John Wesley caught hold of his father's hand and Bobby Lee followed. They went off toward the woods and just as they reached the dark edge, Bailey turned and supported himself against a gray naked pine trunk, he shouted, "I'll be back in a minute, Mamma, wait on me!"

"Come back this instant!" his mother shrilled but they all disappeared into the woods.

"Bailey Boy!" the grandmother called in a tragic voice but she found she was looking at The Misfit squatting on the ground in front of her. "I just know you're a good man," she said desperately. "You're not a bit common!"

"Nome, I ain't a good man," The Misfit said after a second as if he had considered her statement carefully, "but I ain't the worst in the world neither. My daddy said I was a different breed of dog from my brothers and sisters. 'You know,' Daddy said, 'it's some that can live their whole life out without asking about it and it's others has to know why it is, and this boy is one of the latters. He's going to be into everything!'" He put on his black hat and looked up suddenly and then away deep into the woods as if he were embarrassed again. "I'm sorry I don't have on a shirt before you ladies," he said, hunching his shoulders slightly. "We buried our clothes that we had on when we escaped and we're just making do until we can get better. We borrowed these from some folks we met," he explained.

"That's perfectly all right," the grandmother said. "Maybe Bailey has an extra shirt in his suitcase."

"I'll look and see terrectly," The Misfit said.

"Where are they taking him?" the children's mother screamed.

"Daddy was a card himself," The Misfit said. "You couldn't put anything over on him. He never got in trouble with the Authorities though. Just had the knack of handling them."

"You could be honest too if you'd only try," said the grandmother. "Think how wonderful it would be to settle down and live a comfortable life and not have to think about somebody chasing you all the time."

The Misfit kept scratching in the ground with the butt of his gun as if he were thinking about it. "Yes'm, somebody is always after you," he murmured.

The grandmother noticed how thin his shoulder blades were just behind his hat because she was standing up looking down on him. "Do you ever pray?" she asked.

He shook his head. All she saw was the black hat wiggle between his shoulder blades. "Nome," he said.

There was a pistol shot from the woods, followed closely by another. Then silence. The old lady's head jerked around. She could hear the wind move through the tree tops like a long satisfied insuck of breath. "Bailey Boy!" she called.

"I was a gospel singer for a while," The Misfit said. "I been most everything. Been in the arm service, both land and sea, at home and abroad, been twict married, been an undertaker, been with the railroads, plowed Mother Earth, been in a tornado, seen a man burnt alive oncet," and he looked up at the children's mother and the little girl who were sitting close together, their faces white and their eyes glassy; "I even seen a woman flogged," he said.

"Pray, pray," the grandmother began, "pray, pray . . ."

"I never was a bad boy that I remember of," The Misfit said in an almost dreamy voice, "but somewheres along the line I done something wrong and got sent to the penitentiary. I was buried alive," and he looked up and held her attention to him by a steady stare.

"That's when you should have started to pray," she said. "What did you do to get sent to the penitentiary that first time?"

"Turn to the right, it was a wall," The Misfit said, looking up again at the cloudless sky. "Turn to the left, it was a wall. Look up it was a ceiling, look down it was a floor. I forget what I done, lady. I set there and set there, trying to remember what it was I done and I ain't recalled it to this day. Oncet in a while, I would think it was coming to me, but it never come."

"Maybe they put you in by mistake," the old lady said vaguely.

"Nome," he said. "It wasn't no mistake. They had the papers on me."

"You must have stolen something," she said.

The Misfit sneered slightly. "Nobody had nothing I wanted," he said. "It was a head-doctor at the penitentiary said what I had done was kill my daddy but I known that for a lie. My daddy died in nineteen ought nineteen of the epidemic flu and I never had a thing to do with it. He was buried in the Mount Hopewell Baptist churchyard and you can go there and see for yourself."

"If you would pray," the old lady said, "Jesus would help you."

"That's right," The Misfit said.

"Well then, why don't you pray?" she asked trembling with delight suddenly.

"I don't want no hep," he said. "I'm doing all right by myself."

Bobby Lee and Hiram came ambling back from the woods. Bobby Lee was dragging a yellow shirt with bright blue parrots in it.

"Throw me that shirt, Bobby Lee," The Misfit said. The shirt came flying at him and landed on his shoulder and he put it on. The grandmother couldn't name what the shirt reminded her of. "No, lady," The Misfit said while he was buttoning it up, "I found out the crime don't matter. You can do one thing or you can do another, kill a man or take a tire off his car, because sooner or later you're going to forget what it was you done and just be punished for it."

The children's mother had begun to make heaving noises as if she couldn't get her breath. "Lady," he asked, "would you and that little girl like to step off yonder with Bobby Lee and Hiram and join your husband?"

"Yes, thank you," the mother said faintly. Her left arm dangled help-lessly and she was holding the baby, who had gone to sleep, in the other. "Hep that lady up, Hiram," The Misfit said as she struggled to climb out of the ditch, "and Bobby Lee, you hold onto that little girl's hand."

"I don't want to hold hands with him," June Star said. "He reminds me of a pig."

The fat boy blushed and laughed and caught her by the arm and pulled her off into the woods after Hiram and her mother.

Alone with The Misfit, the grandmother found that she had lost her voice. There was not a cloud in the sky nor any sun. There was nothing around her but woods. She wanted to tell him that he must pray. She opened and closed her mouth several times before anything came out. Finally she found herself saying, "Jesus, Jesus," meaning, Jesus will help you, but the way she was saying it, it sounded as if she might be cursing.

"Yes'm," The Misfit said as if he agreed. "Jesus thown everything off balance. It was the same case with Him as with me except He hadn't com-mitted any crime and they could prove I had committed one because they had the papers on me. Of course," he said, "they never shown me my papers. That's why I sign myself now. I said long ago, you get you a signature and sign everything you do and keep a copy of it. Then you'll know what you done and you can hold up the crime to the punishment and see do they match and in the end you'll have something to prove you ain't been treated right. I call myself The Misfit," he said, "because I can't make what all I done wrong fit what all I gone through in punishment."

There was a piercing scream from the woods, followed closely by a pistol report. "Does it seem right to you, lady, that one is punished a heap and another ain't punished at all?"

"Jesus!" the old lady cried. "You've got good blood! I know you wouldn't shoot a lady! I know you come from nice people! Pray! Jesus, you ought not to shoot a lady. I'll give you all the money I've got!"

"Lady," The Misfit said, looking beyond her far into the woods, "there never was a body that give the undertaker a tip."

There were two more pistol reports and the grandmother raised her head like a parched old turkey hen crying for water and called, "Bailey Boy, Bailey Boy!" as if her heart would break.

"Jesus was the only One that ever raised the dead," The Misfit con-tinued, "and He shouldn't have done it. He thown everything off balance. If He did what He said, then it's nothing for you to do but throw away everything and follow Him, and if He didn't, then it's nothing for you to do but enjoy the few minutes you got left the best way you can—by killing somebody or burning down his house or doing some other meanness to him. No pleasure but meanness," he said and his voice had become al-most a snarl.

"Maybe He didn't raise the dead," the old lady mumbled, not knowing what she was saying and feeling so dizzy that she sank down in the ditch with her legs twisted under her.

"I wasn't there so I can't say He didn't," The Misfit said. "I wisht I had of been there," he said, hitting the ground with his fist. "It ain't right I wasn't there because if I had of been there I would of known. Listen lady," he said in a high voice, "if I had of been there I would of known and I wouldn't be like I am now." His voice seemed about to crack and the grandmother's head cleared for an instant. She saw the man's face twisted close to her own as if he were going to cry and she murmured, "Why you're one of my babies. You're one of my own children!" She reached out and touched him on the shoulder. The Misfit sprang back as if a snake had bitten him and shot her three times through the chest. Then he put his gun down on the ground and took off his glasses and began to clean them.

Hiram and Bobby Lee returned from the woods and stood over the ditch, looking down at the grandmother who half sat and half lay in a puddle of blood with her legs crossed under her like a child's and her face smiling up at the cloudless sky.

Without his glasses, The Misfit's eyes were red-rimmed and pale and defenseless-looking. "Take her off and thow her where you thown the others," he said, picking up the cat that was rubbing itself against his leg.

"She was a talker, wasn't she?" Bobby Lee said, sliding down the ditch with a yodel.

"She would of been a good woman," The Misfit said, "if it had been somebody there to shoot her every minute of her life."

"Some fun!" Bobby Lee said.

"Shut up, Bobby Lee," The Misfit said. "It's no real pleasure in life."

INTERPRETATION

1. This story, like "A Rose For Emily," presents us with a shocking piece of pathology. Viewed objectively, the story is an account of how a homicidal maniac slaughters a family of ordinary, innocent people whom he happens to encounter on the road. How does the author interpret this special situation as a comment on general human values? (Of course, in so far as the story is coherent, everything in it will bear on the answer to this question, but especially important for an answer is the dialogue between the old lady and The Misfit. Study very carefully this dialogue and then try to make a statement about the theme of the story.)

2. What is the character of the old lady? Pleasant or unpleasant? Admirable or unadmirable? Selfish or unselfish? How does her character bear on the interpretation of the story?

3. The story can be said to be in two parts—the long first part dealing with the trip, and the second part after the encounter with The Misfit.

What, if anything, holds these two parts together? How does this connection between the parts relate to the theme of the story? In connection with this we may say that the encounter is pure coincidence—The Misfit just happens to come along at the moment when the family has the accident. We have said that, in general, dependence on coincidence is a fault in fiction. What about this instance? Does the fact of the coincidence bear on the theme?

4. What is the significance, if any, of the scene at the highway restaurant?

5. What responsibility does the old lady have for the family's disaster? Can we detect a pattern here? If so, what does it mean?

6. Let us suppose that the old lady were of unusual intelligence and were a completely devout Christian. What effect would this change have on the irony of the conclusion? In thinking of this question go back to the dialogue between the old lady and The Misfit. Which of the two, the sane woman or the maniac, is the more deeply involved in the religious question?

7. What significance for the story lies in the fact that the old lady feels that she has come down socially?

8. What impression do you have of the family in general? How do you relate this impression to the theme of the story?

9. What is the significance of the old lady's last words to The Misfit? For plot? For theme?

10. Work the answers to the questions above into a little essay of interpretation.

Biographical Notes

SHERWOOD ANDERSON (1876–1941) was born in Camden, Ohio. His father was an aimless, improvident wanderer, a talker and teller of tales, a type that appears in Anderson's fiction. Anderson had a limited formal education, served in Cuba during the Spanish-American War, worked as manager of a paint factory in Elmyra, Ohio, then as an advertising copy writer in Chicago, where he became a protégé of the Chicago group of writers, including Carl Sandburg and Theodore Dreiser. He achieved fame with his collection of stories *Winesburg, Ohio*, in 1919; and with *The Triumph of the Egg*, two years later, became generally recognized as a master of that form. His other work includes novels, autobiography, memoirs, verse, and journalism.

MARCEL AYMÉ (1902–) is a distinguished French novelist and playwright. His schooling was irregular—he detested school—and he had a go at various jobs before he found his vein as a writer. He achieved great success as a young man and at the age of twenty-seven his fourth novel won the Théophraste Renaudot prize for the best novel of the year. He is noted as a stylist and as a satirist. His principal novels that have been translated into English include *The Green Mare*, 1938, *The Miraculous Barber*, 1951, and *The Secret Stream*, 1954. *Across Paris*, 1959, is his first volume of short stories to be published in English.

ISAAC BABEL (1894–1939?) was born in Odessa, Russia, of a lower middle-class Jewish family. As a young man he went to St. Petersburg and lived as an impoverished Bohemian. Maxim Gorki was the first to encourage Babel by printing two of his volumes. During the Revolution and civil war, Babel fought with the cavalry. In 1923 he began to win success with short stories published in magazines. He published *Odessa Tales* in 1924 and a brilliant collection, *Red Cavalry*, in 1926. Since 1936 there has been no mention of his name in any Soviet publication. It is believed that he may have died in a concentration camp in 1939 or 1940.

HONORÉ DE BALZAC (1799–1850) was born at Tours, in France, to a prosperous family that abandoned him to a monastic school, and for years neglected him. After his school years he spent a long period in Paris, in dire poverty, struggling to learn the craft of writing, reading prodigiously and writing, under various pseudonyms, a dozen novels, which he later repudiated. When he was thirty, he began to receive recognition, and in the next twenty years poured out a flood of novels, stories, and plays, more than 350 titles, this in addition to work as a journalist and editor. Some hundred of his novels are interrelated to give a coherent picture of the world of his time, under the title *La Comédie Humaine*, a monumental achievement.

AMBROSE BIERCE (1842–1914?) was born in Ohio, the son of a poverty-stricken, pious farmer, whom he detested. He attended the Kentucky Military Institute for one year, entered the Civil War as a drummer boy, and after being twice wounded, emerged as a brevet major, and went to San Francisco and a career in journalism, where his reputation as a writer was made. But he lived and worked several years in England, and Washington, D.C., as a correspondent for Hearst. His personal life was unhappy, and in 1913 he disappeared into Mexico.

RAY BRADBURY (1920–) was born in Waukegan, Illinois. He comes of a line of editors and publishers, and as a young man began himself to write, producing science fiction. *Dark Carnival, The Martian Chronicles,* and *The Illustrated Man* are representative titles. But quite early—in 1945—Bradbury became interested in writing serious fiction, though his subjects still tend to be concerned with fantasy and the grotesque. *The Golden Apples of the Sun,* from which the story included in this volume is taken, appeared in 1958.

ANTON CHEKHOV (1860–1904) was born at Taganrog, on the Sea of Azov, in Russia, the grandson of a serf. Educated as a doctor, he rarely practiced his profession, but devoted himself almost from the first to literature. His stories found a ready public, and in time exerted a profound effect on that form in all countries. Though his first play, *Ivanov,* belongs to his middle twenties, it was more than ten years before his second, *The Sea Gull,* established him as a dramatist. From that time, though he was increasingly plagued by ill health, he devoted himself chiefly to the theater, his other plays being *Uncle Vanya, The Three Sisters,* and *The Cherry Orchard,* which have had an immense influence on the modern drama.

JOHN COLLIER (1901–) was born in London, was privately educated, began writing verse at nineteen, and was soon being published. For several years he was poetry editor of *Time and Tide,* but his reputation is based on his stories.

STEPHEN CRANE (1871–1900) was born in Newark, New Jersey, attended a military school and, briefly, Lafayette College and Syracuse University. Perhaps his training as a journalist on the New York *Herald* and the *Tribune* was the most significant influence in forming his scrupulously realistic notion of fiction. Crane was enormously precocious, writing two of his most impressive books before he was 25, *Maggie, a Girl of the Streets* and *The Red Badge of Courage*. He was a master of the short story and a famous war correspondent, covering the Spanish-American War and the Greco-Turkish War. His verse is, however, undistinguished. He died abroad, in self-imposed exile, feeling himself rejected by the American life of the period.

WILLIAM FAULKNER (1897–) was born in Mississippi, of a family distinguished in the political history of the state. Perfunctorily and briefly he attended the University of Mississippi. He served with the Canadian Air Force in World War I, and in the years before literary recognition came, worked as a barn-storming aviator and at various odd jobs. Since then he has operated a farm and done a good deal of script writing for Hollywood. He is a passionately devoted hunter, and the world of hunting appears over and over in his work, most notably in his masterly long tale, "The Bear." *Sanctuary* brought him his first recognition, but his best novels are probably *The Sound and the Fury, Light in August, Absalom, Absalom!* and *The Hamlet*. He has written some of the most memorable short stories in our literature and one play, a dramatization of his novel, *Requiem for a Nun*. He has received the Nobel Prize.

BRET HARTE (1836–1902) was born in Albany, New York, of Dutch and English ancestry. His father was a school teacher, and perhaps this fact, coupled with years of illness in childhood, led to the boy's extensive reading in the English classics. He began work at thirteen to help out the family, and by sixteen was self-supporting. At nineteen he went to California, where he worked as a teacher, apothecary clerk, tutor, express messenger, type-setter, and editor, all the while writing stories and poems. The frontier life of California gave him his characteristic subject, a subject of interest to the eastern part of America and to Europe. After a brief period as editor of *The Overland Monthly*, which he had founded, and as a professor at the University of California, he went East for a triumphal lecture tour, and on to England, where he cut a figure in literary circles. He was consul at Crefeld, Germany, and at Glasgow. He died in England.

ERNEST HEMINGWAY (1898–), born in Oak Park, Illinois, the son of a physician, served in World War I as ambulance driver, and later with the Italian Arditi, and after the war, worked as a foreign correspondent. In the 1920's, he made a sensational impact with his highly individual stories

and his two early novels. *The Sun Also Rises* and *A Farewell to Arms.*
In the midst of his literary career he returned to journalism as a correspondent covering the Spanish Civil War, an experience reflected in the
famous novel *For Whom the Bell Tolls.* He received the Nobel Prize in
1954.

O. HENRY is the pen name of William Sydney Porter (1862–1910). O.
Henry was born in Greensboro, North Carolina, attended school there until fifteen, when he went to work in a drug store, and at the age of twenty
went to Texas. In Texas he worked as a clerk, draughtsman, bookkeeper,
bank teller, and journalist, editing a humorous weekly and then going to
the Houston *Daily Post* as a columnist and cartoonist. In 1895 he was in-
dicted for embezzlement from the bank where he had been teller, and
though his guilt was, probably, only technical, he fled to New Orleans,
and thence to South America and Mexico, where he travelled with the
notorious Jennings brothers, on money they had stolen. Two years later,
because of the illness of his wife, he returned to the United States, and
after her death stood trial, and was sentenced to five years in the Columbus,
Ohio, penitentiary. In prison he began his serious career as a writer, and
upon being released for good behavior, went to New York to become a
professional fiction writer. He was enormously prolific, enormously successful, and a consumer of enormous quantities of whisky. He died at the
age of forty-eight, of tuberculosis.

SHIRLEY JACKSON (1919–   ) is a native of California, but more recently has
lived in the East. She has written novels and essays, but is best known for
her stories.

JAMES JOYCE (1882–1941) was born in Dublin, and first won fame with his
collection of stories called *Dubliners.* The title is significant, for in all his
subsequent work, including the celebrated *Ulysses* and *Finnegan's Wake,*
the city of Dublin is the vital fact. Joyce's influence has been prodigious,
and some critics are inclined to rate him as the most significant novelist of
the century.

RUDYARD KIPLING (1865–1936) was born in Bombay, India, his father, an
artist, being curator of the museum at Lahore. After attending school at
the United Services College, in Devonshire, England (the scene of his
Stalky and Co.), he returned to India, and became, at seventeen, an under-
editor of the Lahore *Civil and Military Gazette,* beginning the career of
journalism that helped him learn Indian life and form his sharp and succinct
style. Some of his best work was done in his early years, for example "The
Man Who Would Be King," which was written before he was twenty-five,

and world fame came early to him, both as a poet and writer of fiction. He received the Nobel Prize in 1907. He travelled widely, and lived for several years in Vermont (he had married an American woman).

RING (Ringgold Wilmer) LARDNER (1885–1933) was born in Niles, Michigan. He began life as a sportswriter, and much of his fiction reflects the world of sport. He is famous for his vigorous use of the vernacular, for his introduction of new types into fiction, and for a humorous and sardonic tone. In addition to his many short stories, he collaborated in two plays, one with George M. Cohan and the other with George S. Kaufman.

D. H. LAWRENCE (1885–1930) was born in Nottinghamshire, England, the son of a coal miner. For a time he taught in elementary school, trying to find himself as a painter and writer. With recognition, he became a wanderer, partly from curiosity and restlessness, and partly in the vain attempt to cure his tuberculosis, travelling in Europe, Mexico, Australia, and the United States. He was an enormously versatile writer, producing stories and novels, books of travel, criticism and essays, and poetry. By the time of his death, in Vence, France, his reputation seemed permanently established.

CARSON MCCULLERS (1917–) was born in Columbus, Georgia, as Carson Smith, McCullers being the name of her husband. At seventeen she went to New York with the intention of studying music at the Julliard Foundation, but drifted into part-time jobs and attended night school. She began to publish stories, and when she was twenty-three, her first novel, *The Heart Is a Lonely Hunter,* made a sensation. In addition to two other novels, and a number of stories, she has written two plays, one of which, the dramatization of her novel *The Member of the Wedding,* has had a considerable success.

KATHERINE MANSFIELD (1888–1923) was born in Wellington, New Zealand, with the name of Kathleen Mansfield Beauchamp. She attended Queen's College, in London, edited the college magazine, studied music and became a competent cellist, and later toured as a super in opera. Her first stories appeared when she was twenty-two. She married John Middleton Murry, the critic, collaborated with him and D. H. Lawrence in founding a review, *The Signature,* and continued her own writing. By 1920 with the publication of the volume *Bliss and Other Stories,* her reputation was made. For several years she had been suffering from tuberculosis, and died at the age of thirty-five, in France, where she had gone for treatment.

GUY DE MAUPASSANT (1850–1893) was the son of a Paris stock broker and the godson of Gustav Flaubert, who supervised his literary training. From the age of thirty Maupassant was an acknowledged master of the short story, and in ten torrential years produced some thirty volumes, including two world-famous novels. Maupassant had inherited severe nervous disease, which was aggravated by drugs, dissipation, and over-exercise. After an attempted suicide, he died of paresis.

FLANNERY O'CONNOR (1925–) was born in Savannah, Georgia. Her novel *Wise Blood*, published in 1952, received wide attention. Her stories, which had been appearing in the quarterlies and little magazines, were collected in 1955 under the title *A Good Man Is Hard to Find*. She has held grants from the National Institute of Arts and Letters, from the Ford Foundation, and has held a Kenyon Fellowship in Fiction. She makes her home in Milledgeville, Georgia.

FRANK O'CONNOR (1903–) was born in Cork, Ireland, and attended the Christian Brothers School there, but was too poor to go to the university. He began to write early, worked as a librarian to maintain himself, and attracted the attention of literary men like Yeats and AE (George Russell). His reputation is based on his stories, but he has also written verse and a critical study of Turgenev.

LUIGI PIRANDELLO (1867–1936), though living much of his adult life in Rome, was a Sicilian by birth and heritage. Through a long unhappy marriage, and a long and uncongenial career as a teacher, Pirandello produced an enormous amount of work in the short story, the novel, and the drama. Recognition, however, did not come until he was in his fifties, and then the fame of his plays *Six Characters in Search of an Author* and *As You Desire Me* overshadowed his great achievement as a writer of fiction. He received the Nobel Prize in 1934.

KATHERINE ANNE PORTER (1894–), a descendant of Daniel Boone, was born in the little community of Indian Creek, Texas. Brought up in Texas and Louisiania, she was educated in small convent schools. Her formal education ended at seventeen, but she continued to read widely with the passionate desire to become a writer. After some newspaper work and various nondescript jobs, and years of publishing occasional stories, she found distinguished recognition with the publication of the collection of stories *Flowering Judas* (1930), which has now become a classic of our time. Her other collections, which have maintained her high level of performance, are *Pale Horse, Pale Rider* (three short novels), and *The Leaning Tower and Other Stories*. She has published one book of essays, and some translations. She has travelled widely, worked as a script writer for moving pictures, lectured, and taught. She has received a number of distinguished awards.

JAMES PURDY (1923–) was born in Ohio, and attended the University of Chicago, as well as universities in Mexico and Spain. His collection of stories *Don't Call Me by My Right Name* (1956) was received with unusual enthusiasm by many critics. He is the author of a novel, *Malcolm.*

WILLIAM SANSOM (1912–) was born in England and attended schools there and on the continent. *Fireman Flower*, his first collection of stories, appeared in 1944. Since that time he has published over a dozen books, including several novels, *The Body*, 1947, *The Face of Innocence*, 1951, and *A Bed of Roses*, 1954. Other important collections of his stories include *The Passionate North*, 1950, and *A Touch of the Sun*, 1952.

IRWIN SHAW (1913–) was born in Brooklyn and was educated at Brooklyn College. During his college years and immediately afterward, he worked at a variety of jobs, but he had an early success in the theater and as a script writer in Hollywood. He has produced a number of stories, three novels, and his work for the movies and the stage.

JESSE HILTON STUART (1907–) was born in W-Hollow in the mountains of eastern Kentucky. He attended the Lincoln Memorial University at Harrogate, Tennessee, and after a year's work at Vanderbilt University, he taught school. His first volume, *Man with a Bull-Tongue Plow*, was a collection of poems and attracted wide attention on its publication in 1934. Since that time Stuart has become better known as a writer of stories and novels. He held a Guggenheim Fellowship in 1937 and was awarded a prize by the Academy of Arts and Sciences in 1941. A serious heart attack has prompted him to write his autobiography.

JAMES THURBER (1894–) was born in Columbus, Ohio, a city that appears in a number of his stories. After graduating from Ohio State University, he began newspaper work in Columbus, but shortly went to France, on the Paris edition of the *Herald Tribune*. In 1926 he began contributing to *The New Yorker* magazine his famous series of drawings, stories, commentaries, and sketches, which have established him as a distinguished stylist and one of the foremost humorists of our time. He has done, in collaboration with Elliot Nugent, one play *The Male Animal.*

EUDORA WELTY (1909–) was born in Jackson, Mississippi, where she continues to live. She was educated at the Mississippi State College for Women and at the University of Wisconsin; and for a short time, she studied advertising at Columbia University. Though her first ambition was to be a painter, she began to write as a child. With her first book of stories, *A Curtain of Green* (1941), she was widely acclaimed for an extraordinary talent. Since that time she has published a number of novels and collections of stories, and has received general recognition, including the Howells Medal awarded by the American Academy of Arts and Letters, and the Pulitzer Prize.

THOMAS CLAYTON WOLFE (1900–1938) was born in Asheville, North Carolina. He attended the University of North Carolina, where his major interest was in play writing, an interest which he subsequently pursued at Harvard. His fame, however, was achieved in the novel. *Look Homeward, Angel* (1929) made a profound impact. Later novels are *Of Time and the River*, *The Web and the Rock*, and *You Can't Go Home Again*, the latter two published posthumously.

Glossary

ABSTRACTS: Abstractions are qualities and characteristics isolated as pure ideas. A piece of *sugar* is a concrete substance with its own qualities but we may *abstract* (literally *draw away*) from it *whiteness, hardness, sweetness.* Literature characteristically deals with the concrete rather than the abstract, and also the specific rather than the general. All of which is not to say that ideas, which are capable of being stated abstractly—love, courage, justice—are not involved in literature, but such ideas rarely emerge as abstractions; rather, they are incorporated in the concrete elements—in the case of fiction, in the particular characters and situations and events. The general observations that one may abstract from the particulars of a story—observations about human nature or about life—are not to be taken as the equivalent of the story. The abstraction—and the generalization are something less than—merely a part of—the concrete particularity of the story itself. See p. 230.

ACTION: A series of events having unity and significance. See pp. 51–54.

ACTION STORY: A story in which the principal interest lies in plot suspense, such as adventure or detective fiction. See pp. 29–30, 51–54.

ALLEGORICAL: See ALLEGORY.

ALLEGORY: An allegory is a kind of narrative in which the characters, objects, and events are to be taken, not as real but as standing for some set of ideas. That is, each item in the narrative is equated with some item among the ideas. For example, in Bunyan's *The Pilgrim's Progress,* the character Christian, who leaves his home to journey to the Celestial City, is to be taken as the type of all people who try to lead the Christian life, and each event that takes place on the journey stands for some problem in the spiritual life. SEE PARABLE, and see pp. 47–48, 242–244.

ALLITERATION: Repetition of consonants, particulary of initial consonants as in *lullaby* or "*l*evels of the *l*ake." See p. 38.

ANTICLIMAX: A break in the climatic order of events or effects; a falling off from the expected intensification of effect. See CLIMAX and IRONY. See also pp. 161–162.

ATMOSPHERE: The general pervasive feeling aroused by the various factors in a piece of fiction, such as setting, character, theme, and the like; the general effect of the handling of the total work. To be distinguished from SETTING and from TONE. Considerations of the metaphorical origin of the two terms, *atmos-*

phere and *tone*, may be helpful here. *Tone* is to be referred ultimately to the author's attitude (the tone of voice of a speaker as qualifying what he says) toward what is being presented, whereas *atmosphere* is to be referred to the general qualification provided by the materials themselves (an atmosphere of sunshine, of cheerfulness, an atmosphere of gloom, and the like). There is, however, a good deal of overlapping and vagueness about the use of these terms in ordinary discussion. The student, in referring to a particular case in fiction, should ask himself whether he wishes to emphasize the author's attitude or the mere effect of the materials as such. See pp. 50, 53, 110–113, 169.

CLICHÉ: Usually used in reference to a phrase which has lost its force because of continual use; for example, "in the arms of Morpheus," or "a dull, sickening thud." But the term is also applied occasionally to fictional situations or events which have become hackneyed and stereotyped. The cliché represents one kind of appeal to a STOCK RESPONSE on the part of the reader. But, of course, clichés may be used justifiably by the author, for ironical effect, or because a certain kind of character would normally use clichés in his speech, or for other reasons. In general, it may be said that a cliché is bad when used with the intention of creating a vivid and memorable effect; it fails in such cases because it does not represent a fresh perception. See pp. 38, 268.

CLIMAX: The highest point in an ascending series; in fiction, for example, the point at which the forces in conflict reach the highest intensification. See pp. 55, 136.

COHERENCE: The hanging together—the interconnectedness—of the parts of a piece of fiction. TRUTH OF COHERENCE has to do with the internal consistency of a piece of literature. See pp. 56, 153, 232–233.

COINCIDENCE: An accidental coming together of certain events. (See SURPRISE ENDING.) The use of coincidence is, in one sense, unavoidable in fiction, for the original situation in any story may be defined as a coincidence. But the use of coincidence is, generally speaking, illegitimate when it functions to solve the fictional problem; that is, when the events which bring about the resolution of a plot have no logical connection with preceding events. See pp. 72, 79, 112, 320.

COMPLICATION: The interplay between character and event which builds up a tension and develops a problem out of the original situation given in the story. See pp. 55, 152.

CONCRETE: See ABSTRACT.

CONFLICT: All fiction involves, at one level or another, conflict. The characters struggle against enviroment or with each other (external conflict) or are engaged in struggles with themselves (internal conflict). One important approach to the understanding of any story is to determine the nature of the conflict involved and the pattern that the opposing forces assume. See pp. 52–57, 152–153.

CONNOTATION: See DENOTATION

CONVENTION: Any method, device, or rule that is accepted by explicit or tacit agreement. For example, the fact that the letter *t* shall have a certain consonantal value, or that a touchdown shall count for six points depends upon nothing intrinsic but is determined by convention. All the arts, including that of fiction, make use of *conventions*. For example, the omniscient author's ability to enter into the innermost thoughts of several of his characters depends upon a convention. The author continually makes use of traditional conventions handed down to him from the past. His work, however, is termed CONVENTIONAL in a bad sense when it fails to justify the conventional items it employs by relating them freshly to the new problem.

CONVENTIONAL: See CONVENTION.

CUTBACK: A passage in a narrative which breaks the chronological sequence to deal with earlier events. (For example, the method of "An Occurrence at Owl Creek Bridge" involves a long cutback to explain the situation. See pp. 53–54.

DENOTATION: The exact thing or idea indicated by word. The denotation is not only the primary meaning, but it is the specific and abstract meaning. Scientific prose needs no more than the denotations of words, and the attempt to build up a scientific and technical language is in harmony with this situation. But the CONNOTATIONS of a word are the things suggested by or associated with the word. These connotations, though necessarily vague and inexact (as compared with denotations) are nevertheless powerful and important, and the skillful writer whose intention is literary rather than scientific makes full use of them. See pp. 170–171.

DENOUEMENT: The final resolution or untying of the plot. It sometimes, but not always, coincides with the climax. See p. 55.

DISTANCE: The term is used to mean the degree of detachment with which the characters in a story are viewed. See pp. 87–88, 126–128.

DRAMATIC: Strictly speaking, fictional method is said to be dramatic when the author gives a purely OBJECTIVE rendering of his material, without indulging either in editorial comment and generalization of his own or in the analysis of the feelings and thoughts of his characters. The clearest case of such a method in this book is "The Killers" (p. 258). But in such a story as "The Lament" (p. 183), though the method is less strictly dramatic, the old man's grief is not commented upon by the author until he has presented the grief in terms of action. Where a dramatic method is used the reader must infer the inner situation from the external action and dialogue. But the term is used more loosely to indicate merely the presence of strong tension and sharp conflict in a story or novel; and it is used more loosely still to indicate concrete presentation as opposed to abstract statement.

EPISODE: A separate incident in a larger piece of action. In "The Lament" (see pp. 186–188), for example, the visit to the stable to see the horse constitutes an episode.

EPISODIC: A piece of fiction is said to be *episodic* when there is not a strongly emphasized causal continuity between one episode and the next. Episodic structure is, logically, loose structure, in so far as plot is concerned.

EXPOSITION: The process of giving the reader necessary information concerning characters and events existing before the action proper of a story begins. See pp. 55, 148–150.

FABLE: A tale, usually rather simple and often illustrating some maxim about human nature. See p. 46–48.

FIRST-PERSON NARRATION. See FOCUS OF NARRATION. See also pp. 126–128.

FOCUS: The center around which the material of an imaginative work is concentrated. The focus may shift from moment to moment in a piece of fiction or it may remain constant. For example, the focus may be primarily upon character, upon an idea, upon a setting, or the like.

FOCUS OF CHARACTER: A piece of fiction is not merely a sequence of events. The events are of special concern to some person, or group of persons, involved in them, and the structure of the narrative depends, in one sense, upon the reference to the person, or persons, most fundamentally concerned. See pp. 151–152, 266–267.

FOCUS OF NARRATION (POINT OF VIEW): The focus of narration has to do with who tells the story. We may make four basic distinctions: (1) a character may tell his own story in the first person; (2) a character may tell, in the first person, a story which he has observed; (3) the author may tell what happens in the purely objective sense—deeds, words, gestures—without going into the minds of the characters and without giving his own comment; (4) the author may tell what happens with full liberty to go into the minds of characters and to give his own comment. These four types of narration may be called: (1) first-person, (2) first-person observer, (3) author-observer, and (4) omniscient author. Combinations of these methods are, of course, possible. See pp. 126–128, 266.

FORESHADOWING: The process of giving the reader an intimation of some event which is to follow later in the action.

FORM: The arrangement of various elements in a work of literature; the organization of various materials (ideas, images, characters, setting, and the like) to give a single effect. It may be said that a story is successful—that it has achieved form—when all of the elements are functionally related to each other, when each part contributes to the intended effect. Form is not to be thought of merely as a sort of container for the story; it is, rather, the total principle of organization and affects every aspect of the composition. It is the mode in which the story exists. STRUCTURE and STYLE are also used to indicate the author's arrangement of his materials to give his effect. *Structure*, however, is usually used with more special reference to the ordering of the larger elements such as episodes, scenes, and details of action, in contrast to the arrangement of words, for which the term *style* is ordinarily employed. In the fullest sense, both the terms become synonymous with form, but in this book *style* is used merely to refer to the selection and ordering of language. See pp. 170–171, 272–273, 291–292.

FUNCTIONAL: Having to do with the development of the total effect of a piece of fiction. The term is used in this book to denote those elements of a story which actually play a part in building up the complex and rich unity of a story in contrast to those used merely because they are fashionable, or feed some external interest, or are merely sensational or decorative or engaging.

IMAGERY: The representation of any sense experience. Imagery does not consist merely of "mental pictures," but may make an appeal to any of the senses. In keeping with its insistance upon the concrete and the particular, all literature, including fiction, makes much use of imagery, not only in obvious descriptive fashion but also in figurative language. The most common forms of figurative language are SIMILES and METAPHORS. A *simile* is a direct comparison between two things, and such a comparison is introduced by *like* or *as*. A *metaphor* does not announce the comparison and proceeds indirectly to indicate an identification of the two items involved. Although such details of style may seem trivial in fiction, their effects are subtle and important. Sometimes the fundamental attitude of an author (see TONE), and hence the fundamental meaning of a piece of fiction, may be largely conveyed in terms of such details. See pp. 170–171, 187–188, 272–273. See also ATMOSPHERE.

INEVITABILITY: The sense that the result presented is the only possible result of the situation previously given. It cannot be strictly maintained that inevitability in fiction is absolute, if one is to judge by realistic standards. The element of chance, or what appears as chance, in human affairs is too great to admit of such an interpretation. The term is simply used in most discussions to indicate a high degree of logic in the handling of the development of plot or character.

IRONICAL: See IRONY.

IRONY: Irony always involves contrast, a discrepancy between the expected and the actual, between the apparent and the real. Such contrast may appear in many forms. A speaker uses irony, for example, when he deliberately says something which he does not mean, but indicates by his tone what he does mean. UNDERSTATEMENT—the saying of less than one feels the occasion would warrent—and PARADOX—the saying of something which is apparently untrue but which on examination proves to be true, or partially true—both of these are forms of irony. In addition to such forms of IRONY OF STATEMENT, there are also various forms of IRONY OF SITUATION. The irony of situation involves a discrepancy between what we expect the outcome of an action to be, to what would seem to be the fitting outcome, and the actual outcome. In dealing with this term, the student should always remember that there are a thousand subtle shadings of irony, and must, therefore, not take it in too restricted a sense, for example, in the sense of obvious sarcasm. See pp. 30–31, 71, 87, 137, 182, 190.

LOGIC: In fiction, the relation that exists between character and character, or character and setting. See p. 54. See also INEVITABILITY.

MELODRAMATIC: An effect is said to be melodramatic when the violent or the sensational seems to be used for its own sake without adequate reference to the motivation of the characters or to other elements in the story. But the mere fact of violence, it should be pointed out, does not constitute melodrama. If the violence is logical and meaningful, it is not melodramatic. See pp. 29–30, 302–306.

METAPHOR: See IMAGERY.

MOTIVATION: The purpose, or mixture of purposes, or even the more or less unconscious impulses that determine the behavior of a character. See pp. 29–30, 54.

OBJECTIVE: In relation to fiction, the pair of terms OBJECTIVE and SUBJECTIVE, is used in two connections. In the first, they are used with reference to the author, and in the second they are used with reference to a character, or characters, in the work of fiction. In the first connection, an *objective* treatment by the author implies an attitude of detachment toward the material which is being presented, a refusal to comment and interpret directly. (See DISTANCE, DRAMATIC, and SCALE.) A *subjective* treatment, on the other hand, is one which is highly colored by the author's own feelings and beliefs. Of course, the amount of subjectivity or objectivity is always a matter of degree. Since all fiction involves, ultimately, the author's interpretations, feelings, judgments, and the like, there is strictly speaking no absolutely objective presentation, but we can say that, in terms of method the distinction can be made. In reference to the character, or characters, in a work of fiction, the terms can be applied more absolutely. When there is no direct presentation of the thoughts or feelings of a character, the treatment is said to be objective; when such presentation is made, the treatment is said to be subjective. But most pieces of fiction tend to mix the two methods, some events being rendered objectively, some characters being treated objectively, and some subjectively.

PACE: The rate of speed with which the various parts of the story are made to move, ranging from summary to fully reported scene. See pp. 87–89.

PARABLE: A story, usually simple, which makes an obvious point or has a rather obvious symbolic meaning. The method of parable is closely related to that of ALLEGORY, but the tendency is to use the term *allegory* to indicate a more systematic and complicated structure of equivalents. See pp. 47–48, 242–244.

PARADOX: See IRONY.

PATHOS: The sense of pity. The author, however, must be on his guard to make sure that the pathos in a story emerges legitimately from the situation given. When there is no reasonable basis in character and situation for the pathos, one has an effect of SENTIMENTALITY. The quality of being *pathetic* is to be distinguished from that of being *tragic*. In a tragic situation the sense of pity is complicated by an effect of struggle and conflict. The pathetic effect may be given by the spectacle of a weak person suffering; the tragic effect requires that the sufferer have strength enough to struggle vigorously against his situation. See pp. 72, 187.

PATTERN: The significant repetition—such as the repetition of incidents and events in a plot. See pp. 63, 136–137.

PERSONIFICATION: The attribution of the qualities of a person to an inanimate object or idea.

PLOT: The structure of action *as presented* in fiction or drama. Plot, as PLOT PATTERN, is one aspect of the total design of a story. See pp. 51–58, 136–137.

POINT OF VIEW: This term is loosely used to refer to the author's basic attitudes and ideas; for example, one may speak of a detached point of view, a sympathetic point of view, a Christian point of view. More strictly, the term is used to refer to the teller of the story—to the mind through which the material of the story is presented. The story may be told in the first or in the third person, and the teller may be the mere observer or much more than that. See pp. 126–130, 172, 291–292. See also FOCUS OF NARRATION.

PROPAGANDA: Propaganda literature is literature which tends to state its theme abstractly and tends to insist upon its "message" at the expense of other elements. Usually it can be said that such literature oversimplifies its material in order to emphasize a particular interpretation.

REALISTIC: Having a strong sense of fact or actuality. The term is used in this text to refer to the presentation of ordinary, easily observable details which give an impression of fidelity to experience. *Realistic* is to be contrasted with ROMANTIC, which implies the remote, the exotic, the exaggerated. (There is no attempt in this book to go into the distinction between *romantic* and *classic*.)

RHYTHM: Movement with a recurrent beat or stress. Though prose rhythms are not so marked as those in poetry, most of which is written in *verse*, the rhythms in a piece of prose are frequently important and may indeed be highly expressive.

SELECTION: See pp. 128–129, 291–292. See also FORM and STYLE.

SELECTIVITY: See SELECTION.

SENTIMENTALITY: Emotional response in excess of the occasion; emotional response that has not been prepared for in the story in question. See pp. 72, 163–164, 171–172, 187–190, 211–212.

SETTING: The physical background, the element of place, in a story. See p. 169.

SIMILE: See IMAGERY.

STOCK RESPONSE: The automatic or conventional or generally uncritical response of a reader to some word, phrase, situation, character, or subject in literature. See also CLICHÉ.

STRUCTURE: See FORM.

STYLE: See FORM.

SUBJECTIVE: See OBJECTIVE.

SURPRISE ENDING: An ending in a story that comes with some sense of shock to the reader. (For the grounds for distinguishing between legitimate and illegitimate surprise endings, see pp. 72, 78–79, 87, 102–103, 112.) See also COINCIDENCE.

SYMBOL: An object, character, or incident which stands for something else, or suggests something else, is a *symbol* of that thing. See p. 48 note.

THEME: The "point" or "meaning" of a story or novel. See pp. 30–31, 50, 228–234.

TONE: The tone is the reflection in the story of the author's attitude toward his material and toward his audience. (It is to be distinguished from ATMOSPHERE, which see.) See pp. 36–38, 50. See also SENTIMENTALITY.

TRAGEDY: See PATHOS. See also pp. 30–31, 306.

UNDERSTATEMENT: See IRONY. See also p. 126.

UNITY: The sense of wholeness or oneness. See pp. 1–2, 54, 56, 153.